Ferdinand V. Hayden

Ferdinand V. HAYDEN

Entrepreneur of Science

James G. Cassidy

UNIVERSITY OF NEBRASKA PRESS : LINCOLN AND LONDON

The frontispiece: Ferdinand V. Hayden, U.S. Geologist (1829–87). Source: Portraits 9, USGS Photographic Library, Denver.

Library of Congress Cataloging-in-Publication Data
Cassidy, James G., 1957–
Ferdinand V. Hayden: entrepreneur of science / James G. Cassidy.
p. cm. Includes bibliographical references and index.
ISBN 0-8032-1507-X (cloth : alkaline paper)
1. Hayden, F. V. (Ferdinand Vandeveer), 1829–1887.
2. Science and state – United States – History – 19th century 3. West (U.S.) – Discovery and exploration – History – 19th century 4. Geologists – United States – Biography I. Title.
QE22.H3 C37 2000 338.97306′09′034–dc21 99-058427

Contents

Illustrations

PHOTOGRAPHS

following page 178

MAPS

Acknowledgments

Finally, I reach the most pleasant of the many tasks involved in producing a book. In the course of researching, writing, and revising I have incurred innumerable debts to individuals and institutions whose assistance and support were indispensable, and I take great pleasure in thanking all those who have contributed toward whatever is worthy in this book. First among the individuals, I must thank Robert Kohler, my graduate school advisor at the Department for the History and Sociology of Science at the University of Pennsylvania, whom it has been a privilege to know and from whom I have learned much about how to study and write history. My thanks go out, as well, to three historians who took the time to read and carefully comment on various drafts of all or most of the entire manuscript: Mike Foster of Denver, Colorado; Ronald Rainger of Texas Tech University; and particularly Vincent Capowski, my former colleague in the history department at Saint Anselm College, who is now enjoying a much-merited retirement.

¶ None of this work would have been possible, however, without the support and indulgence of my monastic community at Saint Anselm Abbey in Manchester, New Hampshire. Their interest in, and support of, my work has been a constant encouragement. Two members among them deserve special mention. Rev. Placidus Riley, OSB, read and provided copious comments on virtually two entire drafts of the manuscript, insisting that I state what I mean in plain English. I also thank Bro. Andrew Thornton, OSB, for his generous assistance in translating. I am also grateful to those communities that provided this wandering monk with a home for my periods of study and research: the Brothers of the Christian School at West Catholic High School in Philadelphia; the Augustinian Friars at the former Saint John's Priory, in Washington DC; and the parish community of Our Lady of the Rosary in West

Philadelphia. And I thank the members of the community of scholars with whom I work in the history department at Saint Anselm College, who have also been a great source of encouragement and the best of colleagues.

¶ Like all researchers, in the course of my research I had occasion to call upon the services of a number of libraries and librarians, and I am pleased to say that I found almost all of them more than eager to be of any possible assistance. Several in particular stand out: Jeanne Welch and Ila Parnell of the interlibrary loan department at Saint Anselm College's Geisel Library; the exceptionally gracious and helpful staff at the American Philosophical Society, who made the elegant surroundings a delightful place in which to work; Karen Stevens and Linda Rossi at the Academy of Natural Sciences of Philadelphia, which has granted generous permission to quote extensively from the Hayden-Leidy correspondence; William Deiss, Susan Glenn, and their associates at the Smithsonian Institution Archives; and Carol Edwards at the USGS Field Records Library at Denver. I am also grateful to the Geological Society of America, whose Research Grant No. 4165-89 enabled me to visit libraries and archives in Colorado and Wyoming, as well as view a great deal of the country in which the Hayden Survey operated.

¶ Last, and most importantly, I must thank my parents and brothers and sister and their spouses, who have all been most courteously patient and interested in when my book would finally be published. While it is perhaps not the sort of "western" that some of them might have been most interested in reading, they have all been supportively impressed that I undertook the project in the first place and have eagerly looked forward to its completion. Thus, it gives me great pleasure to dedicate this book to them, and I trust they will forgive me for not mentioning them all by name.

Introduction

Hurry up as the Golden Opportunities [are] passing. —William Henry Jackson, quoting Hayden, *The Diaries of William Henry Jackson*

On 2 March 1867, the next-to-last day of its second session, the Thirty-ninth Congress approved funding for two geological surveys in the American West. In one, Congress followed an established pattern; in the other, it experimented in a new direction. In what Henry Adams later called "almost its first modern act of legislation," Congress authorized the secretary of war to direct a "geological and topographical exploration of the territory between the Rocky Mountains and the Sierra Nevada mountains." Five days later, the twenty-four-year-old, Yale-educated geologist Clarence King, who was simultaneously the primary promoter and beneficiary of the legislation, received a letter giving him charge of the Geological Exploration of the Fortieth Parallel. The letter informed King that he could expect to receive one hundred thousand dollars to finance the work for three years and authorized him to engage two assistant geologists, three topographic aides, two collectors, a photographer, and necessary camp assistants. Supposedly, Secretary of War Edwin Stanton also advised King to leave Washington for the West as soon as possible, as four major-generals coveted his place.[1]

¶ Phineas W. Hitchcock, territorial delegate from Nebraska, proposed the second survey, on behalf of the new state of Nebraska. Hitchcock asked, and Congress granted, that "the unexpended balance of the appropriations heretofore made for defraying the expenses of the legislative assembly of the Territory of Nebraska" be "diverted and set aside for the purpose of Procuring a geological survey of Nebraska, said survey to be prosecuted under the direction of the commissioner of the general land office." At breakfast a week later, Spencer Baird, assistant secretary of the Smithsonian Institution, self-appointed "Survey Manager" for the federal government, and ever on the lookout for opportunities for scientists, read the bill and "immediately went to Mr. [Joseph] Wilson," commissioner of the General Land Office, to present the claim of one of his favorites, Ferdinand Vandeveer Hayden, for the position. Wilson seems to have been convinced almost immediately and asked Baird to submit his recommendation in writing, which he did the same day. Baird then wrote Hayden, who was in Philadelphia delivering his course of lectures on geology at the University of Pennsylvania, telling what he had done and advising him to apply in person; the position was almost certainly his if he wanted it.[2]

¶ Hayden did want the spot. It was virtually the fulfillment of a dream he had had a dozen years earlier—a grand geological and natural history survey of the whole Nebraska Territory—and he moved quickly to secure the position. Having done that, Hayden then exhibited great political skill in developing his niche in government science and maintained and enlarged his place through unabashed appeals to patronage and popularization. However, this eventually compromised his science to such an extent that the leaders of American science combined against him and forced the suppression and replacement of his survey with one modeled on proper scientific standards.

¶ Such, briefly, is the traditional account of how one of the largest civilian scientific bureaus of Gilded Age America—the United States Geological and Geographical Survey of the Territories, better known as the Hayden Survey—began, grew, and declined. However, as Mike Foster has recently shown in his biography of Hayden, much in the traditional account is inaccurate. In great measure, these inaccuracies derive from Hayden's political and scientific opponents, who had the good fortune to outlive him. But in almost equal measure, as Foster also shows, the inaccuracies that have substituted as the history of Hayden and his survey are due to Hayden's own lifelong tendency to rewrite his history to make it appear more attractive.[3] Yet the real history of Hayden and his survey is at least as interesting as the received account, as well as much more instructive on a number of elements of mid-nineteenth-century American history.

¶ In this book, I will examine the history of the development of the

Hayden Survey in the context of five main themes. One is the continuing rapid industrialization of the United States in the post–Civil War years. The second is the simultaneous and related exploration, settlement, and development of the trans-Mississippi West. The third is the history of American science during these years. The fourth connects the first three: the role of the federal government and its support of the economic development of the West through the patronage of science. Finally, the fifth theme is the popularization of science in mid-nineteenth-century America.

¶ The decades following the Civil War constituted a transitional period for American society as the nation underwent the rapid and diverse changes that accompanied the emergence of modern America. The pace of industrialization and economic integration continued to accelerate as the United States developed into one of the world's most important manufacturing powers. At the same time, Americans continued their relentless push westward, laying physical claim to half a continent. Both of these conquests—economic and territorial—found support from a federal government that had only recently learned to exert itself to an unprecedented level of activism in peacetime national affairs.

¶ America's industrialization and its settlement of the trans-Mississippi West are intimately connected, as recent works by historians of the West make clear. Far from attempting to consider western history in isolation, these historians argue that the region's history only makes sense in terms of its "connectedness" and "complex linkages" with the eastern states and the rest of the world. At the same time, these new scholars of western history do not ignore the elements that make that history unique. Among the most important of these, they identify the place itself. The West was different, very different, from the eastern half of the United States, and western historians and environmental historians, and particularly those who are both, insist that the land itself must be seen as central to its history.[4]

¶ On one level, this focus on the land is simply the sine qua non of conquest: ownership of the land was taken from those who previously possessed it. On a deeper level, Americans had to come to terms with the land, had to learn how to live on it and with it. Wallace Stegner, who spent most of the twentieth century living, musing, and writing on the West, asserted that coming to terms with the region required four changes from an eastern perspective. The "first and hardest," he wrote, "was to learn all over again how to see." Then it was necessary to "learn to like the new forms and colors and light and scale" of the western landscape. The third step was to develop the literary and visual languages to communicate the appreciation of the western environment, while the final stage required "train[ing] an audience that would respond" to those languages.[5]

¶ This process of adaptation to the West points to two themes that are important for this book. The first is the very idea of process. Recent western historians, in focusing on the West as *place*, do so as a place undergoing *processes* of change. In this, they retain Frederick Jackson Turner's insight of the frontier but reorient it to focus "not on a single region but on many regions undergoing parallel historical change." Some find a key to western history in "common social and economic processes," as different local frontier places "gave way to the stabler, more coherent areas we know today as the regions of North America," that is, parts of an integrated nation. Focus on the processes through which places passed directs attention to the fact that the same places, and the West as a whole, could be successive frontiers—a trappers' frontier, a mining frontier, a transportation frontier, a ranching frontier, a farming frontier—each bringing its own processes to bear and affecting the way people saw the West.[6]

¶ These different frontiers represented different opportunities to different individuals, provoking in turn different interests in the West. In their efforts to seize these opportunities, the men who developed the West in the latter half of the nineteenth century "imitated the nation as a whole by moving [the West] quickly into a capitalized, industrialized economy." This perspective reveals the settlement or "conquest" of the West to have been "a literal, territorial form of economic growth" and a "concrete, down-to-earth demonstration" of the nation's industrial incorporation.[7] Yet these processes of change did not occur willy-nilly or in a vacuum. They were the actions of determined individuals, who, when possible, secured political support for their goals and actions. One important way in which the federal government manifested its support for the economic development of the West was by underwriting numerous geological, geographic, and mapping surveys of the western territories.

¶ The second theme drawn from the process of adaptation to the West follows Stegner more closely. Nineteenth-century Americans incorporated the West into more than their economy. They also incorporated it into their conception of national identity. In the process, Americans learned how to think about a region that was very different from familiar eastern standards of what was beautiful, natural, and suitable for human habitation. Recent studies by art and cultural historians have pointed to dramatic changes in attitude toward nature during the nineteenth century, as artists and authors learned how to see and present nature in new ways, thus taming the threatening wilderness and transforming it into a national heritage. Federally sponsored surveys of the West played an important role in underwriting this transformation, and Hayden's survey was no exception. In fact, two of America's most significant visual artists of the period received important career boosts from positions on the Hayden Survey: the landscape painter Thomas Moran and the photographer William Henry Jackson.[8]

¶ The various transformations that marked the emergence of a modern industrial nation also called forth new conceptions of American society itself. This process has been described as a virtual "incorporation of America," a phrase that refers to a "reorganization of perceptions as well as of enterprise and institutions" that led to "the emergence of a changed, more tightly structured society with new hierarchies of control." Other historians have pointed to the emergence of a culture of professionalism, as various groups laid claim to preference by virtue of a particular expertise important to society at large.[9]

¶ Scientists were not immune to the changes occurring around them. Like so many of their fellow citizens, they also struggled to define their role in a changing society, both as individuals and as social groups. Their tasks in this respect were complicated by rapid changes taking place within their own scientific communities, as educational standards rose, new theories and techniques came into play, and entire new disciplines and subdisciplines emerged from what had been in the eighteenth century a more unified scientific culture. Perhaps in no field of science were the changes more dramatic than in the old discipline of natural history, which was fracturing into at least three separate disciplines, each yielding a variety of specialties. As it did so, the practitioners of the new fields engaged in increasingly sharp competition for the scarce resources necessary to support careers in their chosen professions. Moreover, this competition took place within a context of change in the very conception of the appropriate standards of a professional scientist. Increasingly, those who made science their life's vocation distinguished themselves from amateurs who had long constituted an important block of popular support for scientific endeavors. ¶ It used to be a fundamental theme in the history of American science that Americans have been traditionally indifferent to supporting research in basic science, especially in the nineteenth century. However, this thesis was always coupled with an assertion that Americans have also had a lively interest and strong faith in applied science as being useful and appropriate for a democratic nation. In this understanding, applied science was distinguished from "elitist" pure science, with the supposed attractiveness of applied science attributed to an expectation of economic rewards. Reappraisal of the "indifference" thesis has led to greater recognition of the volume of basic or pure science that nineteenth-century Americans supported, which was fundamental to the explicitly supported applied sciences. Historians of science now adopt a more nuanced approach to the appeals of scientists of the period, recognizing their entreaties for what they frequently were: pleas for more money and rarely balanced, unbiased presentations of the situation.[10] In spite of this reappraisal, however, there have been very few studies of how new social spaces and financial support for science were created in nineteenth-century America. Louis Agassiz's success in Boston, which resulted in a virtual personality cult; sizable benefactions such as the Peabody bequest and the Sheffield Scientific School at Yale; and Alexander Dallas Bache's success in building the United States Coast Survey stand out primarily because they were exceptional cases. ¶ Yet while there is much broader recognition on the part of historians of science that the development, practice, and diffusion of science are inextricably social, there remains a continuing need to direct attention to many of its social processes, especially those going beyond intralaboratory communication. This is particularly the case for the processes involved in the popularization of science in light of the widespread agreement that science is "the most potent instrument of persuasion in our culture." One of the more powerful means of effecting that persuasion is through the "enrollment of interests," and those historians of science who have been looking at relationships of patronage and the making of careers have made profitable use of this concept, for patronage involves more than money.[11]

¶ In recent years, more and more historians of science have begun to examine the mechanisms and impact of patronage on the development of scientific practice. This increased attention is clearly due to a heightened awareness of both the ubiquity of patronage in the history of science and its complexity. Patronage in its simplest terms is virtually essential to the full-time practice of science; unless an individual happens to be independently wealthy, some outside source of support is necessary. But patronage rarely occurs in simple terms. Instead, recent studies of patronage and science clearly indicate that the two have more often had a complex relationship because patronage arises from a conjunction of intersecting interests. While necessary for the scientist, patronage almost always serves the interests of the patron as well. As such, patronage shapes possibilities. To gain the favor of the patron, the would-be client must somehow attach his or her interests to the patron's interests, and numerous studies of how patronage functions have pointed to scientists' promises of "useful" or "practical" results in return for support for their research.[12]

¶ Yet the patronage relationship goes beyond financial support. A closer look at the efforts of scientists to make careers in nineteenth-century America clearly reveals that in seeking patrons, they sought more than money. They also sought the respect for themselves and their work that would assure them secure status in their society and enable them to establish the means to manage their own disputes. Hayden's career as head of one of the most successful geological surveys of the Gilded Age sheds light on many of the issues involved in that quest. An examination of it is particularly valuable because, while patronage was a central concern of nineteenth-century American science, and remains so for modern science as a whole, most studies of scientific patronage relationships and their impacts on the making of scientific careers have examined them in the European context.[13]

¶ In his efforts to create a new career pattern in science, Hayden had to appeal to and rely upon federal patronage. Though he had a few successful patterns available as examples—most notably that established by Bache as head of the Coast Survey—the particular way in which Hayden sought to put them together partook of both old and new. Perhaps nothing illustrates this better than the fact that Hayden recognized no limits to his survey's mission of exploring and describing the West. Virtually everything about it could fall under his purview and be of interest to him: its geology, its geography, its weather, its plant and animal life, its inhabitants, its scenery, its economic potential. At the same time, he sought to make it all—or at least parts of it all—interesting to potential patrons.

¶ Hayden promoted the West and its possibilities in order to promote his scientific program of exploring the West. As he did so, he reached out to a variety of interests and deeply influenced the way late-nineteenth-century Americans viewed the West and acted toward it. Historians of nineteenth-century American science already know of Hayden, though perhaps without a full appreciation of his true significance, but those interested in how Americans came to develop what Stegner called the new ways of seeing, liking, expressing, and responding to the West should also take another look at his influence. In the Hayden Survey, science intersected with American society in the latter half of the nineteenth century to such an extent that promoting western tourism and establishing a national park at Yellowstone went hand in hand with efforts to elaborate the region's geology, understand its natural history, and promote its settlement and the nation's economic development. That interpenetration was an important part of the context for the development of scientific disciplines and the elevation of their social status.

¶ This book presents a study of a career in science. An examination of this career provides a window on the ways in which a new niche was elaborated for science in the federal government. It also illustrates how issues as diverse as tourism and professionalization in science interacted with the evolving relationship of government patronage and a struggle for public legitimacy in Gilded Age America. In fact, a study of Hayden and the Hayden Survey provides an especially good vantage point from which to study the interrelationships of these themes, since Hayden functioned where many of them interfaced: as an employee of the federal government working in the West and practicing a rapidly changing and professionalizing science. I will not argue that Hayden's was a typical government bureau. In some ways it was quite atypical, not least in the degree of success it enjoyed winning funds from Congress. However, for that very reason, it makes an interesting case study of the elements that contributed to success as a bureau—and perhaps still do.

¶ When he assumed responsibility for the survey of Nebraska in 1867 at thirty-eight years of age, Hayden was an accomplished natural history collector and explorer and a highly competent field geologist with nearly a decade's experience in exploring the western territories. Yet his success in obtaining this latest opportunity need not have meant much for the history of American geology and natural science. It might have been simply one more local survey, undertaken with a small annual appropriation. In that case, that might have been the end of the story, and there would be little to write about. But there was a great deal more to it.

¶ By means of his survey Hayden came to exercise an important influence on the development of American science. He grasped the opportunity the survey of Nebraska presented and transformed it into one of the largest civilian scientific bureaus of the Gilded Age. Under his direction, the United States Geological and Geographical Survey of the Territories spent nearly seven hundred thousand dollars in the next dozen years, exploring and mapping thousands of square miles and publishing a veritable library of scientific reports, bulletins, and memoirs on topics ranging from geology and geography to natural history, archaeology, and ethnography. He became one of the best-known scientists of his time, and the Hayden Survey was renowned in the Western world as one of the most successful and generously funded government geological surveys in existence. It was a success story worthy of the Gilded Age, and it might not be too much to consider Hayden a robber baron of science. Though he did not operate on the scale of the builders of the railroads or other great industrial empires of the period, like them Hayden positioned himself to pick up opportunities "on the cheap," many made possible by concessions won from the government.

¶ Though Henry Adams considered the legislation for the King Survey as one of Congress's "first modern act[s] of legislation," in fact, King's survey represented an older, established tradition. Hayden's was a new departure for the federal government, wholly civilian in concept and in direction. Further, when King's survey was completed four years after its start, that was the end of it; all that remained was the completion of the final reports. Hayden's survey, however, had a future, and even his enemies agreed in later years that the United States Geological Survey (USGS), established by Congress in 1879, owed its existence in large measure to Hayden and the Hayden Survey, even though King was named its first director.

¶ In spite of this, historians have generally ignored Hayden. He not only suffered the misfortune of being passed over for the directorship of the USGS—making him seem one of history's "losers"—but his health soon went into a serious decline, eventually leading to his death in 1887 from locomotor ataxia. The isolation brought on by this debilitating disease and the dependency it induced hardly left him in any position to promote his own cause. His competitors held the field and have since found champions among historians.[14] Hayden has only recently found a biographer, and there is still plenty of room for a full study of the survey he directed for twelve years. This book should be viewed as an effort toward that latter aim. It is an attempt, first, to understand Hayden as a public entrepreneur of science and a remarkably successful director of a federal bureau of science, and, second, to seek a grasp of some of the elements that made the Hayden Survey one of the most admired geological surveys of its time in the world.

¶ Hayden's success can be attributed to a number of factors, not the least of which was quite simply his ability in and enthusiasm for science. But more than that, his success as the creator and leader of a survey derived from his skill as an entrepreneur combined with an extraordinary talent for self-promotion. Though he was a gifted geologist, an observant naturalist, and a highly successful collector of natural history specimens, Hayden's most significant impact on American science was as a builder. By sheer force of personality and persistence, Hayden succeeded in selling the federal government something it was not at all sure it wanted. In the process, he created a secure niche for several branches of science within the federal bureaucracy and built new possibilities for scientific careers. As many of his contemporaries recognized, and at least a few were willing to credit, Hayden was the one man most responsible for the creation of the USGS as a civilian bureau within the Department of the Interior. While few historical works have viewed bureaucrats or scientists as entrepreneurs, this study examines someone who was both from just such a perspective.[15] I argue that Hayden's career and survey can only fully be understood in terms of his entrepreneurial skills.

¶ In very general terms, entrepreneurs are opportunists; they are expansion-minded, "irrepressible enthusiasts" willing to employ every conceivable device within their own personal limits to attain their goals. Hayden certainly fit that description. His college classmates remembered him as "very industrious" and "very enthusiastic in what he undertook." One identified "his crude ambition" as "his strongest bent." Hayden's subsequent career indicates he did not abandon his ambition when he left college. One colleague from his survey years characterized him as "a dynamic, intense man." His quest for fame and fortune was that of someone driven and bordered, at times, on the crude and duplicitous; he frequently had to get his more influential and diplomatic friends to come to his rescue and smooth ruffled feathers.[16]

¶ Important as ambition is, however, it alone is not enough for success. Any study of the would-be entrepreneur must look to elements of his or her personal operating style vis-à-vis the organization's needs and the conditions in which it attempts to function. Hayden's success as an administrator of science rested on his ability both to develop, promote, and expand his project and to cope with the mundane but fundamental matters of everyday management. As we shall see, Hayden's case is similar to the laboratory "boss" whose duties reveal a "businessman's view of science." [17] Hayden's work made the work of the survey possible. But it is also vital to remember that success as an entrepreneur of science in the context of civil service is not measured in terms of personal riches and money. Instead, the equivalent rewards are appropriations and control, the expansion of authority, and the enhancement of fame and glory as a scientist. Yet these too are heady rewards, well worth the efforts of those ambitious for them.

¶ A study of Hayden's efforts to gain these rewards sheds light on the nature of government-funded science. Though this study pertains most specifically to Gilded Age America, it also offers insights into the relationship between applied and pure research, between research and popularization, and between science and its patrons while also addressing issues of management style. We will see how the various stances adopted on the question of federal patronage of science implied competing visions of science and the place of science in the federal government. We will also see how the making of careers is structured by the society in which people operate and the options they have or perceive they have in that society. At the same time, this study of the development and elaboration of a niche for government science illustrates a number of features in the changing environment for science in the United States and the federal government. It will become clear that, together with a more sophisticated understanding of what science could provide, there was also a narrower focusing on what sorts of science government would support. The changes that occurred reflected changes within both the nation as a whole and the scientific community during the mid–nineteenth century as a result of industrial and institutional developments at a multitude of levels.

¶ In approaching this study from this perspective, I owe a debt to the insights of the social constructionists of scientific knowledge, especially Bruno Latour. Latour has advised us that in our historical and sociological studies of science we have to focus upon *science in action*, attending to the process, not the product. I accept this as a starting point as I do his theme of the enrollment of interests, that is, the necessity of scientists or other actors to enlist allies to keep the action going in the direction in which they wish it to proceed.[18]

¶ Yet even as we focus on entrepreneurial activity, it is impossible to understand Hayden except as a working scientist, nor is it possible to understand the Hayden Survey except as a working scientific institution. Therefore, we must explore both of these elements: what it meant to be a working scientist in the natural history tradition, since Hayden was first and foremost a naturalist; and what sort of work the Hayden Survey did, since one of the best ways to understand scientists and their institutions is to examine the work they do. And in this, too, the Hayden Survey presents a particular advantage since the science it practiced was a field science rather than a laboratory science. Until very recently, most studies of scientific practice have focused on lab-based sciences. Yet, as a recent collection of essays makes clear, the study of scientific practice in the field opens up a particularly useful perspective for examining a variety of questions about the social relationship of science.[19] I begin, then, with three introductory chapters. The first introduces the context of science in the Gilded Age. The second consists of an introduction to Hayden as a "frontier naturalist," focusing especially on his training in the natural history tradition and his background prior to his appointment to head the survey of Nebraska in 1867. Finally, chapter 3 considers his directorship of that survey as being representative of his scientific practice.

¶ The next five chapters focus on the Hayden Survey as a scientific institution. They begin with the social environment in which the survey was created and then move on to consider some of the more important challenges its director had to face if the survey was to survive and flourish. These include the tension between the claims of patronage and professionalism, issues of personnel management and the need to manage competition and function as a team, and publishing—the production of a scientific product. Chapter 4 explores how Hayden secured financial support from a Congress hardly remarkable for its willingness to invest in scientific research. Chapter 5 focuses on the survey's patterns of hiring and examines Hayden's recruiting practices, which had to accommodate the realities of political patronage and the demands of scientific professionalism. Chapter 6 examines issues of personnel management, that is, the details of Hayden's role as the head of a corps of scientific workers. As such, that chapter looks at what work in the field was like, what could go wrong and what it might take to make things work. The tendency to think of science in terms of men in white coats and pristine labs can cause us to overlook such fundamental elements of field sciences as the terrain and the weather, human relations on extended tours, and the special factors of the West during that period, such as Indian troubles.

¶ The study then begins to come full circle with chapter 7, which reminds us that the survey's work was not done until its results had been worked up, published, and presented to its sponsor—the federal government and the public. This chapter views all "published" products—preliminary reports, final monographs, maps, photographs, tables, models, and the like—as part of one project, which included not only those items produced officially by the survey but also those produced with survey assistance in other outlets, whether strictly scientific or "popular." These latter included articles in journals and newspapers,

William Henry Jackson's photographs and Thomas Moran's paintings, and the immensely popular Hayden Survey contribution to the Philadelphia Centennial Exhibition. Though some survey studies and publications were more clearly directed to specialist scientific or economic interests, they all served to answer interests in the West.

¶ Finally, in the final three chapters I will show how the survey itself played a role in its own decline and examine the paradox of how the downfall of the "virtual master of the scientific situation in Washington" occurred just when geological science was finding a more secure position in the federal government. Hayden's fall from grace involved changing standards in the scientific establishment as well as a changing of the guard—in both government and the scientific establishment. Chapter 8 examines how Hayden sought to defend and protect his survey from criticism and competition directed against it, particularly by other survey leaders and their allies. Previous studies have viewed Hayden's downfall as the result of his inability or unwillingness to adapt to the changing situation in federal science. In chapters 9 and 10, I argue that that was not the case at all, nor is it the best way to understand his ultimate displacement as the leader in government-sponsored geology. Rather, Hayden and the Hayden Survey, as well as their influence and impact on the practice of science in the United States, should be viewed from a different vantage point. His success should be seen as that of an entrepreneur who was manifestly a man of his time—a time filled with "Golden Opportunities," as he loved to say.[20] In this light, even though he was finally rejected by those in power on the dawn of a new age, they built largely on foundations he laid.

¶ In all of this, there can be little doubt that the practice of science in an organization such as the Hayden Survey had elements and requirements common to the practice of any science, such as need for specialized knowledge and personnel, for communication, for resources, and for scientific data. The work of the Hayden Survey encompassed basic and applied sciences in the fields of geology, paleontology, botany, zoology, topography, and ethnology. However, the Hayden Survey was also an organization, a bureaucracy, and Hayden had to be a bureaucrat as well as a scientist. He was, as he titled himself, "Geologist-in-charge," and he had to attend to the needs of a federal bureau of science. In 1867, when Hayden was named United States Geologist for the survey of Nebraska, an opportunity was presented to him. It was up to him to make something of it; he had to take advantage of the occasion provided and keep it alive. How he did just that is the subject of this book. But as with everything in history, the Hayden Survey emerged from and developed within a specific context that provided both opportunities and limits. Any study of its development must begin with a survey of that context.

Ferdinand V. Hayden

ABBREVIATIONS

AAAS	American Association for the Advancement of Science
AAG	Association of American Geologists
AAGN	Association of American Geologists and Naturalists
AJS	American Journal of Science
APS	American Philosophical Society
MCZ	Museum of Comparative Zoology
NAS	National Academy of Sciences
UPRR	Union Pacific Railroad
USGS	United States Geological Survey

1

Geological Surveys in Mid-Nineteenth-Century America

It is the duty of the State Geologist to . . . advise other persons where they may expend their energies in search of minerals with some prospect of success, and on the other hand to advise them against expending money in geological formations barren of metalliferous ores or other economic products. —James Hall to B. W. Kumler, n.d.

George Otis Smith, then director of the United States Geological Survey (USGS), noted in 1918 that "even a Federal Bureau must be considered a product of evolution." Smith was thinking at the time of the USGS and how its original range of operations, methods, and personnel were for the most part drawn from the surveys that preceded it.[1] The same can be said of the United States Geological and Geographical Survey of the Territories. It developed out of a prior tradition of state and federal geological and natural history surveys, whose own evolution was shaped by and had an impact on two distinguishable groups: the scientific community of nineteenth-century America and the larger society of which it was a part and in which it sought to define its role. ¶ Ever since the publication of A. Hunter Dupree's pathbreaking *Science in the Federal Government*, historians have been well advised to take a closer look at nineteenth-century American scientists and evaluate them in terms of their goals and possibilities. For some time now, historians of science have recognized the importance of patronage in the relatively early development of geology as a scientific discipline in America. Largely as a result of geologists' success in attracting public patronage, by the 1830s American geology was coming to a recognized maturity, far in advance of most other branches of American science.[2] ¶ Patronage provided geologists with more than financial resources to conduct their scientific investigations. In Western culture, patronage and nobility have gone hand in hand. The former implied a personal, human relationship by which the patron shaped the status and identity, as well as the career, of the client. In a very real fashion, the patron gave the client a status and identity the client would not otherwise have had. In theory, the patron gave because he or she was in a position to do so, not in order to receive something in return, which would have been crass materialism and beneath the nobility of the patron. In return, the client gave the patron honor by reflecting the honor the patron was already presumed to have and making it even more apparent by doing admirable things in the patron's name, deeds made possible through the patron's notice and gift. Yet because patronage was a personal relationship whereby interests were conjoined, a mutual negotiation of interests was possible. Patronage did not have to be a static state. Wise clients nourished their patronage and kept it alive so it could change and develop. A sign of a talented client was that his or her relationship with his or her patron improved.[3]

¶ Patronage has been described as "the social system of pre-institutionalized science" and the only context in which scientific knowledge could be created in Renaissance Europe, since it was the only social system in which high culture existed. But the key here is the special attribute within the patron's gift and which the client sought—power, which was "not a *thing* but a *process*," the ability to "*do* things for the client." Scientists' knowledge is most impressive when they have access to power, when they are able to do things.[4] And American geologists, like their scientific compatriots, wanted to do several things.

¶ The courtly patronage of Renaissance Europe could not be simply transposed into the democratic culture of the United States. But scientists did find a way to translate the core of the patron-client relationship, for it is clear that while geologists were engaged to pursue their patrons' interests, they also pursued their own interests. What they wanted to do had everything to do with the state of their science in American society. They had more in mind than securing funding. Their very scientific careers were at stake.

¶ It would be a mistake to view science as a uniform profession in the first half century of the United States. Rather, science was a variously populated, indeed almost a multicultural, terrain in nineteenth-century America, and it became an increasingly contested territory as the century wore on. For most of its devotees in those years, science was not a profession—at least, not in the modern sense of the term whereby the practice of science was a person's particular lifework, acquired through specialized academic training and furnishing the means to a livelihood. The situation was more complex, and historians of science now customarily divide the early-nineteenth-century scientific community into three groups: researchers, practitioners, and cultivators. Only the first two resemble the modern notion of scientific professionals, that is, individuals dedicated to advancing scientific knowledge and/or remuneratively employed in scientific occupations. But these two groups were greatly outnumbered by the cultivators, who were people with enough interest in science to be attentive to it as amateurs.[5]

¶ Science was of interest for two reasons. It was part of the tradition of "polite learning." Moreover, the knowledge to which it laid claim might be useful, perhaps even economically rewarding. Insofar as science was part of polite learning, some awareness of science was part of the culture that might be expected of any educated gentleman or lady. In a democratic and increasingly literate nation like the United States in the early nineteenth century, this usually meant those of the middle class or better. Cultivators of science distinguished themselves by going further, by perhaps joining a local scientific society, attending lectures, or contributing toward the collections of a local or distant museum. The scientific society, public lectures, and local museum were all likely to be parts of local civic boosterism, together with the founding of an academy or college and other institutions intended to advance local culture and the prestige of the city or community. These institutions, in their turn, helped create and support a social climate propitious for the development of science. Serious cultivators of science were also apt to enter into correspondence with serious researchers or perhaps collect for them as well. But the status of cultivator did not necessarily, or even usually, entail any extensive academic training in science, let alone employment in a scientific occupation, for the simple reason that neither was generally to be had in the United States in the early nineteenth century. Rather, in the first decades of the century even most of those who should be denoted scientific practitioners and researchers were self-taught and hard-pressed to find scientific employment.[6] In fact, obtaining scientific employment was one of the chief concerns of would-be practitioners of science.

¶ Yet in spite of the paucity of opportunities for scientific employment, one of the important findings of scholars of the history of science in antebellum America is its vitality—a vitality that found vigorous encouragement in a broad social support. Historians now recognize that a lot more science was taught in American antebellum colleges than the educational reformers of the latter third of the nineteenth century ever credited. By the 1830s, a rising generation of scientists, most with academic degrees and some advanced training in science, increasingly obtained during a European tour, was competing for control of American science.[7]

¶ In no field of science did the competition grow more fierce than in natural history. So many different disciplines and specialties have developed out of natural history—botany, zoology, ornithology, mammology, comparative anatomy, physiology, the various branches of paleontology, to say nothing of mineralogy and the various specialties of geology, to name only a few—that it is somewhat difficult to imagine them as all having been part of a unified approach to the natural world. But until the late eighteenth century, natural history was a relatively integrated trinity of sciences. Before they divided into the three disciplines of geology, botany, and zoology during the course of the nineteenth century, the disciplines had been united in having all been parts of a concern to identify, distinguish, and understand everything in and on the earth. The drive to do so resonated deeply in nineteenth-century English culture, a resonance that found strong echoes in America. There, as in England, of all the branches of natural history, geology was the first to truly capture public attention. Ornithology and botany were close seconds, while various branches of zoology followed closely behind in popular fads of their own. As these studies advanced beginning in the latter part of the eighteenth century, it became increasingly difficult for individuals to presume to cover the entire range of natural history, and depth of knowledge in a single or limited number of areas began to substitute for breadth of familiarity as the mark of the man of science.[8]

¶ Under the same sort of pressures that resulted from developing specialization, the very category of "naturalist" itself began to fracture in the first third of the nineteenth century, giving rise to distinctions between "field" and "closet" naturalists. Insofar as they were "serious" scientists, members of both groups shared a common goal to discover, describe, and name new species. The site of their labors could differ, however. Field naturalists collected their own specimens, while closet naturalists described specimens that others had collected in the field and only occasionally collected them themselves. Indeed, as the skills and knowledge required to recognize and describe new species became more demanding in various areas of natural history, some field naturalists found themselves demoted to the status of collectors. The distinction in status was important. While a field naturalist or collector won a reputation largely for success in locating new species, the discovery could not be considered official until the specimen was properly described and published. To do so required familiarity with all of the relevant literature dating back to Linnaeus, as well as the related specimens to be found in museums and private collections. The time required to gain and maintain such familiarity had much to do with the development of "field" and "closet" specialties. So, too, did the fact that fieldwork imposed its own demands for skills—particularly fieldwork at some distance from centers of European and American civilization.[9]

¶ In the first decades of the nineteenth century, however, it was still quite possible to be simply a natural historian. It was, in fact, quite chic. In the age of "Humboldtian science"—marked by a concern with accurate measurement of the earth and its biology—natural history became fashionable. There were several reasons for this popularity. For one, natural history could tap into a tradition of natural theology that grew in strength in America as a consequence of the Second Great Awakening. It could also tap into the commercial and curious interests of the age of exploration and Jacksonian expectant capitalism. And no less useful, its promoters were also able to exploit a scientific consciousness awakened by the heightened literacy that resulted from the spread of education.[10]

¶ That geology and natural history were popular proved immensely useful to would-be professional scientists, since it helped them achieve their own interests. Fundamental among these were their research interests. American geologists had a number of highly interesting scientific problems to engage their attention, problems that had direct relevance to the issues European geologists debated and studied. The questions of the elevation of mountain ranges and the correlation of geological stratigraphy were the foremost issues. Additionally, American geologists possessed an advantage in that they had virtually virgin territory in which to pursue their investigations, while they kept their eyes on results of European, particularly English, efforts.[11] At the same time, they sought a respect for themselves and their work that would assure them secure status in their society and enable them to establish the means to manage their own disputes.

¶ In the first half century after independence, American scientists experienced great difficulty establishing their own independent competence vis-à-vis Europe. While Americans had remained a part of England, their reliance upon British resources had not been a serious stigma; after independence, not only did patriotism make the situation a problem, but distance and expense made it hard to participate. Appeals for new patrons were appeals to fill in the gaps left by the loss of older patrons as well as the needs of an increasing number of new potential clients. In the new situation, American scientists yoked science to enlightened patriotism, promising economic and cultural benefits, and drew a contrast between the British government's allegedly "magnanimous" policy toward its scientists and the obscure status and miserly support scientists suffered in democratic America. It was a theme that would remain constant for most of the nineteenth century.[12]

¶ While American geologists continued to look to Europe for their scientific standards, they recognized that their own practice suffered from a number of institutional and social weaknesses. Early-nineteenth-century America had virtually no stable scientific press until the founding of the *American Journal of Science and Arts* in 1818 (and even after its founding *Silliman's Journal*, as it was known, remained one of the few enduring regular scientific publishing outlets until midcentury). Throughout the antebellum period, scientific education remained woefully deficient by European standards and provided few opportunities for scientific research. Moreover, the pursuit of a scientific career generally afforded slim financial remuneration. The overall goals of American scientists, then, were to improve their social status within American society, strengthen their connections with and standing within the larger scientific community, and win more resources and opportunities for the pursuit of their studies. And for those who sought to devote themselves to scientific research, a particular goal was the control of resources and opportunities, especially in view of what they considered to be the American public's weakness for scientific charlatanism.

¶ Yet even winning recognition from European scientists came with risks of its own. For instance, American geologists preened themselves when Charles Lyell combined an invitation to deliver a series of lectures in Boston in 1841 with a decision to make use of the opportunity to tour American geology. For geologists who had been hard at work on local and state surveys, the opportunity to escort England's most eminent geologist to some of America's most interesting geological sites was a chance to show off their local knowledge, try out their own ideas, receive advice from an acknowledged expert, and share some of his limelight when he cordially and generously praised their work in his lectures in America and letters home to the Geological Society of London. Nor did his lectures do the popularity of geology and geological surveys any harm. On the contrary, they were so well received in Boston that Lyell repeated them in New York and Philadelphia during the winter and returned for two more lecture series, in 1845 and 1852. But praise came at the price of Lyell announcing their ideas to the world. From the first, some American geologists, jealous of their own discoveries and concerned to retain the credit they needed for their own scientific reputations, particularly to continue government support of their surveys, worried that Lyell might simply steal the results of their work. As it turned out, he did not and was more than generous in encouraging and praising American efforts, but the concern geologists exhibited testifies to their insecure status and their lack of control of their own careers as well as the standards relevant to them.[13]

¶ For their part, the public patrons of science were probably not so much impressed by the fact that geology was a field of vigorous intellectual debate by 1800 as that it also bid fair to have immediate economic utility. Seizing on this utility, the legislatures of nearly every state, beginning with North and South Carolina in 1824, sponsored geological surveys for the identification and discovery of their state's natural resources. Geology also received impetus from the industrial and transportation revolutions initiated in America following the War of 1812, with the building of canals and railroads. As had been the case in England, such construction projects not only served geologists by providing opportunities to explore below the surface of the earth, but the search for coal also provided them with occasions to demonstrate the utility of their science. Simultaneously, the discussion surrounding the surveys and their possibilities helped to popularize geology and make it, in the words of an April 1834 issue of *The Knickerbocker*, the "fashionable science of the day" and "a necessary part of practical and ornamental education."[14]

¶ From the mid–eighteenth century, governmental patronage of natural history surveys had rested on economic interests, and the state geological surveys were no different. The surveys of North and South Carolina set the pattern, pointing to agricultural interests and hopes of discovering useful mineral resources. To these purposes, many states soon added natural history surveys that called for the identification of botanical and zoological "productions," with the obvious expectation that such knowledge would be useful. Nor were state geologists to confine their concerns to items of general interest. They were also directed to consider the interests of any of the state's inhabitants—as in the case of the state geologist of Maryland, whose duties included "at those seasons not suited to the active prosecution of the geological survey, to analyze and ascertain the qualities and properties of all specimens of mineral substances or soils left at his office or residence for that purpose by any citizen of the State and taken from any portion of the territory of the State." Finally, every survey called for the careful and timely preparation of maps and reports to be presented to the legislature, with a view to their general dissemination. James Hall of the New York State Geological Survey came to know the various aims of such surveys well, and he identified six duties of a state geologist: to examine the geological formations and map them, to identify mineral resources and communicate his findings to the public, and to take into special consideration the expressed desires of local residents and offer them advice on practical matters.[15]

¶ This expectation that geologists could offer advice not only on the mineral resources of a region but on practical matters of special interest to local residents had a great deal to do with the popularity and development of geology in the young United States. As historians now recognize, the assumption that Americans were indifferent to the promotion of science may be broadly valid as regards "*basic* science," but this indifference should be ascribed to a "strong belief in *applied* science whose practical usefulness appealed to a people laying the foundations for civilized life in a wilderness." This hope that geology would yield results of economic value was a part of a "republican ideology" in which science was linked to craft skills and thus seen as applicable to utilitarian goals in such a way that it could be identified as a means of satisfying the "everyday needs of ordinary people." Rather than a form of esoteric knowledge, science could appear as directly related to popular knowledge, useful to the wider populace, and thus highly appropriate to the growth and development of a democratic society. Scientific men and practical men could both contribute to the development of the country, the one making known the resources of the land and the other making their exploitation feasible.[16]

¶ Theory and practice did not always join so neatly, however. Nor did all of the geologists' patrons understand what the geologists were doing, or why. Geological theories competed with craft traditions, and frequently enough came off second best. When they did, the scientists could hardly avoid seeming "prolix, academic, speculative, sometimes undeniably incorrect, and, worst of all in the eyes of local wise men, time-consuming and impractical." Negotiation between patron and client offered a solution to those scientists astute enough to recognize and accommodate the need, and they found a number of ways to win and retain local support. One of the simplest was to seek out the local wise men during the course of the survey, use them as local guides, and thank them profusely for their assistance in the written reports. Focusing on useful economic discoveries could divert attention from failures and mistakes. The inclusion of a glossary of geological terms helped make final reports more intelligible to nonspecialists. Finally, it was sometimes possible to explain why it was simply impossible or poor economy for the state geologist to devote his time and efforts to his original instructions, and why a different course had been adopted instead.[17]

¶ In adopting such techniques to firm up their patron-client relationships, geologists were simply pursuing their own interests. They had to reach out to a public audience to attract patrons. Fortunately for the scientists, Jacksonian America provided a growing public audience for science, making it possible to combine public advocacy for the support of science presented as a means of advancing popular education with the possibility of augmenting the scientist's own income through public lectures, a popular form of entertainment in the Jacksonian era. Some scientists, like Louis Agassiz, were able to combine the popular interest that public lectures helped create with their own charismatic appeal to win unprecedented local support for their scientific enterprises.[18] Yet for most American scientists this was not a real option, and they remained men possessed of skills in need of materials and opportunities for research. They also remained an available pool of potentially willing scientific laborers and supporters for those who were able to mobilize them. For many, work on government surveys provided just the sort of opening they sought. What these potential clients required was access to patronage, something they sought in various ways.

¶ One of the most obvious, and frequently successful, means of gaining patronage, particularly at the state level, was personal advocacy by scientists. Many state geological and natural history surveys, for instance, had their initial inspiration in personal appeals. These were framed as suggestions from local college professors who saw conducting a survey as a remunerated means of facilitating their own research. Alternatively, the survey might be proposed by a local scientific society, as scientific cultivators sought to nurture an environment for the sciences in nineteenth-century America, and particularly those sciences that fell within the natural history tradition. Local societies not only helped encourage and focus scientific efforts, but they also served to diffuse an appreciation for such efforts in their communities. In either case, the argument made to the legislature usually focused on the economic and educational benefits that might be expected, though there can be little doubt that scientists had not forgotten how their own interests stood to benefit as well.[19] With public backing for their scientific research, scientists found themselves in a stronger position to advance their other career interests of strengthening their control of the scientific community and undergirding its infrastructure.

¶ Scientists had two major interests in strengthening their scientific communities and their control over them. Not only would a stronger community be of direct assistance in facilitating their research, but control of a stronger community would also give researchers more control over their careers and greater influence over the patronage that supported them. Both goals are evident in the actions surrounding the first efforts toward establishing national scientific societies in the antebellum years. As George Daniels has clearly demonstrated, in the period from 1815 to the early 1840s the American scientific community quickly became quite well developed, self-conscious, and articulate in expressing and advocating, if not always successful in achieving, its own interests.[20]

The first members of the scientific community to organize themselves on more than a local level were the leaders of state geological surveys, who attempted to found a society of genuinely national scope to support their own efforts: the Association of American Geologists (AAG), organized at Philadelphia on 2 April 1840. Five of the eighteen founding members of the AAG represented the New York State Geological Survey, whose Board of Geologists had given birth to the idea of a national society as a means of communication among American geologists then engaged in state geological surveys. As members of the largest and most important of the state surveys then in existence, their desire for such a society reflected self-interest. Since the geological formations of New York extended into Pennsylvania and Massachusetts, New York geologists were interested in establishing a uniform system of geological nomenclature that would correlate various local nomenclatures throughout the American surveys and correlate the American nomenclature with that of Europe. Such a society would also assist them in learning of the experience and views of colleagues and coworkers in neighboring states. Yet the AAG soon—and perhaps inevitably, if it was to survive—outgrew its small and narrow origins and goals, expanding into a broader conception and membership. At their third meeting, in 1843, the membership recognized this fact by changing the society's name to the Association of American Geologists and Naturalists (AAGN), which became the parent of the American Association for the Advancement of Science (AAAS) in 1848.[21]

¶ Despite its brief life, the AAGN accomplished several important objectives. Foremost among these, it provided a forum where professional geologists—and to a lesser extent other naturalists—could meet with their peers to exchange views and present the results of their research. The AAGN's success as a society, which was exhibited by a growing roster and generally dependable participation at its annual meetings, not only demonstrated the viability of such a society but also provided an answer to the question of whether or not a similar society with broader scope might be successfully organized. However, the society's members were also alert to the potential of their annual meetings to arouse local public interest in science, and they sought to use these gatherings to bolster public support for their research interests. In this, the AAGN was much less successful. Nor were they able to deal adequately with another thorny issue of importance to professional scientists: gaining hegemony over both scientific amateurs and charlatans.[22] Both of these concerns remained problematic for its successor organization as well.

¶ The transformation of the AAGN into the AAAS did not mark the coming of age of American science as a profession so much as a determination to continue the quest toward that goal by promoting a scientific esprit de corps. As such, the new organization fit in well with the goals of the so-called "Scientific Lazzaroni," who promptly targeted the AAAS for "capture." The Scientific Lazzaroni—or scientific beggars—hold a charmed place in the lore of nineteenth-century American science. They were a select group of only nine permanent members, whose sole public raison d'être was as a dinner club that would gather at least once a year to "eat an outrageously good dinner together."[23] Yet they and their critics agreed there was a hidden agenda as well: to promote their own conception of professional scientific standards.

¶ The Lazzaroni sought to do this in two ways, by advocating public and private support for scientific research and by promoting the scientific careers of individuals whom they considered qualified. Their methods directly addressed what they viewed as the two basic problems in contemporary American science: too little support for science and "charlatanism," which frequently wasted the existing support because the public was so susceptible to it. As Joseph Henry put it to Bache, the challenge "the real working men" of science faced was to "put down quackery" before quackery "put down science." As self-identified true scientific laborers, the Lazzaroni took upon themselves the task of raising American scientific standards by promoting education in science, the formation and direction of scientific societies and museums, and the creation of scientific positions—to be filled with promising individuals of their own selection.[24]

¶ From the first, the Lazzaroni not only joined and took an active part in the AAAS, but they also took upon themselves the task of ensuring the exclusion from its leadership of any "pretenders to science." However, they soon discovered the difficulties inherent in attempting to reconcile elitist values with democratic institutions, for the AAAS was a basically democratic institution whose more numerous amateur members were not always eager to follow the directions of their scientific "betters." The issue is a perennial one, particularly in weak and nascent scientific communities, since it involves establishing the very things such communities lack: a set of common standards by which to judge the competence of the members to contribute to the enterprise. In this case, in the opinion of the self-identified elite, entry into early-nineteenth-century American science was too open. This might be very well in its place, because it made possible the recruitment of talented individuals and because cultivators of science might be very useful in contributing their mites to the efforts of experts. But such a situation was definitely not to the liking of scientific professionals and researchers as they sought to secure their place, particularly given the transformations underway in natural history as it became increasingly specialized.

¶ Yet if the Lazzaroni as a group found it difficult to exercise effective scientific leadership, several of them were highly influential as individuals. None of them was more influential than their "Chief," Alexander Dallas Bache. Chief of the Lazzaroni was at best an honorary title; the origin of Bache's true influence derived from his effective use of his position as director of the United States Coast Survey from 1843 to 1867. From its beginnings in 1816 until Bache's appointment as director, the U.S. Coast Survey suffered under poor political management. Its first director, Ferdinand Rudolph Hassler, initially proved so unresponsive to his political patrons that after only two years in office he was removed and the survey placed under the navy's direction. In its turn, the navy proved unqualified to carry out the survey, and Hassler was reappointed in 1832. Though a highly competent scientist, Hassler remained irascible in his dealings with nonscientists—and particularly with Congress. As a result, though the Coast Survey was revived in 1832, its vitality suffered while Hassler remained at its head because of his inability to function effectively within the patronage world of Washington politics. His successor, Bache, suffered from no such disabilities.[25]

¶ Exceptionally gifted with the talents and connections necessary to succeed where Hassler had failed, Bache labored patiently within the political structure of Washington. His West Point education and army experience enabled him to appreciate military officers' perspectives and work with them instead of against them. At the same time, his social standing as a grandson of Benjamin Franklin and a leader in the Philadelphia intellectual community helped him gain a hearing for the public support of science. Bache also knew the necessity of fostering political patronage. He gave congressmen something they could take home to their constituents, such as quickly produced maps or plans for maps in their own districts. He also made wide use of newspapers to keep the survey before the public eye and encouraged district survey employees to adapt themselves to the needs and interests of local residents. Nor did he neglect his ties with or obligations toward the scientific community. Rather, Bache worked to gain the support of scientists by equating his aims with their interests, all the while reassuring them that they need not feel threatened by the Coast Survey's growth and that he was bending all his efforts to promote the growth of American science generally.[26]

¶ Yet Bache believed progress in American science required that a small class of elite practitioners, men who for the most part had acquired European degrees or training and devoted themselves to serious scientific research, gain leadership positions in the country's national institutions. Once he obtained control of the nation's most important scientific institution—the Coast Survey—he wasted little time in seeking to augment his hegemony. In December 1846, Bache helped define the qualifications for the secretary of the Smithsonian Institution in such a way that virtually only one man in America, Joseph Henry, fitted the position. He then proceeded to pressure his friend and fellow Lazzaroni to apply for the job. Following the founding of the AAAS in 1848, Bache and fellow Lazzaroni members maneuvered for effective control of the society. By making discreet use of the patronage and support that the Coast Survey could provide—in positions, stipends, and loans of equipment—Bache promoted the scientific work of those he approved of and provided connections to a larger research world for college professors. His greatest coup, however, was his joint success with Louis Agassiz of translating their long-cherished dream of a federally chartered National Academy of Sciences (NAS) into a reality early in March 1863. The fledgling society would have to wait a long time before it would consistently exercise anything like an important influence, let alone a dominant one, in American science, but its founding planted seeds that eventually bore important fruit.[27] One of the first of these had a direct impact on Hayden's own career.

As geologists and their natural history colleagues labored to achieve the sort of security and position of influence Bache was able to construct for himself, they did so under a handicap he had not had to face. Bache's discipline and charge were relatively unified and focused on producing accurate maps of the nation's coastline and coastal waterways. Natural history, by contrast, was in the process of fracturing into a series of separate disciplines (including geology) with a variety of goals. Ironically, success in attracting patronage for natural history served to hasten the fracturing, which made the pursuit of patronage all the more competitive.

¶ Louis Agassiz announced the dawning of a new era for natural history in the United States even as his arrival and decision to settle in Boston helped initiate it. Though he remained an inveterate collector of all sorts of zoological specimens—so much so that he was never able to describe more than a small fraction of his collections—almost from his arrival in America in 1846, he began to seek to turn naturalists' attention from merely discovering and describing new species to a search for "the fundamental relations among animals," the new science of comparative anatomy. According to Agassiz, the former work of natural historians would no longer suffice to win Americans the respect they sought in the scientific world. It had become instead, he claimed, "almost the lowest kind of scientific work."[28]

¶ Agassiz's announcement sounded both a challenge and a call to arms. It was a challenge to naturalists of an older generation, many of whom were still active, whose education in natural history had been mostly self-taught and whose careers had been dedicated to exactly what he now termed "the lowest form of science." But it was a welcome call to arms to a younger, more academically and research-oriented generation, who welcomed one of Europe's most illustrious naturalists to America as much for his representation of the most modern thinking in European science as for his skill at charming patrons and convincing them that science was worthy of their support.[29] To both groups, the timing of Agassiz's arrival was significant.

¶ By the 1840s a generation of Young Turk naturalists was coming to maturity in America and ready to make its bid for control of natural history. These men were distinguished from their elders by their possession of a greater degree of academic training, which had frequently included some time in Europe. Their ambition to be accepted as peers by the leading naturalists in Europe primed them for Agassiz's prescription for American science, and they were ready to accept his demotion of the practices of the old-school field naturalists. As the younger generation gained influence, members of the older generation found it harder to gain access to publication and to collections, even collections they had made. In short, the professional standing of field naturalists changed as they were increasingly considered to be "hired collectors," incompetent to be the scientific "authors of their own discoveries."[30]

¶ The whole issue revolved on the questions of who had the authority to speak for science and how that authority could be recognized. These issues are not unfamiliar ones for historians of science, but they have been more frequently examined in the European context. There, social class was quite clearly used as a bootstrap to credibility by means of appealing to the presumed greater inherent trustworthiness of a gentleman's testimony. But questions of authority and credibility were also important in democratic America—perhaps even more so in a society where class distinctions could be less overtly invoked by reputation-conscious scientists. Since geology was already a high-culture science by the 1820s, American geologists had particular reason to be anxious about their status vis-à-vis Europe, and all the more reason to seek to impose standards of practice on American science—which had been one of the founding aims of the AAG.[31] Their naturalist brethren had no less reason to follow the same route out of concern for their own scientific reputations.

¶ Yet as the would-be leaders of American science sought to exercise and impose their own standards, they frequently met with resistance and rebellion from those who found themselves counted among the lower ranks. Unsurprisingly, a situation that was already highly competitive in the search for position and support could easily become contentious, even as it remained important for the scientific community to put forward an image of unity. In an environment where reputation, both with the public and with one's colleagues, counted for so much, one could hardly do too much to protect it. At the same time, however, it would not do to risk it needlessly. With such considerations in mind, scientific disputes were not unlike duels, which implied a code of honor among gentlemen. Since they could only be settled within a gentlemanly community, their conduct had to take care not to offend the standards of that community. Though insult might be given, it had to be done carefully, without impugning the proper honor due a member of the community. To do otherwise was to risk ostracism from the community.[32]

¶ These considerations were not mere academic concerns. They were a matter of careers, careers that depended on reputation. The development of the practice of scientific consulting in geology in Jacksonian America provides a good example of how this was so. Consultants occupied a position at the intersection of science and industry, giving them a responsibility to both sides. But the ethics of consulting quickly came down on the side of science, calling for an appearance of disinterestedness rather than seeming to tailor reports according to the interests of clients. So much was this the case that even clients found it in their interest to seek honest reports. Though they naturally sought to place reports in their most favorable light and accent positive elements, clients also recognized that in engaging a scientific consultant they were hiring both expertise and credentials, the credibility of which rested on the consultant's reputation.[33]

¶ What geologists and naturalists lacked was a strong institutional base in which they could develop and assert their standards. In this regard, Bache's success in developing the Coast Survey as an institutional base for the support of scientific research and the influencing of science policy was something of an anomaly in antebellum America. The anomaly, however, illustrates how "the actual role of the scientist in the federal government was always roughly the same. Scientists executed politicians' mandates except in those rare instances in which a scientist could develop his own political ties with public decision-makers."[34]

The more usual pattern for support of science on the part of the federal government was short-term, relatively small-scale projects oriented to utilitarian goals.

¶ The federal government called on the services of scientifically trained men in a variety of ways in the antebellum period as it sought to fulfill growing obligations to an expanding country. Early in its history, the federal government recognized a number of responsibilities vis-à-vis the western lands, which belonged to the United States yet were not part of any state. Foremost among them, and following the example provided by the Northwest Ordinances laid down by the Continental Congress in the mid-1780s, were the supervision of settlement on the public lands and the orderly disposal of a national resource for the public good. From these flowed a number of corollaries, many of which could only be accomplished through some sort of survey. Orderly disposal—whether through sale or otherwise—demanded mapping surveys to determine and record clear title to the land. Responsible disposal required knowledge of the land and its resources, and the Land Ordinance of 1785 set a precedent in directing that one third of the mineral lands in a territory be reserved for the use of the federal government—an order that presumed some sort of natural resources survey.[35] "Disposal" meant settlement, which imposed more demands and responsibilities upon the federal government. Chief among them were communication and protection; both demanded roads for transporting the mail and moving military forces and their supplies, and road construction also presupposed some sort of surveying.

¶ Besides practical reasons, strategic concerns also led the federal government into surveys of the public lands. As William Goetzmann long ago pointed out, nearly every one of the federal surveys into the American West conducted during the first half of the nineteenth century had military and/or territorial implications. Most of these surveys aimed at "spying out the land" in all the senses of that term, for much of the land was already occupied and claimed—by Spanish, Mexican, and English authorities, as well as by Native American peoples—and rarely were they kindly disposed toward exploratory surveys of the western lands. The government, therefore, turned to the army to accomplish the tasks.

¶ It did not do so without reason. Not only did the army need the results of such surveys to carry out its defense obligations, but it was one of the few institutions in early-nineteenth-century America that employed individuals who possessed the rudiments of technical expertise necessary to undertake such surveys. Throughout the early nineteenth century, the United States Military Academy was the only school in America offering academic training in engineering. When the technical demands of the job were set alongside the obvious need for protection to accomplish the mission, it was only logical that Congress should call upon men who had received some training for such a mission and were already in government employ. Necessity and frugality united to form policy.

¶ The tradition of federally supported expeditions of discovery was nearly as old as that of surveys for reason of sale of public lands. It found its precedent in the explorations of Meriwether Lewis and William Clark at the beginning of the nineteenth century (1804–6). The tradition inaugurated by Lewis and Clark continued in such surveys as those led by Zebulon Pike in 1805 and 1807, Stephen Long in 1819–20, Benjamin Bonneville in 1832–34, John Frémont from 1842 to 1848, and the Pacific Railroad Surveys in the 1850s.[36]

¶ The various surveys that the government ordered provided more than answers to the questions and needs of actual and potential residents, speculators, and government agencies at different levels. They also provided opportunities for scientists. Reconnoitering the land and its resources provided opportunities in the exploring and collecting sciences, such as astronomy, hydrography, terrestrial magnetism, meteorology, topographical mapping, geology, botany, zoology, and anthropology. Besides requiring men qualified to draw up accurate maps, military expeditions were also in need of personnel knowledgeable enough in other branches of natural history to make serviceable collections and to work up and publish the results. For this, they depended largely on civilians, since expertise in most of these areas went beyond the training and inclination of most army officers. But to take advantage of the opportunities the surveys presented, individual scientists needed to make contact with their sponsors and leaders. While local professors of science might loom large enough in a city to gain access to state officials, making contact with the federal government could be a different matter. At this level, it was frequently important to have someone play an intermediary role as a power broker, someone who could make introductions between naturalists and collectors and would-be patrons and occasionally intervene to mediate or resolve disputes.[37] In this situation, one of Joseph Henry's earliest assistants at the Smithsonian quietly crafted a niche for himself in which he partially substituted for the lack of a national institutional base for natural history. In the process, he had a broad impact on the development of natural history in America.

¶ Born on 3 February 1823 in Reading, Pennsylvania, Spencer Fullerton Baird developed from an early age a passion for natural history, and particularly for ornithology. Baird received his first tutoring as a naturalist from an older brother, William. This was followed by some more formal training while he was a student at Dickinson College in Carlisle, Pennsylvania, from 1836 to 1840 and a few medical courses in anatomy. But most of his training was more informal, either self-taught or through connections he established with other naturalists through correspondence, introductions, and visits. Baird had a prodigious capacity for work, and within a few years after graduating from Dickinson he built a reputation as a collector and "one of the leading naturalists in America."[38]

¶ Ambition led Baird to Washington and a position at the Smithsonian, where he arrived with a thorough familiarity with the ways of preference. He came from a political family. An uncle had been appointed solicitor of the United States Treasury by President William Henry Harrison in 1841, and Baird's brother William later received a clerkship in that department. While visiting his brother in the early 1840s, Baird became acquainted with the natural history collection of the United States Exploring Expedition, also known as the Wilkes Expedition, after its commander, naval lieutenant Charles Wilkes. The Wilkes Expedition had explored the Pacific Ocean for four years, from 1838 to 1841, ranging from the western coasts of North and South America to the Antarctic to the South Pacific Islands, constructing naval charts and gathering specimens in all branches of natural history to ship back to Washington. The subsequent history of much of these collections became one of the unhappier chapters of federal scientific efforts, as many specimens were lost because improper provisions for their care were made before Wilkes's return to take them in hand. Whatever the collection's condition, when Baird arrived in Washington in the mid-1840s he made bold to seek the position of curator of the collection in spite of his youth. Though unsuccessful, his attempt gave him a practical demonstration of the necessity of political patronage for federal employment. When he began to seek a position as secretary to Joseph Henry a few years later, Henry provided Baird with some very blunt advice on the need for such patronage. Fortunately, Baird could call on all the appropriate recommendations, both scientific and political. The scientific connections he had woven in his career as a naturalist; the political he had from his family and his marriage to Mary Helen Churchill, the only daughter of Brig. Gen. Sylvester Churchill, Inspector General of the Army.[39]

¶ As Henry's assistant secretary, Baird found that he had more than enough to do in his assigned duties of supervising the Smithsonian's publications and international exchange programs, to say nothing of his own first love, the development of a national museum of natural history, which Henry more suffered than favored. But when his duties prevented him from continuing to spend much time in the field collecting specimens, Baird shifted his sights to collecting surrogate collectors. His position and contacts put him in an ideal position to act as a patron and broker, and over the course of his twenty-eight years as assistant secretary Baird built up an extensive network of clients, with whom he kept in contact by means of a heroic correspondence numbering in the thousands of letters each year.[40]

¶ Baird's collectors ranged in skill and experience from beginning amateurs to seasoned professionals, but he was never too busy to add new ones to his collection, particularly those who seemed to exhibit a special promise either in their own talents or in the regions to which they had access. In the latter regard, Baird gave special attention to army and navy officers, whose duties might take them to more distant and isolated regions. He sought to infect such men with an interest in collecting as a profitable use of their free time and as a way of contributing to science. As a patron, Baird took good care of his clients. He assisted them in the work of collecting by giving them instructions and advice, collecting equipment and publications, money to assist with freight costs, and words of encouragement so isolated collectors could feel connected to a larger scientific community. He also assisted them in their careers, putting in a good word for a transfer to another army post, advising on an appropriate path for higher education in natural history, or helping them find suitable employment.[41]

¶ Helping his best clients find scientific employment was one of Baird's specialties. Situated in Washington, Baird was ideally placed to suggest candidates to act as naturalists on government expeditions. He could take advantage of his ready access to Henry and a number of influential legislators who served as regents of the Smithsonian and respected both Henry and Baird, and he had ready access to high army circles, as well, through his father-in-law. He soon appropriated to himself the function of unofficial matchmaker between military personnel with appropriations and civilians with scientific expertise. As his most recent biographers have written, "Soon every government-sponsored expedition included one or more of Baird's 'missionaries,' as he called them, or else a military man who had been detailed to the Smithsonian for a period of training by Baird and equipped with apparatus for collecting and preserving specimens."[42]

¶ Baird's desire to build a national museum of natural history gave him a particular interest in the western expeditions since they traversed the least-well-known sections of the country and thus the region that promised to add the most new specimens to his collections. Fortunately for Baird, the decade immediately following his appointment as assistant secretary proved an especially busy time for federal expeditions in the West, ranging from boundary surveys to explorations of river valleys. But the most extensive effort, by far, was the search for a route for a transcontinental railroad.

¶ The Pacific Railroad Surveys represented the culmination of the federal government's antebellum efforts at surveying the western territories. They arose from the sectional strife of the time. The discovery of gold in California in 1848, the rapid emigration to the region, and its speedy incorporation into the Union in 1850 soon made it desirable to connect California to the rest of the states by means of a railroad. Yet the construction of a railroad to California presented economic and political problems that were exacerbated by the North-South sectional divisions. To build a railroad across the uninhabited plains, deserts, and mountains west of the Mississippi would be prohibitively expensive for private capital. Government assistance of some sort would be necessary, and even the government was unlikely to construct more than one railroad. For all that, however, there was probably enough support for a railroad. The sticking points were the route and the location of the eastern terminus.

¶ Northern politicians, especially Senator Stephen Douglas, plumped for Chicago, while those southern politicians who supported a federally assisted transcontinental railroad pushed for New Orleans. To everyone involved, it was obvious that if there was only one railroad whichever city was chosen could expect enormous economic dividends. In the hope of elevating the question above politics, in March 1853 Congress sought to solve the Pacific railroad problem by authorizing simultaneous federal surveys by the army's Corps of Topographical Engineers of all the principal routes—three northern and three southern—in an effort to decide on scientific grounds which of them was the "most practicable and economical."[43]

¶ The expeditions were typical of the period. Military in organization and command, they also possessed a scientific orientation. They generally included a "surgeon-naturalist" and had instructions to make observations and collections of the geology, minerals, and natural history of the areas as well as to conduct a reconnaissance and construct a map of the country's topography. As a result, the surveys quickly evolved into relatively elaborate affairs, as places were set aside for scientific experts, and both foreign and domestic scientists vied for membership in the parties. Yet while they proved a great benefit to scientists, the surveys ultimately failed their political purpose because they demonstrated that, given a willingness to spend enough money, any of the routes was feasible while each presented its own difficulties. To the historian, they also demonstrate a number of other things, not least of which is that the effort to provide a simple scientific solution to a political problem is frequently an ephemeral dream. More immediately to the point, though the Pacific Railroad Surveys represented the federal government's most ambitious effort at surveying its western lands, they, like all the efforts in the preceding half century, remained ad hoc. The surveys were established in response to a particular problem and conceived with a very narrow mission, and for a brief period a great effort was made, but no lasting institutional structure endured past the time necessary to compile the results of the surveys.[44] The post–Civil War surveys would eventually leave a more lasting imprint, albeit one marked very much by the stamp of their antebellum predecessors.

The Civil War marks an important turning point in the history of American science in a number of ways. Some of these are quite well known. The United States Sanitary Commission, established during the summer of 1861, set an important precedent for military-civilian cooperation. The passage of the Land-Grant College Act in 1862 went a long way toward providing initial infrastructure as well as jobs for a generation of American scientists. The establishment of the navy's Permanent Commission of scientific advisors in 1863 sought to gather together in a small body the best scientific expertise available in various governmental and quasi-governmental bureaus, including the navy's Bureau of Navigation, the army's Corps of Topographical Engineers, the Coast Survey, and the Smithsonian Institution, in order to provide the government with information on questions of a scientific character. Finally, the founding of the National Academy of Sciences in 1863, with a charge to provide free scientific advice to the government whenever called upon, marked a potential for increased collaboration between policymakers and the nation's scientific elite.[45]

¶ At the same time, the war interrupted some of the government's accustomed scientific activities. With the outbreak of war, for instance, the army quickly called a halt to its surveys of the West, and most of its topographical engineers were reassigned to armies in the field. The interruption caused some initial hardships and inconvenience to civilian scientists who might have preferred both to avoid the war and continue their investigations, but it ultimately proved fortuitous to the cause of civilian science, since with the conclusion of war America was a changed nation—changed both by the war itself and by legislation passed by the Republican Party during the war.

¶ We have already seen that throughout the antebellum period the struggle for government funding for surveys was almost always linked to some overtly useful purpose—the obligation to defend settlers on the frontier, the need to locate wagon or post roads, the discovery of routes for railroads. These reconnaissance efforts were easily adapted to include scientific purposes, especially those that might have economic ramifications, such as geology and natural history. For most of these subsidiary purposes, civilian assistants were frequently permitted or employed to accompany the expeditions.

¶ In the postwar period, these economic and utilitarian purposes remained central, but they did so in an environment that had fundamentally changed in three important ways. The first created new or broader opportunities. Although the initial transfer of topographers and engineers to the eastern military districts upon the outbreak of war might have been temporary, it had long-lasting effects on the careers of many of them. Second, the continuing postwar duties of occupying the South during Reconstruction placed a drain on regular army officers and units. Finally, the transformation of West Point education from a focus on engineering and surveying to a more military emphasis in 1866 and the suppression of the Corps of Topographical Engineers that same year further reduced the number of army personnel available for western surveys.[46] The cumulative effect was to create an opening for others to lead western surveys, and the leaders of those surveys were among the first to seize and exploit the new possibilities for civilian science. Moreover, two other significant changes that had occurred during the intervening years greatly expanded the potential for exploiting these possibilities.

¶ The first of these was the new activist posture the federal government adopted during and immediately following the Civil War. Significantly, this new approach included financial support of scientific activity. Though bearing only a remote similarity to the modern financing of scientific research, the increased support represented a new direction for Congress. It was hardly a planned direction since more frequently Congress merely responded to specific pressures, not always conscious of future direction or potential effects.[47] All the same, these modest beginnings planted the seeds of future scientific bureaus, providing them with the opportunity to take root and develop within the federal bureaucracy and, perhaps, come to enjoy a permanent place. The Hayden Survey was one of those seeds.

¶ The other element was the rejuvenation of interest in the trans-Mississippi West. For several decades, small groups of settlers had been moving west. After the war, the trickle became a flood, and the West's population increased threefold within twenty years. While the nation's overall population increased by less than two-thirds during the same period, from 31.5 million to 50.3 million, the population of the trans-Mississippi West jumped from 619,000 to just over 1.8 million between 1860 and 1880.[48] Americans and immigrants alike went West in search of opportunities for a better life. But many who never moved there also developed interests in western lands and opportunities. Three major stimuli to interests in things western were the discovery of commercially exploitable minerals, the completion of the transcontinental railroad in 1869, and simple curiosity, both scientific and otherwise.

¶ Interest in western mineral resources took several forms. The extraction of gold deposits continued at a steady pace of about 2 million ounces per year during the 1860s and 1870s, while exploitation of silver deposits rose dramatically during the same period, from 116,000 ounces in 1860 to a peak of more than 35 million ounces in 1878. Less precious minerals also promised great wealth to those who could find and make use of them, as the Northeast and the Midwest continued their enthusiastic embrace of the industrial revolution. In the 1860s and 1870s, the iron and steel industries were in the midst of rapid expansion and technological revolution. Iron ore production increased by a factor of nearly 1.5 between 1860 and 1880, while pig iron production rose nearly fourfold, from 0.9 million tons in 1860 to 4.3 million tons in 1880. In 1867, the third Bessemer furnace was opened in the United States. Two more followed in succeeding years. In 1868, Andrew Carnegie opened the first of his iron mills. In the same period, the copper, lead, and other mineral industries were just entering the first stages of bonanza development. Rapidly advancing industrialization demanded the ready availability of basic raw materials, and these lay largely in the West. Eastern industrialists were well aware of these facts and thus very much inclined to view the West as the depository of exploitable natural resources. Bituminous coal, the type found in the trans-Mississippi West, was of particular interest, and production rapidly climbed from 8.8 million tons in 1861 to 50.8 million tons in 1880, evidence of the swiftness with which industry responded to the new discoveries.[49]

¶ The transcontinental railroads were a second major factor in the development of the West because they invested huge sums of capital in construction costs. During the Civil War, Congress passed legislation supporting the railways with bonds and land-grant awards. As they laid down their forty-mile sections of track, the Union Pacific, Central Pacific, Kansas Pacific, Chicago and Northwestern, and a handful of other railroads claimed their awards and quickly became the largest private landholders in the West. Inevitably, they were in a position to influence patterns of settlement, and those patterns were rarely adventitious. Not only was every station along their routes a potential nucleus for settlement and a base for prospectors and miners, but the railroads' position as landholders was significantly augmented by two important factors that united to ensure that these became prime lands. First, location contiguous to a railroad was convenient for transporting crops and goods. Second, when Congress issued grants of land to the railroads, it closed to settlement the alternate sections retained by the government, reserving them for sale only after the roads had completed construction through an area and received their full grants.[50] In most cases this took years. In the meantime, Congress ignored a pressing issue but one the railroads quickly recognized: there had to be settlements and farms along the routes if they were to be profitable. The solution lay in the development of railroad lands.

¶ Needing returns on their investments, railroad companies bent every effort to sell their land holdings. They employed two basic strategies: town development and the promotion of agriculture. Railroad towns included settlements bordering the routes that ranged from instant cities and "hells on wheels" to more sedate towns that remained after the construction crews had moved on. But it was the planned communities, which had been surveyed, mapped, advertised, and developed by the railroad companies, that, when successful, not only provided desperately needed capital for the railroads but also served to ensure that the West developed around those same railroads.[51]

¶ However, efforts to attract agriculturists to the railroad towns confronted a severe obstacle—the "myth of the great American Desert." Historians have noted the persistence and the effect of this "myth" of the unsuitability of the trans-Mississippi region to civilized settlement; beginning with the explorations of Zebulon Pike, it was kept alive through periodic repetition, perhaps most frequently by members of the military. To counteract what was by the 1860s a popular "misconception," many of the western railroads quickly linked up with local promotional efforts sponsored by western states, territories, and local communities. On the Great Plains, these efforts sought "to change the image of the plains [in order] to attract settlers." Promotion included an interest in the potential resources available in the vicinity. Eastern industrialists were not the only ones seeking knowledge of these deposits. Westerners were well aware that the economic development of their territories and towns depended upon the discovery and publicizing of exploitable resources, and throughout the West, "little groups of politically minded merchants, bankers, and land speculators . . . thrust their way forward in each city to volunteer a leadership that was crucial not only to the struggling new community itself but also to the much bigger region that was tributary to it."[52]

¶ Besides those who sought to emigrate to the West or invest in the development of its resources, there was also a more general interest in the region, ranging from the scientific to the merely curious. In the nineteenth century, the West "captured Americans' imaginations," serving as "a metaphor for the character of America . . . the quintessential symbol of everything that made the country unique." Enthusiastic promoters tended to emphasize its boundless size and its fertility, while Americans of all classes viewed the region as "a great national storehouse" for the service of the good of all Americans.[53]

¶ At the same time, it was a "utilitarian age," as the naturalists Alpheus Hyatt and Alpheus Spring Packard wrote in 1867. Issuing the first number of their new journal, the *American Naturalist*, they strove "to meet the wants of all lovers of nature." But they recognized that in a "utilitarian age" knowledge was primarily valued insofar as it was "subordinated to the practical advantage as well as to the intellectual and moral elevation of man." They sought to appeal, therefore, not only to "philosophers . . . seeking the truth for the truth's sake," but also to day laborers, the farmer and the grazier, the artisan and the mariner—all of whom might be presumed to have a legitimate interest in what advances in the natural sciences might mean in their own lines of work.[54] It was, of course, rhetorical overstatement, but those same interests might also be harnessed to sell programs in science as would-be clients sought patrons. They underlay much of the success of the men who stepped forward to assume the army's former mantle of leadership in surveying the West in that they all took advantage, in varying degrees, of the elements that shaped the new environment for science in the postwar American West.

¶ While Hayden directed one of the most famous of the western surveys during the decade after the Civil War, he was not alone in the field. The 1870s were the decade of the "Great Surveys," so-called because "they were great in the sense of the vast territories they examined, in their breadth—embracing topography, geology, and the natural sciences—and in the span of years in which they operated."[55] Known after their directors—Clarence Rivers King, Ferdinand Vandeveer Hayden, John Wesley Powell, and George Montague Wheeler—the King, Hayden, Powell, and Wheeler Surveys between them explored and surveyed most of the remaining unmapped areas of the lower continental United States during the period 1867–78.

¶ The most obvious difference between the Great Surveys and their antebellum predecessors was in organization. Unlike the antebellum efforts, most of these new surveys were under the direction of civilian scientists. The Geological Exploration of the Fortieth Parallel continued the antebellum tradition, but only to a degree. Though under the direction of the army's Chief of Engineers, it was appropriately known as the King Survey since King not only initiated the proposal but described its aims in his instructions to himself. In 1866, when King went to Washington to seek an appropriation for a survey of a one-hundred-mile-wide strip along the route of the transcontinental railroad, roughly paralleling the fortieth parallel of latitude, he sought and obtained the sponsorship and patronage of the War Department. But King was given a free hand in the conduct of his survey. Thus, while under the War Department officially, for most practical purposes the King Survey was a civilian survey.[56]

¶ Hayden's survey was also civilian in inspiration and operation. But it was also radically new in that it was wholly under civilian control and came under the auspices of the Department of the Interior. For the first two years it was administered under the commissioner of the General Land Office. Then, in 1869 the Hayden Survey was placed directly under the secretary of the interior, and over the course of the next ten years Hayden and his men surveyed most of Colorado and Wyoming and parts of Utah and New Mexico while beginning a comprehensive survey of Idaho and Montana.

¶ The Powell Survey, headed by John Wesley Powell, commonly known as Major Powell or simply the Major after his Civil War rank, was another wholly civilian survey. Its roots lay in an expedition Powell led West in 1868. At the time, Powell was a professor of natural science at Illinois Wesleyan University as well as a lecturer in geology and curator of the museum at the State Normal School of Illinois. When he conceived the idea of leading an exploring and collecting expedition to the Rocky Mountains in 1866, after persuading several local Illinois institutions to contribute funds to underwrite the expenses Powell sought advice and assistance from the Smithsonian.[57] Over the next several years, this largely amateur, student-and-teacher venture developed into Powell's explorations of the Colorado River and the Grand Canyon and then into the Geographical and Geological Survey of the Rocky Mountain region. After completing work in the Grand Canyon of the Colorado River, the survey went on to explore most of Utah and the southwestern corner of Wyoming.

¶ One novel and highly significant element in the postwar period, evident in all three of these surveys, was that the expeditions were led by and almost exclusively composed of civilians, with the military only along—when it did accompany the parties—in the role of escort. But this did not mean that the army had abandoned its role in conducting surveys. Besides sponsoring the King Survey, the army could and did continue to argue that it had even more need to conduct surveys for the purpose of preparing suitable maps of the terrain in order to fulfill its responsibilities of protecting the ever-increasing number of western settlers. By 1874, the War Department had no fewer than eight different military departments or districts west of the one hundredth meridian, each of them conducting its own separate surveys and reconnaissances for the use of local troops.[58] It also had a much more extensive effort in the field.

¶ This was the fourth of the Great Surveys, the Geographical Survey of the Territories West of the 100th Meridian, led by George Montague Wheeler, first lieutenant in the Army Corps of Engineers. Wheeler, an 1868 graduate of West Point, had only been engaged in the surveying business for two years when Brig. Gen. Andrew Atkinson Humphreys,

Chief of Engineers, assigned him in 1871 to explore and map "those portions of the United States territory lying south of the Central Pacific Railroad, embracing parts of Eastern Nevada and Arizona" for the purposes of "obtain[ing] topographical knowledge of the country" and "prepar[ing] accurate maps of that section." It was an inauspicious beginning for an ambitious officer; while the trip across Death Valley and up the Colorado River embraced a full share of dangers and hardships, it yielded relatively little useful knowledge. Yet the expedition did lead Wheeler to proclaim that "the day of the path-finder has sensibly ended," and he proposed a grander scheme: the "complete reconstruction of the engineer map of the Western Territories."[59]

¶ Wheeler's proposal won the approval of General Humphreys, who viewed the recent spectacular emergence of the Hayden and Powell Surveys as bureaucratic rivals to the army's traditional dominance in western surveys. Humphreys used every power at his command to promote Wheeler's proposals and, in the brief period of two years, the thirty-year-old first lieutenant became the head of an entire bureau of army exploration, with responsibility for a topographical and geographical survey of nearly half of the United States. However, for the execution of his design Wheeler could call upon only a very few of the officers of the Corps of Engineers and the regular army since the obligations of both stretched their limited manpower extremely thin. He therefore had to rely upon the services of civilian scientists, whom he recruited by relying both upon the tradition of military survey practice and the more recent arrangements that had been made through King's survey, where civilian scientists assisted in army efforts on a quid pro quo basis.[60]

¶ All four of these surveys shared a number of features. They all fit into patterns of activity established in the antebellum period of surveys. They were all mapping and exploring ventures, and they did similar kinds of work. Although they originally employed different techniques in mapping, placed different stresses on geological and geographical investigations and collections in natural history and ethnology, and made use of photography to differing degrees, all of the surveys were involved in similar investigations, and all had to deal with similar problems entailed in the field practice of these sciences in the 1870s. They were also alike in another important respect. Each was largely the work of the individual who headed the survey; each was to a large degree an entrepreneurial activity. King, Hayden, Powell, and Wheeler were not only the *directors* but also to a large degree the *inventors* of their respective surveys. Except for King, each had to act as the *sustainer* of his survey and annually win funds from Congress to continue operations. In other words, they continually had to cultivate patronage by appealing to the various interests people had in the West and their activities. As survey inventor, director, and sustainer, through the 1870s Hayden proved the most resourceful of the four survey leaders. He did so by drawing upon resources and skills developed prior to 1867.

2

The Making of a Frontier Naturalist

I am willing to go any where, for any length of time and labor with the utmost diligence. . . . few obstacles would present themselves which I would not cheerfully overcome, and were it necessary to accomplish my purposes, I could live as the Wild Indian lives and endure any amount of exposure and toil without a murmur. —Hayden to Baird, 16 February 1853

No inevitable destiny propelled Hayden to fame as director of a geological survey. He achieved fame as a result of nearly four decades of experience, opportunities, and choices, as well as by overcoming severe disadvantages in his personal background. At the same time, many elements of his practice, both as a scientist and as director of a bureau, were rooted in the lessons he learned and the patterns he established in nearly a decade of experience in what was at the time the nation's only graduate school for natural history and geology—practice in the field. The training Hayden gained in successive positions during the 1850s equipped him with the skills of a successful collector in natural history and respected geologist and taught him much about cultivating patronage and networking with a wide range of personalities, institutions, and constituencies.

¶ Hayden clearly found his background embarrassing. He therefore invented another, slightly more genteel background. In fact, over time he invented several versions, which did not always agree in the details, making the historian's job all the more difficult. Fortunately, his biographer has unraveled the myths Hayden wove, and they explain much about the man who needed them as substitutes for his true history.[1] Unfortunately, many elements of Hayden's true background remain shrouded in mystery. Not only did he occasionally lie about details, but critical evidence of his past has failed to survive for various reasons—

including, it seems, purposeful destruction. Yet what can be known both arouses curiosity and gives insight into the demons that drove the man to deny much of his heritage and seek to escape his past.

¶ His heritage began with birth out of wedlock. His parents, Asa Hayden and Melinda Hawley, were supposedly married on 26 November 1826 in Enfield, Connecticut, yet no record of the marriage exists. Nor is it likely that their union was ever legally solemnized, even though the couple had three more children before separating permanently in 1838. Adding to Hayden's embarrassment, his father was an alcoholic who had difficulty maintaining a regular livelihood. As a result, the family had no regular residence, though they resided in the western Massachusetts town of Lee longer than anywhere else before his mother took Ferdinand, together with Frances and Henry, his younger sister and brother, with her to Rochester, New York, to stay with her relatives. About two years later, Melinda returned to Massachusetts to file for a divorce, in preparation for marrying John Marchant, of Rochester, New York. Although the Berkshire court dismissed the petition in May 1841, Melinda and Marchant married on the twenty-third of that month anyway. All these factors had ramifications on Ferdinand's upbringing.

¶ Hayden was probably born in Westfield, Massachusetts, on 7 September 1828. His parents' difficulties deprived him of a secure home until he was a teenager. Perhaps the single greatest gift anyone gave him in his first dozen years was a $50 legacy from his paternal grandfather, who divided nearly two-thirds of his $158 estate among the offspring of his own wayward son. Hayden's mother appears not to have felt much affection for any of her children. While preparing to wed Marchant she evidently sought to improve her chances by placing her two elder children, Hayden and his sister, with relatives and keeping only the four-year-old Henry. For Hayden this meant the first serious physical distancing from his family—something he later sought to parallel by distancing himself emotionally from his past.

¶ By at least 1841, when Hayden was about thirteen, he was sent from Rochester, New York, to live with Lucretia Stevens, a sister of his father, and her husband on their farm in Rochester, Ohio. Here Hayden found a secure and supportive home. For the next five years, his aunt accepted him as one of her own. In Rochester he engaged in the sort of things that might normally have been expected to occupy a boy's rural youth: working on the farm, hunting, and studying at a local school. And perhaps here Hayden resolved to make something of himself, to become more than his family had been. Certainly, in Rochester Hayden decided to improve his opportunities by seeking an education at Oberlin Collegiate Institute, as Oberlin College was then known, some fifteen miles down the road.

¶ When Hayden arrived at Oberlin in September 1845 he had just turned eighteen and was virtually penniless but not so unlike many of the young men who would be his fellow classmates. Like many of them, he had to work to put himself through Oberlin. And like many of them he was poorly prepared for entrance into college and was therefore first placed in Oberlin's preparatory department, where he confronted an accelerated program of studies in geography, mathematics, English, elementary Latin and Greek, history, and the four gospels. Despite his weak background, Hayden thrived at Oberlin and did well enough in his first two terms that he was one of forty graduates of the preparatory department accepted into the college in the 1846 fall term. Four years later, Hayden was one of only thirteen to graduate.

¶ In spite of his academic success, Hayden was an enigma to most of his Oberlin classmates. From the first, he marched to a different drummer. Not that his classmates failed to notice Hayden; they did. But they failed to appreciate him. They remembered him as immature. He seemed uncultivated socially, and his "crude ambition" led him to extremes. One classmate later recalled that "He fairly ran when he walked that he might reach something. Sputtered when speaking that he might get at this or that." They also remembered his amusing habit of falling in love with a new girl nearly every week. Yet Hayden himself seemed a nobody, too impractical, too modest and retiring, "without much apparent force of character" to amount to much in the world.[2] Their recollections say as much about their inability to penetrate and appreciate his persona as they do about Hayden.

¶ Hayden's classmates mocked him for the enthusiasm with which he attacked his studies, for becoming "enraptured" with the study of flowers, and for his romantic infatuations with women. But they failed to appreciate the breadth of his studies or the extent of his reading. Nor did they notice or remember that this supposedly poor speaker joined one of the two literary groups at Oberlin at the beginning of his sophomore year, served regular monthly terms as its secretary and vice president, and was one of three students chosen to speak for the senior class at its anniversary. They also failed to appreciate how the study of natural history might have offered a consoling alternative to a young man with poor self-esteem in the face of Oberlin's pressure to adopt a lifestyle oriented to serious social action. Finally, none of his classmates fathomed the need Hayden felt to be accepted by women, after having been rejected by his mother.[3]

¶ No transcripts or records survive to provide definitive testimony to the courses Hayden studied at Oberlin, nor is there any clear evidence beyond his own statements years later that he acquired a "decided taste for the natural sciences" at Oberlin. Like most colleges of the period, Oberlin offered a variety of science courses, including astronomy, chemistry, anatomy, physiology, mineralogy, and geology. In addition, it seems clear that he undertook extracurricular studies in botany and may have acquired some knowledge of biology or zoology in the same way. Whatever science Hayden studied, he probably did so under the tutelage of George Allen, Oberlin's professor of music, geology, and natural history. Allen was more than a teacher to Hayden. He was also Hayden's first landlord (Allen and his wife rented rooms to Oberlin students) and his first academic supervisor as head of the preparatory department when Hayden arrived in 1845. Finally, Allen served as a father figure for young Hayden. Remembered as a gentle man and noted for his devotion to children and young people, Allen would have made a pleasant contrast to Hayden's own father. He may well have helped steer Hayden from a love of flowers to a larger appreciation of natural history. If he did, it may have been a meeting of kindred spirits, both wanting in self-confidence, who took refuge in the respectable, though impractical, study of God's creation.[4]

¶ Hayden graduated from Oberlin on 28 August 1850, just a few days shy of twenty-two years old and apparently with little idea of what to do for a career. He probably had no notion of pursuing a career in natural science, and it would have been unusual in mid-nineteenth-century America if he had, unless he was thinking of becoming a college professor or pursuing a medical degree. Nor did he look for opportunities in the western expeditions, of which neither Hayden nor Allen seem to have been very aware at the time. Instead, in the year following graduation, Hayden looked to continue earning an income as a school teacher. And rather than immediately abandon Oberlin's comfortable nest, he enrolled in the college's theological department.

¶ The year and a half following graduation constituted an important transition time for Hayden, but also a time of indecision. As he sought to sort his life out or, more likely, waited for his life to sort itself out, Hayden had several good reasons to stay at Oberlin. For one, he was in love and even engaged to be married. There was also the practical advantage of a comfortable environment, made all the more agreeable by the fact that the college waived tuition for students in the theology department while offering continued access to a diverse library collection. Though he may not have appeared all that religious to his peers, Hayden was and remained throughout his life well read in theology and no doubt recognized that the ministry would provide social status as well as the possibility of further pursuing studies in natural history. Finally, for a man still unsure of himself or what he wanted to do, continuing to earn a living in a familiar way probably would have been more attractive than seeking to break into something quite new—particularly when no one he knew seems to have been able to offer any suggestions on how to proceed.[5] Hayden's extended stay at Oberlin was just one of several incidents in his life in which, unsure what choice to make, he continued in the path he knew while pondering, or simply awaiting, his next step. What it would be did not become clear until the autumn of 1851.

¶ The summer of 1851 found Hayden between jobs and back at Oberlin, probably seeking Professor Allen's aid in obtaining another teaching position. This time, Allen led him to something that would prove of more lasting benefit. He introduced Hayden to Dr. Jared Potter Kirtland, professor at the Cleveland Medical School. Through Kirtland, Hayden met John Strong Newberry, a recent medical school graduate rapidly making a name for himself as a geologist and paleontologist. Both men soon became Hayden's newest mentors and patrons.[6]

¶ Why Allen directed Hayden to Kirtland remains something of a mystery. Prior to the summer of 1851 there is little evidence of a serious interest in science on Hayden's part. He was interested but seems to have continued to prefer literature to science. Perhaps Allen thought to take advantage of Hayden's avocational interest in science. At any rate, Kirtland advised Hayden that if he had any ideas of pursuing serious study in natural history he should enroll in medical school, the only outlet for advanced academic training in botany, zoology, and anatomy in 1850s America. When Newberry seconded this advice, he convinced Hayden, who quickly made arrangements to begin studies with both men. Before the year ended, Hayden began attending Kirtland's lectures at the Cleveland Medical School and studying medicine and some geology under Newberry's tutelage.[7] He had also begun his initiation into the scientific community.

¶ During his year and a half with Kirtland and Newberry, Hayden began to develop hopes for a career in natural history. He did much more than listen to lectures at the medical school and assist Newberry as a medical apprentice, an assistance grudgingly rendered, according to Newberry's partner. Of greater interest to Hayden than learning the nuts and bolts of medicine were the lessons about geology and fossils that Newberry could impart. Hayden quickly devoted more effort to these studies and to making the acquaintance of naturalists around the country than to his office chores. He spent hours collecting fossils and plant specimens in the local region and initiated an "ambitious correspondence" with naturalists, "picking their brains, asking for scientific books, boasting of his collections." As a consequence, Hayden gained a reputation as "a serious and eager naturalist" among his future colleagues before ever meeting them. These efforts and accomplishments were of no small consequence. As sociologists and historians of science have repeatedly emphasized, science is a craft activity carried on within the context of a community whose members trust one another's competence.[8] To enter into that community Hayden needed to develop both skills and relationships.

¶ Hayden entered the natural history community in the same fashion most any neophyte would—as a collector. And he had a great deal to learn in the way of practical skills. He may have already learned some of his primary lessons in botany from Allen during his time at Oberlin. No doubt Newberry and Kirtland taught him more; Hayden later claimed that under Newberry's tutelage he made enough progress in "fossil Botany" so that he could "readily determine the genera and most of the species" to be found around Cleveland. At the same time, he also made progress in geology, as a result of spending "from 4 to 6 hours per day" in its study. Much of that study was from books, which he borrowed from Kirtland and Newberry or through his correspondence with more experienced collectors and naturalists. In early 1853, Hayden claimed to have "thoroughly mastered several elementary works," including Charles Lyell's *Elements of Geology* (1838), and expected that "by Spring I shall be able to take notes with some degree of accuracy."[9]

¶ Networks such as the ones that Hayden tapped into were an important part of nineteenth-century science. Not only did they augment the resources of local societies and irregular publications, but they also served to help develop national and international communities whereby scientific workers could come to know and trust one another long before they might ever meet face to face. (They remain, in fact, a part of normal scientific practice, as can be seen in the development and operation of the Internet in the late twentieth century.) In becoming a collector of fossils and plants Hayden would have had to learn at least the rudiments of "a thriving set of practices" to gain a reputation as a serious and eager young naturalist.[10]

¶ Among the connections Hayden established during his time in Cleveland by far the most important for his subsequent career was his introduction to the New York geologist James Hall. An old friend of the Newberry family, Hall had encouraged Newberry's interest in natural history years earlier. In the autumn of 1851 he did the same for Hayden. As Hall remembered the meeting some forty years later, Hayden's zeal for collecting impressed him, and the two discussed the possibility of Hall sending Hayden to the Dakota Badlands in the Nebraska Territory to collect fossils. Whatever the exact circumstances, Hall, on the lookout for talent to assist him in his own efforts to gain hegemony in the study of American fossils, invited Hayden to come to Albany when he finished his education in Cleveland.[11] The offer made Hayden's next step obvious.

¶ When he walked away from his aunt and uncle's farm at the age of eighteen, Hayden took few resources with him besides intelligence and a burning ambition to succeed in life and distance himself from what he regarded as a shameful past. In his eyes, success would be measured by acceptance and recognition from others of his accomplishments.

Yet when he graduated from Oberlin five years later, Hayden still did not know what he wanted to accomplish, and it took him another year and a half to settle on natural history. Once he did, recognition from leaders in the field began to come his way almost immediately. Natural history specimens were a growth industry in the mid–nineteenth century, and Hayden showed promise as a collector.[12] Having settled on making a name for himself in natural history, Hayden recognized Hall's invitation as an extraordinary opportunity. He moved quickly to take advantage of it.

¶ He did not wait until he had finished his medical education before contacting Hall. Instead, with still two months to go, Hayden wrote Hall in January 1853, reminding him of his promise and seeking a definite offer of employment. The time proved opportune, and Hall responded with encouragement. He was still thinking of sending someone to the Badlands and promised he would "either give [Hayden] the means of going on this expedition, or upon some other nearer home." Hall sweetened the pot by suggesting that if Hayden wanted to finish medical studies in Albany he would make appropriate arrangements, which would also enable Hayden to assist Hall with his New York fossils. It would be a mistake, however, to view Hall as being philanthropic in offering to act as Hayden's patron—an attitude that would have been quite out of character. Rather, he was acting upon more self-interested motives, though he also described them as "patriotic" as well. The idea for an expedition to the Dakota Badlands had not come to him out of nowhere; it arose out of the recent discovery that the region harbored some extraordinary large fossils as well as from Hall's own need for assistance in working up his collection.[13]

¶ Neither proposal was exactly what Hayden wanted—an opportunity to go into the field as a collector. As his biographer notes, Hayden exhibited a canny prudence in not immediately accepting Hall's offer. Instead, he sought other options, writing in particular to a friend of Kirtland's, Spencer Baird at the Smithsonian, to inquire if Baird could attach him to any scientific expeditions. At the same time, Hayden wrote Hall that though he was eager for anything Hall could do for him, he wondered if it might not be better for him to go to the Badlands the *following* year, while spending the present year studying geology closer to home. In short, Hayden solicited the best offer available.[14]

¶ Luckily for Hayden, acquisitiveness forced Hall's hand when it seemed others were about to skim the cream off the Badlands fossils. After checking with Newberry—for whom Hayden was already collecting fossils—as to the probability of Hayden's success as a collector, and learning that he was likely to prove satisfactory if he had someone more experienced to guide him, Hall offered Hayden a position as assistant to Fielding Bradford Meek, an invertebrate paleontologist working for Hall. Although not quite what Hayden wanted, it was the best offer he received, so he accepted it. As his "terms of agreement," Hayden proposed that Hall pay his expenses in the field plus $150 per month and arrange for him to finish his medical degree the coming winter.[15]

¶ For a beginner, Hayden set a high price on his abilities. What sort of man had Hall engaged? Hayden's letters to potential patrons in this early period reveal a number of important features of his developing character: ambition and idealistic enthusiasm for science admixed with a number of baser qualities. Ambition dominates. Hayden was confident he could perform satisfactorily in spite of his inexperience, and he reassured Hall that "with all modesty, I think I should exceed even your expectations, for obstacles have no terror to me and I trust never will have." Hayden had to convince Hall he could do the job, but "obstacles have no terror" seems extreme and echoes a letter Hayden wrote Baird some three weeks earlier, in which he said that "were it necessary to accomplish my purposes, I could live as the Wild Indian lives and endure any amount of exposure and toil without a murmur." Hayden obviously wanted a position as a collector; he wanted it so much, in fact, that he willingly overcame the obstacle posed by the strict truth. For example, he wrote Baird: "I have taken considerable pains to prepare myself for a collector," rather an exaggeration at that point in his career. In a supporting letter to Baird, Kirtland only went so far as to describe Hayden as "a thorough botanist and to some extent familiar with collecting in most departments of Natural Science."[16] He still had a great deal to learn, and Meek would be his next important teacher.

¶ Eager, enthusiastic, confident, idealistic, ambitious, self-promoting—Hayden was all of these. He was also ingratiating and pleading, all the while bargaining. Obviously putting himself forward, he expressed a willingness to be subservient. Writing to Hall in early March, Hayden claimed that "any decision you may think best to make will please me." Nearly two months later he professed that he would be "very glad to have [Meek as] company, and the reason why I did not say it was I supposed you did not wish to make the additional expense" and then wrote Meek that "it suits me right well" that they would be going to the Badlands together.[17] Hayden presented himself as the ideal protégé, almost too good to be true. Indeed, he was; the image is false. Appearing modest, Hayden was anything but modest in self-promotion. As he pleaded his cause, he bargained, flattered, and wheedled by turns. The man had talents and enterprise. The trip to the Dakota Badlands would put many of those talents to the test.

The Badlands expedition was Hayden's first experience of extended fieldwork and his first exposure to one of the primary realities of expeditionary scientific practice: the myriad tasks entailed in getting into and staying in the field and working there. To a certain extent then it was fortunate that Hayden's first trip up the Missouri River was in many ways a frustrating disappointment since the difficulties provided just so much more education. For one thing, it quickly promised to be much more expensive than expected—largely because the American Fur Company, which provided transportation and promised assistance but had closer ties to competing expeditions, took the occasion to gouge the explorers as trespassers on their private domain. Moreover, the slow pace of transportation up the Missouri frustrated Hayden, impatient as he was to begin collecting. And once they reached their destination, they were only able to collect specimens for three weeks before Indians, who also considered them trespassers, forced them back. Collectively, these experiences provided Hayden with object lessons on the importance of infrastructure to support fieldwork. Pursuing natural history at the edges of empire in the nineteenth century depended upon the assistance of patrons who could provide the scientists with resources of transport and travel. In the Upper Missouri country of the early 1850s, the American Fur Company controlled these resources, and though it was not at all averse to assisting scientific explorations as a means of cultivating a favorable public image, it chose as the recipients of its liberality only those it deemed most likely to help in achieving that goal. At the same time, the Indians, as the other inhabitants of the region, defined limits on field practice by effectively opposing travel. Hayden and Meek had to practice their science and conduct their collecting within the limits of the cooperation they were able to obtain.[18]

¶ In spite of these shortcomings, the trip yielded Hayden some important accomplishments. First, the expedition proved he could succeed as a collector. Equally important for his subsequent career were his working introduction to Meek, which inaugurated what developed into a lifetime partnership, and his initiation into the practice of geology in the western landscape, afforded first by long hours spent on the riverboat gazing at the passing terrain. Yet Hayden could never have become a geologist from the deck of the riverboat. To do so, he had to disembark and engage in what was virtually a "rite of initiation and passage into the [geological] community"; he had to learn how to do fieldwork. He had to learn the basic skills of the craft. Those skills were fundamentally visual skills. Nineteenth-century geology was "profoundly visual from beginning to end." It began with the field geologist's need of a "good 'eye'" for topography, soil, vegetation, rock types, and fossils; continued through sketches and maps made in the field; and culminated in completed maps and sections through which he communicated his findings and conclusions to others. Hayden would not learn all of these skills in a summer, but under Meek's guidance he began to develop a "good 'eye.'"[19]

¶ Geological fieldwork in the mid–nineteenth century aimed at gaining a grasp of a region's stratigraphic structure, and fieldwork focused on tracing the strata over particular areas. But the strata, the different layers of rocks, are rarely easily visible. More often they are obscured by various coverings—grass, trees, soil—and the geological investigator must piece together bits of evidence gleaned from scattered exposures of rocks to extrapolate the existence of rock formations between these points by tracing characteristics in the topography, soil, and vegetation across the country.[20]

¶ When working in new territory, the geological investigator would begin with a reconnaissance, selecting several parallel routes or "traverses" across the landscape that promised to reveal series of outcrops of the strata. While walking over the outcrops, he would note and record the directions of dip and strike of each one. The "dip" of an outcrop referred to the inclination exhibited by the strata, and the geologist would record both the compass direction and the angle of inclination from the horizontal. The "strike" of the outcrop referred to the horizontal direction at right angles to the direction of the dip. At the same time, in the course of his traverse the geologist would also take notes on the types of rocks encountered at the various outcrops as well as the thickness and fossils characteristic of the various strata.[21]

¶ Even the best geologist needed little in the way of scientific equipment to prosecute such fieldwork through most of the nineteenth century. A hammer was almost indispensable and was used for collecting samples of rocks, extracting fossils, and revealing the true character of a rock exposure by knocking off pieces from the more weathered surface. Geologists' hammers came in two basic types, varying according to whether the striking edge was parallel to or at right angles to the handle. For obtaining specimens of rocks, geologists used hammers of the first sort; for collecting fossils, the second. The direction and angle of dip could be roughly measured by sight, but more accurate measurements were taken using a magnetic compass and a clinometer. By the late 1850s, these instruments were combined into a clinometer-compass, an instrument roughly like a carpenter's square, with a protractor to measure angles at the joint, a level on the top half, and a compass on the bottom section.

¶ Other items useful in the field included a small bottle of acid for identifying limestone and a low-power hand lens for field identifications of rocks and fossils. James D. Dana, perhaps the most famous of antebellum America's geologists, advised beginners to include a length of measuring tape as well and admonished that "the field geologist should know accurately the measurements of his own body, his height, length of limbs, step or pace, that he may use himself, whenever needed, as a measuring rod." For more serious collecting of either fossils or mineral specimens, a pick, crowbar, sledgehammer, and even blasting powder might also be added. Finally, no serious geological investigator would think of taking to the field without the best and largest-scale topographical map available, on which he could record the positions of outcrops and other geological features, and a sturdy notebook in which to record detailed observations.[22]

¶ Whether Meek and Hayden had all of these items is uncertain; they clearly had most of them—perhaps minus the small bottle of acid and a measuring tape. They were also well prepared for collecting. For botany, they purchased a large supply of paper and twine as well as a plant press. For entomology, they had a supply of insect bottles. For other branches of zoology they obtained two double-barrel guns, together with shot and powder, and wire for fish nets for catching what could not be shot. For preservatives, they purchased both arsenic and alcohol. For shipping, they bought cotton and plenty of wrapping paper for dry specimens and a supply of kegs for their alcoholic specimens. They also needed camp goods, and they purchased blankets, a kettle, a "mosquito bar," an oil cloth and tent poles for a tent, a lamp, pencils and writing paper, together with tracing linen, an inkstand, and unspecified medicines—all of which would help them take enough civilization into the field to prosecute their scientific labors.[23]

¶ Hayden and Meek traveled up the Missouri River as far as present-day Pierre, South Dakota, and into the badlands of the White River, a tributary of the Missouri, which afforded them the chance to observe the geological structure along the Missouri from Pierre to Council Bluffs, Iowa (see Map 1). With Meek to guide him, Hayden refined his skills in searching for fossils, making initial on-site identifications and relating his specimens to the geological strata and formations in which they were found. Together, Hayden and Meek collected hundreds of botanical specimens, hundreds of invertebrate fossils, and over a hundred vertebrate heads as well as a few specimens of fossil plants. And with perhaps little more than his own enthusiasm to guide him, Hayden collected a variety of amphibians, reptiles, and insects.[24]

¶ Collecting such an assortment of specimens called for an array of skills. From the first, Hayden had proposed collecting "whatever might be of interest," particularly "in other departments of Natural History as Fish, Insects, Shells, etc., for rare specimens," for which Kirtland and others might pay "a handsome remuneration." Hayden suggested that by this means they "might perhaps lighten the expense" of the expedition. Hayden and Meek collected a large series of plants as they made their way up the Missouri, even going out in the evening after the boat tied up for the night and collecting by the light of a lantern. Within a few days after leaving St. Louis they had collected specimens of nearly every species then in flower along the river bottoms. While assistant

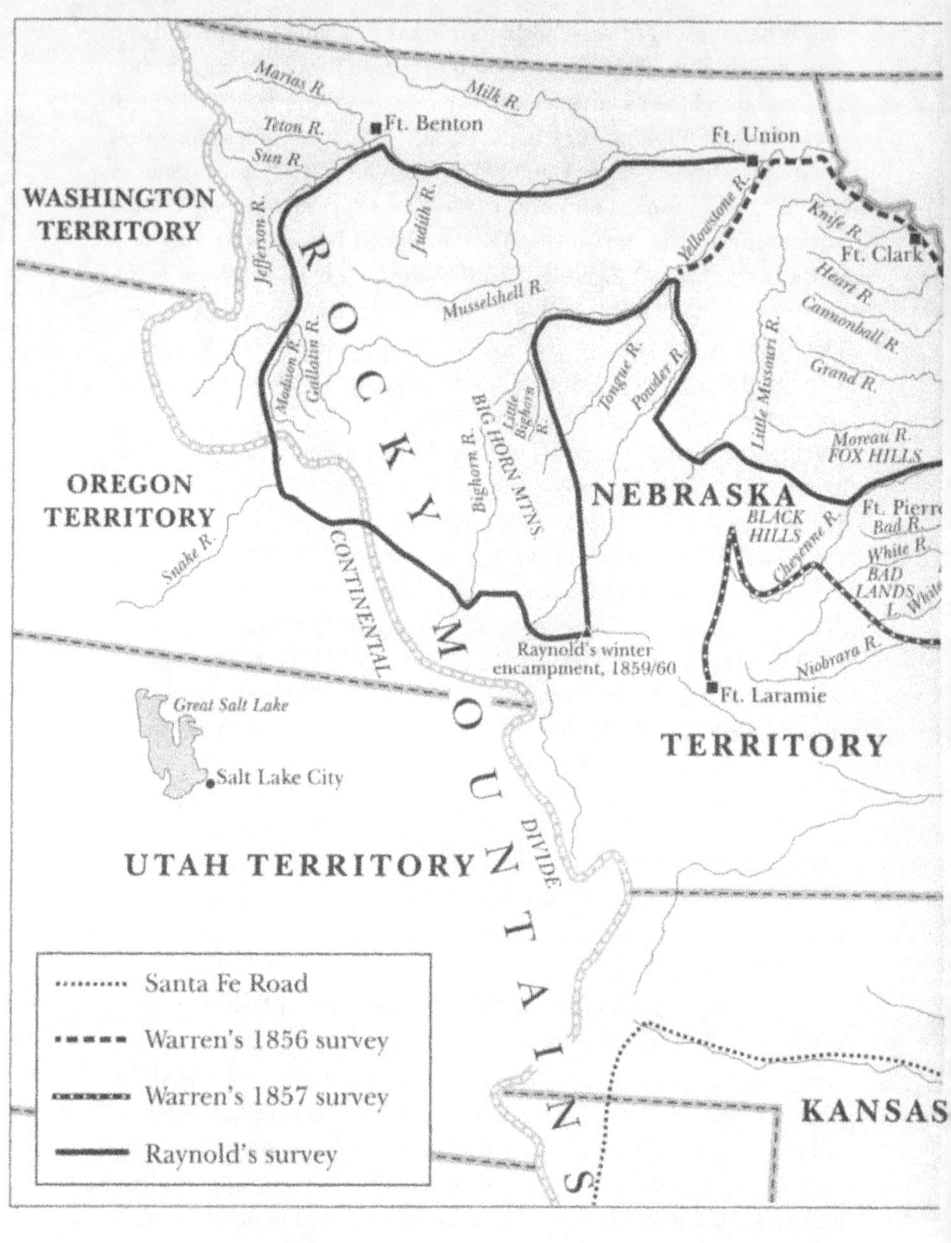
Marias R.
Milk R.
Teton R.
Ft. Benton
Sun R.
Ft. Union
WASHINGTON
TERRITORY
Jefferson R.
Judith R.
Yellowstone R.
Knife R.
Ft. Clark
Heart R.
Musselshell R.
Cannonball R.
Madison R.
Gallatin R.
Tongue R.
Powder R.
Little Missouri R.
Grand R.
ROCKY MOUNTAINS
BIG HORN MTNS.
Little Bighorn R.
Bighorn R.
Moreau R.
FOX HILLS
OREGON
TERRITORY
NEBRASKA
BLACK
HILLS
Cheyenne R.
Bad R.
White R.
BAD
LANDS
Snake R.
CONTINENTAL
DIVIDE
Raynold's winter
encampment, 1859/60
Niobrara R.
Ft. Laramie
Great Salt Lake
TERRITORY
Salt Lake City
UTAH TERRITORY
Santa Fe Road
Warren's 1856 survey
Warren's 1857 survey
Raynold's survey
KANSAS

Red River of the North
MINNESOTA
TERRITORY
Big Sioux R.
Minnesota R.
James R.
Mississippi R.
Floyd's R.
Little Sioux R.
Ft. Randall
IOWA
Council Bluffs
Bellevue
Platte R.
Missouri R.
Grand R.
Chariton R.
Leavenworth
St. Joseph
Kansas R.
Lawrence
MISSOURI
St. Louis
Smoky Hill R.
Lost
Spring
Council
Grove
Cottonwood Cr.
Osage R.
Gasconade R.
TERRITORY

secretary at the Smithsonian, Baird wrote in directions for amateur collectors of natural history specimens that "the collector of plants require[d] but little apparatus" beyond lots of absorbent paper between which specimens were pressed, usually by means of tying a stack of papers between two boards. After removing the dirt from them, specimens were placed between sheets of paper, which were changed regularly until the specimens were dry. Earlier, while still a professor at Dickinson College, Baird instructed his students on the proper method for labeling botanical specimens: "as soon as a specimen is collected, a label should be prepared and placed with it, and constantly kept with it in all its transfers. This label should state the place and time of collection; whether the plant be of land or of water; . . . the kind of soil in which it grows; its name, where found; its uses, if any; . . . the color and odor of its flowers, and any thing else interesting or important connected with it."[25]

¶ Hayden and Meek would have collected rock and fossil specimens with their hammers and most probably would have taken them from rocks in situ, that is, from the geological strata, rather than from stray or free rocks, which would have been of unknown origin. Their rock specimens were probably about fist-sized. Dana recommended that such specimens should be about three by four inches and about an inch thick, with angles squared and showing fresh surfaces all around. Most of their invertebrate fossil specimens were also relatively small, many measuring no more than a couple of inches in length or width. These would have required careful handling so as to prevent them from being broken in the process of collection or transport. They would have wrapped rock and mineral specimens in layers of thick wrapping paper and labeled them, identifying locality and geological stratum where each specimen had been collected. They then would have packed them tightly together in wooden boxes, using wads of paper to crowd everything as tightly as possible. The labels themselves would probably have been numbered, with each specimen keyed to an entry in their field notebooks. There, fuller notes on the specimens would have been entered: items such as the details of stratification, strike and dip, changes or variations in the rocks, and any other geological observations that might have been made. As Dana noted: "A specimen of rock or fossil of unknown or uncertain locality is of very little value."[26]

¶ Dr. Joseph Leidy of Philadelphia, America's foremost vertebrate paleontologist at the time and already very interested in the vertebrate fossils that had been located in the Dakota Badlands, had sent Hall detailed instructions on what a small party should collect: "1. The most important specimens are *Crania, teeth,* and their *fragments.* 2. If the specimens are enveloped, more or less, in a matrix let them remain so, for they carry without injury. 3. Bring no fragments of large bones. 4. Bring no fragments of the long bones whatever, except the joints or articular ends of those which are small in size. 5. Bring no fragments of turtles nor the largest ones even if nearly perfect." No doubt Leidy's instructions led to the emphasis on fossil heads, which seem to have been a simple matter to collect. As Hayden later wrote of another visit to this fossil ground: "We felt very much as though we were in a sepulcher, and, indeed, we were in a cemetery of a pre-Adamite age, for all around us at the base of these walls and pyramids were heads and tails, and fragments of the same, of species which are not known to exist at the present day. We spent that day and the following exploring the cemetery, which the denuding power of water had laid open for our inspection, and many fine specimens rewarded our labors."[27] These too would have been keyed and labeled, recorded in notebooks, and wrapped with several thicknesses of paper before being carefully packed into boxes.

¶ Larger reptiles such as snakes and lizards were usually skinned and then either stuffed—Baird recommended stuffing them with sand, which would have been readily available in the Badlands—or preserved in alcohol. Smaller reptiles and amphibians were best preserved in the field by simply dropping them whole into a barrel of alcohol, a procedure that also worked well for most larger reptiles for collectors inexperienced in the techniques of skinning. Since Meek and Hayden took supplies of both alcohol and arsenic with them, they probably skinned larger animals and dunked smaller ones. Collecting insects depended on knowing where to look and how to catch them. They could be found under rocks and logs and among flowers and plants or attracted with a candle at night. They might be picked up with the fingers, swept up with a small net, or captured in a small jar. Once captured, they could be killed and preserved in a variety of ways. One of the simplest methods was pinning, though it might take a very long time to kill some species. Quicker methods of dispatching them, prior to pinning them into boxes for transport, began with placing them in jars in which they might be exposed to ether fumes or heat. In the latter case, the jars could be immersed in hot water or held over a flame. The methods Hayden used are unknown, but he was familiar with several of these. For example, on a later expedition one of his field companions sketched him at work catching insects with his open hand by the light of a candle and putting them into a small jar. A decade later he asked Baird if the Smithsonian could provide "screw cap cans" and other "apparatus for catching Insects."[28]

¶ Despite their short time in the field, Meek and Hayden brought back a creditable haul of specimens. Their efforts met with the approval not only of their sponsor but also of Baird and Leidy, sponsors of a competing expedition led by geologist John Evans.[29] For Hayden, gaining favorable notice from Baird and Leidy was perhaps the most important accomplishment of the summer's journey. Baird, as assistant secretary of the Smithsonian, and Leidy, a leading member of the Academy of Natural Sciences at Philadelphia, stood in positions to be enormously helpful. Luckily for Hayden, each took a positive interest in him and his career.

¶ When accepting Hall's offer in the spring of 1853, Hayden had written that in going to the Upper Missouri he had "everything to gain and nothing to lose." But upon returning to Albany at the end of the summer Hayden soon realized that to fulfill his ambition "to gain some distinction at least, as a scientific man" he needed more training. His first step was to finish his medical education, which would provide him with scientific credentials. These would help him take his second step, for Hayden had already determined to break from Hall because he was unsatisfied with the amount of credit Hall was willing to share with him for the results of the Badlands expedition. In this, Hayden was being unrealistic. His ambition, fed by the recognition he had received as a consequence of the expedition, did not allow him to be satisfied with the usual rewards due a collector, which was all Hayden had been that summer—and a novice one at that, since Meek had clearly been the expedition's leader. After having a chance to examine their finds, Hall backed away from a promise to help Hayden and Meek prepare a paper for publication and instead decided to put his own name on the report. He listed Meek as coauthor and merely mentioned Hayden as a collector.[30] Hayden wanted more. He wanted the sort of recognition that contributed to a scientific reputation, and he soon concluded that Hall would not willingly aid him in achieving it.

¶ Accordingly, he enrolled at Albany Medical College during January 1854, earning the one-hundred-dollar tuition by working for Hall. But this need not seem strange since Hall had an interest in helping Hayden to a position elsewhere than at Albany. Hall could see that Hayden and Meek, after their experiences of the summer, were becoming close friends. He could also see Hayden's ambition influencing Meek, who was not without ambition himself but was not likely to act precipitately in the absence of Hayden's stimulus. Better that Hayden be helped to depart than allowed to stay and sow discontent in Hall's workshop. Thus, Hall sought to help him find a place on another expedition in the West, writing Leidy soon after the turn of the year that Hayden "would be glad to explore new localities in the region around the present known ones in the Mauvaises Terres." Hall could do "little towards helping him in that direction." Could Leidy do more?[31]

¶ At the time, Leidy could not do much, but that proved of little hindrance to Hayden in the end since Hayden had collected more than fossils the previous summer. He had also picked up a number of friendships, making a very favorable impression on fellow riverboat passengers on the trip up the Missouri, including Alexander Culbertson and John Sarpy of the American Fur Company and Alfred J. Vaughan, the Indian agent for Fort Pierre. While waiting in St. Louis for the expedition to start, Hayden had also won the approbation of Pierre and Charles Chouteau, heads of the American Fur Company.[32] All four could render very practical assistance to travelers in the trans-Mississippi West, and each became important to Hayden's next few years.

¶ Hayden had enjoyed his first expedition and soon sought means to embark on a second. In early January 1854, he composed a long letter to Leidy seeking his "opinion and counsel in a matter . . . of much interest to me" and seeking as well to recruit Leidy as a patron. Writing that he was "anxious to prepare myself for some more permanent position at some future day," Hayden stated: "I am very desirous of studying more thoroughly Natural History as well as Medicine and Surgery, and my mind is directed toward Philadelphia as the best place for me to do so." What he sought, however, was a position on an expedition. He had already written Baird regarding prospects for a position with a government expedition, and Baird had advised him to enter the army as a surgeon. Hayden claimed he was not altogether averse to that since it would enable him to "contribute much to natural history by collections, *at least*," but before he made a decision he wanted to know what Leidy thought of his prospects in Philadelphia: "I would like to ask you how I could get along in Pa. and pursue my studies, if I could make some explorations for the Academy [of Natural Sciences] or do anything to defray a part or all of my expenses?" He had completed his medical studies but graduated "not only poor but somewhat in debt." All the same, Hayden wrote: "I cannot endure the idea of giving up my hopes of doing something in Natural History and I am willing to get along most any way to do so. Might I hope quite positively for some position in an expedition next Spring?" he asked. "I am now ready to go anywhere on any notice, and I feel very anxious to be in the field at [once]."[33]

¶ Hayden reminded Leidy of a proposal previously advanced by Vaughan, the Indian agent. Vaughan had offered to pay all Hayden's expenses from St. Joseph, Missouri, and provide an ample outfit for fieldwork and the use of all the facilities under Vaughan's jurisdiction. Hayden would be allowed to keep half of anything he might collect in a year's time in explorations not only of the Badlands proper but also in the Black Hills of the Upper Missouri, the Fox Hills, and possibly as far as Fort Benton at the headwaters of the Missouri River in present-day northern Montana. As Hayden wrote: "This would give me a chance to explore many new localities, for fossils, also collect many reptiles, fishes, Insects, plants, etc." Should he take up Vaughan's offer, or should he hope for a position "in some public expedition," as he had been advised by Dr. George Engelmann of St. Louis, one of the most prominent botanists in America and founder of the St. Louis Academy of Sciences? Torn, Hayden sought Leidy's counsel, asking if it were likely that Baird would be able to secure him a public post. And if no public posts were available, Hayden was also interested in the prospects of remuneration: "Would a collection from that region sell for any sum? so as to be any compensation for my toil?"

¶ As incentive for Leidy to take an interest, Hayden wrote that if he went out for Vaughan he wanted to have his share of the collection brought directly to Philadelphia and have Leidy examine the vertebrates and Baird the reptiles and fishes. Hayden was confident he could make a "fine collection, much better even than one made the last season, having much longer time." But if Leidy felt it best that Hayden not return to the Badlands, he asked that Leidy mention his case to Baird, who had advised Hayden to secure a post in some government expedition. Hayden claimed that his main desire was "to do that by which I can make the largest and most valuable additions to Natural History by collections." He stated that he had already "spent considerable time in preparing myself to collect well and with discrimination in all departments and now I am giving my attention to Geology altogether, so as to make field notes that may be of some value." In light of his limited experience, Hayden exhibited a cocky confidence, seeking only an opportunity to engage in his chosen pursuit. But then he closed his letter with a strange request: "Please [do] not mention that I have written to you on this subject."[34]

¶ Except for the last line, the letter is clear: Hayden sought advice from a new mentor on what to do next. But why the secrecy? Hall had written Leidy on Hayden's behalf twice in the preceding month, so there was no need for Hayden to hide his actions from Hall. In fact, Hayden was again maneuvering for the best offer. Hayden had already nominated Baird as his next patron. Unfortunately, Baird had nothing immediate to offer, so Hayden was playing off the prospects for a successful venture in partnership with Vaughan against the hope that Baird could provide a government post. The latter was preferable. Not only would it pay better, but it also offered the prospect of doing more for his reputation by granting freer access to publication—hence Hayden's pointed question as to whether a private venture might be made financially remunerable and his expressed desire to do "something in Natural History." Hayden wanted Leidy to put pressure on Baird, but rather than say so outright he revealed his second-best alternative, in the hope that Leidy would see the advantage of seeking to secure all of Hayden's collections rather than settle for half.

¶ Hayden conducted a busy correspondence with Baird into the spring of 1854. By the beginning of March, Hall and Meek were prepared to recommend Hayden for a position as collector on the Missouri geological survey under George Swallow. Though Baird pointed out that Swallow's offer was "better than nothing" and advised accepting it if nothing else presented itself, Hayden thought the salary offered—a dollar a day plus expenses in the field—too little for a man of his experience. Both agreed that Vaughan's proposal was better, and Baird suggested several possibilities for staging grounds for such an expedition: Fort Laramie, Salt Lake City, or Fort Benton as perhaps "best of all." But Hayden had lost contact with Vaughan and requested Baird's assistance in finding him. He also fished for an invitation to come to Washington so he could study under Baird's tutelage. Hayden finally located Vaughan and then called upon Baird to help iron out a new difficulty. Vaughan had originally intended to join Hayden in a collecting expedition; when his own affairs precluded devoting full time to such a venture, he backed away from underwriting Hayden on a solo expedition. Hayden asked Baird to convince Vaughan of the merit in sponsoring just such an expedition.[35]

¶ During the two and a half months before they could resolve affairs, Hayden and Baird went back and forth over various proposals in case the arrangement with Vaughan fell through. Swallow's offer featured prominently as the only sure thing, and when Vaughan's proposal looked lost Hayden went so far as to accept it. Throughout, however, Hayden clearly focused on two objectives: concluding an arrangement with Vaughan or a position on a federal expedition and securing Baird's patronage. Though the first, with its prospect of a large natural history collection, was tendered as an assurance for the second, obtaining the second became a key to the first when Vaughan nearly backed out of the proposal. Thus, Hayden's efforts to recruit Baird's support take on all the greater significance. A year earlier he had pushed to join Hall in Albany; now Hayden pushed to join Baird. He went at it with great tenacity and patience, calmly telling Baird that he considered him his "best and safest" adviser, even as he disregarded the advice Baird offered while pointing out the help he wanted. At the same time, Hayden carefully mixed prodding with stroking; while urging Baird to "make much of" Vaughan in the interests of science, he assured him that a "few words" from someone of Baird's stature would "set him [Vaughan] right." Nor did Hayden fail to offer gifts to his intended patron, asking if he could collect and send specimens from the fish being caught at Grandquist Bay and pointing out the "grand prospect" for collecting offered by an expedition such as Vaughan had proposed.[36]

¶ Baird resisted some of Hayden's blandishments. He offered no encouragement for Hayden to come to Washington, but he did agree that prospects for collecting new specimens were much better in the Upper Missouri country than in Missouri and therefore spoke to Vaughan while the latter was in Washington, convincing him to sponsor Hayden on a collecting expedition. In doing so, Baird became Hayden's patron, and Hayden moved almost immediately to augment the relationship. He called upon him for more assistance. With great hopes of making "one of the finest collections brought from the West," Hayden pointed out that he would need an "extensive outfit" if he was to spend a year or more in the field, and he "suppose[d]" that Baird could furnish "many things" for which Vaughan would "make allowance." First on his list of needs was a map of the region, "as correct" as he could get. Then came a "cheap portable barometer, . . . a thermometer and instruments of that sort"; also, directions for making collections; and money, some fifty to hundred dollars, to use for making out his outfit.[37]

¶ Hayden wanted Baird to "identify yourself with the whole enterprise." Claiming only a verbal agreement with Vaughan, he asked Baird to speak to him again about the terms of the partnership. Then, if things were not in writing at least there would be a witness in case of later disagreements. Baird did better than rely on memory; he got things written down. Vaughan agreed to underwrite Hayden's expenses to the amount of three hundred dollars, and more if necessary for shipping the collections gathered. He also agreed to "see that [Hayden's] expenses were reduced to a minimum" by virtue of his connection with the fur company. In return for Hayden's labor, the two men agreed to equal shares in the specimens collected, with each man free to dispose of his share as he wished. And for his efforts in closing the agreement Baird was promised a share of the booty: "all plants, peltries and alcoholic specimens."[38]

¶ In the spring of 1854 Hayden ascended the Missouri for a two-year stint. His travels took him all the way to Fort Benton as well as excursions along the Yellowstone River and to the badlands of the White

River. If his first trip served as his apprenticeship, this one marked the beginning of Hayden's journeyman period, in which he functioned essentially alone as a collector and observer and thus with broader responsibilities for the success of his expedition. But if he was alone he was not without instructions since both Meek and Baird provided him with notes and suggestions on what to look for and collect. Nor was he without funding from friends back east, from whom he had made repeated requests. In addition to the support provided by Vaughan, several naturalists, including Baird and Engelmann, subscribed to the venture in return for a share of the collection.[39]

¶ The expedition was not without its difficulties. Indian unrest occasionally rendered exploring problematic, while an accident on the way up the river undermined the value of some of his specimens by destroying much of his collecting supplies. In spite of such mishaps, however, Hayden enjoyed the trip and enjoyed great success collecting on his own. The slow pace of progress up to the Yellowstone River in late July and August allowed him to wander off on his own collecting and observing, "with a Bag in one hand, Pick in the other, a Bottle of Alcohol in my vest pocket, and with all a gun to defend myself from Indians and Grizzly Bears." Though the region was "the debatable ground of all the war-like Indians on the Mo.," it was a wonderful country for a naturalist and geologist: "I could always return loaded down with rare and interesting things." During the summer and fall, he sent a steady stream of boxes and kegs of specimens back down the river to St. Louis, telling Baird that Vaughan would direct them to Washington in the spring.[40]

¶ Hayden's journeyman experience continued his education in scientific fieldwork. When he set out, Hayden promised to "endeavor to be as minute, accurate and patient as possible" and on sending off his first collections asked if his labels were "good for anything." Upon receipt of the specimens, Baird soon found reason to critique Hayden's collecting technique. Labels were defective and notes incomplete, and Baird told Hayden that when labeling specimens to be preserved and shipped in alcohol he should use parchment labels, which would not soften and tear as easily as paper labels did. He also advised Hayden to make use of continuous numbers of either individual specimens or lots of specimens. In that way, in case of mishap during shipments, the specimens could be readily identified by reference to lists and notebooks. At the same time, Hayden was attempting to correlate his new geological observations with those of the previous year, repeating sections that he and Meek had done, making new ones, collecting more fossils, and taking advantage of the lowered level in the river to make observations impossible when the water was higher, thereby adding to Meek's notes from the year before. Hayden had already developed a proprietary interest in the geology of the Upper Missouri country. In early March he had written Meek that serving under Swallow would, if nothing else, "give me a foothold in the West which I would endeavor to maintain." And he was pleased to give Meek a preview of a section taken along the river at Fort Clark, for which he had "reasons for thinking that it will reveal some important facts." As he became more familiar with the Upper Missouri region, his interest in the country only increased, and as he made his way back east at the end of 1855 he laid plans to return to the Badlands the following summer.[41]

¶ Hayden's second expedition also contributed to his training in elements other than the strictly scientific. During this period he learned more about collecting not only specimens but also collaborators and supporters for his scientific enterprises. Hayden had already made several friends during the previous summer who remained in positions to help him, particularly Culbertson and Pierre Chouteau, who provided him with free passage and shipping on fur company boats and helped cover his daily expenses for the better part of his two years in the field. While their assistance was not entirely disinterested, since they expected to share in the financial return to be realized from his collecting, Hayden's skill and enthusiasm played important roles in winning and keeping their support.[42]

¶ Laying over the winter of 1854–55 at Fort Pierre, Hayden must have been something of a curiosity to the traders. But sitting still was not one of Hayden's strengths; he rarely did it willingly or well. When the weather prevented him from collecting natural history specimens, he divided his time between teaching the children at the fort, collecting vocabularies of Indian tribes in the region, and writing letters to friends, colleagues, and patrons back east. Besides informing them of his activities, Hayden wanted to know if they had received his letters, if they would send him journals and scientific papers, if the collections he had sent on ahead had arrived safely, if there were any prospects for him on a government expedition the following summer, and why they failed to write him as frequently as he wrote them. He particularly wanted his friends to remember that he remained in need of steady employment. A variety of possibilities suggested themselves to Hayden's mind, including joining Meek on a survey in Missouri or gaining an appointment as an Indian agent. The most promising, for a time, came from Baird, who arranged for Hayden to join Lt. Gouverneur Kemble Warren, of the army's Corps of Topographical Engineers, in his expedition to Nebraska Territory in spring 1855. Though Warren was amenable, Hayden was not at Fort Pierre when Warren and his men arrived, and in the end Hayden was left with nothing more than a vague promise of inclusion in an expedition the following year.[43]

¶ By then, Hayden had already discovered a more intriguing possibility. Warren's expedition was connected not only to the army's concern with the Sioux, who resented recent intrusions into the Dakotas, but also to the Pacific Railroad Surveys authorized by Congress in March 1853. Though the law required a report to Congress within ten month's time, that was an impossible task, and while 1853 saw six reconnaissance surveys in the field, final reports necessitated supplementary surveys over the next couple years. The surveys and the excitement they stirred over the possibility of a railroad heightened interest in the newly organized Nebraska Territory. Speculators and residents quickly appreciated how a survey of the territory's resources might contribute to potential development of the region, and before the end of 1854 Nebraska politicians were discussing the idea. Hayden heard of it while visiting the territorial capital of Bellevue and quickly proposed himself as the person to direct such a survey.

¶ Aware that funding would eventually have to come from Washington, Hayden wrote several enthusiastic letters about the proposal to Baird into the winter of 1854 and strongly urged Baird to use whatever influence he could to support the idea. He repeatedly inquired if there was any news regarding government appropriations for surveying or exploring expeditions in the Nebraska Territory and informed Baird that local citizens were getting up a petition for such an appropriation. Hayden did his part to promote the cause, writing articles for local newspapers "setting forth the importance of such a movement," lobbying key local political figures, and donating specimens to a new territorial museum—all ways of simultaneously promoting the idea of a survey and keeping his name before the public. He even went so far as to put together "a small Box of nice Specimens well labeled, for Senator [Stephen A.] Douglass" to be presented to him by "an intimate friend" of the senator. In focusing on Douglas, Hayden showed a good instinct for presenting gifts to those with power. As chairman of the Senate's Committee on the Territories, Douglas was at the height of his political influence and determined to use it for the development of the West. There was hardly a politician within Hayden's reach better situated to assist him. For his part, Baird thought the idea of a geological survey of Nebraska a "very good one," and recommended that Hayden spend the winter in Bellevue where he could keep in touch with the legislature. Even if the appropriation should fail, he would still be able to get up the river early enough in the spring so as not to lose much time.[44]

¶ When prospects for public funding faded, Hayden did not give up. After returning to Fort Pierre for the winter, he continued to discuss the possibilities with Charles Galpin, the post's *bourgeois*, the local representative of the fur company and head of the trading post. In February 1855, Hayden wrote both Baird and Leidy asking their opinions of a new proposition. Galpin had offered to underwrite Hayden in a natural history survey of the Nebraska Territory for a period of eighteen months. In return, Galpin hoped "to realize a fair percentage on the capital invested," and Hayden also hoped "to realize something from my labors." What did they think? "Could the sum of three or four thousand dollars be raised among the various Institutes of our land, and Scientific men, for such an object? Would Government pay a fair price for such a collection? Could it be divided into sets and sold in Europe so as to make it worth while?" Unfortunately for Hayden's hopes, while both men agreed that such an expedition "would prove in the highest degree of benefit to science," they were "doubtful" it could be accomplished. But they did look forward to examining Hayden's collections.[45]

¶ So did a lot of other people—too many. While Hayden was highly successful in collecting some six tons of materials, including more than a half ton of invertebrate fossils he wanted to work up with Meek, there were more lessons he had to learn about collecting. Just as he relied on eastern friends to sponsor his collecting, Hayden also depended upon them in working up his results. While natural history was breaking into specialties in geology, zoology, botany, and various subspecialties of paleontology, Hayden remained an all-round collector developing a specialization in geology. He came back laden with collections that ranged from birds and their eggs to hundreds of plants and tons of fossils, to snakes and fishes, assorted bugs and insects, and pelts and minerals. He required the assistance of a variety of skilled specialists to describe his specimens, and he divided his share among Baird, Meek, Leidy, Engelmann, Newberry, and the St. Louis Academy of Sciences. Yet the very extent of his collection led Hayden into rashly promising the same parts of his collection to more than one person, a practice that soon got him into trouble. Further, his desire to celebrate his accomplishments and have them recognized led him to leave much of his collection open to public display in St. Louis, until Meek reminded him of the need to keep his new specimens confidential until they had had time to describe them and assure proper credit for his work.[46]

¶ Ignorance of the second lesson, though important, had fewer repercussions than promising identical privileges to more than one person—which he did, for instance, in the cases of Newberry and Hall as well as Leidy and Baird. That practice needlessly angered and antagonized essential patrons and coworkers. Hayden's biographer finds the mistake nearly inexplicable, the result of either extreme carelessness or forgetfulness, or both, but clearly Hayden's fault in either case, and he explains this in terms of Hayden's frequently being "impulsive, self-centered, and remarkably blind to the effect he had on others," traits that "frequently created similar dilemmas" for him. Yet it is also clear from the way Hayden ultimately sought to resolve the conflict that he just as frequently relied on others to extricate him from the difficulties in which these character traits enmeshed him. For instance, while writing that he would be glad to let Baird describe the rodents he had collected, Hayden told Baird that he also felt under obligation to Leidy, to whom they were promised, and suggested that perhaps Baird could better arrange matters with Leidy. Baird resisted this notion, but in the end Hayden left it up to Baird to resolve. There would be many such instances in the future when Hayden would rely upon the good offices of men such as Baird or Leidy to smooth feathers he had hastily ruffled.[47] But while he would continue to use access to his collections to broaden support among scientists, seldom would he forget to check with current collaborators who had a prior interest in them.

¶ Upon returning from the Upper Missouri, Hayden needed a place to live and work. He wanted to work up his invertebrate fossils with Meek, but Meek was still employed by Hall, while Hayden had cut his ties to Hall when he left him in 1854. Yet Hall wanted to retain links to Hayden, hoping to gain access to his fossil plants, so he offered the pair the use of his office. By this time, however, Hayden was unwilling to stand in Hall's shadow, and he refused Hall access to the fossil plants, ultimately deciding to offer them to Newberry. But he did go to Albany during the early months of 1856 to work with Meek and make plans for their future. Having already decided to make a name for himself independently of Hall, Hayden urged Meek to join him. When Hall returned, he grew furious at what he considered Hayden's ingratitude and treachery, and ties between the two were severed for several years.[48]

¶ By this time, however, Hayden had found new employment. In February 1856 he took up Lieutenant Warren's offer of the previous year and made arrangements to return to Nebraska Territory the coming summer. At the same time, Warren asked Hayden to prepare a report on the investigations he had already made in the Nebraska Territory and offered Hayden and Meek a chance to publish their current work together. This left Hayden with several projects going concurrently. He had to write up his report for Warren, supervise the continuing arrival and disposal of his collections from St. Louis, work with Meek on the invertebrates, and begin preparations to head west a third time—and he had little time to conclude any of them. He spent only three weeks with Meek rather than the two months he had planned, and he ended up leaving his report with Baird, asking him to see it through the press, before he rushed off to join Warren in early April.[49]

¶ Warren was a careful and conscientious officer. He hired Hayden as "geologist and naturalist" at a salary of one thousand dollars per annum, as well as allowing him the cost of transportation to and from the field and his subsistence while "*in the field*" (emphasis in original). Only Warren's assistant topographer, at one hundred dollars per month, received more. What sort of man was Warren getting, to make Hayden the second-best paid civilian in his expedition? Warren wanted a scientist familiar with the Upper Missouri territory, a feature made thoroughly clear in his request that Hayden contribute an essay to his report on his 1855 expedition—the one Hayden missed. Hayden's contribution to Warren's 1855 report reveals that in Hayden he got exactly that: an observant and competent collector as familiar with the region as any naturalist in the nation. Hayden's essay exactly fits his description of it: "A brief sketch of the geological and physical features of the region of the upper Missouri, with some notes on its soil, vegetation, animal life, &c." He began with a quick outline of the principal tributary river systems of the Missouri, moved to a similar outline of three main geological systems, and then went on to provide some information on the soils, flora, and animal life of the region. At the same time, the essay reveals two other features about its author. His "notes" on the region were thoroughly attuned to the interests of prospective settlers, while his insertion of a comparatively lengthy description of a journey into the White River badlands not only "present[s] an idea of the country on White river, and the modes of travelling [*sic*] on the prairie" but simultaneously showcases Hayden's competence as a plainsman.[50]

¶ As a result of practice and with Meek's help, he was also becoming a geologist. Hayden's three weeks in Albany resulted in the eventual production of four joint publications with Meek. The bulk of the articles comprised descriptions of new species of invertebrates described from the fossils Hayden had brought back on his expedition; in fact, the second and third article contained nothing but these. But the first article began with a brief summary of the geology of the region in which the fossils had been collected, while the fourth, and longest, article was prefaced with "some general remarks on the Geology of the country about the sources of the Missouri River." This section, nearly a quarter of the entire paper, clearly relies upon Hayden's work in the field, tracing the passage of geological formations. He had also identified what would become one of the central research questions of his career: the extent and age of a "Great Lignite" formation, first identified in 1849, and which Hayden had also noted in his contribution to Warren's 1855 report. There, Hayden mentioned that the formation was known to extend some eight hundred miles from the mouth of Cannonball River on the Missouri all the way up to the mouth of the Musselshell

River and at least some six or seven hundred miles up the Yellowstone River, noting that he had traced it up the Yellowstone as far as the mouth of the Big Horn River. He estimated it "to cover an area, with very little interruption, of from four to six thousand square miles," stretching across present-day North Dakota, Montana, and Wyoming. Given that field geologists were frequently highly territorial in laying claim to regions for active research, Hayden was potentially laying claim to a huge slice of western land.[51]

Hayden's third trip west was the first to cause him serious frustration. He had operated largely on his own the previous two years. This time he had to adapt his pace to the steady tramping of an army troop, which tried his limited patience. The engagement began well enough. Both Hayden and Warren were eager to accomplish something in natural history, nor were they unsuccessful in this quest, as together they gathered a substantial collection. Hayden also benefited personally when he acquired a new collaborator, James Stevenson, whom Warren hired as Hayden's assistant. Stevenson and Hayden thus began a partnership that proved very important in the future. Yet difficulties emerged. Hayden chafed at delays. Worse, upon their return to Washington, Hayden proved overambitious in claiming credit for the expedition and its results, writing letters to newspapers and granting interviews implying that he led the survey and was responsible for all its successes in natural history. Warren, who had his own career to consider, vigorously protested these actions.[52]

¶ This first experience with army ways led Hayden to seek alternative employment for the following year, that he might resume his more individualistic and independent operations. Convinced that he had enough friends in the West to ease his way once there, he sought means to get there, including appointment as a smallpox inoculator for the Bureau of Indian Affairs, attachment to the Northwest Boundary Survey, and the sponsorship of the Academy of Natural Sciences. Any of these seemed preferable to going out again with Warren. None came his way, and in the end Hayden rejoined Warren for an expedition into the Black Hills. However, two small items indicate compromises. In his official journal for the 1857 expedition, Warren noted in the "order of March" that "Dr. Hayden Geologist and naturalist will go any where his duties call him in making researches." For his part, Hayden carefully credited both Warren and War Department permission in all future publications derived from these expeditions, and the next time an item appeared in the *National Intelligencer* mentioning some of the early findings of the 1857 expedition, Warren was prominently credited as its leader. Hayden also sought to make peace with Warren by asking Baird to call the lieutenant's attention to Hayden and Meek's having named a "beautiful shell," *Mactra warrenana*, after their patron. Naming new species was a privilege of the discoverer and a claim on scientific immortality. Naming them in honor of friends or patrons was (and remains) a special form of gift, and Hayden had already made use of this gift several times to cultivate favor with and express his gratitude to his patrons. He and Meek had named specimens after a number of their patrons and assistants, including Galpin, Culbertson, Newberry, Baird, and Hall.[53]

¶ Before he could be ready to go out with Warren again, Hayden had work to do. He had to sort through his collections and notes and compose a report for Warren, who was in Washington with most of the collection. He had to deliver his newest invertebrate fossils to Meek in Albany and discuss his findings with him for their joint work. He wanted to visit Leidy in Philadelphia, to whom he had promised his vertebrate fossils. Finally, he felt an obligation to visit his family in Rochester.[54]

¶ With so much to do in and near Washington, Hayden decided to take up residence there and associate himself with the Smithsonian Institution. Indeed, he had been leaning in that direction for several years, as the capital was becoming a sort of patronage magnet. The 1850s was a time of busy, relatively large-scale public works in the District of Columbia. An "unprecedented federal spending program" for the city saw the completion of City Hall, the enlargement of the Patent Office, the movement of the greenhouse and botanical garden to the foot of Capitol Hill, the beginning of two large wings and a massive new dome for the Capitol, the establishment of a soldiers' home for Mexican War veterans, the construction of an aqueduct to supply water to protect government property from fire, the opening of a government hospital for the insane, and the construction of an armory for the D.C. militia, as well as the opening of the Smithsonian Institution. All the construction served to make Washington a busy city. At the same time, others sought to build with more than bricks and mortar, seeking to make Washington "the intellectual and artistic as well as the political capital of the United States." The Smithsonian Institution, and particularly its museum, quickly acquired a key place in their program, especially after Secretary Joseph Henry agreed to open its halls to public lectures and meetings of scientific societies.[55]

¶ In the 1850s, the national capital was a natural, if frequently disappointing, magnet for seekers of patronage. This was particularly true for practitioners of natural history. As patron of the Coast Survey and various exploratory expeditions under the War and Navy Departments, Congress had become the single most important patron of American science. Given that patronage remained fundamentally a relationship between individuals and given the individuals Hayden sought to cultivate to support his own scientific efforts, it is not at all surprising that he decided to take up residence in Washington, where he could pursue both his science and his patrons.

¶ Accordingly, upon his return from the West in November 1856 Hayden joined a boardinghouse owned by the naturalist William Stimpson. When he moved there, Hayden entered what amounted to a research school, loosely affiliated with the Smithsonian. Stimpson had been attached by the Smithsonian to the North Pacific Exploring Expedition, a naval expedition of discovery in the Bering Straits and the northern Pacific Ocean, and the China Sea. For boarders, he selected fellow naturalists whom Baird had drawn to Washington by acting as their patron. By all accounts, they made a congenial group, dubbing their home "the Stimpsonian." Though membership changed as men came and went, from the 1850s through the next couple of decades they included some of the most eminent naturalists of the day. Besides Stimpson and Hayden, John Torrey, Edward D. Cope, James G. Cooper, John Strong Newberry, and William H. Dall all belonged to the group at one time or another. When, in 1857, Hayden finally convinced Meek to break away from Hall, he joined their number, taking a free room and an unpaid position at the Smithsonian. The Stimpsonians also provided a core of members for the Potomac Side Naturalists' Club, which Hayden joined in founding in 1858 along with nine other "originators," thus establishing one more link with the intellectual life of the capital city that revolved around the Smithsonian.[56]

¶ Hayden's second expedition with Warren proved even more trying than the first. Though once again they got off to a good start, by the end of the summer he was threatening to shoot Warren. Exactly why Hayden became so upset remains unclear. He wrote to Baird of fears that Warren was going to retain their collection for the War Department, which would have made Hayden's access to its contents difficult. Yet troubles had begun earlier, and Hayden was probably simply responding to strictures Warren's authority placed on his independence. The discord emerged during difficult portions of the march, as Warren struggled to bring both men and collections safely home, while Hayden's focus remained shortsightedly on his own interests in collecting specimens, and he seemed oblivious to Warren's larger responsibilities. Hayden viewed Warren's actions as those of a "*young man*" whose head had been turned by too much authority. Despite the conflict, however, the season proved a success for Hayden, and he was able to add to his geological observations and amass another fine collection to disperse among associates. For his part, while Baird expressed sorrow on learning of the troubles between Hayden and Warren, he also expressed a hope that they would "blow over" and the two would be able to work together for the "interests of science."[57]

¶ Baird refused to get involved in his client's difficulties in this instance, nor did he encourage Hayden's combativeness. On the one hand, this seems in keeping with Baird's own preference to avoid conflicts by simply ignoring opponents whenever possible, in favor of working with more amenable personalities. Avoidance seems particularly likely in this instance. Baird had nearly been badly burned by taking sides in a political dispute against his own boss only two years earlier. With his many contacts throughout the army, he had more to lose than gain in supporting Hayden against the War Department. Finally, his aloofness may also be an early indication that Baird had noticed traits in Hayden's behavior that discouraged him from fighting on his behalf in such cases.[58]

¶ Failing to find a paying position the following season (1858), Hayden convinced Meek to accompany him on a two-month tour in Kansas, which enabled them to gather evidence for their claims about the geological age of the strata along the Missouri River. From mid-August to mid-October they tramped a meandering path through central Kansas, basically following the Kansas and Smoky Hill Rivers about to the middle of the territory before turning southeast toward the Santa Fe Road, which they followed northeast until striking Cottonwood Creek. After following the Cottonwood eastward some thirty miles, they struck north to Council Grove, then back southwest to Lost Spring and then northwest back to the Smoky Hill. They followed the Smoky Hill and the Kansas River back east, this time along their south side, as far as Lawrence, from which they again struck across country back to Leavenworth, where they had begun.[59]

With the repeated expeditions, Hayden's discoveries and Meek's evaluations of the fossils took on increased importance, enabling them to construct two- and three-dimensional geological maps, which was one of the goals of geological surveys. The 1853 expedition had introduced Hayden to the "grand sweep" of geology, providing "his first experience with formations that spread over hundreds of miles and whose composition had to be gleaned from occasional outcrops in cliffs or exposures at riverbanks." His practice as a geologist focused on the "art of quickly identifying isolated features, synthesizing them in his brain with scores of others, then unifying them all into a coherent, dynamic picture." Repeated expeditions provided Hayden with opportunities to hone such skills, as he sought to address questions Meek posed while studying the fossils Hayden had collected.[60]

¶ By the middle of the nineteenth century, geologists expressed their findings in various pictorial manners, which indicated both their observations and their inferences regarding the distribution of the geological strata. The more basic was a two-dimensional geological map, on which the surface characteristics were indicated. Beyond these, geologists also might construct a more theoretical expression, the traverse section, which was "a visual representation of the structure of the superficial part of the earth's crust, as it might be seen if the crust could be cut open in a vertical slice running across country on a particular traverse." This, in turn, might be used to construct another theoretical expression, the columnar section, which was "a visual representation of the sequence of formations in a given area" that indicated the sequence and presumed or measured thicknesses of the strata, together with their rock types and characteristic fossils.[61]

¶ Together Hayden and Meek gathered information to assemble a stratigraphic column and produce a geological map of the Yellowstone–Upper Missouri country far superior to any of its predecessors—partly for the simple reason that Hayden had actually tramped over more of the country than most other geologists. Yet they were only able to do this because they had first developed into true collaborators, with a partnership grounded in a sincere appreciation of each other's skills and the contributions each made to their work together. Hayden was becoming a first-rate field geologist as well as an indefatigable collector in natural history, a combination that led him to seek to embrace and describe regions from the widest environmental perspective. For his part, Meek applied himself to careful stratigraphic studies and was becoming an expert in the invertebrate paleontology of the Cretaceous and Tertiary eras. Between 1856 and 1862, Meek and Hayden coauthored sixteen major articles, articles that formed much of the basis of Hayden's initial reputation as a scientific author.

¶ Such activities drew the two men closer together and helped complete Hayden's initiation into natural history. As he was forced to respond to Meek's probing questions on the specimens, Hayden related his collecting to field observations and matured as a geologist. For example, in an 1856 paper they coauthored, only the first four pages are given over to the material most probably attributable to Hayden, namely, a general description of the geology of the area from which the fossils were collected. In a paper they published five years later, a much larger portion, the first twenty pages, is given to discussing the geology on the basis of both paleontological and stratigraphic-lithologic evidence, as well as attempting to delineate boundaries and characteristics of geological formations and series. The on-the-spot observations of rocks and strata mentioned in the 1861 paper have to have come from Hayden. While the integration with material from a wide reading of paleontology may have come largely from Meek, these were issues of concern to Hayden, and he can be expected to have done homework on them in his area as part of his desire to make a name for himself.[62]

¶ Their 1858 tour in Kansas Territory was of a piece in their developing partnership. The papers they published from it focused on the age and boundaries of the Cretaceous strata exhibited along their route, as they pieced together lithologic observations and fossil evidence. As such, it was part of a larger research project into which they had basically fallen with their 1853 expedition to the Badlands, but which they clearly claimed for their own as early as their paper of June 1856. It was also a project that brought them into contact—and occasionally conflict—with the work of other geologists. Most notable among the latter was their former patron and mentor, Hall. He was also at work constructing a geological map covering the same territory, for which he relied upon information they fed him from their own discoveries. Yet when Hayden and Meek learned that Hall was making use of their findings without assigning them what they believed was proper credit, their partnership was strengthened by virtue of a common complaint as well as a common research interest. They vehemently protested Hall's appropriation of their findings, a protest that ultimately led to Meek's leaving Hall's employ and a breach between Hayden and Hall that was never fully repaired. The feud left Hayden with an enduring enemy in Hall, who was not at all averse to whispering poisoned words into the ears of any who would hear them. Since Henry was one of Hall's friends and a recipient of his complaints against Hayden and Meek, Hayden felt a particular concern to justify himself and his actions. He worried about retaining Henry's goodwill and urged Baird to take care to present Hayden's side of the dispute to him.[63]

In May 1859, Hayden joined his last army survey, accompanying Capt. William Franklin Raynolds of the Topographical Engineers to the headwaters of the Yellowstone River, a trip that lasted fifteen months. Though the trip proved rewarding in terms of collections and observations, army discipline continued to rankle. Raynolds and Hayden were oil and water, the first a stickler for discipline, the second used to coming and going as he pleased. Though as usual things seemed to bode well at the beginning, they had hardly started before trouble arose. From Hayden's perspective, Raynolds deprecated the importance of making collections in natural history by remarking that it seemed as if "the Expedition had been fitted out simply to build up the Smithsonian Institution," when its main objects were really "more Military and Geographical." Hayden accused Raynolds of "petty jealousy," at which Raynolds quickly became "quite ashamed." But it was a bad omen, and Raynolds was certainly within his rights to voice questions about Hayden's requirements for transporting his collections.[64]

¶ Hayden's behavior and experiences with Vaughan, Warren, and Raynolds manifest a clear pattern. In each case, he began with excited enthusiasm for the prospects of working with them, and in each case he quickly complained to his patrons when matters did not go exactly as he liked. In no case did he exhibit much self-insight as to the reasons for his difficulties; instead, he put all the responsibility on the other for failing to understand things as he did. Hayden considered the expeditions solely as opportunities for natural history and geology, and he judged men by a single standard, in which helping him equaled aiding science. When he looked at the number of "large wagons" Raynolds was taking, he thought only in terms of how they would "render transportation extensive," and he did his best to excite interest in collecting among other members of the expedition. When Raynolds complained, Hayden shamed him for his small-minded views and justified himself to Baird: "I know perfectly well what to do. I shall pursue a straight forward independent course always at my post of duty and all will come out right in the end." Though he could write that "I think I understand Captain Raynolds better, that he is determined to have his own way," it never dawned on Hayden that the same words applied to him as well and explained his difficulty in working under others.[65]

¶ To enhance security, Raynolds kept the company moving in a traditional military column, but Hayden was accustomed to frequent exploratory side trips to enhance his collections and observations. Normally, these lasted only a few hours and he returned by nightfall, but one night he failed to do so. Raynolds responded with an order forbidding overnight absences without explicit permission. Hayden found the condition limiting. This remained true even though Raynolds seems to have been liberal in granting permission, though occasionally with the condition that since he could not consider a given trip safe he would not accept responsibility for the safety of those undertaking the trip. In light of the real dangers the expedition experienced as it proceeded up the Yellowstone River as well as the fears Hayden expressed of the Indians, Raynolds's concerns and conditions seem more than reasonable. Nor did Raynolds approve of working on the Sabbath, a limitation Hayden found a useless waste of time and ignored when he could.[66]

¶ Within the confines of a winter encampment on the Platte River relations between Hayden and Raynolds improved somewhat, thanks to efforts on both sides. But by then it was obvious they had very different interests. Fifteen months in the field provided Raynolds with plenty of opportunity to observe Hayden. He did not completely approve of what he saw. The two clearly did not see eye to eye on their Christian "duties." Though impressed with Hayden's enthusiasm, Raynolds thought him too ambitious. He seemed to live "only for the world and worldly fame," with his mind set only on "this world's rewards."[67] The observation was perceptive and accurate.

¶ In fact, Hayden's pursuit of the world's rewards was proving quite successful. Even before he departed on this latest expedition he was earning accolades as a geologist and ethnologist. Nominated by Leidy and Baird, Hayden was elected a corresponding member of the Academy of Natural Sciences at Philadelphia in 1856, one of the premier scientific societies in the United States. He also became a corresponding member of both the Boston Society of Natural History (1859) and the St. Louis Academy of Science (1860). His work with Meek helped him gain recognition as a geologist, and a work on Indian languages, which he presented as vocabularies compiled during his winters spent in the West, was published by the American Philosophical Society (APS). Finally, in December 1860 Hayden learned of his election as a corresponding member of the APS, which meant that he had received recognition from most of the more important scientific societies in the antebellum United States.

¶ Hayden remained a junior member in the more prestigious of these groups. The extension of "corresponding" membership was typically a means of recognizing and encouraging the contributions of particularly productive and skillful field collectors. These collectors were linked to the scientific community through the patronage of a regular member of the society who enjoyed full scientific status. But the sort of positive regard in which Hayden was held as a collector, and perhaps a promising scientific colleague, is evident in Baird's emphatic "By all means use my name as recommending Hayden for membership" to Leidy when proposing Hayden for the Academy of Natural Sciences of Philadelphia. Hayden had just returned to Washington with more specimens, and Baird assured Leidy that he would find some of them extremely interesting, including "Quite a variety of saurian teeth, some of which will make your eyes water."[68]

¶ At the same time, Hayden was also winning the esteem of men in the West. For instance, though Isaac Stevens, governor of the Washington Territory and director of the exploration for a northern route in the Pacific Railway surveys in the mid-1850s, had earlier opposed Hall's sending of Hayden and Meek to the Badlands in 1853, two years later he gave Hayden a glowing encomium. Stevens wrote Baird that Hayden had won "golden opinions from all intelligent men, for his persevering labors on the Missouri and its tributaries." Hayden was "a man of the right starch, enthusiastic, forceful and modest"; if the Northern Boundary Survey were to be run another year, "he is the man for its geologist." Stevens so admired Hayden that he gave him a letter of introduction to the trading posts on the Upper Missouri, urging that he be given "any aid he may desire." Like many others, Stevens seems to have been impressed by Hayden's enthusiasm for collecting and exploring. Hayden's zeal remained strong after six years in the field, as is clear from the observations of Dr. Elias J. Marsh, a fellow companion with the Raynolds expedition on the steamboat journey up the Missouri River in spring 1859. Though Marsh found most of the young men in the government party "sociable and pleasant," Hayden particularly captured his attention as "very energetic and active, . . . the moment the boat reaches land he is on shore with his gun."[69]

¶ The Civil War rudely interrupted Hayden's developing career. Returning to Washington in November 1860, soon after the election of Lincoln, and having spent several years traveling in the disputed Kansas and Nebraska Territories as well as winters in Washington, he could hardly have been ignorant of the developing sectional tensions. Yet, surprisingly for a graduate of Oberlin College, an institution known for its militant Christianity, stern morality, social liberalism, and abolitionist stance, Hayden never commented on the issue of slavery until after the election. He then adopted a touch of militant patriotism in some of his letters, but when war broke out the following spring and summer he did not follow it up with active militancy. Instead, as the coming of war dried up the federal government's interest in western surveys Hayden sought other opportunities. For him the war was a problem to avoid.[70]

¶ At first he tried to proceed with business as usual, but with the outbreak of war the War Department called a halt to its western surveys and most of the topographical engineers were assigned to armies in the field. In March and early April 1862 Hayden still did not know whether he would be able to arrange to go west during the coming summer season, and he admitted to Leidy that he had "much to do and ought not to leave the States at all." But if he did not go the coming season, "I shall certainly go the next in order to complete some work which is very important." By the beginning of May he had set his sights closer to home, writing Leidy that "Mr. Meek and I wish to take a tour through the border states for the purpose of studying more thoroughly the Cretaceous and Tertiary formations—especially those of New Jersey. Can you not raise us $25. or $50. to contribute toward our expenses?" In return, Hayden promised to "give to the Academy the results of our labors for publication and one half the fossils." Through contacts at the academy, Leidy found enough funding to support two months in the field. He provided another companion as well, a private student of his, Edward Drinker Cope, who was just turning twenty-two and only beginning what would become a brilliant career as a vertebrate paleontologist. But opportunities to continue with science as usual were quickly evaporating. As Hayden completed the projects he had on hand he was finally forced to focus attention on how to get through the war. He thought first of expeditions, then of enlisting.[71]

¶ Hayden spent the first year of the war finishing work from the late 1850s. He had articles to write on his trip with Raynolds and reports to finish and submit for both Raynolds and Warren. By late summer 1862 Hayden had finished these, as well as several book reviews for the *American Journal of Science.* The latter are more interesting than the former, since in them he pointed explicitly to his hopes for future patronage of science and commented on scientists' needs in such patronage, particularly in high-quality publishing. He had also conducted his excursion with Meek and Cope and paid a long visit to his family. But with no definite prospects for the future his sudden decision to make use of his medical training and enlist as a surgeon of volunteers in October 1862 may have been a calculated attempt to avoid the war, in the hope of winning a posting to the southwestern frontier, where, with luck, he could spend the war collecting in natural history.[72]

¶ Instead, Hayden was assigned to Beaufort, South Carolina, where his charm, medical ability, and administrative talent won the approval of his commanding officers and promotion in authority. By the end of the summer 1863, Hayden had moved up from managing a small hospital to the position of post surgeon and head of the medical staff. At the same time, he took advantage of new opportunities South Carolina presented in natural history and collected specimens and fellow enthusiasts. Finding himself out of touch with current scientific events and resources, Hayden implored his friends' assistance in keeping up to date. He also called for books and materials for making collections and offered local specimens in return, an arrangement with which Baird happily complied since the Smithsonian had little from that region of the country. Hayden also encouraged the cultivation of other collectors, urging that they be proposed as corresponding members of the Academy of Natural Sciences, for which they would surrender their collections.[73]

¶ As an officer, Hayden was both ambitious and entirely comfortable making use of influential friends in Washington who could smooth his way. He also took advantage of ill-defined jurisdictional boundaries to extend his medical authority over all of Port Royal Island. But he was not regular army, and when a regular army surgeon was assigned to Beaufort in autumn 1863 he immediately contested Hayden's authority as a mere surgeon of volunteers. Hayden responded by appealing to friends in Washington who intervened to rescue him yet again. In February 1864 he was transferred to Washington, where he served as assistant medical inspector. Though his new responsibilities kept him too busy to do much in the way of natural history, he did find time to keep his interest alive and join in the monthly meetings of the Potomac Side Naturalists' Club. Finally, in October 1864 Hayden was assigned to the Army of the Shenandoah, in Winchester, Virginia, as chief medical officer of the region, reporting directly to Gen. Philip Sheridan. He remained there until 1 May 1865, when he resigned from the army, eventually receiving the brevetted rank of lieutenant colonel.[74]

Whether they spent the war on the battlefield or behind the lines, a generation of leaders built public careers on their Civil War experience. Hayden was no exception, and though in the midst of his medical duties he continued to dream of the western surveys, his wartime experience continued his education and highlights enduring trends in his developing character. He learned how ambition, charmingly presented, could reap rich rewards in expanded authority. He gained broader and extended experience working within bureaucracy. He made new contacts among people who would be in positions of importance in the postwar years. And he had yet another experience in which an army officer frustrated his efforts.

¶ Yet Hayden would build his career mostly on the experience he had gained before the war. For him, the war had been an unwelcome intrusion into his plans. With its end—even before its end—he looked forward to picking up where he and the federal government had left off four years earlier. With seven years of experience under his belt, he was prepared to continue prosecuting his geological explorations of the trans-Mississippi West. In the years since he had left Oberlin, he had developed from an enthusiast into a scientist. Allen and Newberry had taught him some of the rudiments of natural history collecting and identification; by his own reading and efforts he had taught himself something of the beginnings of geology. During his first ascent up the Missouri, Meek had tutored his development as a paleontological collector and geological observer, while the expedition itself had introduced him to the practical obstacles to field science on the frontier. His year and a half as a solitary collector in the Upper Missouri had also been a learning experience. After his tours with Warren and Raynolds, Hayden knew the territory and its inhabitants and was quite familiar with the variety of interests people had in the West—both as potential settlers or investors or as scientific inquirers.

¶ Hayden had earned his credentials as a scientist of natural history in the only graduate programs available in antebellum America—medical school and practical field experience. His skill as a collector was acknowledged, even by Hall after he had turned against Hayden. If he was not always as careful as he could have been in packing and labeling the specimens he collected, he made up for the deficiencies with the energy he devoted to collecting and the size and variety of his hauls. He had also become an adept geological observer and was becoming a respected author of papers and short reports on the geology of the Upper Missouri country. By the time he enlisted for the war, he had authored or coauthored no fewer than thirty-six separate published articles, reports, manuscripts, or notes related to his researches and had been rewarded with recognition by the peers of American science. Nor were his efforts without a research focus. Though he would never publish a book-length synthesis of his geological investigations, he had identified major research problems beyond simply coloring in the geological map of the American West. At the same time, he remained aware of popular expectations regarding geological surveys, and most of his papers and reports made reference to such interests.

¶ Finally, and far from least important in his antebellum development as a scientist, Hayden had learned how to cultivate support for his activities among influential patrons. His career had been launched by Allen, who introduced him to Kirtland and Newberry. In their turn, they provided introductions to Hall and Baird as well as access to networks of scientific correspondence. Hayden's ambition and earnest eagerness for natural history, as well as his developing skill as a collector, helped him charm senior naturalists and scientists who were in a position to assist him. Moreover, his enthusiasm for investigating and developing the West helped him charm a long list of others who could also boost his career. This list particularly included officials of the American Fur Company and territorial politicians as well as local traders and settlers. Pursuing science literally at the frontier, Hayden needed all the support he could muster.

The immediate aftermath of war left Hayden unemployed but not without prospects. Even before leaving the army, he had begun to make arrangements. Observing that the coming of peace and the assassination of Lincoln left Washington in a confused state, and anxious to return to geology and natural history as soon possible, Hayden decided to look elsewhere for support. He quickly settled on Philadelphia, still the scientific capital of the nation, and assured Leidy that he was "looking to the Academy for my Scientific Home and aiding to build that up." He also looked to Leidy and the academy to aid him, which Leidy soon did, thus setting in motion a plan that gave Hayden a position at the University of Pennsylvania as professor of geology and mineralogy in the Auxiliary Department of Medicine, a post he held until 1872.[75]

¶ Taking a professorship was a natural career move. It offered a respectable position for someone of Hayden's training and experience, though not great financial security—paying only five hundred dollars per annum, plus student fees. However, that could be supplemented by the practice of medicine or other external scientific employment. Hayden chose the latter. His teaching schedule was not overly demanding, and though he seems to have been a competent, popular, and even innovative professor, teaching was not likely to become his first love. Natural history and the West had already claimed his heart, and from early summer 1865 Hayden wrote Leidy that he hoped to return to the Badlands in 1866. He was willing to try teaching but not eager to sacrifice fieldwork for the lecture hall.[76]

¶ Nor was he forced to make the sacrifice. Like other members of the faculty of the Auxiliary School of Medicine, Hayden was obliged to offer at "least thirty-four lectures, . . . three times a week . . . , commencing on the first Monday in April, and ending on the last Saturday in June." The schedule afforded many free months for collecting and exploring. Though Hayden seems to have done a satisfactory job as a teacher, he does not seem to have thrown himself into the work of his faculty. Minutes of departmental meetings indicate he may have missed more meetings than he attended. Nor did he let the academic calendar impede his own schedule. During a meeting in mid-March 1870, when Hayden was again absent, the dean was "instructed to communicate with Prof. Hayden to convey the desire of the faculty that his course of lectures be completed this year at the same time as the others."[77] His practice of crowding his lectures in so as to leave for the West by early June evidently caused dissension among colleagues.

¶ Though Hayden had written hopefully that the federal government would vigorously resume its antebellum western surveys upon the conclusion of the war, his first postbellum survey was a private venture to the Badlands of Dakota, funded partly by the Academy of Natural Sciences and partly out of his own pocket. In company with his old partner Stevenson, Hayden spent August and September 1866 making a circuit of some 650 miles. Leaving Fort Randall, where the Missouri ceases to be the northern boundary of Nebraska, Hayden's small party traveled along the Niobrara River until they were about half way across Nebraska. They then turned north to the Little White River and then westerly to the White River badlands, where they again turned easterly, heading for the Missouri at Fort Pierre. All the while they made geological observations and collected fossils, which they shipped to the Academy of Natural Sciences. Hayden recouped his personal expenses by offering his share of the collection for sale, eventually realizing about fourteen hundred dollars on his investment of six hundred dollars. In doing so, he risked alienating Baird by failing to offer specimens to the Smithsonian. His excuse that he had nothing worth contributing appears disingenuous, however, in light of his suggestion to Professors Dana and Othniel C. Marsh at Yale that he had some important and valuable new finds.[78]

¶ Hayden's duplicity may have been related to his concerns about needing to find a stable source of funding for continuing his expeditions. Aside from his appointment at the university Hayden had no secure employment, and letters exchanged with Baird early in 1867 indicate his predicament. Hearing that Marsh had purchased "a very nice series" of fossils from Hayden, Baird admonished Hayden that if there were duplicates among the specimens that would complete the Smithsonian's series of fossils, "the Acad. should let us have them in return for what we have already purchased and for what they may expect from the Warren Collection." He concluded with a postscript that carried a clear message: "If neither Leidy nor you can give us any thing for the collection it will not be much encouragement for us to interfere to promote the success of another expedition!"[79]

¶ Personal relationships were at the core of patronage, and the exchange of gifts constituted their lifeblood. Hayden had risked a great deal in ignoring his obligations toward Baird, no matter what might have tempted him to do so, and Baird's warning quickly called him back to the realities of his situation. He hastened to reassure Baird of his continuing loyalty and make his explanations. Asserting that he was "as much interested in completing the S.I. collections of Upper Mo. things" as Baird was, Hayden explained that when he left for the West the academy had agreed to pay his expenses. That entitled Leidy to first choice among the collection. Hayden claimed he had performed his part of the bargain but had only received five hundred dollars from the academy, against expenses of eleven hundred dollars, leaving him with a deficit of six hundred dollars. "If that is not returned to me, I shall make a poor thing out of my trip." As for the collection, he wrote: "When Dr. Leidy made his selection there were only 8 or 9 species left, of all of which you have better specimens." Hayden told Baird that if he were to take any of them "they would only be duplicates for you to distribute," while "any specimen represents so much *bread* to me now, that is, if I can dispose of it."[80] It was probably with a sense of relief that Hayden received Baird's letter of 9 March 1867, informing him of the impending geological survey of Nebraska and Baird's own actions on Hayden's behalf.

3

The Survey of Nebraska as the Starting Point

Every body is crazy here about the Survey and it seems to be a great thing to them. —Hayden to Baird, 17 June 1867

A resolution was adopted by both Houses to invite me to speak before them explaining the objects of the Survey. I did so. The pressure was so great on me here that I hardly knew how to refuse. . . . The people at Omaha are crazy on the matter of the Survey. —Hayden to Hon. J. S. Wilson, 17 June 1867

The clause in the 1867 Deficiency Bill providing for a geological survey of Nebraska opened an opportunity to Hayden, and he lost no time in seeking to turn it to his advantage. But translating a clause in an appropriation bill into a geological survey with himself at the head was no mean task. Still more daunting was the hope he quickly expressed that the small beginnings might soon give way to a much-enlarged enterprise. First, however, he had to grasp and exploit the opportunity. Following Hayden in this year—from his quest to gain the position, through his fieldwork and reporting, to his campaign to have the survey continued—opens a window to a number of issues and reveals many elements of his practice that remained recurring features over the years. Many of these themes will be taken up as the particular subjects of succeeding chapters, but four items deserve notice from the start.

¶ First, the Hayden Survey was science carried out within the context of governmental service. Thus, its scientific results were influenced not only because the government was the source of funding but also because government agencies specified objectives, controlled expenditures, and insisted that the results be "useful." However, his warrant could be interpreted very broadly, and Hayden was not slow to take advantage of that fact. Second, Hayden's enthusiasm for the West and for science were characteristic of the man and his work. He sought a large degree of personal independence in carrying out his project. This manifested itself in a tendency to exceed both his appropriations and his authority. While his desire for independence was undoubtedly related to his personal character, it was also the result of the wide scope of his scientific interests, which led to descriptions of projects of all shapes and forms for the future use of the territory. Third, Hayden's natural bent for independence was limited by the constraints of governmental funding and the fact that he had to rely upon the support of others in the pursuit of his goals. Thus, his strategies for circumventing fiscal restraints and enlisting allies and supporters for his projects are of particular interest.

¶ But the most important element is almost so obvious as to escape notice: survey science was largely field practice, which entailed its own particular challenges. To satisfy the scientific demands of the project, Hayden had to recruit the best available scientific talent, inspire them, and keep them working and productive in spite of problems occasioned by government bureaucracy or competing personalities. There were, as well, problems associated with the West itself. As a rapidly developing and changing country, it entailed "live" rather than laboratory environments. Most of the survey's expeditions bore little resemblance to a summer picnic outing. Field practice required a readiness to adapt to circumstances of weather, people, and terrain, many of which could be harsh and life-threatening. Successful practice required a number of talents not generally considered related to the conduct of scientific investigations. But first, Hayden had to win appointment as head of the Geological Survey of Nebraska.

¶ Fortunately, he began with a head start over any competition. He was familiar with the territory and already closely associated with its geology. Baird claimed that he might have "clenched" the position for Hayden during his visit to Commissioner Joseph S. Wilson of the General Land Office if he had been able to show Wilson a copy of Hayden's *On the Geology and Natural History of the Upper Missouri*, but Hayden had "cabbaged" his copy. Baird advised Hayden to "gather up" and send copies of as many of his publications as he could—his memoirs and articles on the region, proofs of the new plates Leidy was having made from Hayden's collections, a copy of Warren's report, and a copy of Hayden's own geological colored map. Baird promised to add a copy of Meek and Hayden's *Paleontology of the Upper Missouri*, which had been published by the Smithsonian, and "send all to Wilson," confident they would make a winning case.[1] Nor were these Hayden's only advantages.

¶ When Congress admitted Nebraska to the Union as the thirty-seventh state on 1 March 1867, some of the new state's leading citizens and politicians already had their minds fixed on the ideal birthday present: a survey of Nebraska's natural resources. Such a survey had been spoken of for several years, and Hayden had done his part to promote the idea as well as his name for survey director. With the achievement of statehood, Nebraska's legislators quickly proposed that the unexpended balance of the state's territorial appropriation fund a survey. And one of Hayden's supporters in the state quickly informed him of the proposal. Even before receiving Baird's letter, Hayden had learned of the proposed survey from Julius Sterling Morton, secretary of Nebraska Territory from 1858 to 1861. Thus, Baird's letter of 9 March 1867 did not find Hayden unprepared. In fact, he had addressed a letter to Baird the previous day, requesting that he recruit Joseph Henry to his cause, write to Alvin Saunders, the governor of Nebraska, and visit the senators and congressmen from the state and enlist their assistance. Hayden urged Baird to tell them "how much it would aid emigration to have a good scientific report of that region." Reminding Baird that the appointment would put him in a "position to do much," Hayden exhorted him to "make a personal matter of it at once."[2]

¶ Hayden moved quickly to muster support for his candidacy, calling upon the various networks with which he was aligned. He wrote Henry at the Smithsonian—"My friend says that with the influence of the Smithsonian Institution I can secure [the position]"—asking Henry to recommend him "as strongly as you can" and assuring Henry of his credentials and ability. He wrote his former patrons in the Army Corps of Engineers—Warren, Raynolds, and Gen. Andrew A. Humphreys, chief of the corps—all of whom proved willing to recommend Hayden "as one eminently qualified" to conduct a geological survey of the state. And he marshaled support among civilian scientists. Hayden's most prominent such supporter was probably Dana, professor of geology at Yale and editor of the *American Journal of Science.* Having published nearly a dozen articles by Hayden on the geology of the Upper Missouri, Dana assured Hayden he would provide "some strong words" of support that Hayden might get the place "for which you are so well fitted."[3]

¶ For his own part, Hayden wrote Commissioner Wilson applying for the position. On 16 March 1867, Hayden sent a memorandum of projected expenses for "the first year of the Geological Survey of Nebraska" that were based on three possible funding levels: thirty thousand dollars, twenty thousand dollars, and ten thousand dollars. Two days later he submitted a second memorandum based on an appropriation of five thousand dollars. On 10 April, Wilson informed Hayden that the available funding "cannot be more than $5,000." In light of this, he asked Hayden to make calculations upon that basis and inform him "if you are willing to begin the work and prosecute it so as to keep within that sum." If so, Wilson wrote, "it is my purpose, . . . to present your name to the Secretary of the Interior as the choice of this Office."[4]

¶ Responding six days later, Hayden promised Wilson that "If appointed . . . I shall deem it my duty to keep my expenses strictly within the limits of the sum designated." Pointing out that the proposed sum would limit fieldwork to only one year, Hayden expressed hope that "with economy and the good will of the people of Nebraska, . . . much good work can be done in that time." Two weeks later, Hayden remained confident that "$3,000 or $4,000 more" would become available from the territorial appropriation, which would enable him to do something the following year. He expressed hope that "some provision will be made to continue the Survey after the first year's labors," yet felt sure that even one year would be time enough "to show the people the great importance of the work."[5]

¶ Hayden's follow-up letter proved unnecessary. On 29 April 1867, upon receipt of Hayden's earlier letter, Wilson submitted for Interior Secretary Orville H. Browning's approval "a draught of instructions for the government of the geological survey" and Hayden's nomination as "the proper person to take the charge of the same." Browning confirmed Wilson's choice on 4 May 1867, and Hayden was notified that instructions would be sent to him "on Monday next." The instructions, dated 29 April 1867, formally appointed "Dr. Frederick [*sic*] V. Hayden" to make a geological survey of Nebraska with the limited appropriation of five thousand dollars, as outlined in Hayden's memorandum.[6]

¶ Hayden's charge was a lengthy one and exhibited the same diverse interests found in the instructions for state surveys. He was directed to investigate the geological formations of the state and determine their order of succession, relative positions, dip, and comparative thickness. He was to search for and examine all deposits of mineral and natural resources, with special attention to deposits of coal, and to obtain chemical analyses of them and of the different varieties of soils. In addition, Hayden was directed to determine elevations in different parts of the state; make "ample collections" in geology, mineralogy, and paleontology; and investigate the agricultural potential of the different regions of the state together with the prospects for introducing timber into the state. A few days later "supplemental instructions" arrived. Writing that in the course of the survey of Nebraska "you will doubtless meet with many striking and beautiful landscapes, outcroppings, geological strata, organic remains, mineralogical specimens, etc.," Wilson informed Hayden that "I desire that graphic illustrations, as accurate as possible, of such objects be prepared without delay, and transmitted to this Office."[7]

¶ From its beginning then, the United States Geological and Geographical Survey of the Territories, to give it its full, eventual title, incorporated features that characterized its growth and entire existence. Foremost among these was the network of scientists centered on the Smithsonian Institution and largely dependent upon Baird. Not only was Baird one of the first to uncover the opportunity and propose Hayden for the position, but he continued to play an important role in the survey as Hayden continued to look to him for assistance and advice. Two other characteristics are also worth noting at this point: the survey was born with the state of Nebraska, the first new state formed after the Civil War, as part of the nation's continuing westward expansion; and while the survey's duties were liberal, its funding was not.

¶ After receiving notice of his appointment on 7 May 1867, Hayden moved quickly to put his plans into effect. Though his instructions emphasized the need to make sure that expenses did not exceed the five thousand dollars available, Hayden realized that both the term of office of only one year and the meager appropriation were severely limiting factors. Yet he remained optimistic, writing Meek, whom he had already convinced to assist him, "Still something can be done with that," and he began firing off instructions. Hayden had to hit the ground running. Commissioner Wilson wanted him to "get into the field as soon as possible." Moreover, the prospect of a geological survey created excitement in Nebraska, and Hayden was "troubled with letters continually." As he put it: "The people are in a great stew. . . . It will not do for me to delay. There is too much excitement and it may turn into complaints."[8]

¶ For assistance, Hayden turned to his usual collaborators: Baird, Meek, Leidy, and Stevenson. Wilson's pressure on Hayden to begin work in the field, even though high water would probably present difficulties so early in the season, introduced an immediate complication. With obligations at the university, Hayden could not leave before late May. But he could send others out ahead of him, and he turned to Meek, who already planned to join Charles A. White, state geologist of Iowa, in a geological tour across that state. Hayden prevailed upon Meek to extend the tour into Nebraska and meet him at Omaha or Nebraska City about 1 June.[9]

¶ Besides lining up personnel, Hayden also had to equip his expedition as inexpensively as possible. For collecting equipment, he turned to Baird for help, having already alerted him that, with only five thousand dollars available, he would "expect much aid" since he would have to do "a great work with small means." After receiving his appointment, Hayden again wrote Baird, asking for anything he could supply—materials for catching insects, boards for binding plants on, anything that might enable him to economize.[10]

¶ Unfortunately for Hayden, Baird did not have much assistance to offer since the Smithsonian had already been called upon to supply equipment to several other expeditions that season. Nevertheless, Baird promised to do what he could, at the same time appending a postscript that made the quid pro quo evident: "I of course take it for granted that the Materials collected are to come to S.I." Heartened by the promise of assistance, Hayden hastened to assure Baird that he intended to send all his collections in zoology and botany to the Smithsonian. He only wished to reserve to himself the prerogative of designating the person to work them up. Yet even in this Hayden had few definite plans and was prepared to rely upon Baird's advice. And there was one more favor Hayden sought from Baird: assistance in getting a permit from Gen. Ulysses S. Grant giving permission to draw provisions and matériel from army posts at cost, which would enable him to stretch his limited funds even further.[11]

¶ Hayden departed Philadelphia for Nebraska on the evening of 28 May and almost immediately ran into difficulties—both political and practical. Though already aware of the enthusiasm the survey was exciting in Nebraska, upon arrival in Omaha Hayden found the people "crazy on the matter of the Survey." Invited to address the Nebraska legislature for the purpose of "explaining the objects of the Survey," he did so, probably gladly. However, he explained his actions to Wilson differently: "The pressure was so great on me here that I hardly knew how to refuse. It was not done at my instigation, but on the contrary I was urged on every hand." Notwithstanding Hayden's protestations, it is likely he was not telling Wilson the whole truth but wanted to have it both ways, balancing his appreciation of the value of publicity with the potential threat that popularity could become a liability if he eclipsed his superior.

¶ It was even unclear who his employer was. As he put it, "No one seems to know exactly whether I should be called state or U.S. Geologist." The confusion over the appointment, apparent in March, had not dissipated, and the situation was not helped by the Nebraska legislature's having passed a bill calling for a geological survey. Hayden wrote Wilson that "this year the 'bill' has been revised and changed so as to incorporate it with the U.S. appropriation under your charge if it passes." However, Hayden said he intended to try to stay out of the limelight: "I think I shall remain in the field until the close of the year, without stopping more than a night or so in a place, so that the excitement will cease as far as I am concerned." At the same time, he planned to make use of the excitement to the survey's—and his own—advantage, adding: "I desire to write one or two letters to the people of Nebraska desiring them to make observations, collect specimens, and send me such *notes* as are valuable for the Survey." Indeed, he had already written one such letter "under my own signature," though he assured Wilson that he had been careful to "quot[e] from your instructions." But if the people of Nebraska were confused as to Hayden's title and if he had resolved "not to explain the matter unless asked," Wilson had no doubts. Nor did he hesitate to clarify the matter, reminding Hayden to whom he owed his loyalty. In the opinion of the General Land Office, so long as Hayden was employed by the federal government "no divided relation" could be permitted.[12]

¶ A more pressing practical problem arose from the fact that Hayden's letter from Grant had not arrived, and he found he had no funds at his disposal. His instructions were explicit. He would be paid his salary in quarterly installments and be reimbursed for expenses. But no money would be advanced. Hayden soon found this complicated matters, leaving him with an even more pressing need to economize, and he began to write Baird daily about the looked-for letter from Grant. He also wrote Leidy, thinking that the letter might have been sent to any of several addresses in Philadelphia, and he asked Leidy to "visit all these places at once and send me my mail." The nub of Hayden's predicament was that "*Without authority the quartermaster will not do a thing*," and the problem was the more galling because he could see the post had everything he needed. The commander was even willing to provide an escort if he wanted one but only on receipt of proper authorization. As usual, Hayden fretted and worried, writing Baird: "I am afraid you sent your letter to Phila. Who knows when I shall get it?"[13]

¶ After a two-week delay, Grant's letter finally arrived. When it did, Hayden's mood quickly shifted, as upon its receipt the quartermaster furnished him with all he wished. He was given the use of five horses, and at least once during the season he purchased "subsistence stores" in Omaha, including cans of peaches, jellies, over a hundred pounds of hams, and ten cans of oysters.[14] It even looked as if the Nebraska legislature might appropriate something to aid him, and Hayden was optimistic that his collections with Meek would be large. Nor had Hayden wasted the time spent at Omaha, in spite of the frustration of imposed waiting. While there, he rendezvoused with Meek and Theodore Gill, a zoologist at the Smithsonian and at Columbian College in Washington, who had also accompanied White on his tour across Iowa. After spending a day or two reporting their findings to Hayden, Meek took a short trip on the Union Pacific Railroad (UPRR)—probably to search for fossils in the cuttings of the railway beds—while Hayden, as collector, spent some time "visiting various localities of interest."

¶ It seems Hayden originally planned to keep Gill with him for part of the summer, but Gill ended up returning to Washington and the Smithsonian before Hayden started his summer's travels. As far as Hayden was concerned, it was just as well since he had found Gill an "entire failure" as a collector and "*utterly unfit for field work*." What the exact problem was is unclear. Perhaps the two men just did not get along in the field. Perhaps Gill slowed Hayden down. Or perhaps fieldwork (or field life) was not his forte. In any event, on 17 June Hayden pronounced his outfitting complete and his party ready for the field.[15]

¶ Hayden set out mindful of his instructions from the Land Office, which had pointed out the desirability "that the portion of Nebraska situated South of the Platte River be examined first." He therefore began with a southward tour from Omaha "to examine the tier of Counties along the Mo. returning through the next tier." With him, he had Meek, as assistant geologist, paleontologist, and collector, and three other men—his old partner in collecting, James Stevenson, and two laborers. Meek only remained with Hayden for the first part of his summer's travels. Upon arrival at Rulo, a small town on the Missouri near Nebraska's southern border, in the middle of July, he left Hayden to do the remainder of the season's fieldwork alone. Yet even after returning to Washington to begin studies of the fossil collection, he stayed in touch by mail, asking Hayden to follow up findings or investigate geological matters about which Meek was uncertain.[16]

¶ With a wagon to transport supplies and their collection, the five men set out from Omaha on 18 June and headed south along the Missouri River, examining "with considerable care" the counties bordering it—Douglas, Sarpy, Cass, and Otoe (see Map 2). After detouring to the west to examine Lancaster County, Hayden arrived in Nebraska City on 1 July, where he took "the first opportunity which has presented itself to me to report to you [Wilson] the progress of my explorations." Stopping only briefly, Hayden continued south, passing through Nemaha and Richardson Counties, then turned north to

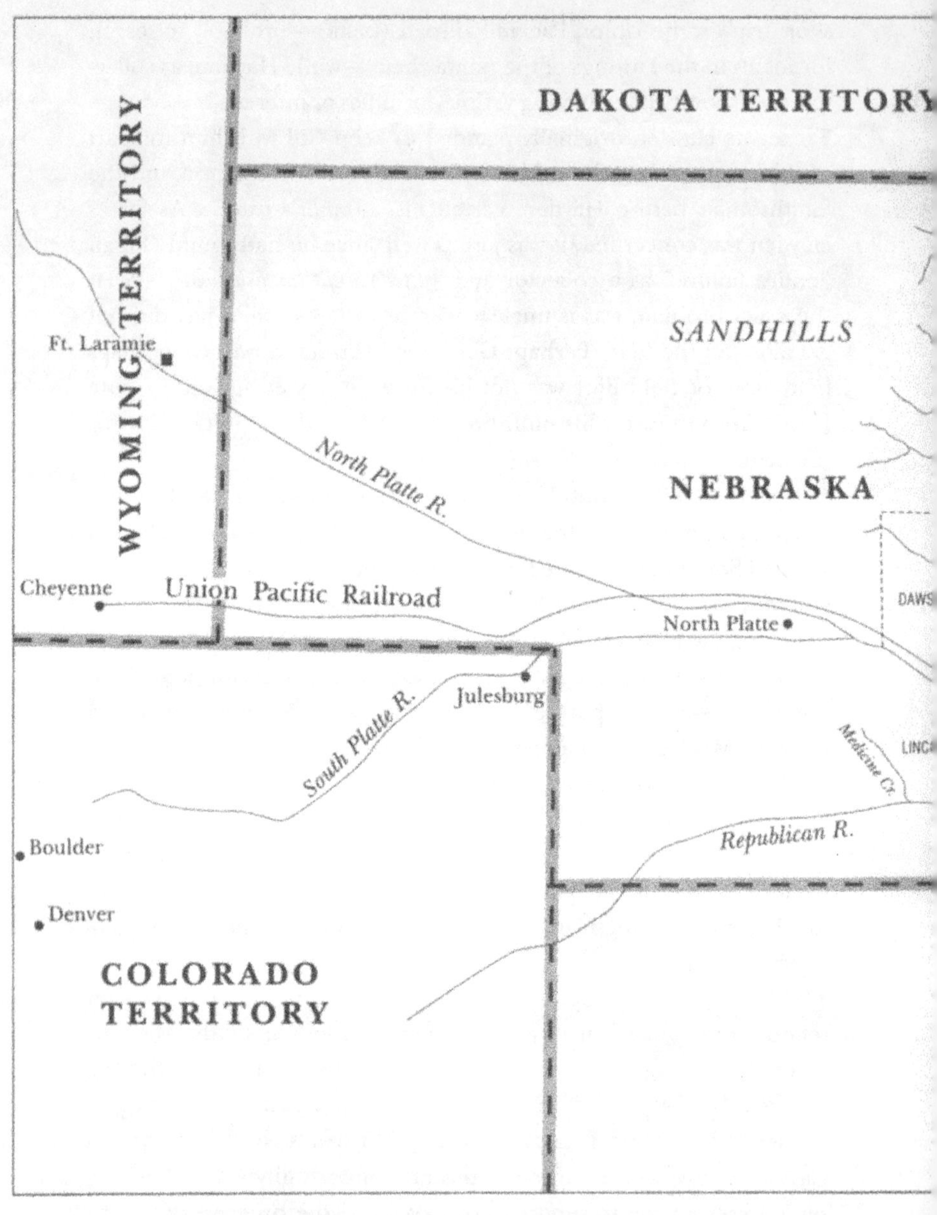
DAKOTA TERRITORY
WYOMING TERRITORY
SANDHILLS
Ft. Laramie
North Platte R.
NEBRASKA
Cheyenne
Union Pacific Railroad
North Platte
Julesburg
South Platte R.
Medicine Cr.
Republican R.
Boulder
Denver
COLORADO
TERRITORY

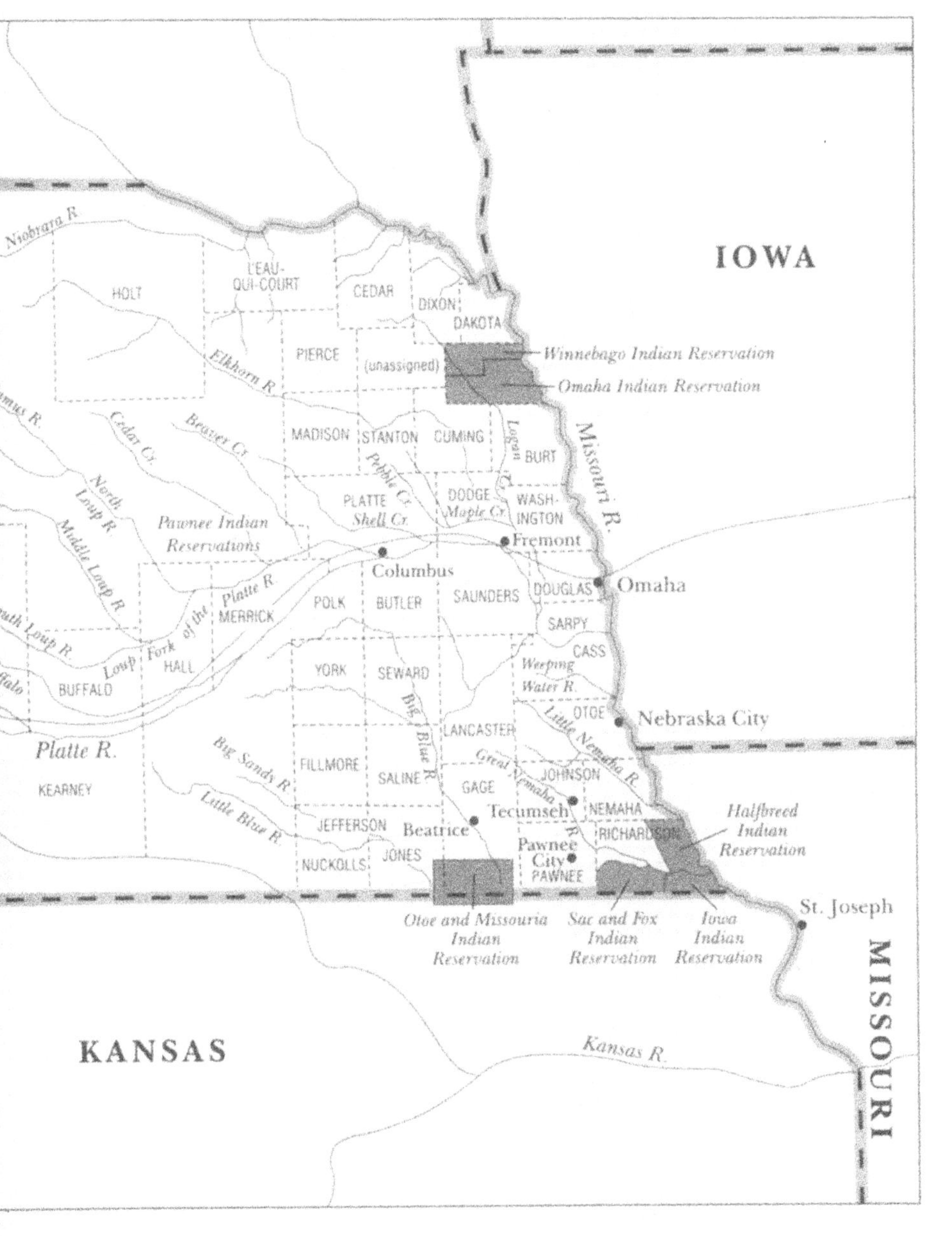

IOWA
KANSAS
MISSOURI
Niobrara R.
HOLT
L'EAU-QUI-COURT
CEDAR
DIXON
DAKOTA
Winnebago Indian Reservation
Omaha Indian Reservation
PIERCE
(unassigned)
Elkhorn R.
MADISON
STANTON
CUMING
Logan Cr.
BURT
Missouri R.
Cedar Cr.
Beaver Cr.
North Loup R.
Middle Loup R.
Pebble Cr.
PLATTE
Shell Cr.
DODGE
Maple Cr.
WASH-INGTON
Pawnee Indian Reservations
Fremont
Columbus
Omaha
DOUGLAS
SARPY
POLK
BUTLER
SAUNDERS
MERRICK
Platte R.
Loup Fork of the Platte R.
South Loup R.
HALL
BUFFALO
YORK
SEWARD
CASS
Weeping Water R.
OTOE
Nebraska City
Big Blue R.
LANCASTER
Little Nemaha R.
Platte R.
KEARNEY
Big Sandy R.
FILLMORE
SALINE
Great Nemaha R.
JOHNSON
GAGE
Tecumseh
NEMAHA
Little Blue R.
JEFFERSON
Beatrice
RICHARDSON
Halfbreed Indian Reservation
NUCKOLLS
JONES
Pawnee City
PAWNEE
St. Joseph
Otoe and Missouria Indian Reservation
Sac and Fox Indian Reservation
Iowa Indian Reservation
Kansas R.

survey the next western tier of counties—Pawnee, Johnson, and Lancaster—which brought him back to the Platte River, where he again turned south through the third tier of settled counties.[17]

¶ From Pawnee City, Hayden continued west to the Big Blue River, which he followed north to Beatrice, inspecting Gage County. Leaving Beatrice at the end of July, he went west to the Little Blue River, which he followed northwest as far as the Big Sandy River, "which is as far as the Indians will permit me to go." This enabled him to report on Jefferson and Nuckolls Counties. He then turned east again, returning to the Big Blue and following it upstream before cutting over to Tecumseh, in Johnson County, where he arrived on 8 August. From there, Hayden made his way back to Omaha, arriving by 22 August and staying about a week to "recruit my animals." At that point, he reported that "My Wagon team has travelled over 500 miles in a straight line within the past two months, and my own travel in my investigations has been over 1200 miles."[18]

¶ Leaving Omaha a second time, Hayden proceeded to investigate the counties north of the Platte River. He went up the Missouri as far as the Niobrara River, which took him to a point about due north of his furthest point in his western explorations of the southern counties. Then he went across country to Columbus "by way of Logan, Elkhorn, Maple and Pebble creeks," gaining "a pretty good idea of the Elkhorn basin," and arriving in Columbus about 24 September. From there he proposed to return to Omaha by rail to resupply and then return to Columbus and proceed west up the Loup Fork of the Platte, examining the country and collecting "some of those interesting fossil bones, if the hostile Indians will permit."[19]

¶ A couple of weeks later, however, Hayden wrote from Julesburg, Colorado Territory, that he had broken off investigations in Nebraska, sent some of his men home, and returned his horses to the army. He had changed his plans to go up the headwaters of the Loup Fork because of the unavailability of army troops for protection: "As this region is the great thoroughfare for several tribes of hostile Sioux, Gen'l. Potter [commander of Fort Sedgwick] thinks it is not advisable for me to make the trip [without the troops]." Hayden had gone up the Loup Fork "as far as it was prudent for me to go" and then crossed it and the Platte and followed the Platte east through Butler and

Saunders Counties, while his wagon came down on the north side of the Platte. After completing his tour of Saunders County, Hayden recrossed the Platte and examined the western portions of Sarpy and Douglas Counties, making his way back to Omaha. By this point, Hayden wrote, his team had traveled about 1,025 miles, "while my own examinations have led me over two or three times that distance."[20]

¶ Thwarted in his plan to visit the fossil beds at the headwaters of the Loup Fork, Hayden decided to spend "a small portion of time" examining the country along the line of the UPRR, which had recently extended as far as Cheyenne, in Wyoming Territory. He decided to pass "from Station to Station" on the way back to Omaha "and get all the facts I can" and then "start down the Missouri from Omaha in a skiff and study the bluffs at low water." During October, he took a western tour "along the U.P.R.R. and other places," and on 2 November informed Wilson that he was headed for Omaha. He reached Omaha by 7 November, sold his outfit at auction as instructed, and left on the eighth to travel down the Missouri, hoping to be in Washington by the twentieth but not arriving there until early December.[21]

¶ As Hayden toured the state, making "ample collections in geology, mineralogy, and palaeontology to illustrate the notes taken in the field," he carried with him several copies of Land Office maps of Nebraska, on which he colored in the geological formations in the field "to ensure the strictest accuracy." He found most of Nebraska to be a rolling land, with much of the country covered with a superficial deposit of yellow marl—a mixture of clay, sand and limestone—which gave a "beautiful undulating outline to the surface" with "gentle slopes" but afforded "only now and then an exposure of the basis rocks. . . . rendering the investigation of the geological structure . . . more complicated and difficult." This was one reason why Hayden gave his "first attention" to the river counties since they presented "better exposures of the rocks than any other counties in the State," though he found even these "by no means good." Hayden supplemented observations along the river banks with investigations at quarries and sites where borings had been made in search of coal or wells sunk for water. For example, an artesian well at Omaha and a boring in Nebraska City helped him establish the succession of geological strata to a depth of 382 feet, and his investigations enabled him to determine several sections across the southern counties as well as general sections of the state's Cretaceous and Tertiary rocks.[22]

¶ Hayden and his assistants also made collections in plants, fossils, insects, birds, and fishes, the last two being of particular interest to Baird. The results were quite impressive, at least in quantity. Although able to employ only three collectors and laborers rather than the five or ten he originally proposed, by the beginning of July Hayden had forwarded six boxes of "fossils and Geological specimens" and was able to tell Wilson that "Our collection now is a fine one. We adding many daily [sic]." By the end of July, Hayden had sent on his tenth box of specimens and decided he would "retain all boxes now until September on account of expense and have a number sent by freight." During the next month, however, his collections began to exceed carrying capacity, and he sent another eight boxes east in late August. He also held yet three more, resolving "to retain all untill the close of the survey and send in mass by freight, as cheaper." At the end of the season, Hayden had yet another ten boxes to ship east. Among them he counted "a huge quantity of fossils—of the Carboniferous kind." Though he admitted he had not made any "striking discoveries," he thought he had done "remarkably well, and gathering much useful information."[23]

¶ After Meek returned to Washington, Hayden once again experienced money difficulties. After two months in the field in Hayden's employ, Meek desired his pay but had difficulty obtaining it. Hayden had to be cautious in handling Meek, who, though highly sensitive to criticism and very reclusive in nature, was also essential to Hayden's work. Writing from Julesburg, Hayden tried to explain the delay and promised to "fix [things] all right so that you can have your pay on the day when I return." He encouraged Meek to work on his report in the meantime and "do all you can in studying up those fossils." He also committed himself to pay for any drawings Meek might have made, promising that "there can be as many plates of fossils as there is material" and urging Meek to "go ahead with your geological report and say all you can." Yet Hayden's remarks failed to address the nub of Meek's complaint, and in the end it took action by Commissioner Wilson to resolve Meek's financial difficulties. Upon hearing of it, Hayden wrote to Meek with relief—"I am *so very* glad the Commissioner fixed that matter for you"—and a promise: "I will make out your accounts for $300 more as soon as I reach W[ashington]. I am *very* glad you are doing so much." But more than money, Hayden pledged himself in a partnership in destiny as well, writing, "Whatever success I have I will always *share* with you and I am anxious you should do the same by me. Our names will be ever identified with the Geology of this country. When I have power I will always do by you whatever you *yourself* will say is right."[24]

¶ Hayden's words held more than a promise. They also contained a plea for Meek's continued partnership and thus hint at the emergence of a new relationship. In the days when Meek worked for Hall and Hayden was a struggling neophyte with dreams of scientific fame, he and Meek had been partners, sharing their talents and dreams. Now Hayden had begun to translate his dreams into reality. Though Meek had achieved no less scientific recognition, Hayden was winning broader fame. Professional success wrought changes in Hayden's relationships, including that with Meek. In the antebellum years, Meek and Hayden coauthored more than a dozen articles, articles that helped build Hayden's scientific reputation. When Meek accepted the position as paleontologist for the Nebraska survey, he included a condition that his results be published in his own name. Just as ambitious as Hayden, Meek seems to have feared that the more political Hayden would receive credit for his work.[25] Thus, when Hayden assured Meek he would always share whatever success he might achieve with him, Meek might very well have received the promise with a grain of salt, focusing as much on Hayden's request: that Meek share whatever success *he* received with *Hayden*. Their relationship cooled, and Meek never coauthored another article with Hayden.

Commissioner Wilson had stated in his instructions to Hayden that he deemed it unnecessary to enumerate Hayden's duties as a "scientific geologist." He relied upon Hayden's "practical experience and well established reputation" and expressed confidence that he would "render an acceptable service to the government and be of great utility in the development of the geological resources of Nebraska and contribute largely to the wealth of the country." Instead, Wilson focused on *economic geology*, calling for detailed attention to mineral resources, agricultural potential, and the feasibility of introducing timber.[26] That Hayden endeavored to meet all these expectations is obvious from the periodic dispatches that Wilson combined into Hayden's report. Hayden was clearly aware of what his employer wanted. At the same time, Hayden remained aware of his responsibilities as a scientist. While he strove to do all he could to contribute to the "development of the geological resources of Nebraska and . . . the wealth of the country," he also sought to stay within the limits of scientific evidence and place the whole report upon an underlying general geological foundation. Together, these factors shaped his investigations and his reports.

¶ From the start, Hayden gave a great deal of attention to the question of coal deposits in Nebraska. He charged Meek to "find out where the Coal beds are which are near Nebraska and try to trace a section across to Nebraska if possible." Identifying the determination of the presence or absence of coal beds in Nebraska as "one of the most important questions," Hayden wrote: "Coal is found about 50 or 60 miles East in Iowa. The beds are nearly horizontal. Can these Coal beds be traced into Nebraska?" Sending Meek ahead of him to Nebraska City, Hayden informed him that a mining company there had sunk a shaft and was saving all its fossils for the survey's investigation. Yet he warned Meek that "this Coal business is most important. In examining the pit sunk at Nebraska City, if you find no signs of Coal, let them down gently, for it will almost kill the Survey, to come out boldly with the statement 'no coal.'" In fact, from his earlier research on the lignite formations, Hayden had good reason to suspect that "no coal" would be the answer. Though he and Meek had both collected numerous Carboniferous fossils from the eastern portion of the state, they had not been able to trace the Carboniferous far into Nebraska.[27]

¶ In spite of these suspicions, Hayden assiduously explored prospects for coal. At Omaha, he investigated and drew a colored section of the geological strata exhibited at the 383-foot artesian well the UPRR had sunk. At Nebraska City, he studied and rendered a similar section of a 346-foot boring made in search of coal. Finding that neither had reached the coal "measures" or strata, Hayden opined that any deposits of coal would be at much greater depth still. That judgment did not entirely please Commissioner Wilson, who wrote expressing the hope Hayden might yet discover exploitable deposits of coal. Nebraskans were also very interested in the "coal question," and Hayden found that the issue "excites the attention of the people more than any other, and they are earnestly asking for a solution of the problem." He attempted to assist them, trying to maintain a measured optimism, but soon decided that "I could not risk my reputation upon any positive statement in favor of the existence of coal at all in this region [Pawnee County], or any workable bed in the State."[28]

¶ Much of the interest in coal derived from the general lack of timber in Nebraska, a feature that had led earlier travelers across Nebraska to conclude that it was a highly unpromising region for settlers and provided Nebraska "boomers" with the challenge of overcoming the region's apparent dearth of fuel. This they did by appealing to presumed unseen mineral wealth. The coal question, then, was already more than a decade old before Wilson's instructions to Hayden took note of it and related it to the region's lack of timber, a relationship Hayden recognized as early as his 1856 report for Warren. The answer he provided was not the one the state's promoters wanted to hear. In reporting on Lancaster County, he wrote that his investigations there "settled an important point . . . for the citizens in this county, that no coal-beds of workable value can possibly be found at a less depth than 1,000 to 1,500 feet beneath the surface, which renders further search for this mineral useless." He "would be glad to find a workable bed of coal for the good people." But though "the almost entire absence of timber would render the presence of coal here a matter of vital importance," he had to conclude "it cannot be. The farmers must plant trees, and in a few years the demand for fuel will be supplied."[29]

¶ As Hayden submitted his periodic reports during the course of his summer's perambulations and became convinced that the search for coal was uneconomical and unlikely to succeed except on a local scale, he stressed more and more frequently the necessity of planting trees in Nebraska. Besides emphasizing the issue in his reports, he spoke on the topic several times during his tour of the state. Hayden wrote that "the greater portion of the more intelligent and thrifty farmers" were already engaged in arboriculture, and he claimed that it was "done so easily that there is no excuse for a farmer to be destitute of fuel after a few years." At the same time, he noted the various kinds of trees settlers had successfully introduced to Nebraska, concluding that "most of the hardy northern trees may be cultivated on these western plains with entire success."[30]

¶ Hayden emphasized the subject of planting trees because of the "popular notion at the East that trees cannot be made to grow successfully on the western prairies, and especially that the climate and soil are unfavorable to the cultivation of the fruits." Admitting that he had also held that notion "until within two years," Hayden now argued that "within thirty or fifty years, forest-trees may be grown large enough for all economical purposes." His conversion may have drawn support from geological history. While he knew that "since the surface of the country received its present geological configuration no trees have grown there," he also knew this had not always been the case. During Tertiary times (a mere thirty-five million years earlier!), "all these treeless plains were covered with a luxuriant growth of forest-trees like those of the Gulf States or South America," including palm trees, sycamores, maples, poplars, cedars, hickories, cinnamon, fig, "and many varieties now found only in tropical or sub-tropical climates." In his opinion, "a sufficient number of experiments" had already demonstrated that it was entirely feasible to restore those forests "in a comparatively short period of time," though he did not think it would happen "except by artificial means."[31]

¶ Planting trees might also yield an additional bonus. Besides supplying necessary fuel and building materials, it might even bring about a change in the climate: "It is believed, also, that the planting of ten or fifteen acres of forest-trees on each quarter-section will have a most important effect on the climate, equalizing and increasing the moisture and adding greatly to the fertility of the soil." Hayden claimed that "the settlement of the country and the increase of the timber have already changed for the better the climate of that portion of Nebraska lying along the Missouri, so that within the last twelve or fourteen years the rain has gradually increased in quantity and is more equally distributed through the year." He predicted this change would "continue to extend across the dry belt to the foot of the Rocky Mountains as the settlements extend and the forest-trees are planted in proper quantities." His suggestion that settlers might change the climate by planting trees linked two important concerns for immigrants to the trans-Mississippi West: fuel and water, both elemental needs. In support of what might seem fantastic claims—though the idea had been published more than two decades earlier—Hayden cited French, German, and English authorities and proposed to show in his final report "that these ideas are not purely theoretical, and that the influence of trees on climate and humidity has been investigated by some of the ablest scientific men in this country and Europe."[32]

¶ Besides the great questions of coal and timber, Hayden had been charged to conduct a general reconnaissance of economic resources of the new state. His reports indicate how wide ranging his observations in this respect were. In Lancaster and Cass Counties he noted that "in the valleys of all the streams, and in numerous other localities, there are low, boggy places which seem to promise peat" and expressed confidence that, in the absence of coal, it would soon become "an object of earnest pursuit and of great profit." At Omaha and "all over Sarpy County," he found "limestone of good quality for economical purposes" and noted "excellent quarries" on both sides of the Platte River "as high up as the Elkhorn." He also reported building stones as "very abundant" all over Pawnee County in the south of the state and observed that "almost every farm has a quarry." And in the northern part of the state Hayden reported on "quite numerous layers, from one to four feet thick, of a very compact massive quartzite, the hardest and most durable rock in the State," which might prove very useful in the construction of contemplated railroad bridges across the Missouri River: "no rock in the State would be so unyielding and durable for abutments as this, providing enough of it can be found."[33]

¶ Hayden also gave attention to potential manufacturing resources. At Nebraska City, he found "potters' clay in abundance" and reported that a pottery factory was about to be established there. He noted, as well, the presence of "numerous beds of sand . . . which are of much value for building purposes" since it could be combined with the yellow marl, yielding "materials for making brick . . . without limit." The lack of fuel presented a serious drawback and raised the question of "whether the making of pressed brick would not prove in this country a success." Settling the question to his own satisfaction, Hayden referred to S. P. Reed, superintendent of construction on the UPRR, as "a most intelligent and liberal-minded gentleman," who reported having successfully made some forty thousand bricks by this method at Fremont, Dodge County. To Hayden's mind, the experiment removed "a great obstacle . . . out of the way of the immediate settlement of a great portion of this State." Finally, Hayden asserted that "should the future prosperity of the country demand it," Otoe and Nemaha Counties contained "abundant materials for the manufacture of what is called in England, and recently brought into use in this country, 'patent concrete stone,'" which he described as a finding "worthy of notice."[34]

¶ Hayden's final major charge concerned Nebraska's agricultural resources. Giving them the same measured, optimistic consideration, he rarely failed to find something favorable to say. After his tour through the southern counties in June and July, for example, he reported on farmers' success in planting trees and raising fruits, remarking that "All kinds of garden-vegetables grow better in Nebraska than in any other region with which I am acquainted." Richardson County, in particular, Hayden found "in some respects the finest county in the State." While the surface was "more rugged than many of the interior counties," Richardson was "fully watered with ever-flowing streams and innumerable springs of the purest water." Moreover, Hayden claimed it was "not an uncommon thing" in the county "for a farmer to have growing 40 or 50 acres of corn and the same number of acres of wheat and oats, and not unfrequently as high as 100 or 200 or each." Although Hayden admitted that the further west he went the poorer he found the soil, he explained that this was a comparative observation. For instance, while the soil in Gage County was not the equal of that in counties along the Missouri River, if the prospective farmer thought in terms of a different crop, it was another matter altogether: "For wheat . . . this soil, . . . seems to be most favorable. . . . [though] the corn and other kinds of grain are not quite as good." In spite of its limitations, he concluded, "too much cannot be said in favor of Gage County as an agricultural and grazing region."[35]

¶ Pushing farther west, south of the Platte, Hayden came to the semiarid plains beyond the ninety-seventh meridian, which Warren had reported as marking the "western limit of ordinary agriculture," beyond which white settlers would have to adopt a pastoral lifestyle. Hayden concurred, remarking that "the greater portion of the western half of the State of Nebraska" would at best be "inhabited sparsely by a people devoted to pastoral pursuits." Even so, he characteristically presented the region in a favorable light. Noting that the "same hills or other portions of the West that appear the most sterile and most deficient in wood and water" were the "favorite resorts" of wild game, wherein they became "exceedingly fat," Hayden predicted that the seemingly "arid, sterile plains" might prove to be "a fine stock-growing country" and the source, one day, of "some of the finest wool in America."[36]

¶ However, not even Hayden could redeem the northwest portion of Nebraska, between the Niobrara and the Platte Rivers. He found travel very difficult in the Sandhills: "the wheels sink deep into the loose sand, rendering it impossible to transport loaded teams through them." And though the water was "usually quite good," it was "not abundant," and there were "many alkaline lakes." Furthermore, there was "scarcely any timber on the whole area." He was forced to conclude that an area of "20,000 square miles forming the northwestern portion of the State is totally unfit for cultivation, and . . . even doubtfully suitable for grazing."[37]

¶ Finally, Hayden deemed it his duty to remark not only on the land but its people as well. Time and again, when he referred to counties in southwestern Nebraska as "the poor man's paradise" with "broad fertile acres, to be had almost for the asking, through the generosity of our Government," he also remarked on the worthiness of the immigrants flocking to this paradise. He noted, for example, that "the inhabitants of Pawnee County belong to a superior class, with respect to their industry and morals" and pointed out that there was "not a locality in the county where ardent spirits are sold as a beverage." And he occasionally had to confess that he was "not a little surprised" at the immigrants' rate of advance, finding even so far west as Jefferson County "a large number of Germans who have taken farms" and "by their industrious and frugal habits . . . made for themselves an independence in the short space of six years." Such comments contrasted sharply with Hayden's observations on the original inhabitants of the land; he claimed that the residents of the Otoe reservation had "the same lazy, improvident habits of the wild Indians further west."[38]

Except for his pessimism about prospects for coal, Hayden's observations and comments were generally well received by the powers that be, both in Nebraska and in Washington. That was fortunate since from the beginning he viewed the 1867 survey of Nebraska as a potential springboard, the beginning of a great work—if he could bring it to a successful completion. To do that, he had to fight off possible competitors, work up his results, and win another appropriation. Even while at work in Nebraska, Hayden tried to keep up with the news in Washington, at least insofar as it might impact him, and he relied on friends like Baird to keep him posted and act on his behalf. For instance, soon after arriving in Nebraska he heard a rumor that Wilson was displeased with some items that had appeared in the Omaha papers. Hayden quickly wrote Wilson, urging that he not "be held responsible for all that appears in the papers." Explaining that he had simply sent "a little note . . . on a curious fossil fish," he contended that his name had been attached to it with the title of "'State Geologist' without my knowledge." At the same time, Hayden also wrote Baird, requesting that he call on Wilson, "get his views and write me." Hayden claimed he should not be held responsible for much of what appeared in the papers and blamed the whole matter on the excitement caused by the survey: "Every body is crazy here about the Survey and it seems to be a great thing to them."[39]

¶ Toward the end of the summer Hayden perceived a more serious threat, perhaps related to this incident, when he heard that Wilson was looking for someone to make a survey of the Montana Territory. Writing Baird once again, Hayden revealed how much he felt a proprietary interest in all of the West, and not just those sections he had already explored: "What is it about the Commissioner wanting some one to go to Montana? . . . Is there any one trying to get my place! Not as geologist of Nebraska, but of the west. I have understood that it was the intention of the Commissioner to keep me in the field for several years. I hope you will watch my interests closely. I do not think the Nebraska Survey will continue after this year and I wish to continue on in different parts of the West. . . . I beg you to write me at once to Omaha and let me know the news."[40] Hayden obviously felt he had only begun his work.

¶ Hayden also began to think seriously about working up his results for his final report. To accomplish this he would need collaborators, a place to work, and, he was sure, more money. Thus, on 6 December 1867 he wrote Wilson asking about prospects for "appropriations for continuance of the geological surveys" and whether a room could be provided for the purpose of preparing his report. Wilson allowed him the use of a room "so long as the same is required for the purpose named" but made no mention of future appropriations.[41]

¶ For collaborators, Hayden farmed out his collections much as he had after previous expeditions, bringing them on to the Smithsonian and then relying on the advice of Baird, Leidy, and others in finding appropriate people to examine them. Meek was already on staff and had charge of the fossil invertebrates. Leidy was Hayden's partner for fossil vertebrates, and Hayden's colleagues from the Smithsonian could handle most of the zoological specimens. Before he was done, he distributed his collections among scientists in at least half a dozen cities, including Horatio Wood, professor of botany at the University of Pennsylvania; Dr. George Englemann, in St. Louis; George H. Horn, a Philadelphia physician and entomologist, then president of the Entomological Society of Philadelphia; Gill, at the Smithsonian; and Samuel Scudder, an entomologist at the Boston Society of Natural History.[42]

¶ This left him needing a chemist and a fossil botanist to complete the analysis of his collections. As paleobotanist, Hayden recruited Leo Lesquereux. Fleeing the political turmoil in Europe, Lesquereux had followed Agassiz to America in 1848 and eventually became one of nineteenth-century America's most important paleobotanists, doing important work for several state and federal geological surveys from the 1850s through the 1880s. When Hayden hired him in 1867, he was already at work on the plant fossils collected that summer by the Philadelphia entomologist, geologist, and naturalist John L. LeConte during a survey along the UPRR in Kansas. Hayden worked out an agreement with LeConte to combine their specimens and have Lesquereux prepare a single joint report on them all. This benefited both surveys since their areas of exploration were roughly contiguous. Lesquereux proved amenable to the proposal, but only after receiving some assurance of compensation—from the present year's appropriations, if possible, or the next year's, if necessary.[43]

¶ Hayden enlisted two chemists with similar arrangements. The first was John Torrey, whom Hayden met at the Academy of Natural Sciences in Philadelphia. Torrey agreed to undertake the analyses of Hayden's lignite samples—a quite soft and brittle form of coal and unsatisfactory for most purposes—on terms Hayden proposed: "hoping you will do what you can in the way of compensation." Torrey did take care, though, to let Hayden know his usual rate was ten to twelve dollars for each sample analyzed, as it was his practice "to make moderate charges."[44] The other chemist was Samuel William Johnson of Yale, who agreed to undertake an analysis of soils. These arrangements regarding compensation proved liabilities for Hayden. Not only were they a gamble for all parties, since the hoped-for appropriation might not be forthcoming, but Hayden had no authority to make such promises.

¶ That did not keep him from seeking the means to fulfill them, however. While his collaborators worked on their reports, Hayden labored to push through a new appropriation for the coming year, seeking twice the previous year's amount. During the summer season in Nebraska, Hayden and Stevenson had met Grenville Dodge, congressman from Council Bluffs, Iowa, and chief engineer of the UPRR. They made a favorable impression. Dodge promised to see to it that the report, once complete, was published at once.[45] Yet Hayden sought more than that, and there can be little doubt that once back in Washington he prodded and lobbied every supporter he could to secure another appropriation.

¶ He received strong support from Commissioner Wilson. In response to a call from the House Committee on the Public Lands for "information as to the practical results of the geological survey of Nebraska, . . . and the propriety of appropriating for the extension of like surveys to other portions of the public lands," Wilson forcefully endorsed Hayden's work. He characterized it as having provided much useful information, both "scientific and practical," and claimed that it would "furnish reliable information not only to our own countrymen, but to the people of other lands who are anxiously examining every source of intelligence preparatory to emigrating." At the same time, Wilson noted that no careful examination of the mineral deposits said to exist in the Rocky Mountain areas had yet been made by men of science and urged that "a geological survey of these districts would at once place the character of these resources upon their basis, give shape to our information concerning them, and place it in an authentic form." He suggested appropriating ten thousand for the purpose.[46]

¶ Hayden's efforts to continue and expand his survey were only partially successful. On 20 July 1868, the day before adjourning for the summer, Congress authorized the commissioner of the General Land Office "to continue the extension of the geological exploration as begun in Nebraska . . . to other portions of the public lands." But the appropriation remained at five thousand dollars. And there was another disappointment for Hayden since Wilson had found he could not be trusted to keep within the constraints of a budget. In March 1868, Wilson had instructed Hayden to discontinue the employment of all his associates as of the end of that month and report all outstanding liabilities. When Hayden did so, he reported liabilities of over $1,300, including $365 for Torrey, Johnson, and Lesquereux, who were to be paid "on condition that the appropriation would permit, or at least need not be paid at present." Learning this, Wilson rejected the vouchers, informing Hayden that he had not received any authority to employ them, "either with said condition or otherwise." He then went on to sketch out a balance statement showing that Hayden had already spent $6,370.31 of his appropriation of $6,637.50, leaving only $267.19 to be applied to Hayden's salary for the year ending 28 April 1868. After this experience, Wilson kept even tighter control over survey expenditures. To Hayden's chagrin, for the 1868 survey "Mr. Wilson made all the appointments and used the whole sum."[47]

¶ These setbacks notwithstanding, most of Hayden's efforts in the 1867 survey were repaid with success. He had demonstrated a generally convincing competence in leading his own survey and had gathered together a corps of scientific assistants impressed with his ability, as well as a corps of political sponsors impressed with his talent and accomplishments. He had made a good beginning. Though the next year opened under the constraint of Wilson's exercise of tighter financial supervision of the survey, this represented a challenge to be conquered. Hayden's method of operations demanded maximum independence. If his supervisor would not grant this, he would simply have to find a new supervisor. But first there was another season of work to be done in the field.

4

Harnessing Interests to Entrepreneurial Science

It is my earnest desire to devote the remainder of the working days of my life to the development of [the West's] scientific and material interests, until I shall see every Territory, which is now organized, a State of the Union. —Hayden, *Preliminary Report of . . . Wyoming*

Whenever a member or Senator asks me for information or to secure any information for him from any person, I make haste to do so. —Hayden to J. Peter Lesley, 30 January 1874 (more probably 1879)

Hayden's 1867 survey of Nebraska marked the dawning of a new sort of involvement of the federal government in geological and geographical science, one not tied to direct military usefulness. A "birthday gift" to the new state, its aims were wholly civilian, directed toward the development of the state in a very broad fashion. Over the next decade, the survey exhibited change with continuity. The campaign for appointment transmuted into an annual campaign for continued and increased appropriations. Enlisting competent collaborators and keeping them reasonably satisfied and productive became more complex as the size and scope of the survey expanded. Accommodating the wishes of government patrons remained an ever-present necessity, as did maintaining the proper balance of "usefulness" in the results of the survey and assuring the prompt dissemination of findings. To these were added the growing burdens of repelling the claims of competitors leading rival surveys and the sharp attacks of critics. But selling the survey to Congress and winning the annual appropriations that were its lifeblood always remained the primary task, a task Hayden accomplished with a degree of success that amazed friend and foe alike.

¶ Upon his appointment to head the survey of Nebraska, Hayden adopted the title "U.S. Geologist." In doing so, he associated himself and his efforts with the authority and purpose of his patron—the government of the United States. At the same time, however, his dreams and hopes for what his survey might become, nebulous though they might have been, went far beyond the broad but definite terms of his appointment. In his first year as director of the survey of Nebraska, Hayden displayed a number of traits that would characterize the survey for the duration of its existence. But to change the survey into something approximating what he had dreamed of and broached to Baird and Leidy more than a decade earlier—a general natural history survey of the whole Upper Missouri region—demanded a variety of entrepreneurial skills.

¶ We have already noted some general characteristics of entrepreneurs. They tend to be opportunists, expansion minded, and willing to employ every device within their power to attain their goals. But understanding entrepreneurs in public service requires examining personal operating styles vis-à-vis the organization's needs and the conditions in which it attempts to function to see how leaders turn "formal authority into effective influence." Hayden had already demonstrated ability as a "self-starter," a successful initiator and promoter of projects, and he had shown some facility to respond to external stimuli. As the head of a scientific bureau, he had to continue to exercise such talents. His survey's future depended upon his ability to identify potential missions for it and cultivate support while countering opposition and criticism. As a leader, Hayden was also responsible for the internal workings of the survey. He had to recruit good men and inspire loyalty among them. He had to foster their professional development, making sure they possessed the technical skills necessary to accomplish the survey's tasks. Finally, as the survey's chief executive, he had to be on the lookout for potential weaknesses in the survey and take action to rectify them.[1]

¶ Hayden's success or failure as a public entrepreneur depended on his ability to respond to several factors in the environment in which he operated. Foremost among these as a client of federal patronage in the early Gilded Age was the federal government itself, characterized as it was by "fragmentation and overlap." He also had to attend to changing public values and opinion and the importance of new technologies. All three provided "fertile ground for entrepreneurship." Yet each presented risks as well. Fragmentation can pose "an important hurdle to sustained and coherent . . . leadership" as well as provide openings "for policy experimentation and for initiative in building political coalitions." Public opinion can be a powerful inhibiting force while remaining eminently malleable, and successful entrepreneurs are frequently those especially adept at "*creating* the 'widespread' public demand to which they appear to be responding." New technology may generate new opportunities, but it also presents the risk of making incorrect choices. Finally, a fourth element was (and remains) crucial for any seeker of federal patronage: "the role of elected officials and their aides in providing political resources and active support."[2] Alliances with congressmen would be key to Hayden's success, but the high turnover among most members of the House meant that Hayden constantly had to cultivate new patrons in Congress.

¶ Beyond these general tasks and risks, we can also ask if there is anything distinctive about the individual character or personality of would-be entrepreneurs. Are some character traits more conducive to successful innovation within the special environment of public service? Studies of public entrepreneurship in the twentieth century suggest three: "a capacity to engage in systematic rational analysis; an ability to see new possibilities offered by the evolving historical situation; and a desire to 'make a difference'—to throw one's energies and personal reputation into the fray in order to bring about changes."[3] The last is especially important since the entrepreneurial civil servant must be satisfied with different rewards than are available in the private sector. Instead of personal wealth and riches, the public entrepreneur's rewards are increased appropriations, expanded authority, and fame and influence—rewards no less heady for being less tangible.

¶ Attention to these skills and traits greatly assists in understanding Hayden's career and the development of the Hayden Survey. For instance, Hayden's ambition for scientific fame led him to identify or claim new missions: proposing surveys of the Nebraska Territory and eagerly laying claim to the survey of Nebraska, as well as arguing for its continuance and expansion. He labored diligently to cultivate external constituencies to support his endeavors. And we have seen how the environment for exploration science in postbellum nineteenth-century America was shaped by a decline in the army's role in the West, which opened a door to expanded civilian activity, the emergence of a more activist federal government, and the dramatic rejuvenation of interests in the trans-Mississippi West in the years after the Civil War. Pursuing his ambition, Hayden expanded and developed his survey by seizing his opportunities and multiplying his markets. One way to understand Hayden is to view him as a salesman who achieved remarkable success selling Congress something it was not always sure it wanted: science.

Though the federal government had long funded reconnaissance surveys, the action of the Thirty-ninth Congress varied the pattern by entrusting such a survey exclusively to civilian supervision and management. As a result, the associated sciences found themselves in a new niche in the federal establishment. Hayden successfully exploited the possibilities this environment presented. How successfully is amply shown by the survey's growth in both funding and organizational complexity over its first five years, as Hayden's annual appropriation rose from five thousand dollars to nearly one hundred thousand dollars, and his organization developed from a single exploring party of five men to a half-dozen parties totaling forty or more scientists and support personnel. Throughout these years Hayden played a crucial role, organizing support for federally funded science in the civilian sphere, weaving together commercial and scientific interests to elaborate a niche in which his survey could develop, and persuading Congress to increase support for his proposals. As a result of his efforts, his survey came to occupy a privileged position in the minds of congressmen, the press, the public, and managers of pragmatically oriented commercial enterprises eager to develop the resources of the West. At first, Hayden's responses to these varying interests were ad hoc. But as he elaborated ways to harness other interests to his own scientific and bureaucratic concerns and cast his plans for the growth of his survey in such a way as to encourage alliances with various western interests, his survey gained greater internal and external stability. Not only did it find a place for itself in its environment—both in the East and in the

West—but it also succeeded in molding that environment to its own advantage.

To win congressional approval for growing appropriations Hayden relied upon support from a variety of constituencies that could make their interests and desires known to their representatives. The growing demand for the survey's various products—its reports, maps, photographs, and specimens—attested to his success in gaining that support through careful cultivation of his "markets." Foremost among them were scientific, business, and trade interests. However, he did not neglect the interests of a more general public, both at home and abroad, for there was a vast audience for information about the West. Both American and foreign scientists viewed the West as a vast laboratory and eagerly sought news of the latest developments there. Some, like Hayden, sought opportunities to go West themselves. Others sought reports and collections for themselves and for their schools, colleges, and societies. The interest of the merely curious ranged from the scientific to the romantic, with heavy emphasis on the aesthetic. Editors of newspapers, journals, and travel magazines eagerly solicited accounts of things new and marvelous. Illustrated publications anxiously pursued striking or remarkable photographs. Editors of specialty and trade journals sought the latest authentic intelligence of the West.

As we shall see in this and later chapters, Hayden tapped all these interests and translated them into congressional support by developing a program to meet all these diverse needs. Structuring his efforts in terms of specific interest networks increased his chances for success by increasing the size and diversity of his potential audience and enabled Hayden to become one of those exceptional scientists who succeeded in establishing "his own political ties with public decision-makers." There can be little question that in 1867 Hayden executed politicians' mandates; that is exactly what he was hired to do. His instructions for the survey of Nebraska owed as much, if not more, to the expectations of the General Land Office as they did to Hayden's own contribution. What was important was that he executed the mandate skillfully enough to persuade Wilson to argue for the value of the survey's "practical results" and the utility of extending similar surveys to other portions of the public lands—in other words, to get Wilson to adopt Hayden's mandate.[4]

¶ Hayden's proposal to extend the survey into the Rocky Mountains was designed to appeal particularly to mining and railroad interests and anticipated harnessing them to a program extending over several years' duration. In arguing for continuing the survey and doubling its appropriation, Wilson picked up Hayden's points and stressed the probable economic benefits of a careful examination by men of science of the region's mineral deposits. But it was Hayden's plan, presented in terms Wilson could appreciate and use to convince others. The "first idea," wrote Hayden, "should be to construct a geological map of the country . . . and upon this basis to build as great and varied economical and practical results as possible." Besides working out all the geological formations in their chronological order, the geologist should also make "a careful examination of the quantity and quality of all coals, ores, or [*sic*] iron, copper, silver and gold, . . . with careful statistics in regard to the thickness and extent of the beds or veins, and the best methods of working the same." Hayden called for securing all such information, together with agricultural and climatological data, "with as much minuteness as possible."

¶ That Hayden was well aware of the important role that the self-interest of various potential constituencies could play in influencing political support for his funding needs is clearly shown in a marvelously plainspoken paragraph in the same letter. His plan, he said, rested on several "facts." First, he observed that along the lines of the UPRR "the facilities for traveling and the protection from Indians are quite good." Second, "whatever resources there are, whether mineral or agricultural or other, they will soon be in demand." Finally, with such a plan, "the influence in congress of this great body of men [the UPRR] is secured for future appropriations, as also the influence of Colorado and Wyoming." As an example, he pointed to Clarence King and the Geological Exploration of the Fortieth Parallel. King had just completed a report on the Comstock Lode and now "the influence of the Nevada Senators are entirely for him." And yet, while Congress supported Hayden's plan, a problem developed when Wilson decided to keep tighter reins on the personnel expenditures and personally appointed all Hayden's assistants and assigned their salaries and period of employment. These restrictions on his liberty go a long way toward explaining why, during the following winter, Hayden labored to have the appropriating legislation for 1869 place his survey under the direction of the new secretary of the interior, who just happened to be an old Oberlin College classmate, Jacob D. Cox, rather than under the Land Office.[5]

¶ In 1869, with his appropriation doubled, Hayden transferred operations to Colorado. His enthusiasm for western explorations continued to increase, probably spurred by an unrecorded private expedition Hayden made at the end of the summer that year. Boarding a Union Pacific train in Wyoming and traveling all the way to California, Hayden persuaded the railroad to allow him the use of a handcart so he might travel at his leisure and stop to examine outcroppings exposed by the railroad cuttings. This was the first time Hayden traveled across the entire Sierra Nevadas. The experience had an "expansive" effect, broadening his geological vision and instilling in him something of a "scientific manifest destiny."[6]

¶ The following spring Hayden presented to the House Committee on Appropriations a plan for the geological and geographical exploration of the territories of the United States that looked forward to the gradual preparation of a series of geographical and geological maps for each of the ten territories. Accepting his proposal, Congress increased his appropriation to twenty-five thousand dollars, enabling Hayden to begin making long-term plans. He incorporated the basic outline of his plans into his 1870 annual report, in which he summed up the changes he had seen in the West and expressed a desire to dedicate his life to the region's development:

> My explorations of the country west of the Mississippi began in the spring of 1853, prior to the organization of Kansas and Nebraska as Territories, and I have watched the growth of this portion of the West year by year, from the first rude cabin of the squatter to the beautiful villages and cities which we now see scattered so thickly over that country. We have beheld, within the past fifteen years, a rapidity of growth and development in the Northwest which is without a parallel in the history of the globe. Never has my faith in the grand future that awaits the entire West been so strong as it is at the present time, and it is my earnest desire to devote the remainder of the working days of my life to the devel-

opment of its scientific and material interests, until I shall see every Territory, which is now organized, a State of the Union.[7]

¶ Hayden's vision straightforwardly allied science to economic development. Though neither unique nor original in this respect, it possessed a political potential that Hayden assiduously cultivated, skillfully identifying new missions and programs for his organization while developing and nourishing constituencies of support. At the same time, the vision needed a bureaucratic incarnation, and Hayden's efforts to perfect his organization and increase his control over his environment should be viewed in terms of this requirement.

¶ By laying forth such a long-term program, Hayden strove to give his survey—and his life—stability. The time for such stability had long since come. In 1870, Hayden would turn forty-two. It was time to settle down in a career, especially since he had become engaged to marry Emma Woodruff, whom he had met in 1867 during his first full year in Philadelphia and whom he eventually married on 9 November 1871. Though little is known of their married life together, according to Hayden's biographer his marriage was "the most significant event" of his life during the time he spent in Philadelphia. That says a great deal, given that these were also the years during which the Hayden Survey was born, had its first great public successes, and underwent explosive growth. And yet the statement is probably true since marriage—and the determination to marry—gave Hayden something he had never before enjoyed: "a calm and satisfaction to [his] personal life."

¶ The Haydens' life together was a quiet one, with few close friends. The daughter of a prominent Philadelphia merchant, Emma Woodruff was probably an accomplished young woman in her own right when, at the age of twenty-four, she first met Hayden, and she retained her individuality, neither losing herself in his identity nor becoming a collaborator with him in his science. She preferred Philadelphia to Washington or the West, and the couple generally maintained a residence there, to which she retreated while Hayden journeyed, though she did occasionally accompany him west for brief periods while expeditions were organized. Marriage did not utterly quiet Hayden's restless character or his drive for success. Probably nothing short of death could have. But marriage did provide a more stable center for his life and firmly attached him to at least one person who, to the end of her life, years after his own death, retained a very evident devotion to him.[8] And plans for marriage may very likely have served as a stimulus to give order and stability to the rest of his life, his survey.

¶ As long as he had to depend upon small annual appropriations, Hayden had to content himself with limited goals. As he won increased funding, his ambitions, plans, and corps of workers expanded. There is a marked contrast between the first years of the survey, when Hayden did much of the fieldwork himself with only Stevenson and two or three collectors to assist him, and the campaign of 1869, when he took the field with nearly twice the number of personnel, including an artist, an entomologist-botanist, a chemist-mineralogist, and a zoologist. But Hayden was nearly caught in a catch-22 situation. To realize his ambitions he needed much more money than Congress was accustomed to give, yet gaining increased funding depended upon proving the value of his work. But the value of his work was related to the quality of the assistance he could afford, which directly depended upon the funding he had. For instance, though his appropriation for 1870 was "very liberal compared with those of former years" and enabled him to add several new positions to his corps, Hayden decided he could not afford to engage a topographer despite his plan to prepare a series of maps. He thus admitted that the expedition "was able to contribute little of importance toward the improvement of our maps."[9] Caught between the desire to collect as much material in the form of specimens and information as possible and the need to effect a stringent economy, he sought to escape the dilemma by giving priority to personnel who would accept low wages or, particularly in the early years, by recruiting volunteers who would work for rations and expenses in the field. Both helped extend the time that could be spent in the field.

¶ During its first four years the survey enjoyed fairly steady growth as Hayden became increasingly adept at "wringing money from tightfisted congressmen."[10] From eastern Nebraska he moved to the Front Range of the Rocky Mountains, where he visited several of Colorado's mountain parks (large, open meadows within the mountains), crisscrossed Wyoming, and made flying visits into Utah and New Mexico. In the process, he won increasing notice and acclaim from scientists, speculators, and congressmen. But he did not win the public fame for which he longed, and he still lacked the opening that would allow him to develop the survey into what he hoped it might become. His great break came in 1871, and during its second four years the Hayden Survey made the discoveries and filed the reports that catapulted its director to public acclaim and won him both a greatly expanded survey and influence. In 1871 Hayden "discovered" Yellowstone (see Map 3).

¶ Of course, he did not really discover Yellowstone that year. Long known among mountain men, the region was already a part of western lore. Moreover, in the 1850s Hayden had participated in two attempts to penetrate to its wonders, first with Warren and then with Raynolds. However, each effort had been thwarted by deep snow, and by 1870 the sources of the Yellowstone River remained one of the few unmapped spots on army and government maps. But by then more people were pressing forward to explore and map the region, pushed by at least two motivations beyond simple curiosity: a search for gold and a desire to stimulate financing for the Northern Pacific Railroad.

¶ In late summer 1869, three local Montana residents successfully penetrated to the geyser region. They returned to Helena with tales that excited local community leaders, including Henry D. Washburn, the territory's newly appointed surveyor-general, and Nathaniel P. Langford, a promoter for the Northern Pacific. Later that summer, while visiting Helena, Gen. Philip Sheridan, commander of the Division of the Missouri, promised support for efforts to explore the region, and in August 1870 Langford and Washburn organized a nine-man expedition accompanied by a small military escort headed by Lt. Gustavus C. Doane. The expedition explored the geyser regions for several weeks and returned to write or give accounts verifying many of the area's natural wonders. These accounts were printed in several western newspapers and picked up and reprinted in papers around the country. Given his connection with the Northern Pacific, Langford particularly sought to publicize the region. From the start, he seems to have determined to compose a series of lectures on the party's adventures and discoveries. He also wrote several articles. In the best-known, "Wonders of the Yellowstone," which appeared in the May and June 1871 issues of *Scribner's Monthly*, Langford stressed that the soon-to-be completed Northern Pacific Railroad would open what was certain to become a "fashionable resort" to the thousands of tourists who would flock to

Montana and Wyoming "in order to behold with their own eyes the wonders here described."[11]

¶ After a few trial efforts in Montana that November, Langford headed east to begin a brief career as a public lecturer. He opened the series at Lincoln Hall in Washington on 19 January 1871 with an introduction by that erstwhile promoter of railroad interests, Speaker of the House James Blaine. Hayden was among those in attendance that night, but contrary to traditional opinion it is doubtful that Langford's lecture sent Hayden to the Yellowstone the following summer. Instead, Hayden had already formulated plans for the coming season and seems to have decided for reasons of his own that it was time to tackle the remaining large lacuna in his explorations of that part of the country. He hoped to unravel the region's geography by tracing its four great rivers to their sources and thereby unify the geological fieldwork he had pursued for over a decade and a half. Having moved west from the Nebraska survey, across the Front Range and into Wyoming, it made sense for Hayden to turn to the Yellowstone—particularly as upstarts threatened to trespass on ground he considered his own. If in doing so he could make use for his own purposes of the public and congressional interest those same upstarts had aroused, so much the better. The interest may have helped, but Hayden knew as early as 13 February 1871 that the House Appropriations Committee had recommended forty thousand dollars for a scientific expedition to explore the region, a significant increase over the previous year's twenty-five thousand dollars.[12]

¶ Nor was Hayden the only one who concluded even before Langford's lecture that the Yellowstone merited a second look. General Sheridan had decided so as well. Even as he sent out Doane's small escort, Sheridan intended to dispatch a larger expedition the following summer if the findings of Doane's expedition supported the marvelous tales. Sheridan remained resolute in his purpose even when Congress authorized Hayden's larger expedition, and on 26 June 1871 he ordered Capts. John W. Barlow and David P. Heap to carry out a six-week reconnaissance of the Yellowstone region. Hayden would not be there alone. The army would have its own expedition there as well, in spite of the fact that Hayden already had permission for an escort of troopers from the Second Cavalry.[13]

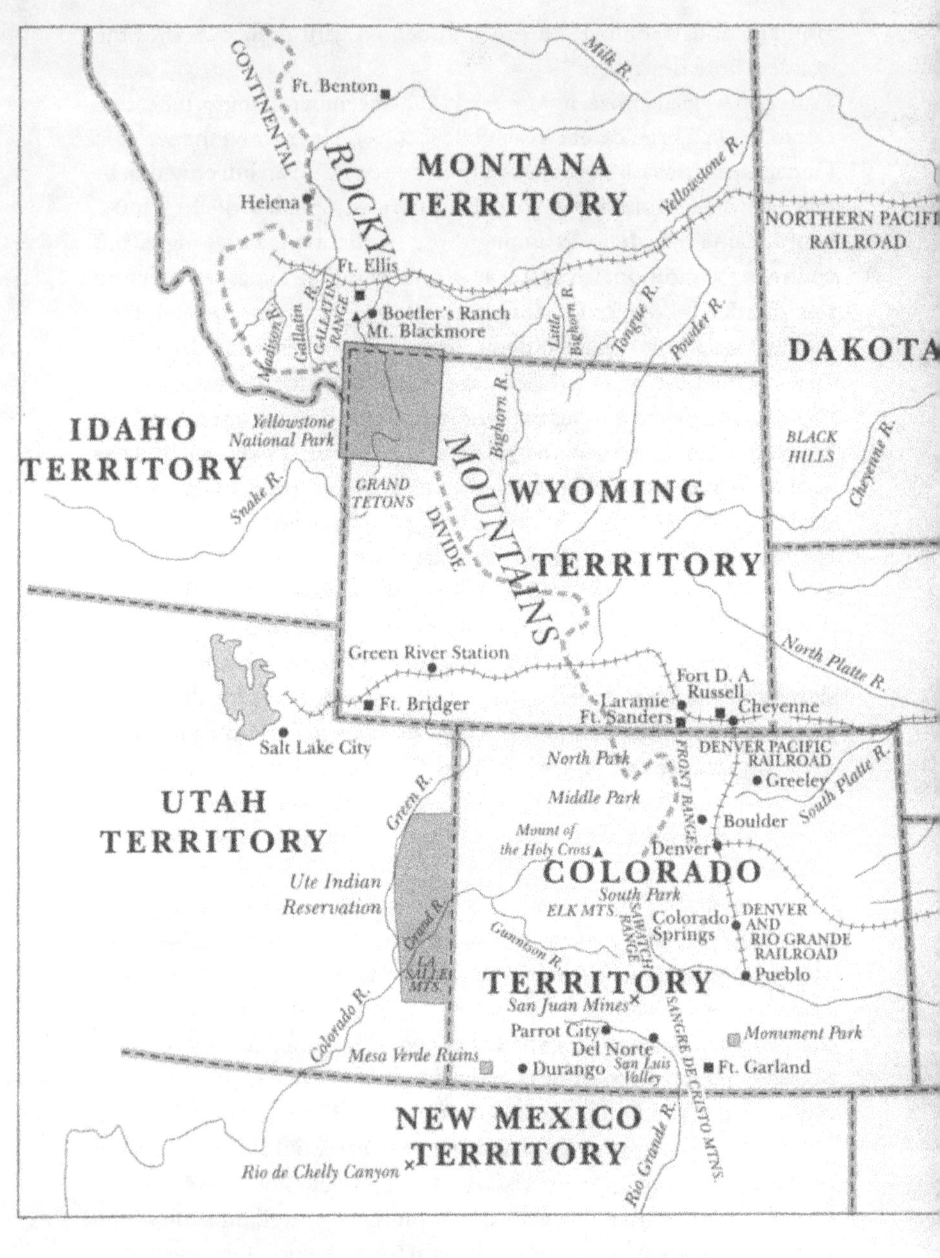

MONTANA TERRITORY
IDAHO TERRITORY
WYOMING TERRITORY
DAKOTA
UTAH TERRITORY
COLORADO TERRITORY
NEW MEXICO TERRITORY
ROCKY MOUNTAINS
CONTINENTAL DIVIDE
NORTHERN PACIFIC RAILROAD
DENVER PACIFIC RAILROAD
DENVER AND RIO GRANDE RAILROAD
Ft. Benton
Helena
Ft. Ellis
Boetler's Ranch
Mt. Blackmore
GALLATIN RANGE
Milk R.
Yellowstone R.
Madison R.
Gallatin R.
Little Bighorn R.
Tongue R.
Powder R.
Bighorn R.
Yellowstone National Park
GRAND TETONS
Snake R.
BLACK HILLS
Cheyenne R.
North Platte R.
Green River Station
Ft. Bridger
Salt Lake City
Fort D. A. Russell
Laramie
Ft. Sanders
Cheyenne
North Park
Middle Park
FRONT RANGE
Greeley
South Platte R.
Boulder
Mount of the Holy Cross
Denver
Green R.
Ute Indian Reservation
Grand R.
LA SALLE MTS.
South Park
ELK MTS.
SAWATCH RANGE
Colorado Springs
Pueblo
Gunnison R.
San Juan Mines
Colorado R.
Parrot City
Del Norte
Monument Park
Mesa Verde Ruins
Durango
San Luis Valley
Ft. Garland
SANGRE DE CRISTO MTNS.
Rio Grande R.
Rio de Chelly Canyon

TERRITORY
James R.
Yankton
Missouri R.
NEBRASKA
Omaha
UNION PACIFIC
RAILROAD
Platte R.
Republican
R.
KANSAS PACIFIC
RAILROAD
Smoky Hill R.
KANSAS
Arkansas R.

¶ The 1871 Yellowstone expedition was Hayden's largest to date, and he added a number of people to his party, including his first topographer, Anton Schönborn, a colleague from his days with Raynolds. He also engaged the services of A. J. Smith as assistant topographer and Albert Charles Peale as assistant geologist. A recent graduate of the Medical School of Pennsylvania, Peale would become a regular member of the survey corps. In all, twenty men composed the "scientific" party, accompanied by approximately fifteen employees who served as teamsters, laborers, cooks, or hunters.[14]

¶ The expedition was a huge public relations success, not least because of the number of visual artists Hayden included in his party, which allowed him to bring back a large number of dramatic images. Even before the party's return, it generated considerable interest in the East and drew the attention of eastern newspapers such as the *New York Times,* which expressed the hope that a party composed of "scientific observers" would provide "trustworthy, exact, and comprehensive" information on "one of the most wonderful tracts of the American continent." There were other interests as well. Langford and other members of his expedition had conceived the idea of petitioning Congress to reserve the region as a national park, and the Northern Pacific Railroad quickly perceived advantages in having along its route a tourist area to compete with "that far inferior wonder the Yosemite Valley and big trees." Before long, one of the railroad's commercial agents urged Hayden to recommend the area as a park in his official report.[15]

¶ Hayden eagerly joined the ranks of the petitioners and seems to have been the first *public* promoter of a national park. He advocated the idea in articles in *Scribner's* and the *American Journal of Science* and vigorously lobbied Congress, helping to secure passage of legislation that established the country's first national park, an accomplishment he proudly reported in his 1871 annual report issued in spring 1872. The very publicity resulting from Hayden's survey proved useful to park lobbyists, and his reward followed in due season. The success of the Yellowstone expedition solidified his position. His appropriation mushroomed to seventy-five thousand dollars, plus an additional ten thousand dollars for preparing illustrations for his reports, which enabled him to put a much larger force into the field.[16]

¶ In 1872 the survey returned to the Yellowstone region with "two large and well-equipped parties . . . each provided with a geologist, topographer, astronomer, meteorologist, with their assistants." Each party had, besides, "a number of young men [who] acted as collectors of objects in natural history." Hayden also fielded four smaller parties that year, led by paleontologists Leidy, Cope, Lesquereux, and Meek, each of whom conducted specialized investigations. As Hayden explained, it would be "a part of the policy of the survey to invite distinguished specialists to examine some of the more obscure and difficult problems in the geology of the West."[17] In adopting this policy Hayden clearly exhibited several traits of the successful entrepreneur: identifying new missions and interests as well as developing and nourishing external constituencies, while enhancing his organization's technical expertise. However, the increased scale and scope of work also brought problems. Hayden's organization lacked a strong bureaucratic structure; to give the survey stability, he had to address its structural weaknesses.

Hayden was a natural enthusiast, bursting with plans and exhibiting a winning personality when he wanted to. But he was not a natural administrator, and in summer 1872, the first time he had more than one party operating in the field, he found that "the burden of executive duty" diverted much of his time and energy from "purely scientific labors." Consequently, his personal report was "much less elaborate and important than heretofore."[18] Notwithstanding the burden of executive duties, Hayden saw the survey's growth as the realization of his ambitions, and he began to take steps toward transforming the survey into a permanent organization in which a man, rather than just making a seasonal outing, could fashion a career.

¶ First he devised a plan that would require several years to complete. Congressional approval of the plan would constitute, by implication at least, more permanent approval of the survey. Then he recruited a lieutenant who could assume some of the burden of administration, particularly in the "topographical branch" of the survey, its weakest suit, and also help give shape to the plan. Clarence King's survey had just concluded its fieldwork, and Hayden found in James Terry Gardner, King's friend and deputy, just the man he needed. A veteran geographer with ten years' experience, Gardner had learned his craft under Charles F. Hoffmann, chief geographer for Josiah D. Whitney's California Geological Survey. He had then worked with King for four years on the California survey, before becoming King's chief topographer on the survey of the fortieth parallel.[19] When he joined the Hayden Survey, he knew precisely what a topographical survey entailed. To achieve these goals, he systematized the fieldwork of the next three years.

¶ Following Gardner's recruitment, the United States Geological and Geographical Survey began to assume its mature institutional form. Up to this point, though Hayden had proposed preparing a series of geographical and geological maps of each of the territories, the survey had not followed a unified plan. Instead, each summer's outing was more or less ad hoc, going wherever it seemed the most interesting problems could be found. This afforded Hayden a good deal of freedom as, among other things, he sought to cultivate congressional alliances—a vote for an exploration of Wyoming this year in return for a promise to survey South Dakota the next. Yet it was not a method calculated to build support on the basis of a continuing operation. Gardner's arrival helped change this, and in the early months of 1873 he and Hayden elaborated an ambitious plan. Though Yellowstone had been rewarding, the difficulty of transport and the fact that the Sioux were in a hostile mood in much of the region in which the survey had been working convinced Hayden that future operations in these regions should be postponed until the extension of rail communication and the pacification of the Indians had been accomplished. Instead, he proposed to move south to the Colorado and New Mexico Territories and, commencing with the southern limits of King's survey, make a systematic survey of Colorado with the goal of preparing a comprehensive geological and topographical map of the territory.[20]

¶ There were other advantages in moving to Colorado, advantages Hayden chose not to publicize in his annual report. Hayden had insisted for some years on the need to prepare more accurate maps of the regions he was surveying, and he had done a fair job of providing such maps for the Yellowstone region. Colorado was even more ripe for maps and surveying. Railroads were expanding into the territory, and prospectors had increasingly called attention to its mineral riches. Hayden himself had contributed to this in the 1860s and in doing so had linked himself with both railroad and mining interests. Renewing that partnership could prove rewarding. He had already sampled the geology there and had a good idea of its prospects. Investigating Colorado's geology could answer a number of needs. Hayden needed favorable attention to keep appropriations flowing, and he had good reason to believe that in Colorado he could win the scientific laurels he desired and the public attention he required.[21]

¶ Gardner modeled the work of the Hayden Survey on that of King's. He divided Colorado into three parallel districts—North, Middle, and South—and assigned teams to each. Gardner himself conducted a primary triangulation of the whole field, "connecting and harmonizing" the work of the other parties. Besides the party headed by Gardner, the other surveying parties each included a topographer with an assistant and a geologist, together with two packers, a cook, and usually one or two assistants who also acted as collectors in natural history. In addition, the survey usually fielded three other parties: a quartermaster's party, usually directed by Stevenson, who had become the survey's executive officer; a photographic party headed by William Henry Jackson, which also embraced several naturalists and collectors and which ranged the entire area "gathering such information and procuring such views as will be useful to all the other parties and to the public generally"; and a party, typically headed by Hayden, to investigate problems of special interest or complexity.[22]

¶ Well aware of the value of Gardner's work, Hayden was pleased with the reorganization, remarking that the survey was now "complete and compact, and prepared for the systematic work for which it is intended." Yet it could also be "enlarged at any time to meet the needs of the Government." The addition of parties would in no way affect the "integrity" of the organization since each party was "complete in itself" and might be sent "to any portion of the public domain as the needs of the [Interior] Department may require." The reorganized survey was virtually the bureaucratic incarnation of the desire Hayden had expressed in his annual report three years earlier: a corps ready to make "thorough astronomical, topographical, meteorological, geological, and botanical researches, and to develop the mining and agricultural resources" of the continent, from the Arctic Circle to the Isthmus of Darien.[23]

¶ Yet the survey still lacked one element: a promise of permanence. Thus, when he described the new organizational structure created by Gardner, Hayden took the occasion to argue for guarantees of permanence and increased funding to support salary increases for staff members. As he put it, for the survey to "continue to command the respect not only of men of science, but of the intelligent world generally" demanded "the very highest order of talent." Yet attracting and retaining such talent required imparting to recruits "a confidence in the permanency of the work" and paying its officers "in proportion to their abilities." [24] At this point, however, the survey had reached a plateau in its growth and received no further significant increase in its appropriations. And so, notwithstanding Hayden's conviction that each professional assistant was worth 50 to 100 percent more each year, he had no way to grant such raises. But much of this was mere rhetoric; there was no real need for such increases in pay. Hayden already paid what were recognized as very good wages; moreover, they were only part of what enabled him to attract and keep talented men. The other part was the opportunities he afforded them. To ensure that he could continue to provide those opportunities, Hayden labored at shoring up external support as well.

Hayden's expectations that the interests of railroads and the men of the territories of Wyoming and Colorado could be turned into support were not disappointed. His supporters included army officers, local business and civic leaders, and editors of local papers. As he gradually built his organization, he gave careful attention to their desires in an effort to establish active alliances with them. The most important of Hayden's supporters were probably the western railroads. Many of them happily granted free passes for his party, saving the survey "hundreds of dollars." [25] Yet more important than the money they helped him save in the West was the money they could help him obtain from Congress.

¶ Even during the survey of Nebraska, Hayden's work and enthusiasm gained him the support of one railroader who also happened to hold a seat in Congress: Grenville Dodge, the Union Pacific's chief engineer. To Dodge, it made sense to assist Hayden with free passes over the Union Pacific, "especially when you are out here writing it up." "Writing it up" was only one incentive for railroad support. The survey could be of practical assistance as well. In the beginning, Hayden thought that the railroads would be zealous supporters of a geological survey, even to the point of turning over to his survey the results of their own investigations and collections of practical data for the use of pure science. In this he seems to have had mixed success. The railroads appear to have been much more on the receiving than the giving end of the bargain, probably due to a desire to keep tight control over information that might prove instructive or useful to competitors or investigators in evaluating the construction of routes. But in spite of this limitation, Hayden could still unite with them in promoting settlement in the West, which addressed the railroads' need to convert grants of land into cash and traffic and gave them an interest in collecting and diffusing "information" regarding the resources present and how they might be exploited.[26] In this respect, the interests of Hayden and those of the railways had much in common and enabled him to enlist the cooperation of some railroad personnel to contribute to the survey's reports.

¶ Hayden's reports offered the railways a practical motive for supporting his survey: publicity. R. S. Elliott, the Kansas Pacific Railroad's first "Industrial Agent," responded to just this incentive when, in January 1870, he wrote Hayden that he had just completed an article for Hayden and would send it along in a few days, after affording "the President and Directors of this Railway time to look it over if they care to do so." The article, a "report on the industrial resources of Western Kansas and Eastern Colorado" in which Elliott promoted the railroad lands as eminently useful for agriculture and not so arid as generally believed, was published in Hayden's fourth annual report. Probably more important to Hayden was the feeling of cooperation such actions helped engender, as when Elliott wrote: "I trust that Congress will give you all the funds you need to prosecute your valuable labors, and finally to publish the results in becoming style."[27]

¶ Hayden's relations with the railroads were not confined to their industrial agents and those who labored to entice settlers to their western properties. He also came to know, and perhaps form friendships with, executive officers. No doubt he endeared himself to them with offers to "serve [them] in Washington." Walter Hinchman of the Lake Superior and Mississippi Rail Road Company asked Hayden to favor him with copies of the latest "Government maps of the Territory West of the Mississippi River," such as those Hayden had already sent to Robert Lamborn of the Denver and Rio Grande Railway Company. It is clear that when Hayden laid out his plans for the survey he often did so with reference to the activities of the railroads. For instance, when Hayden transferred his operations from the Yellowstone area to concentrate on the Colorado Territory, he was well aware that several railroads were in the process of developing and expanding into its mountain valleys.[28] The survey he proposed was just the thing to appeal to a railroad executive, as an incident in the history of the Kansas Pacific Railroad reveals.

¶ The Kansas Pacific reached Denver in 1870, the same year the Denver Pacific linked the city with Cheyenne and the Union Pacific. However, just when Denver seemed assured of becoming Colorado's transportation hub, the Atchison, Topeka and Santa Fe Railroad began to push into the southeastern corner of the territory, threatening to siphon off traffic and the mineral riches of southern Colorado to Kansas City. At that point, William Palmer, construction boss and manager of surveys for the Kansas Pacific, proposed an unprecedented plan. Previously, all the western railroads had followed an east-west route. Palmer suggested constructing a narrow-gauge line from Denver south along the base of the Rockies to Mexico City, envisioning a number of mountain branches to tap resources of stone, timber, minerals, and farmland in the interior valleys. This new railroad, the Denver and Rio Grande, was incorporated on 27 October 1870, and the city of Colorado Springs was launched the following year, a pure case of railroad promotion.[29] Was it mere coincidence when, two years later, Hayden proposed a survey that would provide the sort of topographical information that would help locate trackways as well as promising sites for the mines, ranches, sawmills, and farms of which Palmer dreamed?

¶ The evidence is suggestive. In late 1871 and early 1872, Hayden enjoyed friendly relationships with officials of both the Kansas Pacific and the Denver and Rio Grande. In August 1873, Lamborn of the Denver and Rio Grande wrote that he had received Hayden's recent note "and soon afterwards had an opportunity of urging upon Senator Morton [Oliver Morton, a leader in the Republican political machine of Indiana] the importance of your survey. He seemed fully to agree with me and I think will be friendly to any work proposed for the Rocky Mountains." Nor is it surprising that Palmer later requested a copy of the *Atlas of Colorado*, writing, "we are doing a lot of RRd planning just now," and "it would doubtless prove of more service to us just now than at any other time."[30] If Hayden had good scientific reasons for surveying Colorado, he also had good practical reasons for doing so.

¶ Hayden also formed alliances with mining concerns. They had a natural interest in geological surveys, and Hayden sought to establish the same sort of information exchange with the mining companies that he had effected (albeit with limited success) with the railroads. But this was even more difficult to attain with mining interests because of the intense rivalry among them and their reluctance to reveal information of any utility to potential competitors. Still, though the survey's files do not record much success in these endeavors, Hayden did find mining engineers willing to exchange copies of their maps in return for reports from Washington. At the same time, the mining press exhibited a keen interest in the Hayden Survey and in the early years gladly supported his efforts.[31]

¶ The point of these alliances with business interests was simple. Almost all of Hayden's operations were calculated with an eye to their effect on Congress, and he had not spent more than a decade in Washington without learning that there were a variety of ways to develop political ties with decision makers. Having the good will of the chief engineer of the Union Pacific, who also happened to have a seat in the House, was one way. Enjoying the favor of railroad executives such as Leland Stanford, Collis Huntington, and Charles Crocker—three of the Central Pacific Railroad's "Big Four"—was a second.[32] But Hayden did not think of resting there, and he developed other friends in Congress as well.

¶ One of the more important of these was John A. Logan. Logan had been a representative from Illinois to the Thirty-sixth and Thirty-seventh Congresses, before resigning to serve in the Union army from 1861 to 1865. During the war, one of General Logan's staff officers was James Stevenson, Hayden's companion in his antebellum expeditions. During their years together Stevenson and Logan developed what was reputed to have been a warm personal friendship. This indirect relationship between the survey and Logan expanded when Hayden engaged Cyrus Thomas, who happened to be married to Dorothy A. Logan, the congressman's sister, as entomologist and agriculturist for the survey in 1869. Hayden cemented the connection by means of a personal friendship with Logan, which certainly did the survey no harm in its early years. Writing Baird at the end of the 1869 season, Hayden exulted: "Genl. Logan is much pleased with my success and asks Mr. Thomas if I would like to go again. He says he intends to keep me at this business, which suits me." Logan was in a position to keep his promise. Following the war, Logan developed a commanding political machine in Illinois, won election to the Fortieth and Forty-first Congresses, served on the Ways and Means Committee, and became one of the new leaders in the Republican Party. In 1871, he won a seat in the U.S. Senate. Though he lost the seat in 1877, he remained a force in Illinois politics and won the state's other Senate seat in 1879, serving two more terms.[33]

¶ Other significant "friends at court" included Henry L. Dawes of Massachusetts, James A. Garfield of Ohio, Aaron A. Sargent of California, and Washington Townsend of Pennsylvania. Dawes was elected to the Thirty-fifth Congress in 1857 and served until 1875. His steadily increasing influence earned him appointment as chairman of the House Appropriations Committee in 1869 and of the Ways and Means Committee in 1871. In 1875, Dawes won a seat in the Senate, which he held until he retired in 1892. Garfield served in the House from 1863 to 1880, when he was elected first to the Senate and then to the presidency. Though it took him several years to learn how to accomplish anything in Congress, in 1871 he succeeded Dawes as chairman of the House Appropriations Committee, holding the position for four years. Hayden thus took confidence to "strike out as free as we can" when he heard Garfield assert publicly that Hayden's explorations "would be continued as long as there was any of the Public Domain to be explored." Even when the Republicans became the minority party in the House, Garfield quickly emerged as one of the party's leaders and by 1877 was widely acknowledged as the foremost Republican member of Congress. Sargent, first elected to Congress in 1861 and again in 1869 and 1871, served on the Select Committee on the Pacific Railroad. In 1873, he took a seat in the Senate, serving on the committees on naval affairs, mines and mining, and appropriations—all of which had an interest in the American iron and steel industry. Townsend took a seat in the House in March 1869 and served four terms, retiring in 1877. During his tenure, Townsend served Hayden's survey most importantly as chairman of the Committee on Public Lands when it reported on the problem of duplication in the Western surveys in 1874. The two men developed a warm personal relationship, and Townsend, both while in office and after retirement, gave Hayden political support and counsel.[34]

¶ Though evidence is scanty—he probably did most of his lobbying in person—Hayden clearly had special relationships or understandings with these men and others as well. Nonetheless, Hayden's basic relationship with congressmen always remained one of dependence, as their client. Thus, when he arranged for forwarding copies of the scarce February 1872 issue of *Scribner's Monthly*, which contained Thomas Moran's woodcuts of the Yellowstone and Hayden's account of the 1871 expedition, it was with an eye to influence as much as to please. In some of these relationships, however, there is also evidence of genuine friendship and mutual influence. For example, when Moran was attempting to sell his large canvas of the Grand Cañon of the Yellowstone to Congress, he asked Hayden to use his influence with Dawes and Garfield to arrange for the House to purchase it. But evidences of friendship much be interpreted with caution. The reason is plain in a statement Hayden made to J. Peter Lesley, who as director of the second geological survey of Pennsylvania, secretary of the American Philosophical Society, and professor of mining and then dean at the University of Pennsylvania's Towne Scientific School was one of Hayden's most important scientific supporters. Hayden's claim that "whenever a member or Senator asks me for information or to secure any information for him from any person, I make haste to do so" clearly reveals a disposition to provide any service to those who had a vote affecting his and the survey's future. When Hayden obliged Sargent by obtaining a stereoscope for a friend, it might have been merely a cordial favor or just one more example of Hayden's willingness to do whatever was necessary to carry on his expeditions.[35]

¶ Hayden could offer congressmen more than magazine articles and stereoscopes, however. A clipping from the *Yankton Press*, "the leading Republican Paper of Dakota," serves as an example. Pointing out that while the federal government had "shown its liberality toward Nebraska and Wyoming, as well as most of the Northwestern Territories, . . . by making ample appropriations for geological surveys," the article complained that "nothing of this character has been done for Dakota." Now that all their neighbors had been served, its author hoped "the pioneers of Dakota" would finally be remembered and "be granted this aid from the government" and expressed the conviction that "our Delegate will present this matter to Congress at an early day." The delegate, Moses K. Armstrong, concurred, and in sending the clipping he reminded Hayden of a conversation they had had the previous spring in which he had informed Hayden that the citizens of Dakota felt "much neglected," having unsuccessfully petitioned Congress for such a survey for ten years. He reminded Hayden as well of Hayden's statement that "during the ensuing year—1872—your labors would be directed to Dakota" and asked, "Will you please inform me if this is your present intention, under the next appropriation of Congress?"[36]

¶ The people of Dakota Territory wanted a geological survey—or, more accurately, they wanted the maps and reports that such a survey would produce, and they wanted them for very practical reasons. As the *Yankton Press* noted, such reports served to "advertis[e] the country," and many would-be settlers and investors valued them highly. While minding the Washington office of the survey during the summer of 1873, Cyrus Thomas wrote Hayden that orders for his *Sixth Annual Report* were coming in "by the hundreds." Indeed, demand for Hayden's early reports exceeded the supply, and they were so eagerly sought that in 1873 the secretary of the interior authorized a second edition of the first three reports, which constituted "a compliment," supporters of the survey noted, "seldom accorded to a government document."[37]

¶ Patronage operates as a gift economy, a quid pro quo. In his antebellum years, the most important gifts Hayden had the power to give to patrons were the specimens he collected. As head of his own survey, he remained a client but could now give other highly desired gifts as well: reports, maps, and photographs. Every request represented a vote of confidence in Hayden and his work, and requests poured in from a wide variety of voters. While the distribution of the bulk of reports was not under Hayden's direct control, he possessed a great deal of influence in determining who should receive them, especially when the items sought were of the more "limited issue" variety, such as the *Atlas of Colorado* or the quarto monographs that formed his final reports. In ordering publication, Congress assigned each member a number of the publications to distribute as he thought best and placed the bulk of the remainder in the charge of the Department of the Interior. Besides arranging for copies for his authors, Hayden was able to submit to the secretary of the interior the names of individuals and institutions to whom he wished copies of reports to be sent, a prerogative that gave Hayden leverage and influence both immediately and subsequently. Immediately, Hayden could send copies to known supporters and those who might be interested in his work. Later, when congressmen had exhausted the reports under their own control, they usually had to apply to Hayden to obtain additional copies for constituents, thus binding themselves to at least an implicit recognition of the perceived value of his work and his power to facilitate their response to voters' requests.

¶ Congressmen's appeals to Hayden ran the gamut from photographs for daughters of friends through requests for reports and specimens for colleges and schools in their districts (an especially important element for the new western colleges and normal schools), to requests for scientific advice. Most typically, though, they wrote on behalf of or endorsing the requests of constituents, both individuals and institutions.[38] Among the latter, requests on behalf of schools abound in the letters of the Hayden Survey and were frequently addressed directly to Hayden himself.

¶ One example clearly illustrates several aspects of the relationship. In March 1874, W. E. Wilson, instructor in natural sciences and Greek at the Nebraska State Normal School, extended the institution's thanks for two volumes "sent by request of Hon. L[orenzo] Crounse," the state's "Representative at Large," thanks that he deemed were due Hayden as much as Crounse. The acknowledgment included a request. Having learned that Omaha High School expected a collection of fossils and other materials from Hayden, Wilson asked: "Would it be imposing too greatly upon your generosity to this state to ask a similar favor for the Normal School?" Arguing the merits of the school's case, Wilson claimed that they had nearly 350 students listed in their catalogue, with classes in natural history every year, and that the school was "rising rapidly in public estimation." Further, since its students went forth into all parts of the state to teach he believed "a collection placed here would reach more of the people of Nebraska than by being placed any where else."[39] The quid pro quo is clear: by supplying the school's need for instructional teaching materials Hayden could impress a greater number of people with the results of his survey.

¶ Though Hayden readily responded to such requests from congressional patrons, he also established genuinely warm and friendly relationships with some of them. The easy relationship between Hayden and Townsend found expression in the frequent presentation of mementos of expeditions, such as geyserite specimens and photographs and stereographs for distribution to friends and schools. But in time the number of requests compelled Hayden to change his method of dealing with them. At first, he relied upon the Smithsonian Institution to assist him since it had taken as part of its educational mission the distribution of scientific publications and specimens to various scientific and educational institutions in the United States and abroad. As time went by, however, Hayden found that the press of business—his and theirs—necessitated making his own provisions. The tone of a letter from Rep. James Monroe reveals his difficulty. Noting that Oberlin College had not received a promised box of minerals, Monroe asked pointedly, "What is the matter? Have they gone astray somewhere on the Railroads, or did you find it inconvenient to furnish them to the Colleges in my district?"[40]

¶ Monroe was one of Hayden's friends. A member of the faculty at Oberlin, he remembered Hayden from his student days there and recommended graduates of the school as candidates for the survey. The two men also seem to have developed a personal friendship as well, but the failure of the expected delivery threatened their cordial relationship. At the beginning of 1872, Hayden had promised to send boxes of minerals and fossils to both Oberlin and Wooster Colleges "immediately," so it is hardly surprising that when they had not arrived more than a year later Monroe inquired about them somewhat testily. Nor is it surprising that Hayden quickly took action to remedy the matter. The undated annotation on the letter, "These have been sent," tells part of the story. Hayden followed the matter up and wrote Monroe from Colorado that he had been informed that the people at Wooster University were pleased with the mineral collection they had received. He explained the delay as the result of the Smithsonian having "too many irons in the fire to attend to us promptly" and promised that in the future he would take charge of distributing the survey's collections himself.[41] Hayden realized congressmen wanted tangible results for their support, not excuses.

¶ Besides the requests that came from or through the hands of congressmen, many more requests for reports and publications came to the survey directly, from scientists and amateur naturalists, colleges and librarians, scientific and literary societies—all providing testimony to its popularity. Many of the letters testify to an active networking campaign on Hayden's part. For instance, in "Circular No. 2" issued from the Office of the U.S. Geological Survey of the Territories in 1872, Hayden wrote that he was "desirous of securing, by exchange or purchase, the publications of foreign countries on Geology, Paleontology, and Natural History generally, to aid in the formation of a library of reference, for the use of the survey." He also enlisted the aid of those with scientific connections in Europe in consummating agreements for exchanges. For example, the expatriate Swiss geologist Jules Marcou informed Hayden in November 1874 that he had written to his "old friend Prof. Herder" of Berne, Switzerland, recommending such an agreement between the Swiss Geological Survey and Hayden's survey. Marcou promised to advise Hayden on others, writing that he was "in relations with great many [*sic*] leading geologists in Europe, Asia, Australia, South America, Mexico and even Africa." On the home front, Hayden initiated exchanges with the Museum of Comparative Zoology in Cambridge, Massachusetts; the Peabody Academy of Science in Salem, Massachusetts; the Minnesota Historical Society in Saint Paul, Minnesota; and the Peabody Institute of the City of Baltimore, to name only a few.[42]

¶ These developments represented an institutionalization and expansion of earlier arrangements for sending copies of survey publications to various parties who requested them. Exchanging publications was a normal practice among authors. Since Hayden was the "author" of his reports, people seeking them naturally wrote to him, just as he naturally distributed them as he thought would do him the most good. Being closely associated with Baird, who had charge of the Smithsonian's publications and its network of scientific exchanges, Hayden soon became part of this network, sending books, maps, and photographs abroad with the Smithsonian's packages.

¶ By 1874, Hayden was sending hundreds of publications overseas, but he was not always receiving the looked-for response. That year, for instance, some five hundred copies of Leidy's monograph on ancient vertebrates went "to Europe and other points out of America," including "every important journal in Europe," as well as all those individuals whom Leidy had wished to receive a copy. Yet Hayden found the dilatory rate of acknowledgment discouraging and worried that no one was taking any notice of the work, something he did not want to think about after sending it to "every scientific man of importance and every society in Europe." It was nearly a year before he reported to Leidy that though he was not receiving much in the way of personal acknowledgment he did "see it noticed in nearly all publications of learned Societies." This experience helps explain Hayden's request that Leidy look into the value of such an expensive investment during his 1875 tour of Europe: "Please look into the importance of various learned societies in Europe, so as to estimate the weight of our sending so many books abroad continually. . . . I am sending tons of books every year. Where do they go?"[43]

¶ Sending "tons of books" abroad was a vulnerable political tactic and had to be balanced by building domestic support as well. The practice helped satisfy the interests of scientists and others who thought in terms of an international audience for American efforts, but politicians found their votes in this country. Recognition of such realities is implicit in Hayden's statement to Leidy that besides all those copies sent abroad, "every Library in the United States will get a copy, that is all of importance and many of not much importance." The latter, while perhaps of little academic renown, were important to the congressmen in whose districts they were found, and so requests from the Randolph Graded School in Randolph, Ohio, were honored as well as those from the library of Cornell University.[44]

¶ The relationships Hayden built up with various scientific faculties and societies stood him in good stead in the support he received from them in 1874 and 1878, when he and the survey were under attack.

Yet he sometimes had to be reminded of the need to nurture alliances, as when Leidy wrote that he was going to present two of the geyserite specimens Hayden had given him to the Academy of Natural Sciences in Hayden's name, explaining "I want to keep up your interests there." Or again, when Lesley rebuked Hayden, asking, "Why haven't I rec'd a copy of your report? and why have you not sent one yet to the A.P.S.?" and adding that he had already seen it noticed in *Silliman's* and different newspapers.[45] Not only do these examples point to a tendency to carelessness in Hayden's personal relationships because of his haste to expand operations, but they also reflect his weakness in failing to nourish consistently his natural constituencies.

¶ Hayden also established working relationships with the press, taking care to ally the survey with publications that shared interests in elements of its work. First, of course, was the scientific press. Dana, editor of the *American Journal of Science and Arts*, was an old friend of Hayden's and as such quite willing to write regular letters supporting the survey and keep the AJS open to articles on it and its work. Other scientific editors also solicited articles and notices from Hayden. For example, when Alpheus Hyatt and Alpheus Spring Packard sought to establish the *American Naturalist* as a magazine for the "educational market," they sent Hayden a prospectus and asked for the use of his name as one of their contributors. They also requested an article, "simply and purely upon scientific grounds," and were pleased when Hayden agreed to contribute to their venture. Soon thereafter, they requested "a series of articles from you, and scraps of geological news from time to time as you make new discoveries."[46] The relationship eventually led to Packard's joining the survey and becoming one of Hayden's most loyal supporters.

¶ Hayden also developed relationships with other types of journals and newspapers, including the *American Agriculturalist*, the *Prairie Farmer*, the *Chicago Tribune*, the *New York Galaxy*, and the *Colorado Miner*. His communication with the secretary of the Maine Board of Agriculture, Samuel L. Boardman, to establish an exchange of publications, yielded a bonus when Boardman wrote, "I am glad you have written to me—for I may possibly be of some service to you." He explained that he was editor of "the *Maine Farmer*, a journal of over 13,000 circulation, which we send regularly to our delegation in congress" and added that he was personally "very well acquainted with Senators Morrill and Hamlin and Speaker Blaine." Boardman promised to write an article supporting Hayden and send them marked copies; he would also have a friend visit Blaine personally.[47] The offer could hardly have come at a more fortuitous time, with the War Department then vigorously attacking Hayden and his survey.

¶ Relations with commercial or industrial interests could be straightforward. Sometimes they were simply a matter of requesting information on natural resources. A more common request was for copies of the survey's maps. These came from both government sources, including the chief topographer in the camp of Hayden's archenemy Lieutenant Wheeler, who sought a copy of the *Atlas of Colorado*, and private sources such as commercial publishers of maps, who were eager to remain current with the most recent explorations. The heaviest demand, however, was from those engaged in settling the western territories, including land speculators, miners, railroads, and others. For example, A. H. Clements wrote from Denver that "Myself and Brother have established ourselves on Bear River in N.W. Colorado in Trade and are using our best endeavors to promote settlements in that country"; they would be "very glad to have one of your late maps of that country." B. C. Adams of Greeley, Colorado, requested one of Hayden's maps "as soon as they are out." He wanted "to get the location of the towns South and West of this place and the most direct wagon roads to them." Just starting in the refined oil business, he planned to "run teams regularly to all of the towns I can reach and think one of your charts very nice for referance [*sic*]."[48]

¶ Those in the mining industry also thought the maps very nice for reference. M. C. Kelley wrote from Chicago in the spring of 1876 that he had borrowed one of Hayden's maps the previous summer during a visit to the San Juan mines in Southwest Colorado and found it "invaluable." Having just purchased several mines in the area, Kelley was now "in extreme need" of one of Hayden's maps. He also wanted some geological reports and buttressed his request with the statement: "Being personally interested in the geology and development of that country they would be of more use to me than almost any other person, and better promote the intention of the Gov't surveying there than while lying upon the dusty shelves of eastern libraries."[49]

¶ Finally, some sought information on western ranching or farming settlements. For instance, E. F. Gooding of Elgin, Illinois, sought a copy of the report on Montana, explaining that he had started a ranch there and was "anxious to learn all I can in regard to the Country, its animals, Birds, etc., etc." M. Anker wanted Hayden's "views relative to the profits of Cattle Raising in the West and particularly in New Mexico." Anker, speculating that Hayden would "no doubt" recall him in connection with mining enterprises in the Leavenworth Mountains of Colorado, was certain Hayden's views on cattle raising would prove "of great service" and assured Hayden that he would "duly show my appreciation."[50]

¶ The requests for assistance poured in year by year, mounting into the thousands. Each one represented a vote of confidence in Hayden and his survey. Yet in spite of this, Hayden's reputation has long suffered since many historians have attributed the survey's maturation and perfection to Gardner, minimizing Hayden's role. Without detracting from Gardner's contributions, Hayden's role remained a centrally important one. Each year, in the battle for a piece of the congressional appropriations pie Hayden convinced Congress of the survey's "practical and tangible results," securing and even enlarging his slice. The long tradition of federal- and state-supported explorations probably helped, but in the end Hayden had to win over the legislators. In this, he relied on his experience, which had taught him what to collect and what to appeal to in order to obtain financial support. As pointed out in chapter 2, the 1850s constituted a formative period for Hayden. During it, "he made a variety of alliances, . . . [and] learned to construct partnerships to support his projects." It was, in effect, an "education about what aspects of Western geology were of interest to the public."[51] Out of this variety of seeming disparate elements, Hayden created a niche for his enterprise, a place in which it could thrive and grow. Yet growth also depended on the survey's personnel. If money was the lifeblood of the survey, they were its flesh and bones, filling out its structure and doing its work.

5

Positions, Patronage, and Professionals

I have not troubled you lately about your appointments, but I really wish you would take with you this season the son of Mrs. Briggs. —Henry S. Dawes to Hayden, 5 April 1877

With my absolute deafness . . . I must work for money *and you must excuse me for this necessity.* —Lesquereux to Hayden, 2 May 1872

Every publication of the U.S. Geological and Geographical Survey identified Hayden as "Geologist-in-charge." Hayden was more than a government employee. As geologist-in-charge, he was head of a bureau that over the course of its life span employed more than 250 people in various capacities. To enjoy any degree of success as a federal entrepreneur of science, he had to staff and direct this enterprise so as to reconcile the tension between professionalism and politics, ensuring the survey's technical competency and internal harmony as well as meeting the demands of congressional and executive patrons. And while he always remained a client of his federal patrons, his position made him a patron and power broker as well. Success depended on how he used that power.

¶ Professionalism was vital. If Hayden wasted his appropriation on personnel who lacked the expertise to help him accomplish his tasks in a timely manner he would soon be undone. But politics were no less important, since he would be no less undone if his men could not deal professionally with one another and the political realities that formed an important part of the context of their work. Politics and professionalism met in the question of patronage, and the potential conflict between the demands of political patronage and the need for professional and scientific competence was an annual concern as the survey filled out its personnel roster.

¶ Patronage was a well-established culture in nineteenth-century American politics. As one of the chief means of securing and perpetuating party organization it became all the more important in the 1870s as the federal bureaucracy nearly doubled in size, growing from fifty-one thousand employees in 1871 to one hundred thousand in 1881.[1] The Post Office Department and customs houses, especially at major ports such as New York, represented the greatest patronage plums. But almost any federal position was subject to influence, and the Hayden Survey, though providing positions for only a handful of employees, was no exception. Hayden had used political influence to gain his own appointment, and in making appointments he had to reckon with the same system. To survive within the context of Gilded Age politics, Hayden had to accommodate it. However, to maintain his scientific reputation he could not afford to let political patronage compromise the survey's scientific work. Fortunately, the survey encompassed diverse needs, ranging from muleteers, cooks, and general laborers through "collectors" of all manner of natural history objects, which required minimal training, to the more specialized scientific positions of topographer, geologist, paleontologist, ornithologist, entomologist, botanist, and zoologist. And even the more specialized positions could use assistants to help in carrying equipment, recording measurements, or packing specimens.

¶ This ability to offer employment to people with a relatively wide spectrum of skills was one of the survey's strengths, and Hayden made use of it to attract support from political as well as scientific patrons. It was a practice no less entrepreneurial than his efforts to obtain funding. His recruiting patterns enabled him to build support within a variety of constituencies as he drew personnel from two rather distinct, though occasionally overlapping, sets of networks. One was the political network focused in Washington but important to each senator and congressman back in his home state or district. The other was an ever-increasing series of scientific and professional networks. For Hayden, the most important of his scientific networks were his long-standing relationships in Philadelphia, at the American Philosophical Society and the Academy of Natural Sciences, and in Washington, centered on

Baird and the Smithsonian Institution. Over time, he also established other contacts with most of the important scientific faculties and societies in the nation. Together, the different networks afforded Hayden both political support and the personnel necessary to conduct his survey's operations.

¶ As the survey's organization evolved over the years to satisfy the new tasks Hayden set for it, the changing composition of the corps of skilled scientific personnel set new limits. As he committed himself to multiyear plans of operation, freedom of choice narrowed and posed the danger that he might lose support when he was unable to satisfy patrons' and clients' expectations. Hayden and his men had to exercise increasing diplomacy to manage both the survey and the environments in which it operated. While Hayden recruited personnel and support through the twin networks of political patronage and professional-scientific institutional support, these were not airtight distinctions, as scientists could be political and have political connections. Nevertheless, distinctions can be and were made between politically sponsored applicants and those with scientific pretensions or ability. Hayden required higher standards of the latter, though political connections never hurt.

One problem Hayden did not face was a shortage of applicants. From the beginning, he was "flooded with applications from every quarter," and survey correspondence contains hundreds of letters of application. His difficulty lay in deciding whom to choose given budgetary, political, and scientific constraints. Applications and recommendations came from an array of sources. Some applications were spontaneous and personal; others came at the suggestion and sometimes with the support and recommendation of Hayden's acquaintances or from scientific and academic colleagues such as Baird or Dana. Still others arrived with the endorsements of those already associated with the survey.

¶ First, there were the applicants with political sponsors. Some of these seem to have been looking only for adventure, a summer in the out-of-doors, and a chance to travel. They were frequently willing to go as volunteer assistants, seeking only to have their expenses paid in return for laboring in any capacity. Others sought payment as well, and in a letter to Commissioner Wilson, Hayden referred to both sorts of cases. Unable to take a candidate proposed by Wilson, Hayden wrote: "There are as many persons engaged as the money will permit. . . . Mr. Brewster's son goes out as a Volunteer Asst. without *one cent* of expense to the Survey."[2]

¶ Several unwritten principles seem to have been operative in Hayden's appointments of patronage applicants. Aside from the obvious fact that who one knew counted heavily, at least three other factors were also important. It helped if the applicant had some sort of training or experience and could present some "scientific" credentials. Many applicants referred to having had some courses or interest in natural history, and several offered college professors as references. While testimonials from politicians could not be dismissed as "so much waste-paper," as one disappointed applicant wrote, Hayden felt free to inform at least some officials inquiring on behalf of friends that the best way to apply for a position on the survey was to file an application, "sustained by letters of well known scientific men, and await an opportunity." "Letters from politicians *only*," applicants were told, "would not amount to much." Two additional concerns were at least as important as training for the political candidates. The first was a willingness to go as a "volunteer" without expecting any salary, as Hayden found that it cost him a hundred dollars for each month he kept a man in the field.[3] The second was that volunteers had to carry their weight. Hayden expected his "young men" to work—an expectation that broke upon some of them as a rude surprise.

¶ Some of the young men, upon learning of the necessity of working, came down with mysterious illnesses, though fooling nobody in the party. William Rush Taggart quickly dismissed one case in a letter to his sister, bluntly informing her that W. A. "Monty" West, "could not have sickened on Alkali water as we had none the entire trip; in fact were hundreds of miles from any except a little here which is not used. He was too lazy to scratch himself and got tired of the party when he found that some work was expected of him." Hayden was equally dismissive. Though lavish in his praises to congressional sponsors when their protégés turned out well, he could also forthrightly inform them of his disappointment in other cases. As he wrote Representative Monroe, sponsor to both Taggart and West, "Mr. Taggart turned out well and will reflect credit on you and your efforts on his behalf. West did not."[4]

¶ The "volunteers" included a number of sons and nephews of congressmen. Chester Dawes, son of Henry Dawes, accompanied Hayden to the Yellowstone in 1871 together with William B. Logan, nephew of Sen. John Logan, and three others with similar connections. Returning to the Yellowstone the following year, Hayden again took along "a number of young men [who] acted as collectors of objects in natural history." "Billy" Logan made a return appearance as "secretary," going out with Arthur E. Bingham, whose father was perhaps Judson D. Bingham, assistant quartermaster at Washington, and J. S. Negley, almost certainly the son of Congressman James S. Negley of Pennsylvania.[5]

¶ Nor did Hayden receive such applications only from Washington families. "Monty" West had also sought to accompany Hayden's parties to the Yellowstone in 1872; though not a scion of official Washington, West had good connections to that society. When his father wrote to inform Hayden that his son was "very anxious to join your expedition to the YellowStone," he did so from the supreme court rooms of Columbus, Ohio. Seeking only practical experience for his son in the "geological, botanical and other information which the Expedition will afford," West told Hayden his son should be "regarded and should understand himself to be, a regular member charged with all the duties thereof." Wages "signifie[d] nothing." Nor was the young man without qualities to recommend him. His father described him as "a youth of 20 years—Six feet six Stature—reasonably robust—and of sufficient capacity to stand at the head of his class (Junior) in the University." For further questions regarding his fitness, Hayden was referred to West's professors at the university at Wooster, the "Hon. M. Welker, late M.C."—and the elder West's friends, "Genl. Delano of the Interior Department [Hayden's superior], Genl. Cox late of the same [Hayden's former superior, who wrote a "warm letter in his behalf"], Hons. Jas. Monroe, S. Shellabarger and Senator Sherman." With all this support, West was appointed a "general assistant," though his efforts eventually left much to be desired.[6]

¶ As Hayden's fame and the size of his parties grew, so did the number of applications from congressmen for their sons—and sometimes for themselves, as true guests. Among the numerous applicants, Rep. William S. Holman of Indiana wrote on behalf of his son William S. Holman Jr., who felt "highly honored in being the only congressional offspring on the Survey" in 1875. Sen. James L. Alcorn of Mississippi sought a place for his sixteen-year-old son and informed Hayden that he had "mentioned the subject to the President who promised to bespeak for me the place." John C. Bullitt of Philadelphia wrote much as Judge West had; he wished his son might "have the benefit of such an experience" and declared that "if these appointments should in any wise depend upon political or official influence I can obtain it," yet "preferred writing to you [Hayden] direct first." Indeed, no one who knew anyone in Washington seems to have been reluctant to seek an opportunity for his heir. T. H. Baker wrote from the Clerk's Office in the House of Representatives on behalf of his son, stating that he would have the application endorsed by "the entire Tennessee delegation and especially by my friends and neighbors"—Sen. Isham G. Harris of Tennessee and John D. C. Atkins, chairman of the House Appropriations Committee.[7]

¶ A second category of patronage applicants sought scientific posts, one example of which was mentioned in the previous chapter: Cyrus Thomas, brother-in-law to Senator Logan. In these cases, however, Hayden looked for more than political endorsement to recommend the candidate. Thomas did have some credentials, if no scientific degree, being largely self-taught in natural history. Having taken up the study of entomology in the early 1850s, he had contributed articles on economic entomology to the *Chicago Prairie Farmer*. After his first wife (Logan's sister) died in 1864, Thomas taught for a brief time and then entered the ministry before joining Hayden in Wyoming in 1869. While he took Thomas on that summer, Hayden did not keep him without seeking advice "relative to [his] standing . . . as an entomologist" and was probably gratified to learn from Baird that "Mr. Thomas occupies a high position among his fellow naturalists, and that his original investigations into the habits of the insects of the West, and his published memoirs generally, have been of much importance in advancing the interests of agriculture."[8] This, with his work, proved sufficient, and he stayed with the survey in various capacities until 1873.

¶ All the same, Thomas's case was somewhat atypical. Those of Edmund Burritt Wakefield, W. S. Atkinson, Joseph Savage, and Walter

Platt were more representative of scientists proposed by congressmen. None was advanced on the basis of a family tie. Rather, they were individuals known to their sponsors as men who could use the job and might prove useful to Hayden. Nor did all come with glowing recommendations. When Representative Garfield recommended Wakefield he did so with some reservations. At the time, Wakefield was waiting to see if he would be "called" to Hiram College—of which Garfield was a graduate, former president, and now a trustee—and seems to have been teaching there on a temporary appointment. Garfield told Hayden that "in order that you might not have any burdens laid upon you, growing out of any request of mine," he had written a "confidential letter to the President of Hiram College, asking him if he thought Prof. Wakefield would be of service to you, and whether he could be spared long enough to make his stay with you of any value." President Hinsdale had responded that "they would regard it as a great favor to the College, if the Prof. can go with you and that though he is young and may not be of much if of any scientific value to you, he will be an intelligent, energetic and faithful assistant in anything that you may ask him to do." Taking all this into consideration, Garfield advised, "I do not think you ought to pay him much more than his expenses" but was willing to leave that up to Hayden.[9]

¶ As the 1872 Yellowstone expedition's "meteorologist" Wakefield proved highly satisfactory to Hayden. Far from paying him not much more than expenses, Hayden asked Wakefield if he would be satisfied to have his year's salary set at "a clear and even $1000," practically matching what the young man counted on receiving for a year's teaching at Hiram including preaching and lecturing in the surrounding area besides. Hayden also offered him a permanent position with the survey, which Wakefield turned down, disliking the long absences from his wife such a position would require, even though Hayden promised he would " 'do better by me than that College'—and I guess he would."[10]

¶ Atkinson also came to the survey from Hiram College, where he was a professor of mathematics and astronomy, though under different circumstances. When poor health necessitated that he give up teaching as least temporarily in 1873, Atkinson asked Garfield to speak to Hayden about the possibility of a position. He was turning to the survey more as a last resort after having unsuccessfully sought employment in Hiram and "deeply regret[ing] the necessity of being absent from my family . . . for so long a time." He informed, or perhaps reminded, Garfield that he had gone with the survey in 1872 (probably in one of the smaller paleontological groups), felt that "the trip did me great good," and hoped it would be of "still greater benefit this year" since he would be setting out "with much greater strength and vigor."[11]

¶ Garfield passed the letter along to Hayden with the request that "if it is possible to oblige" Atkinson Hayden attempt to do so. Atkinson is not listed as a member for the 1873 season but was offered a position on the survey in 1874 as Gardner's assistant in establishing the baseline and the primary triangulation for the *Atlas of Colorado*, a position for which his mathematical and astronomical ability would seem to have fitted him. Atkinson accepted gladly enough, but since he was making the trip "partly with the view of restoring my lungs" he had some reservations and asked Hayden "whether or not the difference of temperature at base and summit of the mountains will be so great as to render it inadvisable to me to undertake [the job]." However, Atkinson professed his willingness to "leave the kind of work that I am to do entirely with you."

¶ Atkinson also seems to have overcome his reservations about the extended absences involved, or perhaps he had given up all hopes of returning to teaching, for he wrote that he was coming to Hayden "in a little different way from that in which Prof. Wakefield of this place accompanied you two years since." Where Wakefield had been "obliged to be back here [at Hiram] at a given time," Atkinson had "leave of absence till winter, and if I like the work, find it good for my health, etc., and can suit you I am a candidate for continued employment." He did indeed accompany the survey the following year as assistant topographer to Henry Gannett, but that was his last year with the Hayden Survey. Perhaps he lost his taste for such employment when Indians shot his mule from under him.[12]

¶ No matter their training or connections, it was impossible to accommodate every applicant, as the case of Frederick W. Bond, "friend and connection by marriage" of Rep. Stephen A. Hurlbut of Illinois indicates. In a letter to James Stevenson, Hurlbut proposed Bond, "a Civil Engineer thoroughly educated, and of several years practical experience in the field." Hurlbut said he knew Bond to be "an excellent draughtsman and a fine mathematician" in need of the position and "fully competent for whatever he will undertake to do, of good habits, active and industrious." He assured Stevenson that if he gave Bond an appointment he would not regret it, for in Bond the survey would gain "a good officer, do a favor to a worthy family and oblige personally, your obt. servt." Yet Bond failed to gain a position with the survey. By 1878, positions were hard to come by, and few openings for skilled personnel were created each season. Nor may personally obliging Hurlbut have meant much; though a member of the Forty-third and Forty-fourth Congresses, in 1878 he was not a member of the Forty-fifth Congress and in no good position to return the patronage quid pro quo.[13]

The exchange that was operative in patronage appointments points up an important feature of Hayden's role as head of the survey. Though still a client, he was also a broker of patronage, in a position to act as a patron for others but always in a way that would serve his interests as well as theirs. Fellow scientists who sought access to his survey as a means to employment, career advancement, or research materials naturally come to mind as recipients of such patronage, but Hayden also bestowed his patronage on a number of other individuals who accompanied the survey as his guests. They included newspaper correspondents, artists, and some scientists. In each case, Hayden had good reasons for taking them along, and though the practice was sometimes later attacked as an abuse, in most instances those individuals probably more than repaid his investment in returns to the survey.

¶ Rivalry for publicity and public support led the directors of each of the western surveys to invite, or at least welcome, journalists to accompany their parties and write about the scenery and their adventures. Hayden embraced the practice. Better-known correspondents who accompanied the Hayden Survey as guests included Nathaniel P. Langford in 1872 for *Scribner's*, William N. Byers in 1873 for the *Rocky Mountain News*, William D. Whitney in 1873 for the *New York Tribune*, and Cuthbert Mills in 1875 for the *New York Times*. More frequently, however, "working members" of the survey wrote the newspaper and magazine articles. Albert Charles Peale contributed to the *Philadelphia*

Press and *Illustrated Christian Weekly;* Robert Adams Jr. to the *Philadelphia Inquirer;* Charles Aldrich to the *Chicago Inter-Ocean*, under the pen name "David Grey"; and Ernest Ingersoll to several papers, including the *New York Tribune*, the *New York Herald*, and magazines such as *Scribner's*, *Appleton's Journal*, *Forest and Stream*, and *St. Nicholas*, a popular children's magazine.[14] Besides reporting the progress of the survey, their letters and articles both stimulated and responded to a widespread interest in the West.

¶ Artists accompanied the Hayden Survey as both guests and employees. Thomas Moran was doubtless the most significant in the first category. Moran began his career with the Hayden Survey as a patronage appointee to the 1871 Yellowstone expedition, though one whose links were not political. Instead, one of his patrons was the Scribner's Publishing Company of New York City, for which he was an illustrator. Moran had drawn the illustrations for *Scribner's* article on the Doane-Washburn expedition to the Yellowstone that had played a role in winning support for Hayden's own Yellowstone expedition. But since no artists had accompanied the Doane-Washburn expedition, Moran had only written accounts and a few primitive sketches together with his own imagination as sources for his drawings—quite enough to spark a desire to view and work from the actual scenes of the western wonders. Moran sold the idea to Richard Watson Gilder, managing editor in charge of the art department at *Scribner's*, who encouraged him to go West. But according to Moran's daughter, it never occurred to the artist to ask Gilder for financial assistance. Instead, he appealed to Alvred Bayard Nettleton of Philadelphia, an associate of the Philadelphia banker Jay Cooke, who was deeply involved in financing the Northern Pacific Railroad. Nettleton informed Hayden that he would "confer a great favor by receiving Mr. Moran into your party when you start for the Yellowstone Country."[15] Hayden did so gladly. In turn, Moran's paintings would serve Hayden admirably.

¶ William Blackmore represented a third class of guests. A British solicitor who specialized in railroad and mining securities, Blackmore was a land speculator and railroad promoter as well as a scientist and philanthropist. Hayden first met Blackmore in the course of his 1868 expedition during his tour of the Union Pacific line in Wyoming, while Blackmore was simultaneously scouting opportunities for purchasing land-grant claims and obtaining Indian photographs. The two got along well from the start. Hayden found Blackmore "a most delightful traveling companion," while Blackmore quickly enlisted Hayden's professional services for a geological survey of the Sangre de Cristo Grant in Colorado and New Mexico, a land-speculation scheme. Blackmore hoped that Hayden's report would be a vital factor in convincing potential European and American backers. When he finally "pulled through the 'Colorado matter,'" Blackmore not only sent Hayden an early wedding gift of five hundred dollars as a "slight recognition of my appreciation of your valuable services" but also informed Hayden that he and the other owners of the "United States Freehold Land and Emigration Co." had granted Hayden ten thousand dollars' worth of stock in the company.[16]

¶ Blackmore had hoped to accompany Hayden on his first visit to the Yellowstone region in 1871, but business prevented him from doing so. The following year, however, he eagerly made plans to join the expedition with his wife and also arranged for his seventeen-year-old nephew, Sidford Hamp, to accompany Stevenson's party for the season. It was Hamp's first visit to America, and he thoroughly enjoyed his position as "topographical assistant" responsible for hauling along the odometer. Exaggerating to his mother that his position "was applied for by about 2000 (two thousand) men," he knew how lucky he was. Meanwhile, Blackmore did more than keep Hayden company. By providing additional funds to equip and supply the survey's photographer, he extended the range and quantity of the survey's visual documentation. Hayden acknowledged his indebtedness by bestowing the Blackmore name on a newly discovered mineral, *Blackmorite*, and on a mountain in the Gallatin Range near Bozeman, Montana, in honor of his friend's wife.[17]

¶ Notable scientific and academic figures composed a final category of guests. Sometimes these individuals contributed to the work of the survey, as when Asa Gray and Sir Joseph Hooker, two of the world's foremost botanists, accompanied Hayden during his 1877 expedition. Though Hayden claimed before a congressional committee that it was a "common thing to receive distinguished men as guests" on expeditions such as his, when he invited Gray and Hooker to join his party he could not have been unaware that the presence of two world-renowned figures of science would also prove advantageous to himself and the survey. Gray's letter accepting the invitation pointed out one of them. Writing that

spending some weeks touring the West as Hayden's guests would be a "delight," he wanted to know "how far and in what way we could be turned to account in serving you." Gray suggested that "two such veteran botanists" might be able to do "something" for Hayden's reports by their reconnaissance. Indeed they were, and Hayden pointed to their names as adding luster to his reports. Nor did their support stop there. After their journey, both men readily lent their support in testimonials for Hayden in his continuing battles for appropriations.[18]

Patronage functioned by benefiting different interests. Through a careful distribution of positions among influential political, business, and scientific figures, Hayden ensured continued funding and support in these key constituencies without seriously impairing the ability of the survey to accomplish its work. At the same time, patronage entailed risks, and Hayden had to balance the political support that could be derived from it against potential objections regarding shortcomings in his corps, particularly in the large number of amateurs who served as collectors. The potential for problems is apparent when the names of "collectors" or "assistant" naturalists are compared to those of men known to have won their positions mainly through patronage. As William Henry Jackson ingenuously commented, "for some reason that never became entirely clear to me all newspaper men, as well as any other persons who had no specific qualifications, were carried as naturalists."[19]

¶ Some of the newspaper men, like Ingersoll, were actually quite competent naturalists. Others developed a real interest in natural history while accompanying the survey. For example, when applying to go out with the survey for another season, E. A. Barber told Hayden that he would be "better prepared for making collections than I was last year, as I know exactly what ought to be taken to preserve and collect objects in Botany and Zoology." And there were the "young men." Though some were college youths who had taken some courses in natural history, not all were. Walter Platt was perhaps one of the more exceptional cases in this regard. A student at Yale's Sheffield Scientific School, Platt was sponsored by a neighbor, Rep. Stephen W. Kellogg, on the understanding that he had made botany a "specialty" and might be of "some service" to Hayden. Platt seems to have turned out very satisfactorily and returned with "many pleasant remembrances of our conversation, and of the good counsel you [Hayden] so often gave us boys." Two years later, about to graduate from Yale, Platt wrote to Hayden "anxious to go out on your party and collect plants or insects again," though with more experience this time following two years spent studying botany and zoology.[20]

¶ But Platt was probably more the exception than the rule. Given the number of amateur collectors and what might be termed "collectors-in-training," it is hardly surprising that upon distributing his collections Hayden often received less than complimentary remarks on the specimens' condition. One who frequently criticized the condition of the plants he received was Thomas C. Porter, professor of botany and zoology at Lafayette College in Easton, Pennsylvania, from 1866 to 1897 and from 1869 to 1874 the survey's chief botanist. Porter perceived a good deal of room for improvement in the survey's collecting of botanical specimens and hoped that in the future Hayden would "see to it that *complete, good specimens with flowers fruits* and *radical leaves* are secured, wherever possible and that they be *well dried*." Though aware of "the difficulties that must be overcome in the field" he felt "an expert will manage to conquer most of them." In March 1872, Porter even went so far as to propose his own "first-rate botanical collector" for the survey, an "old assistant" who had done "much good work" in years past and, moreover, someone of "great industry, tact, and perseverance" with "considerable experience in field-work." Porter was sure he would "gather a splendid pile of plants in the best condition possible."[21]

¶ Hayden listened to such advice and did upgrade his corps of collectors when he could afford it. He appears almost to have engaged in a frenzy of hiring degrees and reputations in 1872 when he supported expeditions by Cope, Leidy, Lesquereux, and Meek, while at the same time he continued to seek some of the best talent he could obtain for his main parties. Yet Hayden's use of amateur collectors should not be too quickly dismissed as old-fashioned in an era of professionalizing science. Influential figures in the American scientific establishment continued to support a policy of using more or less amateur collectors, and no less a personage than Baird advised Hayden that in selecting collectors the important consideration was not an individual's "high reputation" but to obtain "those who may work hard. A few energetic men like [George N.] Allen can supervise the collecting for the whole corps, and the specialists can take their share at the end of the campaign."[22] It would be unfair to consider Hayden opposed to professionalism. Rather, it was a matter of allocating funds and meeting diverse demands, recognizing that some positions could tolerate less prior training than others.

¶ Some positions, however, demanded trained personnel, and as the survey's appropriations grew and its program expanded, the number of such positions increased. Yet as Hayden's own career illustrates, expeditionary science called for a special blend of skills: familiarity with science united with the ability to live on the frontier. Though these were not always "an incompatible combination which attracted and produced strange men," contemporaries recognized that not everybody with expertise in the one was competent in the other. The point was tacitly conceded when the experts who studied and described the specimens collected on the expedition did not themselves venture into the wilderness, though they frequently offered directions for collecting. The same was openly accepted in recruiting efforts when referrals were sought, as when Lesley wrote Hayden, "You asked me a year ago to find you a topographer of a peculiar kind. . . . I have just found exactly the man you want for your next survey." Yet it would be a mistake to view the survey's field-workers and its authors of scientific monographs as distinct, segregated groups. Many fell into both classes. For instance, most of the authors of the survey's quarto series of specialist monographs were also field-workers during several seasons. Moreover, natural history was a field science. Working in the field was part of its ethos, and almost all of the survey's scientists expressed this ethos, agreeing with Hayden that "it [was] necessary for a man to do a certain amount of field work to throw the true spirit into his memoir."[23]

¶ In seeking skilled personnel Hayden first turned to the people and networks with which he was most familiar—Baird and the Smithsonian Institution, Leidy and the Academy of Natural Sciences of Philadelphia, and others whom he already knew, such as Dana. He had done this when seeking assistance in working up the reports on the specimens collected during the survey of Nebraska, and in subsequent years he collected recruits through the same channels he used to distribute specimens. In that first year, Hayden called upon Meek as one of his scientific assistants in the field and, through Meek, White of Iowa and Gill from the Smithsonian. For additional assistance to work up the collections he relied on Leidy and Baird, who took parts of the collection themselves and helped him find appropriate people for the rest.

¶ The second year, when Commissioner Wilson assigned all the expenditures for personnel, represents an exception, but in 1869, after Hayden was transferred to a largely independent place under the secretary of the interior, the pattern reemerged. Of those in his enlarged party, besides the three teamsters, a cook, and a general laborer all who can be identified came through Hayden's Washington or Philadelphia connections. There was Stevenson, of course, and Cyrus Thomas. Augmenting the corps, Hayden took along Henry W. Elliott, Persifor Frazer, Edward C. Carrington, and B. H. Cheever. Little is known of either Carrington or Cheever, but the other two were clearly hired for their expertise, though recruited through membership in personal networks. Elliott worked at the Smithsonian Institution as private secretary to Joseph Henry between 1862 and 1878 as well as an artist-illustrator in residence, a capacity in which he had assisted Hayden in 1868. Although he accompanied the survey again the following year, the sketches he brought back and worked up during the two years did not excite much interest, even at the Smithsonian. For such sketches Hayden had to wait until 1872, when he took along a much more promising artist who was also employed at the Smithsonian: William Henry Holmes, whom Hayden judged an artist of "immense" talent.[24]

¶ Frazer was a Philadelphia connection, the son of John Fries Frazer, professor of chemistry and natural philosophy at the University of Pennsylvania and a charter member of the National Academy of Sciences. The younger Frazer possessed one of the best professional educations in Hayden's field corps that year. After graduating from the University of Pennsylvania in 1862 at the age of eighteen and taking a Master of Arts degree there in 1865, he went to Europe to continue his scientific studies, attending the Royal Saxon School of Mines at Freiberg from 1866 to 1869. After returning to the United States he took an appointment with Hayden, who referred to him in the annual reports alternately as "mining engineer and metallurgist" and "chemist and mineralogist." Hayden may not have known the younger Frazer before 1869, but he must have known his father, either as a colleague at the university or perhaps through occasional attendance at informal Sunday evening gatherings of scientific and literary men hosted by the elder Frazer. The gatherings were "fixtures" among the "scientific and literary men of Philadelphia." John L. Leconte, J. Peter Lesley, Fairman Rogers, and others were "constant visitors," while Alexander Dallas Bache, Louis Agassiz, Joseph Henry, Benjamin Peirce, Benjamin A. Gould, and "many others never failed to attend" when in town. Hayden circulated in such circles, and if he was not at the center neither was he at the perimeter. Frazer later wrote that in the mid-1870s Hayden was "among those who were most regular in attendance."[25]

¶ In 1870, Hayden's appropriation was again increased and with it the size of his corps as he explored along the line of the Union Pacific Railroad with Stevenson, Elliott, and Thomas from the year before. Though his plans included preparing a geologic map of the country surveyed, he decided he could not afford a topographer.[26] Instead, he emphasized natural history and illustrations, with Elliott; a landscape artist, Sanford R. Gifford; and a photographer, William Henry Jackson, one of the most valuable additions ever made to the survey.

¶ Gifford recruited himself. He had come out on the newly completed transcontinental railroad "to 'mine' the landscape" in search of new views of the picturesque and to "capitalize on the current fever of interest in the West and the recent easy access to its scenery offered by the Union Pacific." Gifford met Hayden in Denver and talked him into letting him accompany the survey for part of the summer. But Hayden recruited Jackson, whom he had met the previous year while Jackson was on a photographic tour of the West. Well aware of the impact and popularity of photographs of western phenomena, Hayden had long wanted to include a photographer among his corps. On his way to Cheyenne in 1870 he stopped at Jackson's Omaha studio, partly to renew the acquaintance, partly to view the results of Jackson's work of the previous year, and partly to recruit Jackson for the survey, which he did very effectively. Jackson later wrote that when Hayden called "he spent a long time studying my Union Pacific pictures and the Indian groups

I had photographed near Omaha" and remarked "with a sigh, 'This is what I need. I wish I could offer you enough to make it worth your while to spend the summer with me.'" All he could offer was an expense-paid "summer of hard work—and the satisfaction I think you would find in contributing your art to science." For Jackson, whose hopes of making a photographic expedition that summer had fallen through, that was enough, and he instantly decided on the spot at which to join Hayden, inaugurating a highly beneficial partnership for both parties. Content with the additions, Hayden wrote Leidy that "Gifford, the artist is with us—a good fellow" and that he had added "a first class photographer" to his survey.[27]

¶ The 1871 Yellowstone expedition found Hayden leading what was for him a party of unprecedented proportions, with nearly twenty people in the "scientific" party plus a support staff of fifteen. Besides most of the previous year's corps, Hayden for the first time took along a topographer, Anton Schönborn, once again calling upon personal connections. He had known Schönborn for at least a dozen years, since they had both accompanied Raynolds in 1859 and 1860, and was quite satisfied with his competence: "Schonborn is a capital topographer. He is perfectly at home with his instruments." As botanist, Hayden took his old mentor from Oberlin College, Professor Allen, who had the support of Representative Monroe, and provided him with an assistant, Robert Adams Jr. Another Philadelphia connection, Adams came with the recommendations of the provost of the University of Pennsylvania and of Joseph Jeanes of the Academy of Natural Sciences, but he may have had little need of these. An alumnus of the University of Pennsylvania (A.B., 1869; A.M., 1872), he was a former student of Hayden's geology lectures. Three other recent graduates of the University of Pennsylvania also joined Hayden's scientific corps that year, all of them recent recipients of their medical degrees and all of them former students in Hayden's geology class. George Dixon went out as an assistant to the photographer, Charles Turnbull went as the survey's physician and general assistant, and Albert Charles Peale served as mineralogist. Like Hayden, Peale used medicine as the route to a career in geology and paleontology. He remained a member of the survey for the duration of its existence and later held an appointment as geologist in the U.S. Geological Survey until 1898, when he transferred to the

United States National Museum as "Aid in charge of paleobotanical collections."[28]

¶ The success and publicity of the 1871 Yellowstone expedition won Hayden a large increase in funding, allowing him to expand the scope of his operations even further. In 1872, Hayden had enough money to field two "large and well-equipped" parties, "each provided with a geologist, topographer, astronomer, meteorologist, with their assistants" and "a number of young men [who] acted as collectors of objects in natural history." Fielding two well-staffed parties, instead of the usual one, required more recruiting. While his task was eased by the growing fame of his survey, which led to increasing numbers of applications for positions, Hayden preferred to appoint people he knew personally or who were referred to him by those he knew. To fill out his corps he depended heavily on advice and referrals from the networks of his scientific associates. In addition to the topographer recommended by Lesley, Hayden received inquiries and recommendations from faculty at several colleges and from the heads of other surveys. Charles Hoffmann, formerly head geographer of Whitney's survey of California and then teaching at Harvard; Julius Hilgard of the Coast Survey; Alexander Winchell of the University of Michigan; James Hall; Arnold Guyot of Princeton; and William Adams Jr., director of the Rensselaer Polytechnic Institute, all recommended applicants for the survey.[29]

¶ That Hayden actively sought recruits is clear in a letter from Thomas Egleston, founder of Columbia's School of Mines and its professor of mineralogy and metallurgy. Hayden had visited Egleston and spoken to him about the work in which he was engaged and later wrote seeking candidates. In his letter, Egleston wrote that he had spoken to one of the members of the graduating class of 1871 about the survey and won him over. Now Egleston sought to win Hayden over, writing that "he would like to go and is a capable man" and offering to provide special preparation. "I told him . . . I would see that he had special advantages for study in the departments which will be most useful to your survey and he is anxious to commence work in the direction of which I spoke to you when you were here." For some reason, however, the arrangement fell through, and the man's name does not appear on the season's roster.[30]

¶ Dana also served as a scout for the survey. Though flattered when

Hayden offered to take his son Edward along, Dana doubted he would serve Hayden's full purpose: "he could not pledge himself to continue beyond the year . . . as he has his mind fixed on the European tour."
Instead, Dana nominated Frank Howe Bradley, professor of geology at Knoxville, Tennessee: "as capable a geologist as you will find for the Yellowstone region." While Dana admitted that he knew "nothing as to whether [Bradley] would be inclined to go," he endorsed Bradley as someone with "large experience over the country . . . and likes mountain work. He is careful and thorough, and I believe will do his work well. . . . He likes hard field work." As he concluded his letter Dana wished he could recommend a chemist and mineralogist, the positions for which his son was sought, but "we have none here." His wish came true almost immediately. Before he mailed the letter he learned of a graduate of the Scientific School who "would be an excellent man for you . . . ready to go at short notice." He also promised to keep an eye open for potential recruits in the future: "I will advise you with regard to any recruits here suited for your party whenever the time comes for another organizing next spring. I presume there will be some one or two here, but cannot now speak with certainty."[31]

¶ Even better evidence of the increased scope of the survey's operations in 1872 and Hayden's expanding role as a patron of science is seen in his making it "a part of the policy of the survey to invite distinguished specialists to examine some of the more obscure and difficult problems in the geology of the West." That year, Hayden convinced his paleontological associates to take the field "under the auspices of the survey" in an effort to settle the question of the "differences of opinion in regard to the exact age of some portions of the Cretaceous and Tertiary groups of the West." Four different small groups took the field, led by Meek, Leidy, Cope, and Lesquereux. Hayden sponsored Leidy and Cope on expeditions "studying the ancient lake-basins in the interior of the continent, which [had] become celebrated all over the world for the richness and variety of their vertebrate fossils." He convinced Lesquereux, "our great authority in fossil botany," to make "a careful study of the coal regions of the West." And he underwrote a two months' tour by Meek along the line of the Union Pacific, charging him to approach the question from the standpoint of invertebrate paleontology. Their findings were ultimately inconclusive; Cope and

Leidy argued for a Cretaceous date, Lesquereux supported Hayden's own Tertiary dating, and Meek straddled the issue to a certain extent, arguing that the beds were not uniform and represented both eras.[32] Yet launching these specialized studies marked a coming of age in the survey's maturity and Hayden's own role as a patron for science.

The survey's topographical branch took longer to mature. In the early years, Hayden put off engaging a survey topographer, at first relying on General Land Office maps and then simply not presenting any new maps. But by 1872 he could not avoid the fact that existing topographical maps of the West were "not accurate enough for the delineation of the geology." He employed his first topographer on the 1871 Yellowstone expedition, for which no other maps were to be had, but the results were hardly satisfactory, particularly after Schönborn committed suicide at the end of the season before he could work up his field notes. The data were subsequently given to Edwin Hergesheimer of the United States Coast Survey, who pronounced them "excellent" and agreed to work them up into maps for Hayden.[33]

¶ In 1872, Hayden made a concerted effort to overcome the difficulty of inadequate maps and at the same time make the method of work "more systematic," more of a complete topographical mapping survey than a reconnaissance. This required new expertise, and Hayden engaged topographers and astronomers for the two main parties fielded that year. Adolf Burck and Henry Gannett served in these respective capacities for the party led by Hayden, while Gustavus R. Bechler, assisted by William Nicholson and Rudolph Hering, served in a similar capacity for Stevenson's party.[34]

¶ Apart from their participation in the survey, little is known of Nicholson, Bechler, or Burck. Wakefield noted that Nicholson was a "tall bashful boy." Bechler seems to have been an accomplished draftsman, but many survey colleagues considered him lazy. He may have had the assistance of a congressman or two to secure his position initially, since after Hayden dismissed him in 1878 two members of the House interceded on his behalf. In Burck, Wakefield later remarked with tongue in cheek that the survey "was honored with the presence of a German nobleman. His name was Baron Adolph von Burck. He came to Mexico with the Emperor Maximilian, so he said." Unfortunately, the "Baron" was hardly a success as the survey's chief topographer, as Wakefield's account of Burck's efforts to "measure distances up the Yellowstone by triangulation" illustrates: "In order to triangulate you must have a well measured base line. Burck began his work bravely. The first day he chained off nearly a half mile. The next day he proceeded to verify the measurement and didn't get quite so far. So critical did he become that each day the line grew shorter. We knew from the first that the line *began* at the suttler's shop; at last we found that it *ended* there, and the matter of triangulation was given up."[35]

¶ Hering was another Philadelphian, at the time a civil engineer working on the extension of the city's Fairmount Park. Hering's letter of application is a nearly ideal example in the different themes it exhibits: proper connections, professional training and competency, experience, and, not least, the desire for suitable remuneration. He came to Hayden by way of the recommendation of Julius Hilgard of the Coast Survey. Hering had addressed a letter to Hilgard in mid-April 1872, having heard "that Dr. Hayden intends to make an expedition to the Sources of the Yellowstone River in a few weeks." Hering claimed he had long hoped to join such an expedition and not merely out of a "desire of adventures, but because I know I could be of more use . . . than many that have applied." At the risk of appearing "very 'unmannered'" Hering asked Hilgard, whom he knew was "personally acquainted with Dr. Hayden," to do him "the great favor to mention me and my abilities to [Hayden], . . . and . . . inquire whether it is possible for me to receive an appointment."

¶ For qualifications, Hering claimed good health and experience in a similar expedition in the Carpathian mountains six years earlier. He professed ability "to work with all geodetical instruments, with much precision; am also acquainted with the theories and methods of higher Geodesy and am able to perform the necessary calculations in connection with them." He had "studied Geology 1½ years with Prof. Geinitz in Dresden," where he had attended the Royal Polytechnical School, graduated as a civil engineer in 1867, and become proficient in "topographical and other draughting." And while this was the last year that Hering was likely to be free to undertake such a position, "as I expect to be married thereafter," he wanted it clearly understood that "Of course I would not wish to join as a volunteer, as my finances would not permit it."[36]

¶ Gannett, the final addition to the survey that year, came with Hoffmann's recommendation in response to Hayden's request for "a young man for Topographical and other work." Gannett, asserted Hoffmann, would "just suit." Born in Bath, Maine, he was a graduate of "Harvard mining school" (Lawrence Scientific School, B.S., 1869; M.E., 1870) and had accompanied Hoffmann as one of his pupils on a trip to the Rocky Mountains in 1870. He was later employed at the Harvard Observatory as an assistant making longitude observations, until funding fell short and he had to take a temporary job with the Coast Survey. Though not "a first class draughtsman," he could make "a decent looking map," and Hoffmann was sure he would be "of great service in fieldwork" since he was "active and [took] interest in his work." Hayden followed up the recommendation, but the issue was brought to a head when Gannett informed Hayden that he had received "an official letter from Lieut. Geo. M. Wheeler, . . . informing me that he is in want of an astronomer for the coming season's work." However, Gannett "prefer[red], on many accounts, to be a member of your [Hayden's] party; the country in which you work is, to me, more interesting." The two soon reached an agreement, and Gannett returned to Cambridge for special instruction in preparation for joining the survey.[37]

¶ Hayden has long been criticized for his supposed role in his survey's efforts in topographical mapping. Critics at the time and since have claimed that the initial results of the survey's forays into topographical mapping were "undistinguished" at best and demonstrated that Hayden "clearly lacked the ability to organize his men for a basic purpose of this kind." But it is unfair to expect Hayden personally to have possessed expertise in all branches of the survey's work. Rather, identifying deficiencies and responding to them by enhancing the organization's technical expertise are marks of the successful entrepreneur, and Hayden exhibited both skills when he recruited Gardner in the winter of 1872–73. With a decade of experience in triangulated topographical surveys, Gardner moved quickly to restructure the survey's mapping efforts in line with his own high standards for a "true topographical map for geological purposes"—it ought to "represent the features of the country accurately, and in bold relief" as a veritable "picture of the earth's surface as one would see it looking down from above."[38]

¶ Topographical mapping was quite different from anything Hayden had previously attempted. Putting the new ideal into practice required "the very highest order of talent." Since Gardner was more capable than Hayden at recognizing what was necessary, the task of recruiting the necessary topographical talent fell to him, and he set out to enlist the best he could. Yet the two men collaborated closely in this effort, discussing the qualities they sought. Gardner brought Allen David Wilson to the survey with him; Wilson had learned the art of surveying by triangulation under Hoffmann on the California survey along with Gardner and King. Gardner also made the rounds of Yale, MIT, and Harvard, and his letters to Hayden detailing his visits to prospective candidates provide evidence of what they sought. Given his personal orientation, Gardner focused on topographers, but given the dual nature of the planned survey, they also needed geologists and hoped to find pairs who could work together and combine their talents. They wanted individuals who had experience in the West, preferably in the mountains, or at least had been trained under or recommended by men with such experience. Finally, Gardner was leery of hiring anyone without a personal interview, being "a great believer in what old Vanderbilt calls taking 'a square look at a man.'"[39]

¶ They attempted to recruit some of the most prominent figures in American geology but generally had to be content with selecting from among the best of the newer talent. For instance, Gardner found Dana "so anxious to get out his new *Geology* that it will be very hard to get him into the field." But in making inquiries about present and former students at Yale, Gardner followed up on an application from George B. Chittenden, who had heard from Platt that the survey had a vacancy for a topographer. After an interview and some inquiries, Gardner was "favorably impressed" and reported to Hayden that Chittenden was "highly recommended . . . for your kind of work." After a second interview, Chittenden won a place on the survey.[40]

¶ Going on to Cambridge, Massachusetts, Gardner visited "two young men that have been with [the mining engineer Raphael] Pumpelly"—Archibald Marvine and Storey B. Ladd. Gardner found Marvine's experience impressive. He had visited the South Park of Colorado as a student in 1869, and after graduation from Harvard's Hooper Mining School in 1870 had spent a summer working for Wheeler. Since then, he had been doing topographical and geological work with Pumpelly at Lake Superior. Ladd, Gardner felt, showed "unusual taste as a draughtsman." After visiting with them, he remained favorably impressed: "They both strike me as able and energetic men who would sympathise with the spirit of the party and enter enthusiastically into our plans." He hired Ladd, just graduating from the mining school with a year's experience in topography under Pumpelly at Lake Superior, at one hundred dollars per month. But he was surprised to learn that Marvine was "not a topographer but a geologist." Although he had done some astronomy in the first part of his expedition with Wheeler, in the latter half of the season he devoted himself to geology, and his work with Pumpelly was "exclusively geological." However, J. D. Whitney recommended him highly, claiming he was "much better prepared for responsible work in the Rocky Mts. than any man can be from experience in Ohio alone"—probably a reference to John James Stevenson, whom Gardner and Hayden were also considering. Marvine's declaration that he wanted "to devote his life to pure geology and not touch commercial operations" also impressed Gardner, and he told Hayden that Marvine struck him "as a man who would identify himself thoroughly with your geological work" and, in high praise for Gardner, as "a man that I think you could trust in charge of a party."[41] Marvine joined Ladd on the survey.

¶ Stevenson did not, however, largely as the result of a misunderstanding that led to very bitter feelings that were not explained for several years. An 1863 graduate of the University of the City of New York, Stevenson had been professor of chemistry and natural science at West Virginia University (1869–71), assistant to Newberry on the geological survey of Ohio in 1871–72, and was currently part-time professor of geology at his alma mater. Stevenson visited Hayden in the fall of 1872 and offered his services for the 1873 campaign. Hayden apparently accepted the offer, conditioned upon appropriations from Congress, and promised to discuss the matter more fully during the winter. Instructed to follow up on the matter, Gardner spoke to Newberry about "his Ohio assistants." Reporting that Newberry "spoke of Prof. Stevenson as perhaps the ablest," Gardner felt Hayden "would do well to secure him." However, Gardner doubted that would be possible; Newberry had also reported that Stevenson had made arrangements to go with Wheeler that season.[42]

¶ In fact, as Stevenson later informed Hayden, while he had been contacted and "strongly urged to go with Wheeler as early as January," he "declined to have any communication respecting that matter as I was already pledged to you [Hayden]." The winter passed and Stevenson heard nothing from Hayden. Though Gardner had said he would "be on the lookout for any further information on the subject," apparently he heard nothing contrary to the original report. Even after communicating with Stevenson directly, Gardner seems to have retained the impression that Stevenson preferred to go with Wheeler—a confusion probably caused by the rivalry existing between the two surveys and the secrecy Gardner and Hayden were attempting to preserve regarding their plans prior to congressional action. Finally, becoming "a little anxious," Stevenson wrote Meek, who informed him that Hayden's parties were complete. The situation left Stevenson "very much irritated at such trifling" and led him to say "a good many very bitter things." But it was a double misunderstanding, as Stevenson later admitted. "From what Mr. Gardner said [in later explaining the situation], it seemed clear that you regarded me as acting dishonorably toward you, while I regarded you as acting in the same manner toward me."[43] Unfortunately for Hayden, some of the "very bitter things" said later bore very bitter fruit.

Successful recruiting entailed more than having a position to offer. Attracting and retaining qualified personnel for his expanded survey sometimes required Hayden to compete in ways that had usually not proved necessary in the earlier years. One was financial. When Gannett wrote that he would prefer to go with Hayden over Wheeler, he had no hesitation in adding, "with regard to compensation, I think that one hundred dollars per month, for the first year, is not too much to expect for my services." In fact, it was low, but Gannett was unemployed at the time. Hayden and Gardner were willing to start assistant topographers at $125 per month, and while recruiting Marvine Hayden learned he was "receiving one hundred and fifty dollars a month where he is. He would expect as much with you."[44]

¶ Hayden willingly paid good wages. As he wrote Interior Secretary Delano, if men of talent were "to identify themselves permanently with the survey" they "must be paid in proportion to their abilities," and even Hayden's critics admitted he was generous. Samuel Chittenden, an engineer for the Union Pacific, thought his brother George had gotten "a *very* good place with the Hayden expedition." Though holding a low opinion of Hayden's own ability, he said Hayden "manage[d] to keep good men with him by paying good prices." Even so, Hayden claimed he "could not do much if I paid the real value of this work" and claimed to rely a great deal on the efforts of volunteers willing to work for their expenses or a nominal salary.[45]

¶ Yet to draw a sharp dichotomy between paid and volunteer contributors to the survey would be a mistake. Both were important, and in many instances the deciding factor was whether or not a particular individual had an adequate outside source of income. For example, neither Cope nor Leidy was on salary. Cope had inherited a personal fortune that enabled him to work without pay, and Leidy seems to have had sufficient income from his teaching positions. At the same time, by the second half of the nineteenth century scientists were becoming more assertive in putting a value on their time and expertise as a means of making a livelihood, and a number of those who worked for the survey depended upon it. Though some scientists turned down invitations to become associated with the survey because they felt the terms offered not worth their while, others were glad enough to be associated with the survey for the price of their expenses in the field and in printing. But there were others who, as Lesquereux put it, could not afford to "count [themselves] in the number of those scientific gentlemen to whom [Hayden paid] a fine compliment remarking that they work for love of science only." As for himself, Lesquereux asked "what can I do?" He had given his life to science and "should have obtained some material advantages from it, at least to enable me to work without being troubled by the constant necessity of procuring a living." Then he would be like the others—Leidy, Cope, Porter, or Newberry—who had "such kind of situations, Professorships or other" that enabled them "to pursue science for itself only." However, "with my absolute deafness that can not be and therefore I must *work for money* and you must excuse me for this necessity."[46]

¶ Lesquereux's was a pathetic situation. In December 1870, he wrote Hayden that "for 41 years at least, I have worked for science without caring for any retribution [*sic*] for my labor." But now, he was "65 years old, totally deaf, half blind, without any provision for the future and I can not continue to work in that way." It was also a lonely life: "I have built a small shed for my specimens, use my parlor for work room, take my own room for exposing and comparing specimens and as I have nobody visiting me not even once a year, and as my wife says nothing, there is place enough." However, he enjoyed good working relations with Hayden, who paid him five dollars per day and encouraged him in what he loved to do. One example among many must suffice. In the same letter in which he described his solitary lifestyle, he told Hayden, "It is pleasant to work for you and with you. Not only are you always ready to help your assistants and to furnish informations [*sic*] as soon as wanted; but you encourage them by such confidence and free use of their own faculties in their researches that nothing is left to them but to go ahead with their own work, certain to be appreciated if they do it as well *as they know*."[47]

¶ Meek's social situation was even more extreme. Lesquereux had at least a wife and a son. Meek had no family whatever, and after losing a small inherited estate through a bad business investment he lived a very frugal and insecure existence. His partial deafness, which grew worse with the years, only served to accentuate his social awkwardness and inclination to withdraw. In addition, he suffered from tuberculosis after 1870. Insofar as it was within him, Hayden stood loyally by his friend and his promise to share his success with Meek, but it could be a difficult relationship all the same. Though Hayden manifested solicitude for his friend's health, he was torn by his concern that Meek should finish his "great work." Nor was he ever able to convince Meek to confine his efforts to the Hayden Survey, and he experienced great difficulty inducing Meek to finish work on the fossil invertebrates of the Nebraska Territory. The major stumbling blocks were Hayden's inability to ensure a steady source of income, and Meek's perfectionism regarding his writings and the figures illustrating the work. A further reason was Meek's determination not to be constrained regarding opportunities for research but to remain free to take other work, particularly when Hayden could not pay him.[48]

¶ Among his salaried naturalists, Joel Asaph Allen was perhaps Hayden's greatest bargain. While working as a curator at the Museum of Comparative Zoology (MCZ) in Cambridge, Allen initiated a correspondence with Hayden in 1872, requesting assistance on a paper on the geographical distribution and history of the American bison. Hayden promised to send his notes on the subject, for which Allen was grateful, though he had to wait two years to receive them. Duties at the MCZ, the low salary, and frail health all handicapped Allen's efforts to finish his manuscripts, but early in 1875 he finally reported that a monograph on North American hares was "so far advanced" that he was ready "to make a definite arrangement for its publication." Was Hayden interested in it? Hayden was interested but unable to offer Allen the desired illustrations for this monograph. Yet before the end of spring he enlisted Allen in another project: a series of papers on North American rodents.[49]

¶ Allen's hindrances then became hindrances for Hayden. Allen could not provide manuscript pages according to Hayden's printing schedules. When advised that the printer was ready for copy, Allen responded that whereas this would normally give him "great pleasure" under the circumstances he was "not quite prepared to profit by it." Writing that "the M.C.Z. considers itself too poor to give me a salary on which I can live," he was forced to "look out for other ways of earning money" and prevented from "devoting much time to unrewarding work, such as I suppose work on my rodent papers must be, and devote my pen to something that will bring me a little money." Informed of the difficulty, Hayden presented Allen with a "most agreeable surprise," a check that not only temporarily relieved his financial worries but was also "very gratifying to [Allen] to find [Hayden] willing to place so much confidence in [him]." This marked the beginning of Hayden's subsidizing of Allen's researches and writing, and by the end of the following year Hayden was paying him a monthly stipend of seventy-five dollars while he was engaged on survey work. While Allen remarked that the amount would "satisfy me at present, because this will enable me to get along comfortably with what I get from other sources," it was "only nominal compensation in comparison to the amount of work." Nor was Allen exaggerating. His payments from Hayden worked out to about a dollar per printed page, while rates paid contributors to journals such as *Scribner's* during the period 1865–85 rose from an average of three to five dollars per printed page to between ten to twenty dollars per page.[50]

¶ Hayden annually faced yet another recruiting challenge related to finances as he sought to keep his corps together during the winter. It might have been a simple matter except that his appropriation generally fell short about November or December, and he had to wait until the next session of Congress and hope for an additional sum of money in one of the several "Deficiency Bills" generally introduced to meet such shortfalls throughout the government. During his forty-year career in Washington the astronomer Simon Newcomb had ample opportunity to observe the usual maneuvering. Politically savvy and established heads of departments would ask for about a third more than they wanted; then when Congress cut the money down a third their departments got all they needed.[51] However, those already operating on a tight budget were likely to feel pinched before the end of the fiscal year. Hayden always felt pinched and annually requested more money to meet his deficiency.

¶ While awaiting the new infusion of funds, he had to ask his staff to do without. The young bachelors usually endured the time with a fair grace. Chittenden wrote home in May 1874 that in the summery weather they would "go out rowing, eat ice cream and strawberries and drink soda water in true summer style and borrow the money to pay for them with!" But the delay could also call for a degree of sacrifice not all were ready or able to make. In February 1875, Theodore Gill, Hayden's office manager, tendered his resignation, "sorry to learn that [Hayden was] in such an embarrassed position." His replacement, Elliott Coues, had a rocky beginning due to Hayden's continued financial difficulties. Part of the problem that year derived from 1875–76 being the "long session" of Congress. Since the survey was funded through the Sundry Civil Bill, Hayden regularly had to wait until the end of the session before he received the year's appropriation; that year he had to wait until 31 July. Aware of the coming period of dearth, Hayden began to cut expenses early, writing a "personal" letter to Meek at the beginning of December 1875 asking him to attempt to make do with what Hayden had recently paid him "until July next" and not ask for "*much* more until then." By doing so Meek would greatly assist him; because this was the "long session of Congress" Hayden needed "the strength of what money I have to sustain me." He told Meek he had already made such an arrangement with Lesquereux and explained that he himself would not draw his own salary.[52] Still, not knowing when the next paycheck would arrive cannot have been a pleasant way to work.

¶ In spite of such inconveniences, when Gardner and Hayden finished recruiting for the 1873 season they had assembled a talented team founded on pairs of geologists and topographers. Though there was some turnover during the years as well as rearrangement of the teams, the success of their efforts is evident not only in the organization's basic stability for the life of the survey but also in the subsequent careers of its members, many of whom remained in service with the United States Geological Survey, the successor organization to the Hayden Survey. At the same time, Hayden's recruiting practices went a long way toward developing and nourishing external constituencies to support his goals and the survey generally. They enhanced the survey's technical expertise by recruiting skilled personnel and thus improving its capacity to accomplish those goals, while they simultaneously attached Hayden's interests to those of his political patrons and his scientific colleagues and clients. Hayden's balancing of patronage and professionalism helped him maintain enthusiasm and support in Congress without sacrificing the same among the general scientific community, as evidenced by the fact that many of the best American naturalists, geologists, and geographers were happy to associate themselves with and support the Hayden Survey. But recruiting was only a step toward practice. Hayden also had to create and nurture internal constituencies in the survey, motivating and training his men so that they might identify themselves with the survey. In short, he had to direct their work to success in the field and in the office.

6

Executive of Science

So far as the regular hours are concerned, I beg leave to state my regret at the utter impossibility to keep them, and would remind you of the fact, that no regular hours have ever been agreed upon between us. —Frederick M. Endlich to Hayden, 3 February 1877

The title "Geologist-in-charge" did more than designate Hayden's position and role in the survey; it also aptly described his principal ambition. Hayden identified himself with the survey and desired to be identified with it. Though he wrote Baird in September 1873 that he had "but two objects in life, *My Survey* and the *National Museum*," that was for the sake of winning Baird's continuing favor and assistance.[1] If pressed, Hayden probably would have admitted only one great ambition—his survey—of which he was, and intended to remain, geologist-in-charge. As such, Hayden's responsibility went beyond his personal scientific contribution, extending to the direction of the entire enterprise. He was more than a patron to the members of his survey; he was also their boss and had to take a bureaucratic perspective of the survey and its operations. His executive functions reveal different but no less essential facets of a scientific entrepreneur, as organizer and manager. ¶ Adequate organization had always been requisite for the survey. As the survey developed into a permanent and expanding scientific bureau, problems of organization were not only materially compounded but further complicated by clashes between strong and competitive personalities and the natural desire of recognized scientists for professional independence. In examining the elements involved in Hayden's management of the survey and its work, we must give our first attention to the work environment and the organization of work groups. However, several interconnected issues of personnel management are clearly important as well. Among these are the difficulties of working in teams, notwithstanding an expressed ideal; the need to confront competition; the issue of professionalism, with its ramifications of respect and independence; and, overshadowing all of these, Hayden's desire to be recognized as "Geologist-in-charge."

¶ These themes are all related to his responsibility for inspiring loyalty among his men and fostering their professional development as members of the survey. He had to establish a stable work environment where they could produce work of suitable quality. Hayden did not enjoy total success in these areas. Though his organization generally enjoyed high morale, the demands of personal ambition competed with the need for bureaucratic order, posing several serious problems and threatening his bureau's stability. As geologist-in-charge, Hayden had to fashion solutions to a variety of problems. At first sight, tasks such as providing enough mules, obtaining railroad passes, warding off Indians, or pacifying aggrieved scientists might seem to have little relationship to science. Yet failure to attend to them would have meant that very little could have been done in the way of scientific work. It was no simple thing to put a scientific expedition in the field in working order; it was, rather, a matter of a thousand and one details.

Like every cooperative enterprise, the Hayden Survey required coordination. As its personnel and appropriations grew along with its area and range of operations this need became more acute because of the need to outfit, support, and coordinate the work of several parties in the field at the same time. It seems quite clear that increased order was imposed on the field operations of the Hayden Survey more quickly than upon its Washington office. For instance, at the end of the 1873 season Hayden began a practice of hiring local ranchers to care for equipment and animals from one season to the next and have them ready in the spring. These ranches then became the jumping-off points for the next season's expeditions. Though the practice was instituted because the animals and outfit "could not have been sold [that] fall without great sacrifice to the interest of the Government," it also obviated the necessity of gathering together all the materials needed for mounting an expedition each succeeding year.[2]

¶ The "rendezvous" or spring gathering was usually under the charge of James Stevenson, who served as quartermaster and executive officer of the survey. Going out in advance of the rest of the corps, he purchased supplies and oversaw necessary preparations while the rest of the men arrived from the East in fits and starts. Sometimes they met on the trains coming West. Sometimes they arrived knowing no one and finding everything rather strange until they were met by Stevenson and given a hearty welcome and introduction all around. During the Colorado years (1873–76) Denver was the starting point for major field parties. But since the survey had become too large for the city to afford it comfortable yet economical facilities, the rendezvous camp was established on Clear Creek, "in a grove of cottonwoods, six miles from town," where the tents were pitched, baggage and stores distributed among different divisions, animals brought together, and new hands given their first taste of "roughing it."[3]

¶ The first few days in camp were spent preparing equipment and organizing for the season's campaign. Much of this work fell to laborers, primarily the muleteers, who often accompanied the survey year after year and had the responsibility of caring for the animals and packing all the necessary equipment. Because survey parties so frequently traveled in places inaccessible to wagons, they used few wheeled vehicles after leaving the rendezvous, instead packing all supplies and equipment on mules. Thanks to their greater hardiness, mules were also generally used as riding animals in preference to horses. Yet mules presented their own difficulties, and most of the survey men learned by personal experience the truth of the saying "Stubborn as a Missouri mule."[4]

¶ Almost everything they took with them had to be accommodated to traveling on the backs of the mules or the persons of the men. The only exceptions were some few bottles and flasks of condiments, for which, with some other fragile items, a pair of panniers was provided. Nearly everything else went into a canvas bag that would be securely lashed to one of the mules. The same was true for the scientific equipment; theodolites, plane tables, barometers, thermometers, and chronometers all had to be carried on the men or their mules. So, too, the photographic equipment; and Jackson's darkroom tent, chemicals, plates, cameras, tripods, and the like, usually required two mules to carry it all, except on rare occasions when he could use a wagon.[5]

¶ For Jackson, outfitting for a season's campaign was a major operation. Since contemporary enlarging methods were extremely time consuming and only yielded low-quality prints, it was "necessary to make large plates if you wanted large pictures," and both Hayden and Jackson wanted large pictures. His supply of plates, amounting to two or three hundred pounds or more, varied from five by eight inches up to the almost unheard-of size for expedition photography of twenty by twenty-four inches. The various chemicals comprised a nearly equal additional weight. In the field, the cameras, the chemical boxes, and the rest of the supplies were wrapped in hides, which were tied to the pack-saddle, and a supply of water was loaded on top of the pile. The result could be "a very top-heavy load," requiring "strenuous work of all hands to keep everything right side up" on the steeper trails.[6]

¶ The geologist-in-charge typically arrived in camp just a few days before the expedition was to get under way, at which point preparations swung into high gear. Last-minute purchases were made and packing completed. Assignments and routes of march were given along with any special instructions, and then one by one the parties packed up and set out. As the men broke camp, they cut a remarkable figure, outfitted with Texas saddles; lariats and riding crops; belts containing knives, pistols, and cartridges; and various scientific instruments slung over their shoulders while leading half a dozen or so "kicking, jumping, heavy loaded pack mules." As Chittenden recognized during his first summer with the survey, it was a scene worth writing home about.[7] Yet the season's work had only begun.

¶ One of the elements heightening the romantic appeal of the western surveys was the notion that they operated in the wild West, exploring where no white man had gone before. Aware of its value, Hayden carefully cultivated this perception of the survey. But while it contained a certain amount of truth, a careful reading of Hayden's reports reveals a surprising number of times when he and his party traveled for miles into supposedly unexplored territory only to find settlers or other white people upon arrival at their destination. During his survey of Nebraska, Hayden admitted surprise at finding settlers, complete with thriving farms and growing villages, as far west as he did. Later, when he led his survey into the Yellowstone region to bring back the first "trustworthy, exact, and comprehensive" reports of "scientific observers," they found people resident there. In his report, Hayden referred to the warm mineral springs and speculated that "there is no reason why this locality should not at some future period become a noted place of resort for invalids." In fact, a rough settlement had already been established and was on its way to becoming "McQuirk's Medicinal Springs," one of several squatter's claims that became an issue in the debate about reserving the area as a national park.[8]

¶ Some writers have misunderstood the relevance of the presence of settlers to Hayden's role as an explorer. Peter Hales, for example, makes much of the vanishing wilderness and how the images of the West that Hayden and Jackson brought back were in some respects artificial. But his observation that the survey parties were constantly "stitching in and out" between civilization or settlement and wilderness is of greater importance in understanding the survey's operations. The "vanishing wilderness" in no way detracts from the survey as exploration when Hales's observation is set alongside Goetzmann's characterization of exploring as an activity whose "purposes, goals, and evaluation of new data are to a great extent set by the previous experiences, the values, the kinds and categories of existing knowledge, and the current objectives of the civilized centers from which the explorer sets out on his quest."[9] It is not terribly important whether members of the Hayden Survey were the first on the scene. The important point is that they were *the first of their kind to do what they did upon arrival.*

¶ Nor did the fact that the wilderness was "vanishing" in any way diminish their experience of the wild West or the difficulties posed by the elements. The actual conditions of the work are the significant features. "Stitching in and out" on the boundary of settlement afforded both advantages and disadvantages. As the country became more settled, it made the parties' lives easier. They could go to town occasionally to get a "first rate dinner" or sleep in a hotel or deposit and pick up their mail. It could also make things more difficult. For instance, it was harder to find places to "squat" for a campsite among farm fences and ranches.[10]

¶ The parties had their fair share of the wild West and battling the elements. Some of these were starkly stated in newspaper headlines such as "Experiences of the Last Party of the Hayden Expedition: In the mountains in winter—camping in the snow with the mercury below zero—traveling through a frozen country—sliding down mountain trails—shooting a grizzly—spending Thanksgiving in the open—reaching civilization at last." They also endured their share of discomfort and difficulties posed by the terrain. Chittenden wrote home during the 1874 season that while he had "always gloried in the plains," and still thought them "just as beautiful to day as they were the first time I set eyes on them," he had had "no idea how dry the plains were till we came to work on them. . . . yesterday I rode over thirty miles round in a kind of broken semicircle at my work and never saw a drop of water till I got to camp."[11]

¶ The plains were also windy, and Cope described the effects in a passage detailing the discovery of a dinosaur fossil "under circumstances of difficulty peculiar to the plains." After fruitlessly examining the bluffs for half a day, the paleontologist was finally rewarded with the discovery of several vertebrae preserved within "the protective embrace of the roots of a small bush." Just as he brought his pick into action to secure the fossils "one of the gales so common in that region sprang up, and, striking the bluff fairly, reflected itself upward," resulting in an ironic "conversion of force." No sooner did the fossil-hunter's pick pulverize the rock than the limestone dust was carried "into eyes, nose, and every available opening in the clothing," blinding the investigator and threatening to drive him from the field. To continue work, he was obliged to make a mask of his handkerchief by tying it over his face, after piercing it with minute holes for his eyes.[12]

¶ They also did battle with fire, or at least its effects. A regular feature of the American frontier, fire caused a variety of problems for the Hayden Survey. One was the inconvenience presented to travel. Reporting on explorations in central Colorado's Sawatch Range in 1873, Hayden wrote that winter winds following autumn fires had toppled the timber "in every direction, forming a net-work over which it [was] almost impossible for our animals to pass." Though he found such barriers common in the mountainous portions of the West, he claimed it was "difficult for any one not familiar with this country to comprehend how important an element of hindrance this is in making a detailed exploration of the country. Very frequently we are obliged to cut our path through the logs for great distances, making only a few miles a day." The smoke from fires presented another problem. Sometimes it so obscured the horizon that it prevented topographers from getting the accurate sightings on mountain peaks and other "stations" necessary for making triangulations or determining altitudes. Franklin Rhoda described one fire south of Del Norte, in Colorado Territory. The smoke "extended clear across San Luis Valley to [Fort] Garland over 60 miles [to the east] and even there was thick enough to be troublesome." A heavy haze in the atmosphere could present the same difficulty and frequently prevented work after midday.[13]

¶ In addition to the general trials of survey work, William Henry Jackson, the expedition photographer, had a further host of difficulties to overcome. Frontier photographers such as Jackson required more than technical skills; they also needed "talent, infinite patience, full dedication—and a strong back." The West was hardly suited to the photographic technology of the 1870s. Because the initial problem was to get enough light, the weather and other natural conditions affected the speed of picture taking, and photographers sometimes had to "wait out" spells of bad weather. But when the sun shone it presented other problems. The arid desert atmosphere could shrink plate holders until they literally fell apart, or it could cause damp plate coatings to dry too rapidly. Wet plates also had to be protected from dust and insects, which could ruin images. Photographers had to adapt to the elements: "changes of temperature, relative humidity and altitude all varied the working characteristics of the coatings and chemicals, and photographers had to correct their formulations and exposure and processing times to compensate for these variables."[14]

¶ Once exposed and developed, it remained necessary to preserve and transport the delicate plates home. Jackson endured numerous trials in this regard, but none was more disheartening than the discovery, while on his way to the Mount of the Holy Cross in 1873, that his pack mule had strayed from its place in the train. The packsaddle slipped off and rolled down the mountainside, resulting in the lid coming off the box holding his exposed negatives. Hayden himself found the broken plates scattered down the mountainside and in informing the photographer was at first inclined to admonish him for carelessness. But when Hayden saw how obviously distressed Jackson was, he offered comfort instead, reminding him that he could repair the loss by retracing his steps and replacing the lost plates.[15]

¶ The risk of serious illness and even death were also constant concerns. Hayden's letters from the West frequently remark that all in his party were well—testimony to the prevalence of the concern. Cope came down with mountain fever in September 1872 and was prostrated for several weeks at Fort Bridger. The sickness of one of his packers in 1874 so greatly delayed Gannett from covering his assigned territory that he decided to discharge the man at the next town and pay his transportation back to Denver. During the same season, Hayden was delayed by the serious illness of a member of his own party, J. C. M. Shanks, the son of Congressman John P. C. Shanks of Indiana, and Hayden had to leave the party and take the young man to town where they could await his parents. Still, the only recorded death on a survey party was that of the wife of William Blackmore, who died during the 1872 expedition to the Yellowstone and was laid to rest at the base of the Gallatin Range.[16]

¶ The parties all faced a further hazard in the loss of equipment by accident or theft. Barely a month after starting his survey in the 1868 season, Hayden had to inform Commissioner Wilson that he had met with "a sad loss" that would "cripple" his efforts: four mules and two riding animals had been stolen by "an organized band of thieves." Though he would still be able to accomplish "a good deal," it would not be as much as he had intended nor would his collections of specimens be "nearly as large" as planned. This was not the last time Hayden was thus relieved of property. In 1870, an army lieutenant reclaimed a pony Hayden had purchased at Fort Benton but which the lieutenant claimed had been stolen from him at Cheyenne. In 1876, Stephen Hovey, Hayden's chief packer and wagon master, submitted an affidavit listing all the survey animals that had been "lost and stolen and died since 1868." It revealed that animals were lost almost every season for a variety of causes.[17]

¶ Perhaps one of the most humorous losses, at least in retrospect, occurred to the party led by Bechler. While making his second station of the 1875 season, Bechler looked down "after 4 hours of terrible climbing" only to discover that his camp was on fire. When he finally descended the mountain after completing his observations he found his own tent had particularly suffered; everything in it had been consumed in the flames. But it was the cook who presented "the most pityful sight." The man had had charge of the camp, but while he had been watering the animals the wind carried sparks from the campfire "and set the neighborhood in blaze." The survey was fortunate, losing only a tent, two pair of saddle blankets, and an old packsaddle, yet Bechler wanted instructions as to who should bear the expense of the loss. Writing that "the fellow is poor, awfully poor," he asked "Have I got to charge him with the amount on his salary?" [18]

¶ Finally, the survey also labored under the threat of Indian attacks, though it usually experienced little actual peril from this quarter since the men preferred to avoid risk when possible. Still, the threat was real enough for Scudder to write after Hayden's return in 1868 that he was "glad the indians didn't get your scalp." Four years later, W. H. West wrote to the commander of Fort Ellis regarding his son, who was with Stevenson's party. Noting that his son's letters for the previous two months had "just been returned here from Ft. Ellis" and "as the Indians have been troublesome, I am naturally anxious," West told the commander he would be "obliged to you for any information you may have of the Party." It was also great enough to be one of the reasons for transferring operations from the Yellowstone area to Colorado in 1873. But the threat of Indian danger was nothing new to Hayden. He took it seriously, yet balanced it against enthusiasm for his research and put most of the responsibility for controlling the Indians on the army. For instance, before departing for the Niobrara in 1866 he wrote to Leidy, transmitting his will and appointing Leidy executor of his estate. Hayden admitted that the trip was said to be very dangerous and he had been cautioned against going, but he hoped to get back safely, and if he did "the collection will be a fine one." [19]

¶ In spite of precautions, however, the parties had several adventures with Indians, two of which threatened the lives of the men and resulted in the loss of equipment and animals. One occurred during their last expedition to the Yellowstone in 1878, when A. D. Wilson's camp was fired upon after having blundered into a minor rebellion by members of the Bannocks. The attackers escaped with the survey party's animals and most of their camp equipment. However, there seems to have been no serious threat to their lives, and they were able to recover their instruments, which they had cached, and resume work a few days later.[20] In this, they were much luckier than their colleagues who had been attacked while working in Utah several years earlier.

¶ In mid-August 1875, the survey teams led by Gardner and Gannett were working just across the border on the Ute Indian reservation in Utah in the La Sal Mountains as part of their mapping effort for western Colorado. Having been warned it might not be safe to go on the reservation, the parties joined together in the interest of safety. That yielded a combined total of thirteen men who managed to complete most of their work before they were attacked. But on Sunday, 15 August, they found themselves in a running battle that lasted from Sunday evening until Tuesday night, before the men felt safe. In the process of making good their escape they abandoned all but the barest necessities and only by luck ran into Holmes's party on Thursday, 19 August, as it was making its way to Parrott City for supplies. Joining Holmes, they all went in together and gave the news of their adventure to the nation.[21]

¶ Accounts of the fight were soon on the telegraph wire, which is hardly surprising given the story—high drama in the finest wild West tradition—and the makeup of the combined Gardner-Gannett party. There were at least two newspaper correspondents along, writing for three papers: the *New York Evening Post*, the *New York Times*, and the *Philadelphia Inquirer*. Further, when the party reached Parrott City, Peale noted that "all the boys were busy writing" and sent "special telegrams to the Eastern papers." He himself sent two letters "to the Philadelphia Press, one describing our fight." At Parrott City, they also met a reporter for the *Chicago Inter-Ocean*, who composed an "entirely original" account of the fight.[22]

¶ The episode provoked a firestorm of publicity that Hayden seems to have viewed as a greater threat than the Indian attack itself. The crisis called for all the expertise Hayden could muster in political and public relations damage control. It came on top of a continuing conflict with the Army Corps of Engineers and provided the army with an opening to argue that the civilian scientists ought to be under army jurisdiction because of the obvious danger. It was also coincident with charges of corruption in the Bureau of Indian Affairs and, by extension, the Department of the Interior that were capturing newspaper headlines that summer. Hayden did not need to add to the department's "Indian

1. In 1872, the Hayden Survey fielded "two large and well-equipped parties" to explore into Yellowstone National Park. The assembled corps of sixty-one men are pictured here, after their rendezvous at Lower Firehole Basin. *Source*: William Henry Jackson, 1257, USGS Photographic Library, Denver.

2. One of the "young men" of the survey was typically assigned the task of hauling the odometer. *Source*: William Henry Jackson, 1290, USGS Photographic Library, Denver.

3. Camp scene: George B. Chittenden, survey topographer, stuffing his "war bag." *Source*: William Henry Jackson, 1639, USGS Photographic Library, Denver.

4. Camp scene: William Henry Holmes "writing letters," a regular activity for him and many survey members. The camp scene shows some of Holmes's scattered gear. *Source*: William Henry Jackson, 1291, USGS Photographic Library, Denver.

5. Camp scene: Jackson's 1874 photograph of survey men performing their "Morning ablutions" in a cold mountain stream presents a small slice of what survey life was like apart from those rare times when the men were able to take advantage of an opportunity to sleep in a hotel bed—which in most western hotels was a mixed blessing. *Source*: William Henry Jackson, 501, USGS Photographic Library, Denver.

6. Camp scene: The "Doctor's mess," with, from left to right, Hayden, James Stevenson, William Holman, S. C. Jones, James Gardner, William D. Whitney, and William Henry Holmes, the party that made the first ascent of the Mount of the Holy Cross in 1873. *Source*: William Henry Jackson, 490, USGS Photographic Library, Denver.

7. "Triangulation, summit of Sultan Mountain, San Juan County, Colorado, 1874." Allen David Wilson and Franklin B. Rhoda were one of the Hayden Survey's topography teams. The survey constructed maps by means of triangulation. After selecting three prominent peaks in a region, they measured the angles between them by means of a theodolite, and then used the geometrical principle that when one knows two angles and the length of one side of a triangle, the other angle and two sides can be discovered. Under Gardner's direction, Colorado was overlaid with a network of triangles, into which the work of each topographer was fitted. *Source*: William Henry Jackson, 1111, USGS Photographic Library, Denver.

8. "Topographical work." George Chittenden, topographer, and William Henry Holmes, geologist, formed a team constructing the maps. In his sketches the topographer recorded drainages, elevations, and specific points located with the theodolite, while the geologist colored in geological formations and indicated their relationship to one another in vertical sections. *Source*: William Henry Jackson, 1112a, USGS Photographic Library, Denver.

9. William Henry Jackson and Charles R. Campbell, one of Jackson's young assistants in 1872, are shown "Photographing in high places" on a ledge commanding a view of the Tetons, Lincoln County, Wyoming. The small tent was Jackson's darkroom, where he would prepare the wet plates for exposure and, following exposure, immediately develop them. *Source*: William Henry Jackson, 172, USGS Photographic Library, Denver.

10. This photograph of the Grand Canyon of the Yellowstone, from the east bank, was made during the Hayden Survey's 1871 expedition. *Source*: William Henry Jackson, 88, USGS Photographic Library, Denver.

11. Jackson's photographs of the Mount of the Holy Cross, taken during the 1873 expedition, were perhaps the most popular of all his many photos, uniting popular mythology of the West and contemporary religious sentiment. *Source*: William Henry Jackson, 1248, USGS Photographic Library, Denver.

problems." Instead, he needed the department's steadfast support in dealing with his "army problems."

¶ Hayden weathered the army's attacks upon the survey that the Indian fight publicity provoked, but he also had to endure some ridicule because of it. The next year, when Elliott Coues was recruited from his position as an army surgeon to temporary assignment with the Hayden Survey as an ornithologist, he complained that "Some graceless wag has taken an atrocious liberty with my name, and the joke is current here [in Washington]. He said that Hayden wisely takes Coues [pronounced "cows"] along this year to pacify Sitting Bull!" [23] Fieldwork in the West was not for the faint of heart.

¶ Nor was it for the frail of body. In addition to the dangers of terrain, climate, theft, and hostile Indians, Hayden had to confront difficulties arising from the scientific personnel he wanted to include in the expeditions. Apart from questions regarding the quality of his volunteers and patronage appointments, some of Hayden's most distinguished personnel presented problems of a different sort, not the least being their physical fitness. Of those recruited for 1872—Leidy, Porter, Meek, Lesquereux, and Cope—only Cope was younger than Hayden. Leidy and Porter, though in good health, were both in their fifties, nearly a decade older than Hayden. Meek was a few years older yet and suffered from tuberculosis and partial deafness. Lesquereux was in his sixties, half-blind, and totally deaf. They formed a corps unlikely to relish the hardships of camp life, and Hayden had to mix entreaty with cajolery to get them to undertake the work. He even resorted to a bit of implicit blackmail since he did not hesitate to observe that unless they accompanied the working parties they might find themselves cut off from the survey's collections. For instance, in 1873 Hayden told Leidy that after visiting Columbus, Ohio, and dining with Lesquereux, he had convinced Lesquereux to take the field once again: "He wishes very much to continue in the service of the Survey, so he will go out." [24]

¶ Lesquereux's age and condition hardly encouraged him to look forward to the trips. After having made many of his geological explorations alone, he knew full well the difficulties he could expect to encounter. To entice him into the field in 1872 Hayden allowed him to take his son along as a paid assistant. But even for Lesquereux the trips were not all bad, and upon returning from his 1872 expedition he told

Hayden that it had provided him with "a great deal of valuable informations [*sic*] and materials too of importance." He had also acquired "an exact idea of the formations where the fossil plants are found," without which he "could never have been able to make reliable deductions [or] to compare characters of fossils at diverse levels."[25] Yet even as he hoped a second western tour would serve "as a kind of rest" and a chance to recuperate from the strain on his eyes, before going out he wrote to Lesley that the "purposed [*sic*] expedition gives me a great deal of anxiety. I am too old for such work but I could not well refuse." Not only had he been "urged to go by three letters from Hayden and one from Baird," but after his explorations of the previous year he felt "a yearning to know more of that lignitic formation on which I have made a too long report perhaps."

¶ Lesquereux's hope to contribute "something to the history of our Coal formations, lignitic and carboniferous" provided his strongest incentive to go West again. But his more pessimistic premonitions proved true, and he returned to Columbus at the beginning of September "much tired even sick of a work too hard for my old age."[26] After this experience he did not take the field for the survey again, nor does Hayden seem to have pushed him to do so. Hayden valued the work Lesquereux did for the survey, and he came to recognize that he could only ask so much of some of his more senior collaborators. It was more important that Lesquereux finish his contributions to Hayden's series of final reports. There was plenty of work for him to do without risking his health and ability in an attempt to do even more.

While the "Geologist-in-charge" might decide that some of his associates were past their field-working days, he still had to provide direction to the efforts of the rest of his corps and ensure that they worked productively as a team. These responsibilities became more difficult after 1871 as the increasing numbers of new men hired in the years after the first Yellowstone expedition changed the nature of the survey in several ways. One of the most obvious changes was that the survey became larger, fielding several teams of workers simultaneously. This multiplied administrative and personnel issues for Hayden. Another highly important change, particularly after 1872 and Hayden's decision to produce a geological and topographical atlas of Colorado, was that the survey became more "professional." Though this was probably the only way it could have begun to accomplish Hayden's new program, the change generated a variety of effects. One of the most immediate was the introduction of a new degree of stability into the work. Now, instead of more or less free-floating exploring reconnaissances, a plan required a plodding fulfillment. Stations had to be erected, observations taken and recorded, specimens collected, photographs made, sketches drawn—all in a systematic manner. It was not only adventure; it was also a job.

¶ And other jobs were available. The previous chapter mentioned some of the financial aspects of this consequence, but more than money was at stake in Hayden's dealings with his corps of scientists. There were also issues of professional pride and the desire for independence in work, concerns that lay behind a conscious decision taken in spring 1873 that any "eminent" geologists who joined the survey would enjoy complete freedom to publish their own conclusions as a result of their examinations, even if those views were antagonistic or contrary to Hayden's views. The survey would leave judgment to the scientific world at large. Hayden insisted on only a single proviso: "any geologists connecting themselves with the survey are not to connect with the general affairs of the survey but to undertake special works," in the fashion of subcontractors under special assignment.[27] This provided some distance on both sides, but Hayden soon learned that not only the most eminent scientists could have such professional concerns. So might a number of others, and egos could be bruised in many ways.

¶ The amount and manner of recognition for contributions to the survey's success quickly emerged as an issue. In recruiting new topographers, Gardner believed it necessary for them to go out with him for a probationary period of instruction, to make sure their work met his standards. Chittenden served such a probation. But after learning the business to Gardner's satisfaction, Chittenden wanted greater recognition of the value of his work. Upset that press accounts presented him as "a mere appendage" to Holmes's party, Chittenden sought "a more equal distribution of the credit" and "independent and separate recognition."[28]

¶ The composition of the personnel of the different work parties posed a more fundamental problem affecting the working environment. As Hayden expressed the ideal, "the association of topographer and ge-

ologist [would lead] to benefits for each" and be "a great advantage to the system of fieldwork." Since it was "as yet impossible" to enter the field with a finished topographical map on which to work out the geology, Hayden and Gardner decided that "the union of topography and geology, in one and the same party" would be the best way to furnish the data "for the realization of the full value of the otherwise more or less disconnected observations of the geologist." The topographer would literally draw those observations together on his map. At the same time, Hayden believed the topographer received "equal benefits" from association with the geologist, whose observations would enable him to see more deeply into the "internal structure" of the country, rather than simply dwell upon its surface.[29]

¶ The pairings were made up of individuals, however, and three or four months in the field provided plenty of time to reveal incompatibilities. Generally, the system seems to have worked well, and a number of the scientists became not only collaborators but fast friends, as did Chittenden and Ladd as well as Holmes and Peale. The working relationship between most of the men as partners in a team seems to have been generally harmonious and respectful of one another. Under the leadership of Wilson, even a team including the "volatile" Rhoda and the "somewhat haughty and intolerant" Frederick Endlich "was known for hard work and no fuss."[30]

¶ Other pairings were not as successful. While Wakefield considered Peale, Platt, and Holmes the "pleasantest of comrades," he found Gannett a difficult man to work with and "a dreadfully profane skeptic. Sometimes his talk grates so I can hardly endure it." Bechler posed an even more serious case of someone with whom many found it difficult to work. In his correspondence to Hayden, Bechler presented himself as a hard worker and a good draftsman, but many members of the survey considered him lazy and negligent in carrying out his duties. In the end, Bechler was given his own party, the "Meandering Topographical Party," to carry out measurements along the roads with an odometer. Perhaps this was because no one else wanted to work with him, since no one did until the geologist Charles A. White joined the survey in 1876.[31] Yet as difficult as Bechler could be to work with, his case was a simple one compared to Hayden's biggest personnel headaches, which resulted from an excess rather than a lack of zeal.

¶ As geologist-in-charge, Hayden could delegate some problems, and he was lucky to have a competent executive in Stevenson, who took care of the day-to-day details of getting parties into the field and keeping them supplied. Other problems could easily be dealt with by shuffling assignments according to personalities. But some problems had to be confronted head on. When Hayden and Gardner decided that "the only plan" by which eminent specialists might be enticed to join with the survey was to permit each to publish his own views freely, "leaving the scientific world to judge by the evidence who is right," they did more than express ground rules for freedom of speech. By establishing a framework for dealing with competition between ambitious scientists they sought to make the survey a neutral ground. But it was impossible to keep completely out of the way of ambitions, and Hayden found that he had to deal with them both internally and externally. Two of the most serious cases he had to confront involved some of the most valuable contributors to the survey: Cope and Gardner.

¶ At times, Cope's actions must have been exasperating to Hayden. They threatened to drive Leidy from the survey and seriously complicated relations with Hayden's friends at Yale through a bitter quarrel with O. C. Marsh over priority in the discovery and naming of fossil vertebrates. Cope and Marsh were both determined to make a name for themselves in science, and both had chosen vertebrate paleontology as the field in which to do so. By the late 1860s, it had become apparent that the American West held vast treasure troves of vertebrate fossils, and both men bent their not inconsiderable efforts toward the attainment and control of those caches. Though both were heirs to fortunes, which they exhausted in their scientific efforts, they also found it convenient to ally themselves with the federal surveys scouring the West. Both were single-mindedly ambitious, and both were willing to employ ruthless, even unscrupulous, means to attain their goal of scientific immortality through naming, describing, and systematizing fossil vertebrates. Having either of these men associated with his survey made it almost inevitable that Hayden would be drawn into the fray. Although Cope in many ways exacerbated the situation for Hayden, an underlying tension already existed.

¶ Hayden's involvement in the competition in this branch of paleontology predated the scientific activities of either Marsh or Cope. It derived from his association with Leidy, the third great figure in mid-nineteenth-century American vertebrate paleontology. In 1856, as Hayden was returning from the Nebraska Territory, he promised Leidy the privilege of examining all vertebrate collections made during his western explorations. At the time, the promise helped assure Hayden of Leidy's continuing support, but Hayden later found that keeping it entailed hard feelings on the part of some of his other friends, particularly Marsh, with whom Hayden enjoyed good relations when Marsh began his own work in the later 1860s. Marsh occasionally bought fossils from Hayden—as did Cope—and Marsh wrote letters supporting Hayden's candidacy for the position of geologist for the survey of Nebraska.[32] However, when Marsh began his own western expeditions in 1870, he and Hayden soon found themselves competitors.

¶ Both men were aggressively ambitious. When Marsh sought to monopolize the field in vertebrate paleontology, Hayden resisted the intrusion, contending that the western fossil fields belonged to him "by right of occupation." Marsh proposed a collaboration by which he would give Hayden a notice of his finds for Hayden's next *Report* in exchange for permission to describe any vertebrate fossils found. Hayden, no less ambitious than Marsh, replied that "all fossil vertebrate remains that I ever collected in the world" were promised to Leidy, Hayden's "best and oldest friend," who could do with them as he chose. Wary of being anticipated by Marsh, he urged Leidy to look over the specimens quickly, and "if there are any new species, . . . describe them before Prof. Marsh returns."[33] Then, in mid-October Marsh erupted "in a terrible rage," claiming Hayden had followed him and "taken the cream off" an expedition that had cost Marsh some twenty thousand dollars. Hayden objected that he had merely "followed my official instructions," but the incident left him suspecting that Marsh had not found much for his expense and efforts.

¶ Initially, Hayden hoped the whole matter would blow over, but forgiveness was not in Marsh's nature. Learning that Marsh still felt he had been taken advantage of a month later, Hayden reversed himself and asked Leidy to delay publication of the new species until Marsh had a chance to visit, explaining that he did not wish to have Marsh's "ill will." But that was impossible. Leidy had already published the descriptions. No stranger to ambition himself, Leidy had no intention of waiting. Rather, he reinforced Hayden's initial stance: Marsh was out of line, behaving childishly, asserting rights he did not have. Like Hayden, Leidy viewed the issue in terms of a collector's prerogative to do as he wished with his collections.[34]

¶ To expect the affair could be smoothed over was unrealistic. By this time, both Cope and Leidy were firmly in Hayden's camp, while Cope and Marsh were already maneuvering in the opening skirmishes of what would become a very open fossil war. In early April 1871, Hayden wrote Baird of having learned that Marsh planned to go west again the coming summer but was attempting to keep his plans a secret from Hayden, while "ventilat[ing] himself freely every where" in complaints against Hayden. When Hayden sponsored expeditions by Cope and Leidy in 1872 it was almost inevitable that he would be drawn into the dispute. Hayden offered to help Cope in an exploration of the Wasatch, a region embracing the northwest corner of Colorado, northeastern Utah, and the southwestern corner of Wyoming. He also coaxed Leidy into exploring the Salt Lake City area and the fossil beds near Fort Bridger, Wyoming. As a result, three vertebrate paleontologists worked the Bridger Basin fossil fields that summer; by season's end, two of them were complaining to Hayden.[35]

¶ Leidy soon found that working in the same fields with Cope was not always a pleasant experience. Writing Hayden that he had enjoyed his trip west and was "so well satisfied with the result of my labor, that I think I shall take another trip to the west next summer," Leidy said he would rather not work in fields where others were competing so violently. While he could not "reasonably object to Prof. Cope or anyone else going to examine the Bridger beds," he did think that when arranging for two parties to make explorations Hayden ought to send them into "different fields." Immediately contrite, Hayden was caught by his desire to retain the services of both Leidy and Cope. He began by sympathizing with Leidy and promising that in the following year he would "most gladly aid you to visit two localities, neither of which will be visited by any one but you." Yet he also warned that while he would do nothing to aid Marsh or Cope in visiting those localities, he could not hinder their doing so on their own. Hayden claimed he had not assigned Cope any areas in which to work. On the contrary, Cope had already made his plans, and when Hayden asked him to leave the Fort Bridger area to Leidy Cope "laughed at the idea of being restricted to any locality and said he intended to go whether I aided him or not." Since Hayden was "anxious to secure the cooperation of such a worker, as an honor to my Corps," there was little he could do "in as much as I pay him no salary and only a portion of his expenses." Thus, while he could sympathize with Leidy's feelings about working in competition with others, he wrote that "it seems almost a necessity." Hayden even suggested that the experience might help Leidy "sympathize with me a little better in the case of Marsh and others," and his letters to Leidy that summer kept him informed of Marsh's activities and urged rapid descriptions and publication of his own discoveries, lest they be anticipated.[36]

¶ Cope needed no such encouragement. While Leidy expressed a dislike of competition and Hayden occasionally put on an ambivalent face regarding it, Cope openly relished rivalry. While still in the field, he sent preliminary notices of his finds to the printer, "desiring them to print them immediately and have them distributed." As he explained to Lesley, with two other parties working in the same field it was "very desirable" that the Hayden Survey secure all the results to which it was entitled. However, it soon emerged that Cope was a little overzealous in his efforts to secure credit for the survey. Only a week after Cope sent his notices of discovery to Lesley, Marsh wrote, suspicious that Cope had "surreptitiously obtained and examined some valuable specimens of fossils belonging to Yale College." Lesley's response, informing Marsh of the papers Cope had sent from the West, corroborated Marsh's suspicions. Marsh quickly accused Cope of violating scientific procedure and etiquette. The least of his charges was that Cope had reneged on an agreement to share prepublication notices designed to avoid questions of priority in discovery and description. More seriously, Marsh raised doubts about the quality of Cope's scientific work and the integrity of his character and sought to have him publicly chastised by the National Academy of Sciences and the American Philosophical Society.[37]

¶ The Cope-Marsh dispute soon spilled over to affect the survey. Cope consistently maintained that "Marsh's noise is a matter of indifference to me." While recognizing that the attacks were "probably directed as much against you [Hayden]" as himself, Cope urged Hayden not to be alarmed at Marsh's "game of bluff." However, Hayden could hardly afford to take the chance; though Cope sought to gain his support Hayden refused to take sides. And not without good reason, as Gardner testified after visiting Yale in early 1873. One objective of the visit was to win the support of the scientific faculty for the survey's effort to produce a "thorough and valuable piece of work that will stand the test of scientific criticism." Only with difficulty could he gain Marsh's endorsement. As Gardner informed Hayden, Marsh wanted rules established "which shall so define the rights of paleontologists as to prevent this everlasting conflict." Following this hint, Hayden did his best to make peace with Marsh, and after "some plain talk" with him in early April 1873 wrote, "I think we are better friends."[38] Apparently, the two expressed some agreement about Cope's character and his work, and Hayden assured Marsh he would not permit Cope "to put anything of a personal or controversial nature affecting [Marsh] in his Report." But Cope soon provoked new howls of rage from New Haven with which Hayden had to deal.

¶ In December 1873, Marsh wrote Hayden referring to their earlier talk and Hayden's assurance on which he had "fully relied." Marsh claimed to have been "greatly surprised and pained," therefore, to discover in Hayden's latest annual report that Cope had claimed many of Marsh's discoveries as his own and had charged Marsh with making mistakes on points where Marsh claimed to have exposed Cope's "blunders." Expressing confidence that Hayden would never have knowingly permitted publication of these passages, Marsh asked Hayden to ensure that "nothing of the same objectionable nature" would be included in his final report and to have "some fair correction of the more important wrong statements" published in his next volume.[39]

¶ After consulting with Baird and Samuel Scudder, Hayden responded that this was impossible. He told Marsh that both Baird and Scudder agreed that Hayden could do nothing except when Cope made personal attacks. As editor, Hayden "insisted on that" and claimed not to know of "a single personal allusion to [Marsh] that could be offensive in the report." But scientific issues such as "dates, claims for species or discoveries" and the like were matters for specialists. Hayden refused to get involved in such issues, contending "I do not consider myself competent to decide disputed claims." At the same time, Hayden claimed that as editor he had no right to cut out such scientific matters; if he did so Cope "would have a right to censure me much," as Cope alone was responsible for the scientific matter. If Marsh had complaints with the contents in that respect, he should "take up the report and review it, making the corrections." As for the forthcoming quarto report, Hayden told Marsh: "as long as he does not allude to you personally in an offensive way, I can do nothing. If he claims your species, you must reclaim them and present your evidence." But scientific corrections or adjudication would have to be settled by such experts as the two disputants could agree upon.[40]

¶ For all his professed limitations, Hayden did inform Cope of Marsh's complaints, only to receive a cavalier response in a postscript urging him to disregard Marsh's "stock in trade of complaints." Cope claimed to be mystified as to why Hayden was so concerned about the opinions of the people at Yale. But as geologist-in-charge, Hayden had to concern himself with the opinions of the people at Yale, who were a force to be reckoned with in Washington. Caught in the middle, Hayden printed his public response in the next annual report, where he insisted that while each assistant of the survey would be held responsible for the correctness of his statement, no "unkind criticisms" of other scientists would ever receive his sanction for publication in a survey report. At the same time, "difference[s] of opinion among true men of science" were to be expected. These would be decided in time, as the evidence was revealed.[41]

¶ But Hayden was not about to give up Cope. As he explained to Marsh, "Prof. Cope is one of the collaborators of the survey, you are not, and have refused to become such though requested by me to become so many times within the last three years." Though Marsh might "take any course [he saw] fit," Hayden's own course was "plain." One reason was his policy of academic freedom, but that policy rested on pragmatic as well as idealistic principles. Hayden sought to multiply the results of the survey. He was not about to jettison one of his most prolific workers for the sake of someone who had refused to assist his efforts. As Hayden explained to John L. LeConte, whom Cope also offended: "As for Cope, I am friendly to him, . . . He furnishes me much valuable matter for my publications and I shall continue my friendly relations with him as long as I can."[42]

¶ The difficulty remained a lasting one for Hayden, and it would be presumptuous to think there was or could have been any decisive way in which he could have abolished the competition between Cope and Marsh, or even between Cope and Leidy. As Hayden admitted, he could do little to control someone who was not in his pay and was quite set on his course, with or without Hayden. If Hayden wished to take advantage of Cope's efforts, Cope was willing to offer them—but only on his own terms. It was an arrangement of convenience. All Hayden could do was attempt to manage the competition as far as it affected the survey. Toward Leidy, this meant offering him facilities to pursue his studies in areas other than those in which Cope and Marsh were working. Toward Marsh, it meant trying to maintain some sort of amicable relations in spite of Cope's activities and trying to make the survey's publications a relatively neutral venue. Neither was an ideal solution, and he was only partly successful since Marsh broke with Hayden in the spring of 1874. Rather, both solutions were fashioned out of the reality of a scramble for priority of discovery. But they were defensible and they worked, for a time.

The "Geologist-in-charge" faced quite a different conflict in the case of Gardner. Though united in a great scientific work they proved not very compatible partners. The essential problem was that Gardner was a star, not a team player, and the survey already had one star, Hayden, who saw no need for another. While enormously useful to Hayden and the survey, Gardner was also a threat to its unity and represented, in Hayden's eyes, a threat to Hayden's role as head of the survey. They did not break until 1875, but signs of trouble existed from the first.

¶ Initially, Hayden fairly exulted in Gardner. He was "a perfect Trump." There was no "better field worker in his line in the United States." Gardner was "harmonizing all the work." Toward the end of the season, however, Hayden began to observe that Gardner had a tendency "to crowd out the central power," and Hayden "commenced slowly and quickly drawing in the reins." Recognizing "no harm" at present, Hayden told Baird that he "*remember[ed] your advice* and see the good sense of it." From now on "the 'U.S. Geologist-in-charge' will hold the *sole power* as long as he [Gardner] has any connection with the Survey." While Gardner was "a good man for the special duty assigned him," Hayden now saw "why King held the *reins* so tight."[43]

¶ Hayden was upset when he wrote to Baird that September in 1873. Having permitted Gardner to write several articles for the *American Journal of Science*, he was dismayed to find that Gardner had failed to highlight the role of his chief. In Hayden's view this was simply "self glorification" on Gardner's part. He responded by telling Gardner "he must observe the rules as is done in the Coast Survey" and give due credit to his superior. Hayden found Gardner "yields in a moment when the screws are put on," but he was extremely ambitious: "give him a little latitude and he takes the reins." Though Gardner had never written "a paragraph for any thing while with King," Hayden believed "the speed with which we are driving things has stirred up his ambition."[44]

¶ Hayden's problem may have been as much a result of his own failure to establish a clear hierarchy and lines of authority as of insubordination on Gardner's part. But Hayden was not the only member of the survey who had trouble with Gardner that summer. While respected for his talent as a topographer, Gardner was a hard taskmaster, and many of the younger members of the corps complained about him for various reasons. Chittenden particularly chafed under Gardner's tutelage as he perfected his topographical skills, finding him "the most disagreeable, egotistical and thoroughly selfish man I ever worked with." The following spring, Chittenden fairly rejoiced to share the news that "the storm about Gardner has finally burst and he knows from the Doctor's [Hayden's] own mouth just how he stands": that "not a young man was on the Survey who did not complain of him, for his meddlesomeness."[45] Perhaps this had the desired effect of reining Gardner in for a season, but during the 1875 season there were more complaints, one of which directly questioned his integrity as a public scientist as well as reflecting upon his recognition of the authority of the geologist-in-charge.

¶ There were complaints about Gardner's playing favorites in supervising the distribution of equipment at the rendezvous camp. There was a rumor that Gardner was paying his packers more than those in the other parties received. But the most serious complaint against his professionalism arose when Gardner decided to conduct his own small mining survey of the southern coalfields of Colorado. The endeavor was designed to benefit several commercial interests in the territory, particularly the Denver and Rio Grande Railway Company. It was an impolitic decision at best, made without consulting Hayden and carried out without informing either Hayden or Endlich, the survey geologist in whose assigned district the region lay. Though Gardner later claimed he received no compensation for the survey and never expected to, from the character and contents of Gardner's *Report upon the Southern Coal and Iron Field of Colorado Territory* Endlich quickly concluded that "the examinations were not made purely for the sake of scientific truth, but more likely to further the interests of some corporation, with which I do not happen to be acquainted." He considered Gardner's actions "wanton interference" at best. Hayden also suspected Gardner's motives in this action, and before summer's end he accused Gardner of having "sold out" the survey to a private corporation and disgraced it.[46] The storm that arose as a result of the Indian fight that same summer did nothing to improve Gardner's position, nor did the fact that his delay in rendezvousing with Gannett before going onto the Indian reservation was caused by his unauthorized investigation of and preparation of the report on the southern Colorado coalfields.

¶ Hayden's efforts to minimize the damage of the Indian fight left him in a dilemma. When newspapers questioned whether the men had actually been in danger or had simply become frightened and later "told the big story to justify their conduct," Hayden confronted a predicament. On the one hand, it would not do to call his men cowards. But he also had to account for the losses incurred without calling too much unfavorable attention to the survey. Hayden needed to balance the real danger with the claim that the survey could operate safely, and thus avoid giving the army an opening to capture his organization on the pretext of its need for protection. Yet while Hayden sought to maintain a low profile on the issue, Gardner kept calling attention to the incident and defending himself against charges of cowardice or imprudence. By mid-October, even Gannett, initially a strong supporter of Gardner's actions, felt he had "made himself and all of us ridiculous enough."[47]

¶ At this point, the stage was set for Gardner's departure, though Gardner failed to understand the necessity, or at least the inevitability, of it. Instead, Gardner believed himself the victim of Hayden's "inflamed passions" and suspicions that he was seeking to take Hayden's place as head of the survey. As an example of this, Gardner pointed to the appearance in the *North American Review* of a number of articles published during the summer that attributed to Gardner all the honor due the geographical work of the survey as well as its generally improved condition.[48] While the acknowledgment confirmed Gardner's own opinion of his worth, he said it had only inflamed Hayden's jealousy, which, according to Gardner, was always bubbling just below the surface, had led to "one outburst after another" in the past, and only ceased when Hayden "was in trouble and wanted my help."

¶ Gardner claimed that "for the sake of the great work in which we are engaged" he had borne these "abusive tirades" in the past, but now things were more serious. As Gardner viewed the situation, Hayden, piqued by the favorable attention Gardner had received and annoyed by the criticism his newspaper accounts of the Indian fight had drawn, was making a pretext of Gardner's report on the southern coalfields of Colorado to accuse him of "having sold the Survey out to a private corporation." Gardner asserted that Hayden had begun to make these allegations long before consulting with him or giving him an opportunity to explain his actions. Gardner claimed that upon hearing of the charges he immediately went to see Hayden and asked for a chance to clear himself, but Hayden refused to listen, insisting "that he would not believe differently from what he did 'if God Almighty' should tell him it was untrue." Gardner first resolved to wait until the storm passed. However, as Hayden grew "more violent in his abuse, giving rise to a very strong current of feeling against me in the Survey," he decided it was time to leave. Thus, he handed in his resignation, "expressing the wish that if it was agreeable to him [Hayden] I should like to finish the primary triangulation and put the record in an intelligible form, so that the proof of the accuracy of the maps might not be lost." Hayden accepted the resignation but not the offer. Gardner could work up what he had finished so far; someone else would finish the triangulation.[49]

¶ Gardner's version of events, recounted to his mother and a close friend who bore no affection for Hayden, reveals little awareness that Hayden did not have to manufacture all of the ill feeling. If Hayden was to be geologist-in-charge, he probably could not afford to keep Gardner much longer. The survey was a cooperative effort, with room for only one "central power," and Gardner had little idea how many of the men on the survey he had antagonized. While his pretensions and behavior sometimes afforded amusement at his expense, they also provoked resentment by men anxious for their own share of credit and recognition.[50] Most of them could do little more than mutter and complain, but Hayden was in a different position. While he might have been mistaken in thinking Gardner sought to displace him, he was not mistaken in judging the survey now well enough established scientifically that it could get along without Gardner. Self-centered to the end, Gardner never admitted the implications of his "errors in judgement of policy."

¶ Nor was Hayden wrong to accuse Gardner of having "sold the Survey out to a private corporation." Though not a geologist, Gardner's report on the southern coalfields of Colorado was presented as a geological report, lending all the weight and prestige of the survey to it and the companies it benefited. Obviously promotional, it clearly aimed at advancing the interests of the Denver and Rio Grande Railway and its land development company, the Colorado Central Improvement Company. If Hayden did not assign him the task, and Gardner surely would have claimed as much in his defense if Hayden had, then to have undertaken a coal survey within Endlich's district without Hayden's knowledge was more than a minor "error in judgement of policy." It was a clear case of insubordination.

¶ But this was more than a contest of two strong personalities. It also was a matter of making a scientific and bureaucratic career. Gardner had been King's associate during the survey of the fortieth parallel and had seen King make a number of private geological surveys during those years, for which he was well remunerated. In a fashion, his actions in conducting and reporting on the survey of the coalfields of southern Colorado were similar to King's surveys of gold and silver mines. But Hayden had given up making surveys directly oriented to private interests. In earlier years, Hayden had been deeply involved in the very interests Gardner was serving by this survey, yet some opportune congressional advice early in 1873 reminded Hayden that his first obligation was to the economic interests of citizens of the United States. From that point on, Hayden's reports, though continuing to keep a focus on economic possibilities, shied away from promoting particular industrial or commercial interests. They presented the appearance of impartiality and offered information that was open to exploitation by all. Hayden had little incentive to appear too closely linked with particular land or mining speculation interests. Instead, he sought to build a reputation as a neutral bureau. His goal and Gardner's actions could hardly have been more divergent on this issue.[51]

¶ Yet there remains a final question: why did Hayden not simply dismiss Gardner rather than grow ever "more violent in his abuse" of the man? While the ultimate answer to this question remains a matter of speculation, Hayden's actions were signs of weakness in his administrative ability and were probably related to his character. They suggest a lack of self-confidence or inability to discipline Gardner in spite of earlier claims that he "yields in a moment when the screws are put on." Hayden was suspicious of threats to his authority, preeminence, or position, and there was probably more than a grain of truth in Gardner's assertion of Hayden's "ever smoulder[ing]" jealousy.

¶ But Hayden had dealt with threats before and even met them with an impressive degree of patience and self-control. In the 1850s, he and Meek countered threats to their scientific priority from both James Hall and George Swallow, and in the 1860s Hayden counseled Meek to ignore renewed threats by Swallow because their own claims were secure. Just the previous summer he had dealt with the threat posed by Wheeler and the Army Corps of Engineers so convincingly as to make them look foolish and himself the champion of all reasonable civilian scientists.[52] Was this threat too close? Or did Gardner still seem indispensable for some reason? He certainly was no longer essential for the survey's scientific work, as Hayden recognized in allowing him to leave before finishing the final results of his work. Perhaps Hayden wanted to avoid breaking links with the political support Gardner helped command and sought to do so by putting the onus on him to resign from the survey rather than be dismissed from it. If so, Hayden was less than successful in the effort and probably would have done better to discharge Gardner for insubordination. It would have made for a cleaner cut and would have been accepted by most of Hayden's supporters. As for his detractors, there was little hope of convincing them no matter what he did. By handling the incident as he did, Hayden not only let Gardner set the terms but also put him in a position to complain of unfair treatment.

The work of the "Geologist-in-charge" did not end with the completion of the season's fieldwork. The results of the summer's work had to be presented to his public. For this, the center of activity—and the focus of management—shifted to the survey's Washington office, a bustling site that was described by the Washington correspondent for the *New York Times* following a visit in the spring of 1875. At the time, the survey occupied the upper two and a half floors of an office building at the corner of Eleventh Street and Pennsylvania Avenue in northwest Washington. The newspaperman found the survey's artists among its most interesting characters and chose to focus on William Henry Holmes and William Henry Jackson. An artist as well as a geologist, Holmes was using his topographical sketches to construct a scale model of a section of the Rocky Mountain system, complete with the "relative heights of the peaks and ranges, the courses of the rivers, and the more prominent features of the region," all designed "with the strictest scientific accuracy" and intended to "convey . . . a very complete idea of that country." Jackson had his own set of rooms, conspicuous for the odor of chemicals emanating from it. Nearly as skilled with the artist's pen as with his cameras, the shelves in Jackson's office were filled with sketchbooks and albums of photographs. Additional photographic views of all sizes were suspended along the walls, while in the window hung transparencies of mountain scenery. Cameras of various sizes, the tools of his trade as a frontier photographer, were scattered around the room in various places, as were the rifles and cartridge belts "with which every member of the field parties seemed to be provided."[53]

¶ Even from this brief sketch, the anonymous correspondent's description provides a good picture of the sorts of activity that took place in the Washington office. Host to frequent visitors, it was also the site of a great deal of work in topography, drafting, and photography as well as editing and correspondence. And it was the place where a great deal, but by no means all, of the geological reports were written. Most of the natural history work, however, was performed "off-site," by people with institutional connections elsewhere, at various colleges and universities, the Smithsonian, the Academy of Natural Sciences, or other museums. Yet there were exceptions, and Thomas, Gill, and Coues all combined positions as secretary-editor with natural history research or writing.

¶ After the close of each season's fieldwork, usually sometime in November, the parties returned east. Hayden generally allowed them a few days—sometimes as much as a couple of weeks—to visit families and friends before requiring his geological and topographical corps to assemble in Washington and begin working on their reports. In the meantime, the paleontologists, zoologists, and naturalists who had accompanied the western parties returned to their own homes to begin working up their assigned collections of specimens. Others, who had not taken to the field, simply waited to have their boxes delivered. For all, there was much to be done and little time in which to do it.

¶ Lesquereux may stand as an example for those working in natural history since his letters give an indication of the amount of labor involved and its degree of difficulty. The implications posed by the mass of materials collected by the survey take concrete form in Lesquereux's protests against Hayden's insistent calls for manuscripts for his annual reports and Lesquereux's equally insistent appeals that he be paid for his efforts. In December 1870, Lesquereux claimed that his work for Hayden's report on the survey of Nebraska had consumed fifty-three days "and a part of the nights too" in examining and comparing specimens, determining their specific relationships, and preparing plates. Three years later, chastising Hayden for unreasonable expectations, Lesquereux told him: "you do not realize the amt. of materials which have passed my hands for the reports of yours. In the catalogue of yours, 1300 specimens are labeled after examinations. A large number of useless and undeterminable specimens are not in the list. From my own explorations of these two years, I have 1500 specimens also in catalogue. Only those who know the difficulties of identification of fragments of fossil plants may know how much time is necessary for the careful examination of all these specimens."[54]

¶ Meanwhile in Washington, Hayden, with his geologists, topographers, and photographer, was immersed in the multitude of details involved in turning a season's collection of field notes, observations, sketches, and negatives into an annual report of progress. Finished drawings and engravings had to be made from the sketches. Topographical data had to be translated into maps, upon which the geological data could be colored. Field notes had to be reworked into a narrative of the geology of the country. They had only a few frenetic months to produce a report that would impress appropriate members of Congress before the spring round of hearings on the next year's appropriations.[55]

¶ To facilitate all this work, Hayden eventually tried to impose a system of regular office hours on his staff. The effort was less than successful, however, and even led to outright rebellion when in February 1877 the geologist Endlich expressed dismay that Hayden had considered it "necessary to appoint definite hours of work" and sought to be excused from such an arrangement, claiming his "utter impossibility to keep them." Endlich offered to guarantee completion of his maps and reports within the same average time as the other geologists on the survey or any given date Hayden might set.[56] But his social standing and professional pride rebelled at submitting to regular hours, as if he were a mere clerk.

¶ Endlich had some reason for pride. His father had been the U.S. consul at Basel, Switzerland (1857–61), so the family must have possessed political connections. Endlich himself was one of the most polished men of the survey, with a talent for exercising diplomacy among the more cultivated men of Congress. He had political connections of his own; his fellow townsman from Reading, Pennsylvania, Hiester Clymer, was elected to Congress in 1872 and served into the 1880s. Endlich could also boast of a fine education. He was the only geologist on the Hayden Survey who had studied abroad, first at the Polytechnic Institute in Stuttgart and then at the University of Tübingen, where he obtained a doctorate in natural sciences. He later returned to Germany for another year to study at the University of Breslau and at Freiberg, home to a world-renowned mining academy. Upon his return from Europe, Endlich was soon hired by the Smithsonian (1872) as its resident mineralogist, geologist, chemist, and mining expert. In 1873, he also took employment with Hayden when the latter expanded the survey's corps to begin the survey of Colorado. Yet Endlich seemed ambivalent toward Hayden, who was of a lower social class and possessed a less distinguished educational background. On the one hand, he shared with Hayden a competitive personality. He loved a good fight and took delight in the byzantine machinations of the annual contests for appropriations as he lobbied his friend Clymer, who sat on the House Appropriations Committee. But he also displayed an independence bordering on insubordination, as the incident regarding work hours illustrates.[57]

¶ Endlich does not appear to have been a typical example, however. While all of Hayden's men acknowledged him to be a hard taskmaster, most were utterly loyal to him and returned the support he gave them. Their letters suggest that they formed a tight community, and most of the young men got along well with one another and the geologist-in-charge—as long as they kept their sense of humor. A letter from Holmes to Peale, bringing him up to date with the goings-on in Washington, reveals how they humored Hayden's admitted eccentricities: "Hayden is in ecstasies. 'Oh! Oh!' says he jumping clear of the floor with a bundle of them (the illustrations and maps) in his hands. 'My good God, these are *gorgeous, extraordinary—This will stir Europe up to the very bottom.*' Don't trouble yourself about Hayden."[58]

¶ Though there was plenty of work to be done in the winter and spring and little enough time to do it, there was also time for the men to enjoy themselves in Washington, particularly late in the spring as they waited for Congress to make its yearly verdict on their fate. They did so with as much enthusiasm as they toured the West during summers and falls. Besides, whatever the press of the work, life in Washington in the 1870s hardly followed a hectic pace. It was a southern city, and Chittenden for one found it congenial. The building programs of the Grant years had begun to turn the capital into "a beautiful city, *roomy, refined,* and *clean.*" The natives were "delightfully lazy and luxurious," and others were "obliged by the prevailing law of circumstances to be so too. . . . Breakfast not till after eight, a lunch at half past twelve, and then at half past four comes dinner: making the day be included between such narrow limits, no one seems in a hurry."[59]

¶ Hayden, however, was almost always in a hurry. It was one of his most consistent characteristics. He had been in a hurry to make a name for himself in science. He was usually in a hurry to get into the field in the spring. He hurried to cover as much territory, collect as many specimens, and make as many discoveries as possible. And he hurried to get his findings before the public. He pushed himself, his men, and his supporters. He knew that while there was an abundance of "golden opportunities" in the West for men like himself, they would not last forever. To collect them one had to bestir oneself since fortune favored not only the brave but also those who were alert and enterprising enough to take advantage of the possibilities presented to the entrepreneur. Comprehending Hayden in this way leads to the exploration of a number of issues not normally thought of as part of science. But there can be no doubt that they were important concerns of the "Geologist-in-charge." Had he ignored them, the survey could not have survived, let alone grown. As it did grow, dealing with these issues called for an assortment of entrepreneurial skills. While Hayden's recruitment patterns helped nurture important political patrons, gradually increasing professionalism served to enhance the survey's technical expertise, which strengthened its scientific credentials and expanded its constituencies. His management of the survey and its work involved issues of facilitating production by building or maintaining morale among his collaborators, shielding the survey from attacks, and neutralizing or eliminating threats, both from within and without. But all of this was in view of the final product: the documents and other items that could be presented to Hayden's various publics in return for their support and could in turn be used to argue for more support.

7

Publishing and Publicizing

Papers gain nothing by lying in drawers. —Cope to Hayden, 26 November 1873

Every one can understand a picture. —"The Hayden Survey," *New York Times*, 27 April 1875

Shortly after Hayden's death, Archibald Giekie commented that "no one who has not been in some measure admitted behind the scenes of political wire-pulling in the States, can realize what had to be undertaken by the man of science who would obtain and retain an annual subsidy from Congress for scientific investigation in the days when Hayden carried on his explorations." As director of the contemporaneous geological survey of Scotland, Geikie was in a position to know that dealing with government demanded political as well as scientific skills. Not all those who headed geological surveys in mid-nineteenth-century America possessed the combination of scientific and political expertise necessary to enable their enterprises to survive. For instance, while Whitney's survey of California "set the basic foundations for an understanding of the geology of California," its leader made a fatal strategic error in his failure to recognize "the political necessity of publishing intermediate reports of the work of the survey, preferring rather to wait until all fieldwork was completed."[1] As a result, political attacks against supporting pure science in the midst of a statewide recession spelled the survey's death knell.

¶ Hayden did not make that mistake. He knew the importance of promptly reporting his findings, especially on topics of interest to the various groups whose support was essential for the continuation of the survey. He also recognized the value of keeping the survey in the public eye, and he exploited popular interests to advance his survey. Interest in the West was widespread and wide ranging. It included potential for economic development, discovery, and exploitation of its natural resources; prospects for settlement; as well as scientific interests and simple curiosity. The West was a mysterious and unknown place, filled with wonders, a romantic subject. Hayden exploited all of these interests. His practice represented more than a logical consequence of responding to a political environment; it was a mode of science in service of the public interest, wherever that interest might lie. In the process, he helped reveal and explain the West to an eastern (and global) public—a task in which all of the Great Surveys took part.

¶ Its official publications composed the fundamental means for keeping the survey before the public as well as fulfilling the requirements of Congress, but Hayden also kept the survey before the public eye by other means. Magazine and newspaper articles as well as public lectures, all frequently accompanied by illustrations based upon Jackson's photographs, all represented ways of reporting on the survey's activities. The photographs themselves constituted a powerful marketing tool for the survey, as did Moran's paintings of some of the more spectacular features uncovered by Hayden and his men. Finally, the Centennial Exhibition at Philadelphia provided Hayden with a chance to exhibit his wares before a world's fair, an opportunity he exploited to the full. The very breadth of his approach corresponded to the breadth of his own interests and of his various audiences.

Hayden's publication strategy was founded on two basic principles: rapidity and monopoly. Rapid publication of practical results helped create and sustain an impression of usefulness. Monopoly, presenting the survey's findings solely through its own publications, ensured that the survey's results were clearly attributed to it and to its director, highlighting their value to the nation. Success was measured by the demand for the survey's publications, which could be translated into influence with Hayden's congressional patrons.

¶ Mindful of his different constituencies, Hayden brought out a wide variety of publications through his survey, which he grouped into six categories. The first consisted of his "annual" or "preliminary" reports, which were issued as inexpensively produced octavo publications and printed in the tens of thousands in the later years of the survey. Following on the preliminary reports, Hayden added a series of "final" reports—elaborate quarto volumes containing expensive plates illustrating specialized monographic studies. Given the greater expense and more restricted audiences of the final reports, Hayden issued the quartos in much smaller press runs than the annual reports. In 1873, Hayden expanded his publication program to include the first of his *Bulletins*. Designed as an occasional publication to secure rapid dissemination of important or timely information, the *Bulletin* soon evolved into a scientific journal. Published at minimal expense as an octavo with simple illustrations, it was distributed free of charge in large numbers. A fourth group comprised Hayden's "miscellaneous publications," which responded to diverse special needs.

¶ The last two groups of survey publications were the maps and "unclassified publications." Maps quite obviously come to mind in considering a geological and geographical survey, but the public demand for them and Hayden's use of them to broaden his networks of support has already been discussed in chapter 5. The unclassified publications were a rather arbitrary group and were brought together in Hayden's catalog as publications that did not logically fall under any of the other headings and had "no connection, ostensibly or otherwise, with each other."[2] In fact, most of them had only a tenuous connection with the survey itself and were actually the publications of the Entomological Commission, which operated under the supervision of the Hayden Survey. The group also included other items, such as the final report of the survey of Nebraska, a couple of earlier catalogs of publications and photographs, and an early version of one of Cope's reports for the survey. As much as anything else, these publications illustrate Hayden's propensity for "adopting" work that had at best a peripheral connection to his survey. However, since the other publications also exhibit this trait, these unclassified publications can be safely ignored.

Hayden took particular pride in the promptness with which his survey's results were published. Several motives contributed to his policy of rapid publication. In the early years, his superiors' requests that his reports be available for inclusion in their annual reports constituted a primary factor. The need to present proof to Congress of the survey's usefulness, in support of his efforts to gain annual appropriations, was also fundamental. Besides self-interest, Hayden also sincerely desired that the results of the survey's work be useful as immediately as possible. Unfortunately, the rush to get into print held both challenges and hazards for Hayden.

¶ As the size and number of survey publications grew, especially after 1871, managing them became a full-time job that required a number of skills. Not the least was a measure of diplomacy to deal with the competing demands of printers and scientists. As chief executive of the survey, Hayden had to coordinate, personally or by proxy, the disparate elements involved in publication. These included obtaining copy, distributing proofs and getting them returned, meeting the demands of printers regarding both schedule and money, and guiding his various publications through the press and bindery and into distribution. Additionally, he had to satisfy his authors' demands for corrections, reprints, plates, and the like; commission accurately drawn, printed, and correctly inserted illustrations; and secure appropriations to support the work. Though Hayden delegated a number of these time-consuming tasks to a series of editors over the years, there remained details for which he had the final responsibility.[3] Further, while he delegated the tasks, he refused to delegate much authority where money was concerned.

¶ Hayden permitted his scientists a great deal of freedom in working up the results of their investigations. As editor, he accepted the reports and published them; his most proactive suggestion may have been the request that they make their reports both "popular and scientific" in order to widen their appeal to readers. Even in the face of insistent criticism, Hayden did not presume either the right or the expertise to censor or exercise stringent controls over the reports offered to him. Instead, he preferred to let them stand on their own scientific merits, even to the point of publishing in the same volume reports containing contradictory conclusions, as in the case of competing interpretations of the age of the lignite strata in Colorado and Wyoming by Meek, Lesquereux, and Cope. In his own report introducing the volume, Hayden simply summarized their conclusions and made no attempt to decide the question. Nor was it desirable to do so since it best served Hayden's purpose not to impose uniformity of opinion on scientific questions. Not only was he sure the question would be resolved eventually as a result of further study, but his attitude provided his professionals with an incentive to do their best work, while simultaneously pointing out the need for more research and thus more funding for the survey.[4] Rapid publication of the reports was far more important than having initial results that were in complete agreement.

¶ Hayden always seemed to be in a rush to get the reports done. Giving Chittenden permission to remain at home for a few days after a season's campaign, he added: "I hope you can do some work at home." Hayden frankly acknowledged his dependence upon the rapid publication of each season's results. As he told Leidy in September 1870, "my preliminary Report this winter must be a good one." Two months later, he urged Leidy to hasten completion of a full report: "Do not fail in this because I have much at stake." Two years later, following Leidy's western expedition for the survey, Hayden put it bluntly: "I am most anxious that your report be full in order that the results may tell on another appropriation."[5]

¶ The rush to publish exacted a price. The annual reports have frequently been criticized as "shoddy" and "filled with inaccuracies." One source of defects lay in the fact that some of Hayden's geologists had no opportunity to correct proof sheets because they were in the field when the report finally went to press. However, not all of Hayden's authors were willing to dispense with the opportunity to review proofs, and some, such as Cope, insisted on their rights while exhibiting little attention to the needs of printers and editors. For instance, when sending a manuscript for the *Fourth Annual Report*, Cope told Hayden, "*Be sure to let me read proofs* of it," a demand he repeated at least twice in the next few weeks.[6]

¶ Rapid publication also frequently led to an unfinished appearance in Hayden's reports, which was especially apparent in the first two years when the survey was under the General Land Office. Hayden recognized the problem, and in his preliminary report during the second year he apologized for it: "these notes are prepared in the field after the labors of the day are completed, far away from books and collections, and without that opportunity for mature reflection which should characterize a final report." But it was not only the reports written in the field that had an unfinished appearance, and even friendly critics complained of Hayden's writing style. After reading one manuscript in 1869, which was under consideration for publication by the American Philosophical Society, Lesley informed Hayden that he found the narrative style "slovenly in the extreme." Not only had he written the text "straight ahead and at railroad speed," but a copyist had punctuated portions of it into an "unintelligible mass." Complaining that "there is absolutely no system of subdivision '*at all, at all,*'" Lesley pleaded: "I wish to heavens you would give me a very little liberty to correct the proof." Still, Lesley would not have asked for permission to edit the manuscript if he had not seen value in it. He agreed with geologist and fellow APS member John L. LeConte that Hayden's manuscript "contained such important matter that it was a pity it had not been put into a more agreeable dress." In spite of Hayden's "slovenly style," which led Lesley to fear for the society's "belles lettres reputation," he had been "charmed" by the narration and "admire[d] the steady tramp of [the] narrative." Lesley judged that "a *very* little attention to the proof-reading will satisfy everybody."[7]

¶ Most historians who have written about Hayden have mentioned a characteristic lack of systematic detail in his writings. Less friendly critics, though admitting he was often correct in his general conclusions on questions of geology, have noted that "shoddiness became the hallmark of [Hayden's] reports," evidently failing to find much that was charming in his rambling narratives. More sympathetic reviewers have recognized that in adopting a diary style in his writings, Hayden "sacrificed organization for speed in placing his miscellaneous observations before the public . . . revealing the wonders and resources of the West to the widest possible audience."[8] But few have considered Hayden's reports as narrative works per se though this would make it possible to understand Hayden writings on their own terms.

¶ Lesley's remarks on "belles lettres," "charm," and the "steady tramp of [Hayden's] narrative" provide important hints for a true appreciation of Hayden's writing style. Charm and steady tramp are characteristics of one of the most popular literary genres of the late-eighteenth-century English world, a time when scientific writers still aspired to belles lettres style. Travel narratives had become so popular by the beginning of the nineteenth century that a "firmly defined tradition" directed how one was to write down one's observations and reflections.

Critics expected a well-composed travel narrative to join pleasure with instruction as it embraced both science and history. The mixture made the genre a fitting mode for scientific explorers, or scientific travelers as they were more apt to call themselves, and imitated the style of Alexander Humboldt, who set the pattern, and Charles Darwin, his ardent imitator.[9]

¶ Travel narratives were as popular in the United States as they were in England. They were, in fact, one of the first forms of literature on the New World, as European visitors and residents described it, and from the first many of them were works of science. From these beginnings, American natural history essayists evolved their own characteristic genre, which also enjoyed a wide popularity in the mid–nineteenth century. Nor did writers disdain to write in more than one genre, as the careers of Ralph Waldo Emerson, Henry Thoreau, and John Burroughs illustrate. All three wrote in a tradition inaugurated by Gilbert White in his 1789 *The Natural History of Selborne*, one of the most frequently published books in English, with nearly thirty editions between 1789 and 1854. Often used as a standard for writing natural history, White's book began with observations and collections and moved on to cataloging and categorizing before proceeding to interpretive description and generalization.[10]

¶ The travel narrative style presented an obvious advantage to the natural history writer in its relatively easy expansiveness since almost anything observed was potentially fit for inclusion. Aiming both to entertain and to inform, writers received praise for providing "descriptions that are novel in content and clear in the manner in which they portray the country" by taking notice of new places or places that others had not described, or described in the same way. Their accounts were not to be "purely pedantic" but also provide "some image" of the place. At the same time, observation had to be balanced with reflections on the meaning of what was observed, as Darwin did in *The Voyage of the Beagle*. That work was a "combination of field naturalism, personal narrative, travelogue, speculation, and history" that all the while exhibited a marvelous catholicity of interests in natural history: "mountain vistas, the Brazilian slave system, condors, Argentinian politics, Indian names, South Sea missionaries, coral reefs, Noah's flood, the state of the English nation, Handel's music, the future of manufactures in Australia,

Humboldt's *Voyages*, and, of course, the vast problem of the development and disappearance of animal species, all to be readily available for description, comment, and reference." Yet while *The Voyage of the Beagle* is most frequently called a "journal," Darwin himself was "careful to point out that it is in fact 'a history' written 'in the *form* of a journal.'" The distinction reflects the important difference between unself-conscious observation and ordered scientific observation.[11]

¶ That Hayden was not the only American geologist in the middle of the nineteenth century to write in such a mode in an effort to reach a broad audience is clear from the cases of two contemporary examples. Raphael Pumpelly and Clarence King, two of America's best-known Gilded Age geologists, each succeeded in obtaining what Hayden did not: recognition as a literary author. While their success was remarkable, their pursuit of it was not. After completing a report on a geological exploration of China in the early 1860s, a region quite inaccessible to the average tourist, Pumpelly composed a narrative of his travels intended for the general reader. Aiming for the same literary audience Humboldt, Darwin, and Frémont had cultivated, his *Across America and Asia* entertained readers with reports of encounters with strange cultures while serving to popularize geology at the same time.[12]

¶ King did not have to go all the way to Asia for inspiration. His literary imagination found plenty of stimulation in the Sierra Nevadas, enough to prompt what many critics agreed was "the first real literature of the Sierra," *Mountaineering in the Sierra Nevada*, published in 1872. King's "slight book of travel," as he modestly called it, was not a simple travel narrative but a natural historian's book of stories, tales based on his mountain travels. Yet this hardly stood in the way of appreciation. His descriptions of nature and mountain scenery were so well drawn that the work fit neatly in the natural history tradition. Yet admiring contemporaries valued even more his "studies of character . . . because Mr. King is a humorist, and has an evident relish for the type of humor in which the extreme West excels."[13] *Mountaineering* both informed and entertained.

¶ Though Hayden never matched the literary graces of these geological colleagues, he came closest in 1872, the same year King published *Mountaineering*. In that year, Hayden published his first reports on Yellowstone, whose wonders inspired him to use some of his most polished prose to convey in words an adequate appreciation of the sights he saw there. However, he was not invited to become a member of New York's Century Club, the acknowledged center of New York's social and literary life in the mid-nineteenth century, as were King and Pumpelly. Nor did Hayden write up to the scientific standards of King's *Systematic Geology*. Yet none of this need diminish the power of his writing. Hayden wrote not just for scientists, who could generally appreciate the worth of his writings. He also wrote for nonscientists, government bureaucrats, representatives, and a general population of "all classes of intelligent people of our country from Maine to Florida," in whom he sought to instill some appreciation for the values of science. His travelogue style of narrating the route he followed and of reporting the geology as it was uncovered along the way, as well as his remarks upon interesting landmarks and incidents, followed the same style as Darwin's *Voyage of the Beagle*. As with Darwin, Hayden's language was calculated to establish a rapport, leading the reader to visualize and experience the landscape. While a younger generation of professional scientists may not have approved, Hayden's reports fit into an older style of scientific literature, one perhaps more appropriate for a scientist who was also a public servant. It facilitated prompt dissemination of information and possibilities, while also providing general instruction.[14]

¶ Whatever style Hayden adopted, rapid publication posed risks, as he well recognized. As he put it, "an unkind critic" might fault the survey's reports for "defects . . . which might not have existed with delay." But he judged the risk acceptable in view of the good he sought to promote by bringing the results before the public "at as early a date as possible." As for mistakes, which "cannot reasonably be avoided," Hayden advised that "we hope to correct them in future publications."[15] Once again, he balanced his desire to educate broadly with his confidence in the eventual success of the scientific effort. And once again, he took an entrepreneurial risk that success could richly reward but which posed an opening to competitors, should they be able to combine and take advantage of it.

¶ Perhaps the best measure of the success of Hayden's policy is the reception his annual reports met. In the early years especially they received almost unanimous approval, even if there were reservations regarding particulars. Lesley and John L. LeConte were not the only ones who appreciated "the great essential worth" of his observations, which were at times "as surprising as they are important for the higher geological questions of the day." Packard at the *American Naturalist* gladly reviewed his reports "at some length" in an effort to "call attention to [their] value." Dana reposed such trust in Hayden's work that he confidently handed articles submitted by Hayden directly to the printer of the *American Journal of Science* without pausing to review them. It is no surprise, then, that when he thanked Hayden for a copy of his report for 1869, Dana expressed "no doubt of its great value." But Dana also recognized shortcomings in Hayden's work. Complimenting Hayden on the map that accompanied his report that year as a "highly interesting one," Dana pointed out that "Of course you have not traced the Potsdam [formation] around, or along the sides of, all the mountains represented on the map as bounded by it" and asked if, notwithstanding this, "you . . . regard the distribution of it you give as beyond all reasonable doubt?"[16]

¶ The mining and engineering press also took a keen interest in the survey's reports. Hayden made sure that editors of these bureaus at newspapers were regular recipients of the annual reports, as were the editors of such trade journals as the *Engineering and Mining Journal*, and he was no doubt pleased when his efforts to cultivate their favorable attention met with success. William Bross, publisher of the *Chicago Tribune* and possessed of a lively interest in railroad developments, geological features, and the agricultural potential of the northern plains states, acknowledged the receipt of the 1869 annual report with "very great pleasure." He assured Hayden that he had "looked over it with very great interest. The facts you have so graphically grouped together are of permanent and inestimable value," and he promised to send Hayden a copy of his notice in the *Tribune*.[17]

¶ Rossiter Raymond, editor of the *Engineering and Mining Journal* and a supporter of government geological surveys generally, was also a strong supporter of the Hayden Survey in its early years and a man whose opinion counted. After graduating from the Brooklyn Polytechnic Institute in 1858, Raymond spent three years studying in Germany at the Universities of Heidelberg and Munich and the Royal Mining Academy of Freiberg. Following service in the Civil War, Raymond worked as a consulting engineer in New York City; editor and then coeditor of the *American Journal of Mining* (subsequently the *Engineering and Mining Journal*), 1867–90; U.S. commissioner of mining statistics, 1868–76; and professor of economic geology at Lafayette College, Pennsylvania, 1870–81. He soon developed an interest in the relation of government and mining and as editor took special notice of all of the western surveys. Though he did not think much of Hayden as a geologist or mining engineer, neither did Raymond dismiss the survey's reports as valueless. The *Journal*'s review of the *Fifth Annual Report* in 1872 commended Hayden as "an energetic and indefatigable traveller and collector" who had availed himself "of the services of some of the ablest naturalists in the country." Hayden's own report was not so favorably received, however. His statements were deemed too "sweeping" and his theory of the geology of Montana too "simple." Though it might prove "convenient for amateurs," the reviewer noted, "it will need much revision and correction in details."[18]

¶ According to the editor of the *Engineering and Mining Journal*, the value of the survey's reports resided more in the writings of Hayden's collaborators and assistants. Hailing the *Report* for 1873 as "by far the most thorough and valuable of the progress reports of Dr. Hayden," Raymond focused first on the contributions of the entire corps of assistants, all of which he reviewed favorably before turning to Hayden's personal report. Though disavowing any disposition to "undervalue [Hayden's] contributions to scientific literature," Raymond suggested it would be "better for his reputation" if Hayden limited his comments to subjects "with which he may reasonably consider himself well acquainted." But Raymond was not ready to condemn Hayden or his survey's reports for "the small imperfections of a volume so crammed with valuable information." In his opinion, Hayden's strength in fieldwork and ability as an organizer more than compensated for his scientific shortcomings. Relying on the Hayden Survey's "practical results," Raymond judged "the country is well served" by it.[19]

For all their merits and whatever their faults, Hayden's annual reports remained in a real sense "preliminary." Hearing a rumor that a scathing review of his 1870 *Report* would appear in the *American Journal of Science*—he suspected Marsh as either the author or instigator—Hayden complained that it would be "unfair" to review "a mere report of Progress" too harshly. While he believed his annual reports the "full equal to the usual reports of progress of our State Surveys," he did not look to them to serve as the final synthesis of the survey's scientific work.[20] For that, Hayden looked to a separate category of publications.

¶ Though his instructions in 1867 called for both reports of progress and a final report, not until 1872 did Congress appropriate any money "for the preparation and publication of the maps, charts, geological sections, and other engravings necessary to illustrate the final report of the United States geological survey of the Territories." By then, Hayden's plans embraced a series of five monographs. He would have three volumes on paleontology—one on invertebrates, another on vertebrates, and a third on botany. There would be a fourth volume by Hayden on the geology, supported by "profiles, sections, maps and other illustrations." And there would be a fifth volume, consisting of "separate memoirs . . . prepared by several authors" on the contemporary natural history of the areas investigated. Later, Hayden expanded his plans and decided to extend the series indefinitely; it eventually embraced thirteen volumes, of which twelve were printed.[21]

¶ Once funding for engraving and printing was approved, Hayden lost no time in getting the work underway. In one respect, it was already well along as he had had many of the drawings made during the previous winters. But aside from Leidy, who had already begun his manuscript on the *Extinct Vertebrate Fauna of the Western Territories*, most of the other subjects in the series still lacked authors. Hayden knew whom he wanted, however. He asked Meek to take their collections of the Nebraska Territory and the Upper Missouri in hand and promptly recruited Cope, who had increasingly become a collaborator of the survey, to finish working up his "Kansas collections." For fossil botany, he turned to Newberry and Lesquereux; both had done work for him in the past and both had portions of his collections. To begin the memoirs in contemporary natural history, Hayden agreed to publish Thomas's work on grasshoppers.[22]

¶ Initially conceived as final reports on the survey's findings, Hayden soon expanded the series' scope far beyond the limits implicit in such a purpose. In some respects, the expansion seems mundane. So that the reports would be as complete as possible, he instructed authors to include everything regarding the West that was in the areas of their expertise, whether or not the specimens described or discussed had actually been collected by the survey or were even found in the territory covered by the survey's explorations. More significantly, Hayden also determined to reach beyond the work of the survey in accepting manuscripts for publication. In presenting volume 1, Hayden wrote that the reports were "intended to embody the more original and technical results of the survey," yet their ultimate scope was much broader, including elements that could hardly be counted among its results by any stretch of the imagination.[23]

¶ In issuing Packard's monograph on the geometrid moths, Hayden clearly went beyond the work of the survey. Though Packard had received survey assistance, the bulk of his material was collected under other auspices. Yet Hayden felt confident the monograph would meet with "the hearty approval of all entomologists, [and] of scientific men generally." He stated that adopting such outside work was "one of the most important parts of the work of such surveys, second only to their chief object, to seize upon the opportunity of completing such monographs," arguing that "otherwise, materials which individuals and various expeditions have been collecting, may remain for years in private or public museums, or perhaps be destroyed, without any systematic arrangement ever having been made."[24]

¶ Aside from professed practical usefulness, Hayden's policy also served strategic concerns. While the annual reports aimed at a general audience, the final reports addressed a scientific audience. Hayden intended them to serve as examples of the survey's best scientific work, comparable to memoirs issued by prestigious scientific academies and societies. He envisioned them as being useful in "more advanced" studies by specialists in the subjects as well as by institutions of higher education.[25] He expected both audiences to have more appreciation for an exhaustive memoir. At the same time, Hayden's authors appreciated the liberality of vision with which Hayden approached the subject. His policy, then, fostered both internal and external constituencies for his survey.

With efforts for both preliminary and final reports under way simultaneously, it might seem as if the survey had undertaken all the publishing it needed. But Hayden's ambitions led him even further. One of his strategic aims was to highlight the importance of the survey by ensuring credit for its discoveries. In Hayden's opinion, this goal was best accomplished when results appeared in official survey publications. Yet he also recognized the need to ensure priority through *rapid* publication. When these needs came into conflict, Hayden established the *Bulletin of the United States Geological and Geographical Survey of the Territories*, first published on 21 January 1874.

¶ While Hayden had been considering issuing such a publication for several years, the *Bulletin* made its appearance mostly at Cope's persistent urging. In his quest for priority in naming and describing the wealth of fossil vertebrates uncovered by the western expeditions, Cope found Hayden's publication schedule too slow. Cope therefore offered announcements of discovery and first descriptions to other scientific journals, which irritated Hayden, even though in earlier years Hayden had himself readily given brief notices of findings to the scientific and popular press and had urged Leidy to publish his more novel discoveries quickly to ensure credit for the survey. But as his own organization grew and his publication plans matured, Hayden sought to have all of the survey's discoveries come out in its own publications. After investing heavily in 1872 in sending a number of groups west to examine one of the major geological questions concerning the region, Hayden did not want his survey's reports anticipated elsewhere. Thus, when Lesquereux sought permission to publish an account of some of his more "interesting" findings, Hayden refused, advising him that with no competition in his field there was no reason to rush into print and that he should keep all results for the next annual report.[26] Though Lesquereux readily acquiesced in this policy, Cope balked at it.

¶ Cope had been associated with Hayden as early as 1862. By 1870, he had even managed to break Hayden's policy of "first offer" to Leidy of all vertebrate collections. When Hayden began to put his quarto series together, Cope was one of the first scientists Hayden invited to contribute, and he readily agreed when Hayden promised "full illustrations" for the monograph. The partnership got off to a good start. In mid-February 1872, Cope sent the bulk of his "preliminary report" and a year later reported the "literary work" of his report "*finished*" as far as it could be, based on the previous year's collections. "Additions to it can only be made in *the field*," Cope claimed. Since the report could not be published until all the plates were engraved, which would be some time yet, Cope informed Hayden that he had decided to leave for the West and remain there all summer.[27]

¶ By April, Hayden was beginning to worry about Cope. During the preceding winter of 1872–73 Hayden had been attempting to mediate Marsh's complaints against Cope. Suddenly, Hayden found Cope unresponsive. Alarmed, he wrote Leidy that Cope had been "perfectly silent" for the past few weeks and confided his fears that Cope would "fail" him. Hayden believed Cope was sulking because Hayden had refused to take his side against Marsh. But Hayden knew his man and calculated he would "come around" eventually, "if he finds that is the best he can do." So Hayden decided to wait and see what developed. In preparation for the worst, however, he asked Leidy if he thought he would be able to describe the specimens from the plates already engraved.[28] Though Cope did "come round," in the process he and Hayden had to work out an arrangement on publications that would satisfy both Cope's desire for scientific priority and Hayden's desire to ensure that survey work appeared in survey reports.

¶ During the first half of 1873, Hayden had heard a number of complaints regarding Cope's competitiveness. In November, Hayden finally called Cope's attention to how his "race" for rapid publication, with its utilization of a variety of venues for reporting his discoveries, was both complicating relations with Marsh and depriving the survey of deserved glory. Cope responded to the criticisms with two lengthy epistles in which he laid out his reasoning concerning his work and his mode of publishing the results. Rarely one to mince words, Cope bluntly informed Hayden: "You certainly do not see the point in the matter of publication, or you would not have penned your last note." He was particularly insulted by Hayden's use of the words "*haste, rush*" in describing his work and accused Hayden of borrowing them from Marsh. Insisting that his studies were "as deliberate as those of any other person," Cope asserted: "as I value my reputation, I offer nothing for publication until it is as good as my opportunities can make it." But once written "papers gain nothing by lying in drawers."

¶ Cope viewed the situation as publish or perish. Convinced that Marsh and other workers in vertebrate paleontology possessed materials similar to his, and were developing the same sorts of conclusions from them, Cope was certain his competitors would publish their findings as promptly as they could. As their knowledge advanced, their publications would appear even more rapidly, leaving Hayden with an unfortunate choice: "either to publish matter as the results of your survey or of Marsh's, Wheeler's, etc." The reason was simple. If others issued reports "which must cover my and your ground largely," Cope would have no choice but to quote them in his own reports or simply "make catalogues referring to their publications." This he called "*very second hand.*" But if Cope published first, "wherever that be done," Hayden's survey would be credited with the results, "and even if a part has been already printed, your annual report contains the work of *your survey.*" That, he said, "is *not second hand.*"

¶ As Cope presented the situation, early publication was the "only way" the survey could expect to secure credit for its discoveries, and he even went so far as to declare he would prefer not to publish at all if he was to be deprived of the credit due the work. Nor did Cope think Hayden really wanted to be in a position of publishing the discoveries of his competitors. Therefore, he insisted that a policy of rapid publication was "the only way of securing the results to the Survey in the face of rivals." This was the core difference. Unlike those in other branches of paleontology, Cope had rivals. The success of his policy was proved by the fact that "*200* new vertebrates" had appeared as the result of Hayden's survey, whereas if Cope had postponed publications "*nearly every one* would have been anticipated by Marsh."

¶ Cope wanted rapid publication. If Hayden could provide this, he would happily submit all of his papers to the survey. Though Hayden had proposed such an offer, he had never made good on it, even when Cope offered him papers. Lest Hayden insist on his point, Cope issued a double warning: "Supposing you should or could prevent my prompt publication of results, what w[oul]d follow?" The survey's department of vertebrate paleontology would be a "failure" since Hayden would surely decline to publish reports on work done by rivals, and Cope would "turn to a field where I could *secure* the results earned by heavy expense and labor."[29]

¶ This brought a prompt response from Hayden. Still unconvinced that Cope was not in an intemperate "race," which Cope continued to deny, Hayden yielded to the desire to ensure prompt publication, implicitly admitting that this was the only way to guarantee full credit for the survey's discoveries. Cope, meanwhile, accepted Hayden's proposal of a monthly publication. If the journal should not be issued regularly and he had "anything important to publish," Cope professed satisfaction that his priority would be ensured by submitting the article to Hayden as a report of the survey and receiving a note authorizing publication, with which the article could later be prefaced. This, he claimed, should satisfy them both. The work would be published quickly, and it would be published as "*survey work*."[30]

¶ Yet if the *Bulletin*'s beginnings bordered on blackmail, that was hardly any way to introduce it to the public. Instead, Hayden explained the *Bulletin* as if it were all his own idea. He defined it as a means to prevent scattering the survey's findings through publication in diverse journals or other outlets and a natural answer to the desirability of prompt publication of certain materials that might be delayed if issued in the survey's annual reports. Once begun, the *Bulletin* soon evolved from occasional and separately printed pamphlets to a serial, "issued at convenient irregular intervals, as material comes to hand." Nor did Hayden simply wait for material to "come to hand." Instead, he solicited materials he thought related to his own work or of general interest, as in the case of Samuel Scudder, from whom Hayden solicited several articles after 1875. By then, Hayden was convinced of the *Bulletin*'s value, writing Scudder it was "useful as a channel for quick conveyance to the world of preliminary matter."[31]

¶ The *Bulletin* was indeed "useful." Though the *Bulletin* was established as a means for Hayden's employees to establish instant credit for their work and often criticized for the errors contained in its pages as a result of haste or poor quality control, it was "actually a new scientific journal." And though it has been seen as a tool "that made it possible for his men to break the monopoly on scientific publication held by the *American Journal of Science* and its backers in Eastern academic circles," such a view misreads its utility.[32] Hayden retained excellent relations with Dana, and notes and articles from the survey were always welcome at the *AJS*. The issue was not the survey members' access to publication but ensuring recognition for the survey.

¶ Hayden's practice of opening the pages of the *Bulletin* to writers with no connection to the survey other than similarity of interests was related to this goal. Noticing that "the proof that [the *Bulletin*] was needed lies in the vast quantity of material submitted to it" is perceptive but potentially misleading. Hayden's more vociferous critics at the time did not fail to see how accepting such materials served Hayden's purposes. Powell put his finger on two of those purposes when he wrote that among the "manifold" purposes of the *Bulletin* were "keep[ing] a constant stream of matter before the public, calling for constant notices from the scientific journals and reviews," and publishing papers "on precisely the same basis as a contribution is sent to a magazine." Powell clearly recognized that authors willingly allowed Hayden to adopt their papers as the work of his survey in return for rapid and *free* publication.[33] As director of a rival survey Powell expressed strong disapproval of Hayden's policy, especially since it worked to his disadvantage; however, he had no difficulty appreciating how such a policy appealed to scientists as well as served the survey's institutional needs.

¶ The *Bulletin* answered a weakness in the infrastructure of American science. Scientific journals of the period were notoriously undercapitalized and under subscribed. The *Bulletin* had no such problems. Its funding was as secure as Hayden was, and since it was distributed free of charge by the government it possessed a ready-made subscription base composed of those individuals already on Hayden's mailing list, to which he happily added all others who requested copies. He could translate that demand into political support.

¶ The *Bulletin*'s success in meeting these various needs was not lost on Hayden. Reviewing its progress in a "Prefatory Note" for the final number of volume 4, Hayden adopted much of Cope's reasoning as his own. Claiming the *Bulletin* had proved highly successful in answering the need for prompt communication of "new or specially interesting matter," he now regarded it as "one of the most important means to the main ends which the Survey has in view." In the preceding five years, the *Bulletin* had included papers on archaeology, ethnography, linguistics, geology, topography, geography, paleontology, and various branches of natural history. Critics such as Powell bitterly complained that by opening its pages to authors who had little or no connection with the survey, Hayden purchased fame at taxpayer expense and "unlimited access to the Government Printing Office."[34] Such complaints both exaggerated and downplayed the truth. Hayden and his survey were already famous, and contributors sought to attach themselves to that fame. Moreover, a simple review of the tables of contents of the *Bulletins* issued from 1874 to 1878 reveals that the vast majority of the articles were written by survey members and apparently for the reason Hayden cited: rapid dissemination of the "more interesting" discoveries, especially in view of increasing delays in producing annual reports.

¶ The "miscellaneous publications," the survey's fourth general category of publications, consisted of a mixed lot. Hayden described them as issued "on different subjects connected with the West, which are important contributions, but are to some extent compilations." Usually issued in smaller editions than the annual reports, from which they were sometimes extracts, they ranged from tabulations of elevations and meteorological observations to studies in botany, ornithology, zoology, and ethnology. The most popular items were probably the catalogs of Jackson's photographs. Hayden exaggerated slightly when he claimed these "miscellaneous publications" were "all based on the labors of the survey." As in the three categories just treated, Hayden occasionally solicited monographs from people who had no direct connection with the work of the survey, such as Washington Matthews's study of the ethnology of the Hidatsa Indians. He also accepted studies compiled before their authors joined the survey, such as Coues's handbook on the *Birds of the Northwest*. However, in both instances he saw the material as germane to the work of the survey, and in all cases the miscellaneous publications served the same aims as the rest of the survey's publications: dispersing information about the West and the survey's operations and keeping the survey's name before the public.[35]

Hayden's various official publications fulfilled his legal responsibility to report his findings and ensured that they were clearly attributed to his survey. But Hayden did not rest there. He had more than one prescription for fortifying support for the survey, and he made use of a variety of means to appeal directly to public opinion. Newspapers represented an obvious way to reach a wide audience; so did all the weekly and monthly journals aimed at a mass national audience that arose in the latter half of the nineteenth century. Public lectures, while not directly reaching mass audiences, could reach smaller audiences and, through newspaper coverage, larger audiences as well. Even more effective than the written or spoken word in some respects were the striking visual images taken from Jackson's photographs and works by artists like Gifford and Moran. Hayden made use of all of these to build support for his efforts.

¶ Hayden was not unique in using these media. The competition for funds between the different surveys led to a rivalry for publicity and popular support. As a result, all four survey leaders encouraged their men to contribute letters to hometown newspapers and welcomed journalists seeking to travel with the survey parties to write about their adventures and the western scenery.[36] But Hayden was perhaps more willing than other survey leaders to devote attention to ensuring that his survey received good press coverage. One likely reason is that before 1872 Hayden was in greater need of such publicity than his chief competitors, King and Wheeler, who enjoyed the support of the army. Additionally, after 1872 Hayden had more resources to devote to cultivating the press than did his rivals, Wheeler and Powell. Nor does Hayden seem to have thought it inconsistent with his role as a scientist to give advance notice of some findings to local papers. Instead, he seems to have considered it a part of his duty as a public servant.

¶ As the foremost boosters of their towns, editors of local western papers were generally eager to make use of anything that would highlight and direct favorable attention to their regions, a trait that predisposed them to become Hayden's natural allies. For example, Hayden quickly developed a close relationship with William N. Byers, editor of the *Rocky Mountain News*, Denver's first newspaper. By 1859, Byers had settled into "a lifelong career of boosting Denver . . . and promoting his own money-making schemes." When Hayden came to Colorado at the conclusion of his 1867 season, his work was easily fitted into these aims. It was almost a perfect match. Both men were wildly enthusiastic about the West and its possibilities and eager to see it celebrated and developed. A scientist in need of publicity and a publisher in need of a reputable authority who shared his optimism could hardly have failed to combine. Thus, when Byers received a copy of Hayden's letter to a local citizen regarding the "national importance" of coal deposits in the basin between the South Boulder and Clear Creeks, he gladly reprinted it, noting it would be read with interest.[37]

¶ In succeeding years, Hayden remained in close contact and the *Rocky Mountain News* regularly printed articles and letters about the survey's activities. This was particularly so during the survey of Colorado. The first year of that survey, Byers went so far as to accompany Hayden's party for most of the season and sent frequent letters back for publication in his paper. Evidently enjoying the experience, he repeated it for parts of the following season, and when he had to leave the survey for a period in midseason he asked fellow survey guest Professor William Dwight Whitney of Yale, who was writing letters for the *New York Herald*, to take up the task.

¶ In the 1870s, articles about the West made good copy in eastern newspapers. Horace Greeley's celebrated western tour in 1859 marked the beginning of a high tide of interest in a new mass readership. Invited to make use of this interest, Hayden rarely turned down opportunities; rather, he sought them out. As early as 1869, before he set out on the season's explorations, he received a letter on behalf of Greeley from Whitelaw Reid, editor of the *New York Tribune*. Hayden had proposed sending the paper a series of letters regarding the survey's activities. Replying that he would be glad to receive them, Reid advised Hayden "the shorter and more graphic the better." The paper would use all it could, and "of course" pay for them.[38]

¶ Before long Hayden had more requests for such items than he could supply. Late in the 1871 season Reid wrote complaining that Hayden had failed to fulfill a promise to send the *Tribune* notices regarding the expedition to the Yellowstone. He asked, "Why not send me something now?" even if only a quick note as to whether it would be worth his while to send a reporter after Hayden. Nor was Reid the only one who had to remind Hayden to fulfill pledges for articles or letters. Frederick A. P. Barnard, president of Columbia College and one of the editors of *Johnson's Illustrated Universal Cyclopedia*, had to write Hayden several times to secure a promised short article on the "Yellow Stone Valley" for the encyclopedia. This inability to meet the demand for articles may be another reason why Hayden found it advantageous to encourage members of his parties to submit letters and articles to local papers and take professional journalists along in the parties. Still, Hayden took a personal interest in the results. For example, Peale recorded in his diary of the 1871 Yellowstone trip that one day Hayden spoke to him about the letters Peale was writing for the *Philadelphia Press*. "He gave me a sort of lecture on my letter writing," Peale noted, "betting me that I was two [*sic*] scientific." Apparently he was not, though; when a few weeks later a mail delivery brought a copy of the paper with one of Peale's letters in it Peale proudly recorded: "the Dr. thought it very good."[39]

¶ Hayden was not content to rely on the haphazard or irregular activity of "correspondents," however. Letters from Thomas, who had charge of the Washington office during the 1873 field season, reveal an active approach. Responding to Hayden's request that Thomas arrange to have "something" about the survey put in the Washington papers, Thomas told him that "scarcely a week passes without some notice of your movements." However, the papers wanted original copy and stories and did not like to print accounts that had already been published by competitors. Yet all were eager for "anything that comes directly from you or any [survey] member and call upon me every few days to see if I have heard anything farther from you or your party." In this situation, Thomas managed "in a quiet way" to have the expedition noticed every few weeks in both the Washington papers and some of the northern ones as well.[40]

¶ Newspaper editors were not the only publishers interested in stories and accounts of the western surveys. The 1870s constituted a heyday for new journals aimed at a national market. Many survived no more than a few years, and most inflated their circulation figures, but some were genuinely important and won a lasting place in the mass media. *Scribner's Monthly*, *Harper's Monthly*, and *Harper's Weekly*, all with circulations above one hundred thousand, were among the most important in their class, while other popular journals included the *Illustrated Christian Weekly* and *Appleton's Journal*. All of these published articles on the western surveys in the interest of entertainment and education. *Scribner's* solicited an article from Hayden soon after his return from the Yellowstone in 1871, complete with instructions about the sort of material they wished to accompany the woodcuts they were already preparing. Several years later, Lyman Abbott, editor of the *Illustrated Christian Weekly*, wrote Hayden to solicit a series of articles. Having already selected a number of Jackson's photographs, Abbott wanted an extended article on "the *Hayden Exploring Expedition*, telling what it is, how composed, what its work is, what camp life is, what are the instruments; in short giving a dramatic not scientific—a popular not professional account of such an expedition, elaborately illustrated." In the end, Peale composed the account, which ran to four parts.[41]

¶ Cumulatively, these efforts resulted in nationwide reporting on the survey's activities. The letters alone were printed in a number of major cities, including New York, Washington, Philadelphia, Chicago, and Denver, besides being reprinted in an unknown number of local papers across the country. Not all of the stories were accepted at face value, however. Nor should they have been. One reader wrote the *New York Times* of having noticed "with considerable amusement the statement which has appeared in a great many papers concerning 'Hayden's wonderful unknown region of the Upper Snake.'" The cause of the writer's amusement was the apparent belief that Hayden's party had been the first "civilized beings" to visit the spot. Such, said the writer, had also been the opinion he and some companions had held when visiting the same region in 1866, "until we found just inside the vegetation line on a tree three names with date—1836."[42] But aside from such occasional criticism, there was a demand for such stories, embellished as they sometimes were, in keeping with prevailing Victorian tastes in literature and perceptions of the West and its explorers.

¶ Public lectures provided yet another means of reaching and teaching people about the survey's activities. By the mid-nineteenth century, the public lecture had evolved into a characteristic social form in America and enjoyed great popularity as a mark of civilized life. One of the underpinnings of its appeal was its democratic form, presenting almost everyone with the possibility of pursuing "useful knowledge."[43] Since such a philosophy corresponded closely to Hayden's own aims in widely diffusing the "practical results" of his survey, it is not surprising that he made use of lectures to inform people while advancing his own interests. Lectures in science were among the most popular subjects, and good lecturers were in demand and frequently able to put together financially rewarding tours. Even more useful for Hayden, the speaker's reach extended beyond the audience halls since newspapers frequently printed the texts or substance of a lecture. Lectures on the survey thus found an existing social pattern into which they could easily be fitted.

¶ Though it is clear Hayden delivered such lectures, exactly how frequently is not. During the survey of Nebraska, Hayden was invited to speak before the Nebraska state legislature and the general public, and he made use of these opportunities to promote his survey and suggest remedies for concerns of widespread interest. After his Yellowstone expeditions, which made him something of a "minor celebrity," and beginning with the survey of Colorado, he came into greater demand as a lecturer. In the succeeding years, he received invitations from groups ranging from the Philadelphia YMCA to the American Geographical Society to "the ladies of Plymouth Congregational Church" of Lawrence, Kansas, who were attempting to raise funds to retire their church's debt.[44]

¶ Hayden earned a rather generous salary and probably did not have the incentive of Powell or some of the supporters of the Hayden Survey who took to the lecture circuit, at least in part, as a means of earning or supplementing their income. Nonetheless, he clearly recognized lecturing's potential for arousing support for government surveys. In his lecture before the American Geographical Society on 15 April 1874, he concluded with a stirring peroration to that effect: "If the surveys which have been inaugurated by our Government are permitted to continue, we may annually look for fresh and most valuable additions to our knowledge of the geology and geography of the little-explored portions of our great West. May the united voice of the people go up to our legislators in Congress, and sustain them in their efforts to continue them, until it shall not be thrown up to us as a matter of reproach that even Central Africa is better known to geographers than our own great West."[45]

¶ In addition to being informative, lectures were meant to entertain. One clear mark of the successful and capable lecturer was the degree to which he or she accomplished both goals. In this dual aim, aside from his own talents as a speaker, Hayden had a clear advantage in his ready access to Jackson's photographs, which enabled him to make his lectures more informative and more entertaining at the same time. For instance, in an address delivered before a "large audience" at the American Geographical Society in April 1874 Hayden presented an illustrated tour of the West, ranging from the wonders of Yellowstone National Park down the Front Range of the Rocky Mountains in Colorado, with stops including the Garden of the Gods, Monument Park, the Mount of the Holy Cross, and the mining district in Clear Creek.[46]

¶ Friendly critics, at least, judged Hayden's lectures successful and urged him to give more. Others associated with the survey also presented lectures on its work and their adventures, and to judge by their own accounts, these seem to have been popular as well, thanks in part to Hayden's assistance. Recognizing their value for promoting both the survey and its chief, Hayden happily provided them with notes and suggestions as well as the illustrations they invariably sought.[47]

Though aware of the power of words, Hayden was also alert to the power of visual images, and his use of visual technologies was an important part of his publication strategy as he sought to exhibit and explain the West to eastern audiences. Illustrations served a variety of purposes in the Hayden Survey, as they did in the developing branches of natural history as its fields became specialized and professional scientists diverged from amateur naturalists during the middle decades of the nineteenth century. In the process, each group developed its own conventions about the meaning of "nature" and "natural" and how they ought to be presented, textually and visually. While scientists tended to drop narrative elements from their texts in favor of description, naturalists retained such elements as part of their older tradition. The survey functioned in the midst of this changing environment, and Hayden sought to appeal to both sides—responding to his scientists' requests for adequate illustrations while simultaneously seeking to bridge the widening gap by asking that they include narrative elements in their reports. Meanwhile, to readers of government reports "nature" had an even wider connotation: it might refer to the land and all the variables that might affect its potential for settlement and profit; it might be systematized scientific knowledge, handsomely presented courtesy of the federal government; it might be a source of entertainment and patriotic gratification.[48] Together, these presented a broad market for an entrepreneur.

¶ In the early decades of the nineteenth century, the development of new printing techniques gave visual modes of communication an increasingly heightened importance in geology and the natural history sciences. By the 1850s, new techniques in lithography and steel engraving enabled the use, at a much reduced cost, of a comparatively lavish number of prints that were actually superior to copper engravings for many subjects. By midcentury, good quality illustrations were virtually essential elements of scientific texts on natural history and geology.[49] Hayden recognized the substantial impact illustrations could have in making reports and other publications more effective, both in the popular and scientific markets. He also realized that his contributors expected a measure of control over the illustrations used in their reports. However, illustrations cost money, and good ones were expensive. For all these reasons, he manifested constant concern for the number of figures to be made and included in the reports.

¶ Most illustrations in Hayden's earlier annual reports appeared in his personal reports. For instance, the 1871 report had nearly seventy figures, all but one with the report of the "Geologist-in-charge." Only with the 1872 report did illustrations begin to be distributed among the reports of his collaborators. Two factors probably account for the change: the decreasing proportion of text Hayden contributed in the years following 1872 and pressure from his growing corps of professional scientists who very likely expected illustrations. Though survey records contain no evidence of geologists requesting illustrations for their reports, other scientists could be insistent on the matter. As Hayden's contributions to the expanding reports shrank and the number of illustrations continued to grow, his assistants reaped the advantage.

¶ Yet even while Hayden was willing to employ illustrations in his reports, there were realities to consider. Without express appropriations, to do anything beyond relatively inexpensive woodcuts was prohibitive. Further, Meek for one refused to have illustrations done on wood, insisting to both Hayden and Baird that it was "*utterly impossible* to bring out the delicate structures" of invertebrate fossils with woodcuts. While "some kinds of natural history illustrations" might be done in wood, he maintained those of fossils could not and told Hayden "you do not see any well illustrated work of the kind anywhere with wood cut engravings."[50]

¶ Hayden therefore employed two types of illustrations in his publications. Those in the annual reports consisted mostly of woodcuts or electroplates. The *Bulletin*, as a journal of rapid publication, also used inexpensive illustrations. The quarto monographs were a different case, however, and after Meek's expostulation Hayden could hardly think to publish them with less than fine steel or lithographic plates. But given the expense involved, he sought to economize. One way to do so was simply to reduce the number of illustrations to the absolutely necessary. For instance, while advising Scudder about what to include in his monograph for the quarto series, Hayden said he should feel free to "include all fossil insects not previously, properly figured." But he drew the line with those, informing Scudder that "I do not believe in *bookmaking* in itself, that is figuring a second time matter that has already been well illustrated." Yet this did not mean Hayden was uninterested in fine work. Most volumes of the final reports were liberally illustrated with very fine plates, generally presented in a much less crowded format than in the annual reports.[51]

¶ Hayden's efforts to economize also led him to experiment with technologies that promised visual advantages at reduced costs. For instance, two of Coues's monographs on mammals included engravings made from "photographs on wood." Instead of using an artist's drawing, photographs were printed on sensitized wood much as they might be on paper, and the engraver made a woodcut from the print. Introducing the process in 1877, Hayden admitted the results showed "less detail" and did not compare with the best in hand-drawing. But as usual he accentuated the positive, noting that "the cuts possess the merit of absolute accuracy of contour."[52] Another way Hayden sought to economize on expenses for illustrations was by getting others to pay for them. This applied particularly to Jackson's popular western photographs and photographic illustrations, which played a prominent role in the survey.

¶ Jackson's photographs were perhaps the survey's best advertisements. Without doubt, they were its most popular product, and Hayden's use of them was one of his most important means of keeping the survey literally before the public eye. Even before acquiring Jackson's services, Hayden had had some experience with the use of photography as a medium for presenting western views to eastern consumers, both scientific and nonscientific. During his 1866 expedition for the Academy of Natural Sciences, he reported on photographers "passing up and down the [Missouri] river taking stereoscopic views all the time" and requested permission to spend ten or twenty dollars on a series of photographs of "scenery and Indians." They would be of the "utmost importance" in illustrating the geography and geology of this region and "a cheap way of getting an ethnological collection." Convinced, the academy authorized him to spend up to fifty dollars for "photographs, indian relics, &c."[53]

¶ The photographers Hayden observed that summer were among the pioneers in what became in the 1870s a lucrative business in outdoor photography. Still in its infancy in the 1850s, photography came out of the studio during the Civil War, and before long well-financed expeditions, including all four of the Great Surveys, sought to exploit the new medium. In September 1869, the lead article of *Harper's New Monthly Magazine* introduced the general public to landscape photography with "Photographs from the High Rockies," thirteen wood engravings copied from photographs Timothy H. O'Sullivan made for the King Survey.[54]

¶ Perhaps partly inspired by King's efforts with expeditionary photography as well as by J. D. Whitney's *The Yosemite Book* (1868), which contained photographs by Carleton Watkins, in 1869 Hayden decided to issue his own volume of photographs of Rocky Mountain scenery to bolster support for his survey. The result was *Sun Pictures of Rocky Mountain Scenery* (1870). Supported and explained by a text running to nearly two hundred pages, *Sun Pictures* contained thirty photographs by Andrew Joseph Russell, one of the foremost western photographers. The photographs, however, had only the most tenuous connection with Hayden's survey; most had been selected from a portfolio compiled while Russell was an official photographer for the Union Pacific Railroad. Still, the success of *Sun Pictures* was probably instrumental in Hayden's decision to secure the services of a survey photographer and why, after studying the photographs hanging in Jackson's Omaha studio, he wistfully observed, "This is what I need."[55]

¶ Relying on the medium's reputation as a means of faithfully representing nature, Hayden saw photography as contributing directly to the scientific efforts of the survey. As he put it, photographs provided "the nearest approach to a truthful delineation of nature." Yet he also recognized the potential appeal to a large public, and an anonymous review of *Sun Pictures* for the *American Journal of Science* made the scientific element almost secondary. Though asserting that the views had been selected to "illustrate the geographical and geological features of the region," the author claimed they would be "interesting to the student of science *as well as to the artist and the lovers of the picturesque in nature*" (emphasis added).[56]

¶ With advances in the technology of photographic reproductions, a market for photography developed during the 1860s. The development of the Albertype process in the early 1870s provided a commercially feasible reproduction process that yielded high-quality results, setting the stage for a mass market in photographic images. The new industry's most important products were stereopticons. Sold individually or in sets by companies with national distribution networks, these twin-image prints, mounted on cards and designed to be seen through a stereographic viewer, were relatively inexpensive and extremely popular, selling by the hundreds of thousands. With a viewer in virtually every parlor in the country, anyone could enjoy a "breath-taking, three-dimensional effect, an impression which was the next closest thing to being at the scene."[57]

¶ Hayden and Jackson both exploited aspects of this market. Hayden's contract with Jackson allowed the photographer to retain possession of the negatives of his photographs—a trade-off for Hayden's inability to offer Jackson a salary during their first season together. "In consideration" for this privilege, Jackson agreed to provide the government and Hayden with "all the prints, transparencies, etc. that may be required or the use of the negatives in any way that shall promote the interests of the expedition or advance its scientific results," exclusive of commercial use. The arrangement benefited both men. Retaining ownership of the negatives was no small consideration, and Jackson swiftly concluded profitable arrangements with some of the largest publishers and distributors of stereographs in the country. His photographs quickly became popular, though how many of the thousands of prints made from them were legitimate and how many were pirated copies is impossible to know. Still, their rate of survival into the present time "suggests they were among the most popular landscape stereos in America, a necessary part of virtually every stereo collection."[58]

¶ Jackson's commercial dealings also served Hayden. Every legal stereoscopic or whole-plate image mount was imprinted with the survey's stamp and Hayden's name as geologist-in-charge, advertising the fame

of both. While Hayden's friends and supporters occasionally lamented that the value of his reports was not fully appreciated by the great mass of people for whom he labored, as a correspondent for the *New York Times* pointed out, "the work of [the photographic] party is something which interests everybody." This was so, he explained, because "while only the select few can appreciate the discoveries of the geologists, or the exact measurements of the topographers, every one can understand a picture."[59] And it seemed everybody wanted to have them.

¶ The photographs' primary official use was to illustrate survey reports and "promote the interests of the expedition or advance its scientific results," but the phrase was broadly interpreted, and Hayden responded generously to innumerable calls for the photos from various government offices, as well as requests from individuals both within and outside the government. He used them like other survey publications, as items of exchange or gifts to nurture relationships of interest and support. Numerous copies of individual prints went to members of Congress, and survey records contain dozens of letters acknowledging receipt of packages of photos. A particularly expressive, though not unusual, example is the acknowledgment by Congressman Frederick H. Teese. Thanking Hayden for a "very beautiful set of photographs" he promised: "Should it be in my power hereafter to aid you in any way in furtherance of your valuable labors in the cause of science you may count upon such aid."[60]

¶ Besides distributing copies of the prints to congressmen and other official "friends" of the survey, Hayden also disseminated them among other potential supporters. Dana was obviously on Hayden's list as a regular recipient of photographs and appreciated them for their scientific content as well as their picturesqueness. Alexander Agassiz, too, had occasion to thank Hayden for a "beautiful present," a set of "exquisite photographs" of the Yellowstone. More packages went to various scientific societies, such as the American Geographical Society and the Boston Society of Natural History. The purpose of such distribution is clear. In requesting a series of photographs for the Boston Society of Natural History, Ernest Ingersoll, secretary for the society and occasional member of the survey, assured Hayden that "such a donation would be highly appreciated here, and increase the popularity and support of your (and our) enterprise." Nor was Hayden the only Washington official to make such obvious use of the photos as a medium of political currency. The Department of the Interior frequently sent them out in its own name, and Henry and Baird both called upon Hayden for photographs to present to individuals or institutions in the name of the Smithsonian Institution. Even General Sherman requested a series of photographs of the Yellowstone country, which he desired to present to the Earl of Dunraven, who had made "an express desire to receive them."[61]

¶ Hayden also distributed the photographs among the nation's colleges and libraries as educational materials. J. J. Stevenson, professor of geology at the University of the City of New York, wrote in late December 1874, asking if Hayden had any photographs of "glacial action" since he wished to make use of them in his classes. The unusual aspect of this request lies in Stevenson's writing to Hayden rather than Wheeler, with whose survey he was associated and from whom Stevenson "suppose[d]" he could get photographs. Yet he preferred not to ask Wheeler, as "One has to ask for things rather pressingly and humbly at the War Dept." Hayden quickly offered his assistance, asking which particular views were desired.[62]

¶ The press also sought copies of photographs for use in preparing illustrations for articles on the region. Always attentive to the possibility of negotiating a mutually beneficial arrangement, Hayden turned this to his advantage. He offered his photographs to the journals and then requested the use of their engravings for his reports. Though editors frequently demurred, preferring to retain exclusive control of their engravings, they knew when they were being made an offer they could scarcely refuse. Although R. Watson Gilder of *Scribner's Monthly* complained that "it cheapens the illustrations to have them appear in reports, etc.," he also recognized that Hayden was in a position to assist the magazine in the future. Trusting to that eventuality, he convinced the publishers to make an exception and loan their woodcuts. Hayden made similar arrangements with other journals, including the *Illustrated Christian Weekly* and *Appleton's Journal* and its allied series, *Picturesque America*. Frequently, all they asked was credit for supplying the engravings or electrotypes, something Hayden was happy to give.[63]

¶ Finally, railroads asked for copies of photographs for use in promotional pamphlets. Soon after Hayden's return from the Yellowstone in 1871, a vice president of the Denver and Rio Grande Railway Company wrote that he wanted a thousand eight-by-ten copies of "at least *one* of the pictures you had taken along the route of our road, if I can get them at cost. . . . ready to paste in a book." Several years later, when preparing a tourist guidebook on the western states, the Union Pacific turned to Hayden for copies of some of the famous photographs from Yellowstone National Park.[64] In fulfilling such requests, Hayden not only received back the cost of providing the photographs and the goodwill of the railroads, an important political lobby, but he also received the usual free publicity that went with exhibitions of official survey photographs.

While there can be little doubt Jackson's photographs were the single most important imaging medium for the survey, at least in the popular estimation, the paintings and lithographs of Thomas Moran ran a close second. Other artists had traveled West in search of views to paint, but none created quite the impression of "The Grand Cañon of the Yellowstone," the result of Moran's 1871 journey with Hayden. Having gone to see for himself the wonders for which he had made the drawings illustrating Langford's 1871 article, Moran returned with a portfolio full of sketches and studies for watercolors, but determined to "cast all my claims to being an Artist into this one picture of the *Great* [sic] *Cañon*." As he had hoped, his work produced "a most decided sensation in art circles." Exhibited at Clinton Hall in New York in the same manner as the grand works of Frederick Edwin Church, America's foremost landscape painter at the time, Moran's painting was a sensation in May 1872. The reviewer for the *New-York Daily Tribune* received both artist and painting favorably, judging Moran's "Great [*sic*] Cañon of the Yellowstone" second only to Church's famous painting of Niagara Falls.[65]

¶ If that had been all, the effect might have been minimal. But when Moran sold the canvas to Congress later that year, the Capitol Building became home not only to what one art critic considered "the only really good picture to be found" there but to a vivid reminder of the Hayden Survey as well. Additional reminders appeared when Moran received numerous commissions to prepare drawings for a variety of journals and books, including, besides *Scribner's*, *The Aldine*, the nation's leading art journal, and *Picturesque America*, a two-volume set of "well-illustrated articles on interesting places throughout the United States." Moran's work captured the attention of Hayden's competitors as well, and in 1873 Powell invited him to join an expedition to the Grand Canyon, which Moran accepted. He capped this trip with another large canvas, which Congress also ultimately purchased for the Capitol. Yet Moran retained such pleasant memories and gratitude for the assistance Hayden and his men had provided that in the ensuing years he continued to consider himself a member of the survey, and even apologized to Hayden for having joined Powell. For their part, Hayden and his men expressed their appreciation of Moran by electing him an "honorary member" of the survey while encamped in Yellowstone in 1872 and by conducting him on a special repeat expedition to the Mount of the Holy Cross in Colorado so he could make sketches of it. Moran expressed his loyalty in concrete fashion, as a good client to a patron. Learning that his Yellowstone drawings had been used in journals without reference to the survey, Moran made it a condition of publication that "proper credit" be given the survey, thus continuing to put Hayden's name before the public.[66]

¶ The works of western landscape artists and photographers like Moran and Jackson helped Americans come to terms with the western landscape, initially so forbidding and strange. But the images alone were not enough; the landscape had to be described as well, and geologists like Hayden provided the words to make the strange understood, if not familiar. The collaboration between artist and scientist is evident in every request for an article from Hayden or one of his men to accompany illustrations printed by a journal or book. Nowhere is this as clear as in *The Yellowstone National Park, and the Mountain Regions of Portions of Idaho, Nevada, Colorado and Utah*, the result of a joint effort of Hayden and Moran with Louis Prang, nineteenth-century America's foremost chromolithographer. Moran provided fifteen watercolors of well-known western features, the bulk of them from Yellowstone National Park, while Hayden provided two-page descriptions of the scenery and geology for each view. Published as a deluxe, oversized portfolio in a limited edition, the work received high praise on both sides of the Atlantic.[67]

¶ Interest in the western landscape also fed into the development of American middle-class tourism. Sites previously simply strange became transformed into tourist attractions, following upon the elaboration of transportation networks and the construction of local infrastructure for hospitality. At the same time, the needs of tourism nurtured an interest in the land—needs Hayden happily served by supplying both information and illustrations. Science, art, and tourism all met in guidebooks, and together they contributed to the development of a national identity based upon the uniqueness of the American landscape. And for those who could not actually go there, photography enabled them to become virtual or armchair tourists by means of the stereograph.[68] All in all, it made a fertile soil for an entrepreneur like Hayden to plow.

Publicist and promoter that he was, it is no surprise that Hayden fully exploited the opportunities presented by the 1876 Centennial Exhibition. The great national fair held at Philadelphia from 10 May to 10 November provided a spectacular showcase in which to display his survey's work. Thanks to Baird's assistance and advice, Hayden was largely successful in efforts to show his survey to its best advantage there, mounting an impressive exhibition of the results of the survey's labors including maps and charts, photographs, and various natural history artifacts. He did not get much help from the government, though. Congress only reluctantly participated in the Centennial Exhibition, grudgingly appropriating a miserly budget for government exhibits. When, in November 1875, the Interior Department distributed its share of the appropriation among its various bureaus, Hayden was informed that $2,945.30 had been allotted for preparation of exhibits representing the work of the geological surveys. Worse, the department's centennial representative recommended the sum be divided evenly between the Powell and Hayden Surveys. That must have stung since his survey was easily three times as large as Powell's. It left him with only $1,472.65 with which to prepare.[69]

¶ Hayden had bigger plans. To accomplish them he needed more money, so he submitted a request for a supplementary appropriation in which he explained his proposed exhibit. It would include a full series of survey publications: annual reports, bulletins, miscellaneous publications, and monographs as well as numerous topographical and geological maps, some ranging up to seventeen feet in length. He also wished to present for the first time a "general graphic representation" of the survey's findings, utilizing "relief maps, photographs, and transparencies . . . to represent important geographical features, such as would interest not only scholars engaged in the study of physical geography, but the great mass of the intelligent citizens of America."[70] The construction of these "graphic representations" meant a great deal of work for Jackson. Not only did he have to prepare a display of photographs, selected from the thousands of negatives among the survey's collection, but along with Holmes he was charged with fashioning plaster and papier-mâché models of sites of particular interest.

¶ If success is measured in capturing the attention of visitors, the results were highly successful. The survey's assignment to the west end of the federal government's exhibition hall helped, enabling it to utilize its best photographs to splendid effect: "The west end of the building had been constructed for the insertion of transparencies or photographs on glass, and these were of much interest, as being some of the largest views of the kind to be found." Besides the transparencies, the walls of the exhibit booth "were decorated with some of the largest and finest photographs ever taken in the Rocky mountains." Impressive as the photographs were, the models were the stars of the survey's exhibit. They included a model of Yellowstone National Park, "showing all points of interest and routes of travel, and colored to approximate to nature"; a model of Colorado constructed in sections and cast in papier-mâché; and two models of the Elk Mountains, one with the colors of nature and the other "in adjustable sections with the geology laid down." The most popular models, however, were those presenting a panorama of the Mesa Verde ruins, described as faithful miniatures of about a third of the ruins found in the Rio de Chelly canyon in Arizona. One showed the ruins in their present condition while the other presented them as "restored to its probable original state, [with] tiny men and women . . . at their daily work, grinding corn, carrying water, etc." To enhance the effect, collections of glazed pottery and implements obtained at the ruins were displayed with the models.[71]

¶ J. D. Runkle was so impressed with Hayden's exhibit that he borrowed pen and paper and sat at the attendant's desk to write Hayden a letter. A professor from the Massachusetts Institute of Technology, Runkle was visiting with a group of about 350 professors and students from MIT. Declaring that he wanted "to make as much of this exhibit in Boston at the Inst. [MIT] as possible," Runkle asked Hayden, "What is it in your power to do?" Was it possible to obtain copies of "these magnificent views on glass" as well as duplicates of the "admirable" restorations of the cliff houses? If so, he assured Hayden that whatever could be provided would "afford us the most admirable means of illustration in our teaching" as well as the interest of citizens of Boston and all visitors in the work being done in the West.[72]

¶ Nor was Runkle the only one impressed by the models. That same day, Baird also wrote to Hayden on behalf of one of the British commissioners to the exhibition, Professor Thomas C. Archer. Introducing Archer as a "staunch admirer" of Hayden and his "ethnological labors," Baird said Archer was "extremely desirous of having copies of the ethnological casts you are exhibiting in the Centennial." He asked permission to promise Archer the models in the exhibit and was very grateful when Hayden agreed to give Archer the cliff dwellings.

¶ Baird was hardly a disinterested mediator in this donation, however. As one of the U.S. commissioners at the centennial, he lost no opportunity to seek exchanges with foreign exhibitors. His primary aim was to obtain materials for the National Museum, and he proved so successful in achieving this goal that after the centennial the Smithsonian had to put up its first new building to house his collection. His primary currency was exchange in kind. He offered Smithsonian publications and sought similar items from other government offices. Hayden's reports and photographs were much in demand. In asking permission to make the gift to Archer, Baird explained that Archer had already presented "some very valuable specimens of statuary casts" to the National Museum and had promised "great quantities of fossils, etc." to boot. Nor would Hayden be forgotten in the gift giving: "He is going to send you a great variety of publications that he can control, and can get, if you desire it," including "most of the geological works of the British colonies, of which there are a great many volumes to be had here."[73]

¶ Baird was not the only one to encourage Hayden to make use of the Centennial Exhibition to expand his network of scientific exchanges and seek new supporters. Gen. John Eaton, the Interior Department's Centennial Exhibition commissioner, suggested that each of the five judges on "collective exhibits" be presented with a set of annual reports and bulletins, as well as a half-dozen photos. The gift, he advised, would do "much in influencing their decision in favor of the Survey." Baird sought influence in different circles, however, and advised Hayden to distribute his wares liberally to the commissioners representing exhibiting countries rather than to the foreign judges. In a series of letters, Baird solicited materials to exchange with representatives from New South Wales, Brazil, Austria, Sweden, Japan, Russia, New Zealand, Queensland, South Australia, Victoria, the Zoological Society of London, and the South Kensington Museum. All of them, he assured Hayden, would make "satisfactory return."[74]

¶ The favorable reception of the plaster models and Holmes's assurance that there would be "no difficulty in duplicating them" inspired Hayden with an idea for yet another product for his growing enterprise to market. The models always remained a subordinate venture, however, and were never promoted as vigorously as the photographs, which were much easier to reproduce in quantity. Instead, Hayden seems to have relied more on personal appeals to potential buyers, using the income produced by sales to construct additional copies. Still, full or partial sets of six geological and ethnological models found their way to a number of schools and museums along the eastern seaboard as well as in Europe. Arnold Guyot took a set for the Museum of Geology at Princeton in 1877, and Packard ordered a set when appointed professor of geology and zoology at Brown University in 1878. F. W. Putnam convinced the trustees of the Peabody Museum at Harvard to purchase a set that year as well. By the end of 1878, Hayden had enough orders on hand to provide two months' work for his sculptor; he had even managed to sell a set of models as far afield as Berlin.[75]

As a result of all of these varied actions, for a span of years in the mid-1870s Hayden enjoyed great success in translating the disparate items he and his men collected in the West into the political influence necessary to gain the appropriations for continuing his work. For a time, his name became synonymous with exploration and remarkable discoveries. In December 1876, Henry Wood Elliott forwarded an advertisement clipped from the San Francisco *Advertizer and News Letter* advising Hayden that he was "getting notorious." The advertisement, a regular feature, facetiously announced that "Two hundred petrified cats have been found by Professor Hayden in an Aztec village. Each one had a convivial expression of countenance, and each clasped a petrified boot-jack."[76]

¶ That Hayden had become a household name is one measure of his success. Yet the secret of his success as an entrepreneur of science is not hard to find. He offered something for just about everyone. To westerners, he proclaimed the beauty and possibilities of their land. To potential investors and immigrants, he advised where to go and what to seek. To legislators, he supplied photographs, patronage positions, and glowing reports of their districts. To journalists and editors, he was a source of good copy. To the public in the East, his survey delivered beautiful photographs, stereopticons, and paintings of some of the most exotic scenery in the country. And to scientists, Hayden furnished prospects of many sorts. His survey provided employment, materials on which to work, and an outlet for publication—opportunities utilized alone or in various combinations. But Hayden was not altruistic. All of these fed into a feedback loop; in return, he expected recognition and support.

¶ In retrospect, it is hardly any wonder an enterprise offering so much to so many was successful. What is a wonder is that one person was able to develop all of this out of a five thousand appropriation of money left over from territorial expenditures in Nebraska. Hayden was an entrepreneur par excellence. Quick to recognize opportunities for science in the Great West that he loved so much, he was also quick to act on them. Though his survey developed with a number of weaknesses, through most of the 1870s Ferdinand Vandeveer Hayden was a dominant figure in public science.

¶ Yet in the process he also made a number of enemies. By the mid-1870s, Hayden was constantly under attack. He was openly assailed by Wheeler and those allied with his survey and not so openly by Powell, who operated behind the scenes to counter the threat the Hayden Survey represented to his survey. And he was also increasingly under attack from a new generation of scientists—men who possessed college degrees in their specialties and were not physician-naturalists like Hayden. To them, Hayden seemed an anachronism as well as an impediment to their advancement to what they believed was their rightful place at the helm of government science. Finally, there was increasing pressure within Congress to reduce the seemingly wasteful extravagance of supporting three competing and frequently overlapping and argumentative surveys, especially since none of them showed any indication of coming to a conclusion any time soon. When the storm finally broke, Hayden was not caught completely by surprise. Neither was he fully prepared.

8

Competing in a Changing Environment

There is [sic] going to be desperate efforts made outside in the West and from Boston to crowd me out, and take my "warm place" but if my friends adhere to me they will not succeed.—Hayden to Leidy, 31 December 1872

Powell's plots are deep as the devil (with a capital D) and are well designed to do us harm. But . . . Dr. is aroused and when Jim comes back—such counter scheming as they will do—Oh my!—Holmes to Peale, 5 June 1877

Hayden basked in the favorable attention his survey received at the Centennial Exhibition. He was at the pinnacle of his career. After nearly twenty years exploring the West, he had seen his efforts grow from personal wanderings to a government bureau employing several dozen men, including some of the most prominent of the nation's scientists. One of the country's best-known scientist-explorers, his name ranked with those of Lewis and Clark, Zebulon Pike, and John Frémont. To a large degree, he had accomplished his dream of having his name "ever identified with the Geology" of the West.[1] Yet he was not to savor his victory in peace. Instead, he soon faced the most serious challenge of his career, a fight to the finish for his scientific and political life.

¶ As an entrepreneur, Hayden had to do more than build his organization. He also had to protect and defend it against criticism and competition. In the 1860s, an opportunity had opened, enabling him and the other leaders of the Great Surveys to establish claims upon federal science in the American West. In the 1870s, that opening began to narrow, and by the end of the decade it was closing, as the political environment changed. As it did so, the leaders of the various surveys competed ever more intensely for the resources necessary to carry out their work. At the same time, Hayden became a victim of his own success. He had managed to situate civilian science firmly in the federal government, and his efforts contributed greatly to the possibility of making civilian careers in federal science, particularly in geology, topography, and paleontology. By the mid-1870s, a new generation of scientists was eager to capture the territory Hayden had colonized. Graduates of the new scientific schools that had sprung up in the previous two decades, they had dedicated themselves to specialist studies in those disciplines and sought to assume what they felt were their rightful places in those careers. Criticism of Hayden was one way of gaining the control they sought over their careers.

¶ Other factors that had an impact upon the political environment included the change from a Republican to a Democratic Congress, sectional rivalries between the East and the West, and a persistent national recession with growing pressure to reduce congressional appropriations. Together, the complex of changes formed the context within which a continuing rivalry was fought out between military and civilian scientists over the control of federally funded science and between divergent views of what sorts of science the federal government should support, all before an administration exasperated with the scandals of the Grant years and eager to effect changes in the civil service. Gradually, Hayden was finessed out of his position. But his detractors did not accomplish their goals easily. Hayden did not meekly give in, and he had a variety of weapons and allies at his command as he fought what proved to be a rearguard action.

¶ It would be too much to expect that Hayden could have avoided criticism and opposition as he built his organization, and in the 1870s he engaged in three serious struggles for mastery of the western surveys. The first was with the Army Corps of Engineers and the Wheeler Survey and resulted in a congressional investigation of the western surveys in 1874. The second was fought within the Interior Department, as Hayden sought to absorb Powell's survey in a campaign that began in 1874 and continued until the end of the Great Surveys. The third came in 1878, when the House of Representatives decided to refer the whole western survey question to the National Academy of Sciences (NAS) in a final effort to end duplication of work and "secure the best results at the least possible cost."[2] The first and last of these conflicts were pivotal, not only in Hayden's own career but also as marking definitive changes in the practice of federally sponsored science. Both occasioned pitched battles between Hayden and his critics. Though in each case both sides made reference to scientific practice and competence, the battles were largely fought in terms of personalities and practical politics, with charges of fraud and charlatanism and countercharges of cliques and special interests. Behind the combat, though, lay competing visions of science and its practice under government sponsorship. The underlying issues were control and purpose, as the rival parties sought to dominate federal science on the public lands.

¶ To some critics, Hayden seemed too ambitious, too eager to claim credit for himself and his survey for almost everything to do with the West. Some simply laughed at extravagant claims; others protested bitterly when he sought to claim as his own discoveries made by them, sometimes years earlier. To these, it seemed as if Hayden sought to be "monarch of all he surveys." Even allowing for the value of his work and giving due respect for his "real conquests and achievements," as early as 1872 the *Engineering and Mining Journal* commented that Hayden needed to be reminded that "the whole boundless continent ain't his'n."[3]

¶ If Hayden played the part of scientific monarch laying claim to the West, his actions were consistent with nineteenth-century geology and exploration science. With their emphasis on explaining a region of the earth, geology and the natural history sciences were highly territorial. The relative ignorance about the American West had been an advantage when Hayden began his career. It had provided an opportunity to open a territory and lay claim to it while making a name for himself. It was an opportunity he recognized from the first, writing Meek in March 1854 that going to Missouri would "give me a foothold in the West which I would endeavor to maintain." Having selected the region as his research project, he understandably sought to protect his claim.[4]

¶ The trans-Mississippi West was a large territory, but even so it proved too small for the ambitions of those who sought to lay claim to rights to map it and describe it for science and the nation. More exactly, the resources available to do so were too few, and therefore competition for them became intense. The most important resources were men and money, and not enough of either were available. Skilled scientific personnel were essential to the surveys, but they could not be manufactured on demand. Experienced men were in short supply. As the surveys expanded, they competed for the few men available and interested in such work, despite its hardships. Money was just as essential as men, and in the end it could only come from one source, the federal government. So the competition for men and money became a competition for patronage. Each winter, the survey leaders presented their proposals for the coming year, and each spring Congress decided their fates.

¶ Congress, however, might be influenced, which was a primary aim in the competition. Whatever else he tried to do, every survey leader had to influence Congress if he wished to continue in business; he had to convince Congress that his efforts deserved its patronage. Hayden competed for influence in all the ways described in the preceding chapters. He strove to do work that was not only scientifically accurate but also responsive to popular interests and needs. He hastened to perform favors for congressmen and administration officials whenever he could. He cultivated relationships with industrialists, publishers, scientific societies, and college faculties around the nation. When his funding reached a plateau in 1872, even as other survey leaders began to intrude on his territory, he began to compete in other ways, confronting and challenging them for control of western scientific surveys. As he did so, he turned to some of the same means he had always used. He recruited allies, friends, and patrons for the influence they might bring to bear. He strengthened his organization. He expanded his mission, laying claim to increased responsibility and authority over the territory he already occupied. All were ways of maneuvering for an advantage in the pursuit of mastery of the western surveys.

¶ Mastery held the promise of stability. In this, Hayden, like numerous other entrepreneurs, sought monopoly as a means of taming a competitive environment. As early as 1872 he laid claim to all of the territories as his domain for mapping and demonstrated antagonism toward efforts to move in on his claims. Noting that eastern state geologists were preparing a memorial to Congress urging the preparation and publication of a geological map of the states and territories, Hayden told Baird, "Let them take the states and I will take care of the Territories." Though he quickly changed it to, "that is King and Myself, etc.," his first statement was probably a truer expression of his feeling.[5] As he perfected his survey's organization and abilities, he became even more possessive of its, and his, territory and moved to overpower his opponents by either absorbing them or driving them from the field.

Hayden was no stranger to conflict. In 1874, he characterized the growth of his survey as the result of a "painful struggle . . . breasting apathy and some opposition" in pursuit of a secure place in the government and a steady source of funding. The opposition came particularly from the War Department, with its seventy-year tradition of topographical surveys. As Hayden's survey grew, it grew alongside those administered by the Army Corps of Engineers, especially those of King and Wheeler. King's survey had concluded most of its fieldwork by 1872, but Wheeler's was just coming into its own. By 1873, the Hayden and Wheeler Surveys were of roughly equal size. When Hayden proposed that January to transfer his operations to the eastern portion of the Rocky Mountain range in Colorado and New Mexico, he disingenuously informed Secretary Delano that the region was "unoccupied, at this time, as far as I am aware, by any other survey under the Government."[6] The statement was untrue, and 1873 found Hayden's and Wheeler's surveys occupying the same territory, setting the stage for conflict.

¶ Though Hayden later claimed to have had no "official" knowledge of other surveys in the same or contiguous areas that might be duplicating the work of his own, he clearly intended to challenge the engineers on their own ground. Having already written to Leidy at the end of 1872 that he expected "desperate efforts . . . to crowd me out, and take my 'warm place,'" Hayden recruited Gardner in early 1873 as part of a plan to challenge Wheeler's geographical survey by launching one of his own. No sooner had Gardner joined the Hayden Survey than his letters started to bristle with threats toward the Corps of Engineers, to the deep regret of his former partner, King, who reminded Gardner that "every blow at them falls fair on the head of me your oldest friend." At the same time, Hayden and Gardner drew up plans for the construction of a geographical and geological atlas of Colorado and New Mexico.[7] Since Wheeler also planned to survey all this territory, duplication was inevitable.

¶ Opposing the resources of the War Department would require assistance. For this, Hayden and Gardner turned to the Coast Survey. In 1872, Coast Survey Director Benjamin Peirce inaugurated the triangulation of a transcontinental arc to connect the maps of the Atlantic and Pacific systems, which were nearing completion. He anticipated opposition from the army, however, which already had a survey underway that embraced exact astronomical measurements. If approached correctly, Peirce was not likely to scorn a popular and influential ally in the halls of Congress. To win him over, Gardner recruited the assistance of J. D. Whitney, now on the faculty at Harvard and understood to be "very influential with the C[oast]. S[urvey]." Approving of the new partnership between Hayden and Gardner, Whitney agreed "to persuade his friends to support" them.[8]

¶ They sought an alliance with the Coast Survey of equal and independent partners. Recognizing that the Coast Survey was much better prepared to carry out exact astronomical work and establish primary reference positions, they were prepared to build on this groundwork with secondary triangulations in constructing their atlas. To that end, they were eager to "cooperate with the Coast Survey *in Congress and the field*" (emphasis added) and "work as allies with all our strengths and crush all shams." This was just the sort of cooperation Peirce welcomed, having already outlined such a plan in his annual report for 1872. He was happy, then, to point out in his annual report for the following year that Gardner had applied on behalf of the Hayden Survey to the Coast Survey for the accurate determination of several points in Colorado and that "similar requests were made somewhat later in the year, in behalf of surveys contemplated by the States of Wisconsin and Minnesota."[9]

¶ While Hayden and Gardner were laying their plans, maneuvering for allies, and recruiting men for the season's campaign, Wheeler was also busy. The Army Corps of Engineers had already made one attack on the Coast Survey's appropriations for the coming year, something Gardner characterized as the "opening gun." Attempting to recruit personnel for his own survey, Wheeler felt no hesitation in attempting to recruit from Hayden's own corps, infuriating Hayden and convincing him that it was all the more necessary to be sure of the survey's friends.[10]

¶ The controversy broke into the open in the summer of 1873. After martial posturing and saber rattling during the preseason, once in the field the opposing parties commenced serious skirmishing. The accounts that would later be presented to congressional inquirers were contradictory, but 9 July 1873 found Hayden and Gardner with their primary triangulation party and Lieutenant W. L. Marshall, who was leading one of the parties of the Wheeler Survey, meeting in Colorado's South Park to the "surprise" of all concerned. All who were there agreed that the parties camped together that day and held a friendly discussion, during which "some regrets were expressed" that they should all be working the same ground. Everyone also acknowledged that Marshall had stated that he regarded himself as under orders to survey along the main range of the Rocky Mountains and the Arkansas River valley to the west of South Park. But there was no agreement about what happened next.[11]

¶ Marshall laid all responsibility for duplication on Hayden, saying that Hayden first agreed to a division of labor that would have largely prevented duplication and then went back on his word. Hayden remembered the incident differently and denied having made any such agreement. Instead, he maintained that Marshall was not the only one under orders to survey the South Park region. Nor did Hayden consider their efforts to conflict, given the different nature of their investigations. Hayden claimed that he had told Marshall to "go on and publish his maps and reports, and that we would do the same."[12] Notwithstanding the expression of pacific intentions, accusations soon began to fly. Marshall's party charged Hayden with rushing into areas in order to preempt the Wheeler Survey. Hayden's party claimed that Wheeler was sending Marshall to follow them around to provoke controversy, incite a congressional investigation, and ultimately suppress the Interior Department surveys.

¶ Believing conflict with the army inevitable, Hayden had long been making preparations for it. Despite the skirmishes in the West, Hayden focused his main attention on Washington, where the battle would have to be fought. While he continually urged Thomas to keep the survey in the public eye, Hayden was even more interested in news of Washington officialdom. Was the War Department making any moves against his survey? Would the Coast Survey support him? Would the Interior Department champion his cause? Would civilian friends rally behind him? Hayden needed answers to these questions. He claimed Marshall had admitted that the Corps of Engineers "were '*going*' for us next winter" because in their view "the 'Engineers were educated to direct and expend the public monies for science' and . . . civilians were to serve under them." Certain Congress would disapprove of two parties working the same territory, Hayden predicted that though they had "escaped" the engineers the previous winter, "there is no dodging them the coming winter." He asked Baird to give the matter serious thought, "for we will have to strip to the waist next winter." He expected formidable opposition but was not without hope. Yale's William D. Whitney had assured him that "all the scientific men of the country will come to our rescue." Baird, too, hastened to reassure Hayden that if the Corps of Engineers succeeded in interfering with his work it could only be "at the expense of their labors in the same direction."[13] Heartening as this was, Hayden still sought further assurance of support in Washington. He needed to know if the Coast Survey would be for or against him and if the Interior Department would support him.

¶ Thomas reassured Hayden on both points. After a long talk with one of the Coast Survey's officers, he reported that the Coast Survey would stand with Hayden if the War Department sought to absorb the Hayden Survey. Thomas also spoke to one of the clerks in the Interior Department regarding the expected opposition. Having explained that Hayden wanted to know whether he would be "*heartily* supported by the whole influence of the Interior Department," Thomas told Hayden he could "rely upon it, that all are with you—and that they are at work in your behalf." With orders for his sixth annual report "coming in . . . by the hundreds," they were not only prepared to defend Hayden if the War Department should attempt to gain control of his survey, but they even stood ready to counter the move by seeking to have all explorations and surveys not strictly for military purposes placed under the Interior Department.[14]

¶ Hayden also found time in the midst of the summer's fieldwork to contact his congressional patrons. Soon after his encounter with Marshall, Hayden wrote Monroe that "the young Engineers threaten to extinguish us next winter" and told him that "We will look to you for strong aid." Responses were reassuring. Monroe assured Hayden that he could count on him, as did Senators John Logan of Illinois and Aaron Sargent of California. Ready to "fight to the death if necessary," Hayden asserted, "I neither take nor will give quarter."[15]

¶ Though Hayden and many of his supporters nurtured a bellicose mood during the 1873 field season, the real battle could not begin until Congress resumed in December. Even then, no overt notice was taken of the dispute until 15 April 1874, when Rep. Lazarus Shoemaker submitted a resolution calling on President Grant to "inform the House what geographical and geological surveys under different departments and branches of the Government are operating in the same and contiguous areas of territory west of the Mississippi River." The resolution asked whether or not it would be practicable either to consolidate the surveys under one department or define geographical limits for the different surveys to limit conflict and duplication.[16] The House readily agreed to the resolution and sent it to Grant, who asked Secretary of War William Belknap and Secretary of Interior Columbus Delano for their comments. In turn, Belknap sought a report from General Humphreys, chief of the army engineers, while Delano solicited statements from Hayden and Powell.

¶ Everyone agreed that the surveys might profitably be consolidated. Belknap and Humphreys argued that "economy and efficiency would be the result of consolidating all [geographical and geological] surveys under the War Department." Delano, drawing upon the arguments of Hayden and Powell, contended that "in view of the powers conferred and duties enjoined upon the Secretary of the Interior touching the development of agricultural, mineral, and kindred interests in our vast territorial domain, . . . all matter having any relation thereto should be wholly under the jurisdiction of the Department of the Interior." However, neither position made a strong impression upon Grant, who transmitted all five letters to Congress. Admitting the Interior Department's right to control all surveys "made with the view of sectionizing the public lands, preparatory to opening them for settlement or entry," he saw no reason to prefer either department when the object was "to complete the map of the country . . . [and] collect full information of the unexplored, or but partially known, portions of the country." Grant considered the issue of which department should administer the work "a matter of no importance" and suggested the decision should be based on "first, which Department is prepared to do the work best; second, which can do it the most expeditiously and economically." On the basis of the second criterion, he proposed the War Department be given control, but interested civilian scientists quickly noted he had begged the question of who could do the work better.[17]

¶ Grant's report was referred to the House Committee on the Public Lands, chaired by Washington Townsend. Finding the views of the War and Interior Departments "antagonistic" and having no instructions from the House regarding the message and accompanying papers, Townsend's committee decided to conduct its own investigation. Holding hearings between 11 and 21 May, they initially "requested the attendance" of Wheeler, Hayden, and Powell but soon found it necessary to expand the scope of their inquiry and solicited testimony from Humphreys, Delano, and Gardner. They also accepted statements from Marshall and a number of scientific institutions and individuals. Yet the hearing before the Townsend Committee gave Hayden an advantage. Townsend was a close friend of Hayden, while committee member Hiester Clymer was closely connected to the Hayden Survey through Endlich. While there is no absolute evidence, it is highly probable that Hayden Survey men suggested areas on which to question Wheeler, as in Clymer's dogged pursuit of the incongruity of employing civilians to do work for which army engineer officers were supposedly specially trained.[18]

¶ With friends at court, Hayden and Powell quickly put Wheeler on the defensive, even though he testified first. Townsend and Clymer asked most of the questions, requesting details on War Department surveys, and Wheeler repeatedly had to note that he could only speak for his own survey. Initially a very reserved witness, when Wheeler found that Hayden had no hesitation about going on the offensive, he became more forthright in his charges against Hayden and more openly defended his own survey. By this time, however, the civilians had outmaneuvered him. Hayden had begun his testimony by stating simply, "I desire to have placed on record the fact that the civilian side of the controversy before you has not been its author." He then used the occasion to point out the differences between army and civilian organizations and the special nature and requirements of the scientific temperament. Celebrating the work his survey had been doing and the popularity of its reports, he urged the need for continued congressional support, especially now that his survey, which in its skilled and experienced personnel represented many years of service, was a valuable resource to the nation. Hayden pressed his point home by distributing copies of the maps the survey had been producing as well as a variety of photographs. Wheeler, by contrast, had brought no maps with him, only promising to send copies to the committee.[19]

¶ Powell then weighed in on the side of civilian science. Deliberately selecting the worst examples of Wheeler's work, Powell held them up as typical of army surveying, raising doubts about the army's ability to provide accurate maps for its own needs. He even went so far as to assert that civilian surveys could supply all of the army's mapping needs with greater accuracy than the army and at less expense. Though Wheeler sought to regain the initiative, he could not escape three facts: the majority of his scientific personnel were civilians, competent engineering officers were in short supply, and the developments in technique his survey did exhibit were a result of adopting methods pioneered by civilian surveys. Nor did he do his cause any good by responding to the harsh criticisms leveled against his survey's work with personal attacks on Hayden's ability or the character of either Hayden or Gardner. Both men were able to make reasonable responses to his charges, and Hayden could not have sounded more the voice of reason than when he disdained to respond personally to charges against his character, while referring the committee to a dozen letters and memorials from "some of the ablest scientific men in the land" in response to Wheeler's charge of incompetence.[20]

¶ In the end, however, the committee's findings were even less definitive than the president's. Where Grant had ventured that the surveys could be combined under either department, the committee concluded there was "an abundance of work for the best talent of both the War and Interior Departments in these scientific examinations of the Western Territories for many years to come." It recommended only minor changes. Convinced the major problem was duplication, rather than unregulated competition, the committee decided the problem could easily be resolved by assigning different areas to the different surveys. Relying upon the statements of Belknap and Delano, it concluded that "a very brief consultation" between the secretaries of the two departments would suffice to prevent needless duplication.[21]

¶ Despite its shortcomings, the committee's report went a long way toward setting the conflict between the surveys within a historical context. Its summary of their history clearly exhibited the consistent and growing role of civilian scientists in the army surveys, while situating the surveys in the context of the economic and industrial development of the territories and country as a whole. Though the report did not propose an immediate change in the system of surveys, its logic clearly foresaw future consolidation of the surveys under the Interior Department by virtue of its particular needs and the insufficiency of personnel in the War Department. This and the fact that, if not a complete victory, at least the affair did not end in defeat for their survey and civilian science gave the Hayden camp cause to rejoice.

¶ While the Townsend Committee's findings vindicated civilian science in the federal government, that was only one aspect of the situation. Even if the Corps of Engineers was loath to recognize that the nation had changed dramatically since the 1850s, the significance of that change was not lost upon William H. Brewer, professor of geology at Yale and a former assistant on the California Survey. In a letter to the committee, Brewer made a strong point against the engineers by directing attention to the growth of the nation's scientific schools in recent years. Conceding that twenty or even ten years earlier placing graduates of West Point over the western surveys was to a certain degree "necessary," Brewer argued that had been because West Point was then the only school where "a liberal Engineering and Scientific education could be obtained." That was no longer true. By the 1870s, a number of new schools had grown up, and in them "very nearly all of our best younger topographers have been trained." Among such men, Brewer numbered King and two men now with Hayden: Gardner and Henry Gannett. Brewer went on to point out that not only had West Point educated none of the younger naturalists or geologists presently employed on federal surveys, but it did not claim to educate "topographers, nor geologists, nor naturalists, nor even to train men to take charge of geodetic work." Yet these were just the things the scientific schools at Harvard, Yale, and other places did claim to train men for in "long courses of study in the necessary departments." The graduates of these new schools of science had given impetus to the work that had been "so well inaugurated and carried to its present shape." The civilians had even "forced the Army to do work as well," to which Brewer added: "I think they [the army] never claim to do it better."[22]

¶ The changes Brewer highlighted and the committee recognized provided Hayden with strong support in his contest with the army. The Hayden forces could also rejoice in the fact that these same changes were contributing to the end of the army's monopoly of the western survey work. It is all the more ironic, then, that in a very short space of time the same changes contributed to Hayden's own displacement.

The sanguine expectations of the Townsend Committee were soon disappointed. Within days of the report's publication, the first effort at consultation between the war and interior secretaries ran directly into a brick wall. Professing a desire to prevent a repetition of the confusion of the previous season, Belknap sent a memo to Delano proposing that "an understanding should be had between the two Departments, as to the field within which each should confine the Surveying parties under its order." Delano promptly forwarded a copy of the proposal to Hayden for comment, who immediately recognized it for what it was. Belknap proposed that the course of the Union Pacific and Central Pacific Railways be designated as a boundary line and that War Department parties operate south of the line while Interior Department parties operated north of it. This was simply an attempt to make explicit what Marshall had claimed was an implicit understanding at the War Department. Rather than entertain the proposal, Hayden reasserted his own right, even obligation, to survey Colorado, arguing that the territory had been assigned to him in the appropriating legislation and that it was clearly "the intention of Congress . . . that the Survey should continue in Colorado." Wheeler, Hayden declared, did not operate under such restrictions, for "the Act authorizing Lieut. Wheeler's exploration, does not define any area."[23] If either party was to abandon the field, let it be the engineers.

¶ Delano sided with his geologist, and Hayden's instructions for 1874 called for "a continuation of the survey of 1873" in accordance with the appropriating act of Congress. As if to ensure perpetuation of the conflict, Delano added a supplementary note adopting as departmental policy Hayden's proposal for the "construction of an Atlas of the territory of the United States, west of the meridian of 99°30′." With Wheeler's survey embracing the territory west of the one hundredth meridian, the proposal encompassed the entire area of the Wheeler Survey.[24]

¶ Yet it is difficult to see how the recommendations of the Townsend Committee could have put an end to the warfare between the surveys. The hearings and letters had revealed not only the competition between Hayden and Wheeler but also the underlying tensions of the competing efforts to control science and scientific careers. On one side, there was the army's nearly seven-decade tradition. On the other, there was the new generation of civilian graduates of the scientific schools to which Brewer made reference. Rapidly advancing in numbers and self-assurance, they were much less inclined than their predecessors to submit to military direction and demanded the right to control their own destinies. Far from resolving the tensions between military and civilian visions, the committee's report hardly recognized them. Pointing to the "abundance of work for the best talent of both the War and Interior Departments," it preferred to do little more than encourage Congress to give recognition and support to "the value of the services of eminent scientific men in civil life" and promote "a generous rivalry" between the surveys. However, the rivalry was often far from generous. After 1875 it became even more intense, as Hayden strove to defend what he had won from Wheeler while warding off a growing threat from Powell.

One result of the Townsend Committee's investigation was the transfer of the Powell Survey from the supervision of the Smithsonian Institution to the Interior Department. Hayden and Gardner hoped this would enable the Hayden Survey to capture Powell's survey, but although Powell had volunteered that "for the sake of preventing any conflict" it might be well to place him under the Interior Department, he probably intended a position parallel, rather than subordinate, to Hayden. In such a fiercely competitive environment, Powell probably calculated that if Hayden could pose such a threat to Wheeler, who enjoyed the backing of the War Department, his own survey, with its tenuous hold on life, would be better off aligned with a powerful government office than with the relatively insignificant Smithsonian.[25]

¶ Whatever his intentions in proposing the transfer, its accomplishment provided all the incentive Hayden and Gardner needed to begin laying plans. In Congress, they sought to have the appropriating legislation worded in such a fashion that Powell's survey would be combined with Hayden's. In their own offices, Gardner began drawing up plans on how the two surveys could be consolidated. When "technical difficulties" prevented consolidation that year, Hayden and Gardner let the matter rest, temporarily. But Powell did not, and Hayden soon noticed disturbing changes in Powell's manner. The man who found an institutional niche alongside Hayden in the Interior Department was no innocent. Though he had come to Washington as a full-time resident only two years earlier, he did not come a naïf. Over the years, his efforts to extract money and win support for his exploring ventures had given him an intimate acquaintance with the political scene.[26] Just as Hayden had carefully nurtured connections in government and scientific circles, so had Powell. And in a move that would prove decisive, after his transfer to the Interior Department Powell began courting Garfield's goodwill.

¶ Although a minority member of the House following the 1874 elections, Garfield remained one of the more influential Republican members as well as a member of the Appropriations Committee. Hayden counted him as a staunch supporter, but Garfield was also a staunch supporter of the Smithsonian and considered his term as a member of its board of regents from 1865 to 1873 as "the most pleasant duty of my official life." While there is no clear evidence as to the immediate effects of Powell's efforts vis-à-vis Garfield, they were probably furthered when Garfield was reappointed to the Smithsonian's board of regents in 1877. By that time, Powell had restricted his personal studies to ethnology and saw his bureau's future home in the Smithsonian.[27]

¶ When immediate absorption of the Powell Survey proved impossible, Hayden soon discovered in Powell another competitor to his empire. He also began maneuvering to block Powell's appropriations. Powell had nearly completed his survey's task, namely, "The survey of the

Colorado [River] of the West and its tributaries," and he began to cast around for a new claim on life and appropriations. On 23 June 1876, as the House considered the Sundry Civil Bill, Powell sent in an amendment asking that the clause "For completing the survey of the Colorado of the West and its tributaries, by Professor J. W. Powell" be changed to "For the continuance of the geographical and geological survey of the Rocky Mountain region, by J. W. Powell." The amendment's sponsor forthrightly explained its purpose: "in order that the survey may be continued beyond the Colorado [River] region and embrace the whole Rocky Mountain region." This was Hayden's territory, and his supporters immediately called for the substitution of "completion" instead of "continuance." As Rep. William Holman put it: "Let us some time or another bring these surveys to a close."[28] This was just what Powell wished to avoid.

¶ The amendment changing the survey's title passed, but it retained the word "completion," a small victory for Hayden.[29] It was tempered with disquieting news, however, when Hayden learned that instead of taking to the field Powell planned to use the summer to "visit the scientific men of the Country," seeking letters of support and the influence of scientific societies. Hayden had previously heard from a "disaffected member" of the Powell Survey that Powell had hoped to "break up [the Hayden Survey] entirely" during the 1876 season but had been "crippled" by the failure to secure a large appropriation. As a consequence, Hayden began making preparations for a "great battle" during the coming winter.

¶ His plans were simple. By using his influence with members on the House Appropriations Committee, Hayden hoped to have both Powell and Wheeler "dropped out" at the next session. That would begin the "tug of war" in earnest, but Hayden proposed to be prepared. He would have his *Atlas of Colorado* ready to display in opposition to Wheeler's claims, but he knew he would also have to forestall Powell's efforts to build support among the scientific community, especially since he expected Powell to join forces with Wheeler. Thus, Hayden asked his scientific collaborators to help discourage commitments of support to Powell, explaining that whatever aid Powell received would "really [be] . . . against our Survey."[30]

¶ This time, however, the situation was complicated by changes in the political landscape. The 1876 elections had brought in a new Congress and, after a severe struggle, Rutherford B. Hayes as president. Both were strongly inclined to give at least the impression of reform after the scandals of the Grant years. Both also posed a challenge to business as usual on the western surveys. The challenge came first from Congress, but the way the issues developed there helped set the tone for a more serious challenge to Hayden in the Interior Department.

¶ With the continuing depression following the "panic" of 1873, Congress was in an economizing mood, and one of the areas on which it focused was the western surveys. The previous winter, Congress had shown a strong disposition to cut off funding for all scientific surveys. When Holman called for an eventual conclusion of the western surveys, he was not alone. Although the Appropriations Committee finally decided to continue appropriations for the Hayden, Powell, and Wheeler Surveys, many congressmen doubted whether appropriations for any of them were in order "in view of the present condition of the Treasury."[31]

¶ When the same committee reduced the appropriation for the General Land Office surveys, it outraged representatives and delegates from the western states and territories. Montana's Martin Maginnis professed to be "particularly wonder-struck at the power of humbug and successful log-rolling when ingeniously presented and industriously followed up." After voting $145,000 for the Hayden, Powell, and Wheeler Surveys, "chiefly for the purpose of taking photographs and sticking pins through bugs," the House proposed to allow only $200,000 "for the benefit of the actual settlers of sixteen States and Territories." Maginnis claimed he had "no reason to find fault with these geological surveys or these gentlemen who go out there and take photographs of our beautiful scenery." Yet he could not remain silent if, "when the interests of the actual settlers . . . are on the one hand, and this fanciful work of making photographs and handsomely-colored maps on the other, this House makes a mistake when it discriminates in favor of the fanciful and throws the practical work to one side."[32]

¶ The issue was even more stridently contested in the second session of the Forty-fourth Congress. The basic setting remained the same, as many congressmen continued to consider the geological surveys related to the public land surveys. But more ominously for their future, western members increasingly viewed the geological surveys as *competitors* of the public land surveys in the battle for appropriations. The geological surveys were not without supporters, however. Oregon's LaFayette Lane asserted their "incalculable value" and "true economy," claiming that they enabled a more intelligent determination of what areas to survey in the land-parceling system, "thus saving the expense of surveying lands unfitted for cultivation."[33]

¶ Yet as the House discussed the appropriation for the Wheeler Survey on 23 February 1877, John D. C. Atkins of Tennessee raised an issue that threatened all three surveys. Atkins told the House he had "made some little investigation" regarding Wheeler's appropriation. What he found was not to his liking. Though "not opposed to an appropriation" for scientific investigations, Atkins informed his colleagues that they were "making appropriation for duplicate and triplicate work." Reminding members that there were three surveying parties in the field, he claimed that "to a considerable extent" the different parties had been "going over the same territory and making the very same surveys." Worse, the government had been making appropriations for three groups "to make the same report with similar maps." Atkins declared Congress had a "duty to take up this subject and put it into the hands of a committee that will make proper investigation and report, so that the House can act advisedly, and that we may not make appropriations here for three companies doing duplicate and triplicate work, making duplicate and triplicate maps and duplicate and triplicate reports." The matter, he said, "should receive prompt attention next session."[34]

¶ Atkins struck a nerve. Whether he raised the issue on behalf of any of the survey leaders is unclear. However, he raised it during consideration of Wheeler's survey, and he suggested that the proposed appropriations reported by the Committee on Appropriations, with Wheeler and Powell each getting twenty thousand dollars and Hayden fifty thousand, were "a sufficient sum for these purposes." Both facts tended toward Hayden's benefit; the other two surveys would have been crippled, and Hayden would have been that much better situated for any future consolidation. Though Atkins found support for his proposal to consolidate the surveys in the next Congress, the survey proponents all rallied to their respective causes. Wheeler's supporters maintained that there was little duplication of work, even when the surveys covered the same territory, pointing to differences of purpose between his "largely military" survey and Powell's and Hayden's "largely geographical and . . . scientific" surveys. Hayden's partisans, in their turn, claimed that his survey was "valuable in every direction," useful for its practical findings and highly regarded for its scientific work. They stressed the practical and economic utility of geological and geographical surveys, the care with which the work was done, and Hayden's good character as a government employee. In the end, the surveys all survived that year's challenge, and when the bill finally passed Hayden received seventy-five thousand dollars, Powell fifty thousand dollars, and Wheeler fifty thousand dollars.[35] Yet it was evident that Hayden's struggle was far from over, especially since Congress's increased attention to economies and alleged inefficiencies among the surveys was accompanied by efforts at reform within the Interior Department.

Along with their appropriations for 1877, Hayden and Powell also acquired a new secretary of the interior, Carl Schurz. A man of strong moral convictions, Schurz believed his appointment carried a mandate to clean up the department. Though the worst scandals were in the Bureau of Indian Affairs and the General Land Office, the continuing squabbles between the rival surveys also troubled him, and he quickly took steps to put an end to the bickering, especially in his own department. On 19 May 1877, in an interview with Powell and Hayden, he ordered them to come to an arrangement that would put an end to the dissension. Adamant, he instructed the directors to submit their proposals within the next few weeks.[36]

¶ Powell responded within a few days. He began by dividing the work into two categories: geography and geology on the one hand and "subordinate and collateral investigations," embracing natural history and ethnography, on the other. Only investigations in the first category, he explained, could "easily be limited to small and accurately defined areas of territory." In the second, "a proper division of labor and economic publication of results must necessarily rest on some other basis." He then summarized the work being done in the different branches of science by his and Hayden's parties. Throughout, he professed a willingness to cooperate. His personal preference was ethnography, and he devoted more than half of his letter to this subject. Yet he declared a willingness to give even this up and proposed a "very simple" division of labor that would "do no injustice to either of the interested parties." Natural history should be assigned to one division and ethnography to the other. He suggested Hayden take the first, while he took the second.[37]

¶ For his part, Hayden did not relish the prospect of relinquishing any of his work. Nor did he trust Powell's sense of justice. Ever since moving to the Interior Department, Powell had worked to undermine Hayden's position, contacting and allying himself with Hayden's bitterest enemies, particularly Newberry and Marsh. Newberry had long since turned against his former student, perhaps because he considered Hayden insufficiently grateful, perhaps because he thought Hayden too brightly outshone his teacher, perhaps as part of Newberry's having aligned himself with the Wheeler Survey, or perhaps because Hayden had given up on waiting for Newberry to describe the specimens sent to him in the early 1860s and had turned to Lesquereux for descriptions of fossil botany. In any event, by 1877 Newberry bitterly opposed Hayden and sought to do him harm by supporting Powell in the legislative budget battles. Writing Garfield and Rep. Abram Hewitt in January of that year, Newberry charged that Hayden's survey had declined to such a state as "to bring into disrepute all the laudable scientific enterprises of the Government and throw odium upon scientific men." He urged that if it was "necessary to retrench in the matter of Western explorations, there may be some discrimination made between the good and the bad, and the retrenchment may fall where it will do the least harm and the most good."[38]

¶ Powell appreciated Newberry's efforts, which were really only a return for a favor Powell had already done him while simultaneously posing a threat to Hayden. Before leading his disastrous expedition to the Little Bighorn in June 1876, Gen. George Custer had led an expedition into South Dakota's Black Hills in the summer of 1874 exploring for gold. When his investigation verified reports that had trickled back from the region, he set off a gold rush to the Sioux reservation. Given the army's inability to prevent trespassing by gold seekers and the government's unwillingness to enforce the proscription against trespassing, the government ordered a survey of the region to determine its value with the intention of purchasing it from the Sioux. Accordingly, two geologists, Walter P. Jenney and Henry Newton, and a military escort of some 450 men surveyed the region in 1875. Their findings corroborated the prospectors' and Custer's reports, but while Jenney focused on the gold strikes, Newton undertook a more elaborate study of the geology of the Black Hills.[39]

¶Jenney quickly published his findings early in 1876, but one season in the field did not provide Newton with enough time for investigation, and his study remained incomplete and unpublished. In 1876, Powell offered to support a second expedition to the Black Hills so Newton could complete his investigations. In spite of the financial constraints under which he already labored, the offer suited Powell. Not only did this please Newberry, who had first proposed Newton as Jenney's assistant for the 1875 survey of the Black Hills, but it also offered the possibility of upsetting the findings of the only other author of a geological study of that region: Ferdinand Hayden, who had explored there with Warren in 1857. Powell and Newberry even went so far as to claim that Hayden had engineered a delay in publication of Newton's report out of fear that it would reveal deficiencies in his own work.[40]

¶ Learning of Powell's scheming, Hayden countered by recruiting allies to write Schurz on his behalf. At the same time, Powell's actions left Hayden suspicious of Powell's motives in his proposals for the future of their two surveys. Consequently, Hayden evaded Schurz's directive to suggest how the conflict between the surveys could be eliminated. Instead of presenting a proposal for dividing the labor, Hayden asserted that "the organization of [my] Survey is now so complete in all its details, and in such good working order, and its operations have proven so effective, that no material modification of its policy or its purposes seems to be required to insure the greatest efficiency and secure the best results." Far from proposing reductions, he set forth a program calling for expansion in all areas of activity.[41]

¶This was not what Schurz wanted to hear. Insistent, he addressed a letter to Hayden in Denver, informing him that while he had found Hayden's letter "interesting," he "regret[ted] to observe that it does not refer to the distribution of subjects which was agreed upon in my presence between Major Powell and yourself." Telling Hayden of Powell's "frank and fair" proposal, Schurz directed him to "make your choice accordingly, so as to prevent the duplication of work and the causing of unnecessary publication" and submit an "early answer." Forced to make a choice, Hayden responded nearly two months later, reluctantly accepting Powell's proposed division. The Interior Department quickly approved the choice, expressing the hope that "this division of labor will advance the public interests." Hayden Survey geologist William Henry Holmes knew better. Though Powell's plots were "deep as the devil (with a capital D)," Holmes told Peale that the "Dr. is aroused and when Jim [Stevenson] comes back—such counter scheming as they will do—Oh my!"[42]

¶ One of the first fruits of their "counter scheming" was a new proposal to combine the two surveys. Less than a week after accepting the division of labor, Hayden began drafting a letter to Schurz submitting "certain further considerations" with "important bearing upon the case, and which may tend to a more satisfactory adjustment of the conflicting interests involved." If the ideas expressed in the letter were sincere, they represent a dramatic change of heart. Three years earlier, Hayden had admitted that the "first impression of many, in fact of most persons" might favor a plan in which all the geological and geographical surveys in the Interior Department were placed "under one Bureau," but he had gone on to argue that "more mature reflection will show that this is an erroneous idea." Now he wrote that the existence of two virtually identical yet independent surveys under one department was an "anomaly [which] must necessarily result in evils of the first magnitude" when "one Survey, organized upon a proper basis, and conducted after a proper method, would accomplish all that both these surveys, as now carried on, could do, and at vastly less expense."[43]

¶ Hayden argued that combining the surveys would result in twofold savings. Fewer personnel would be needed, and excessive printing expenses resulting from the "natural rivalry" between two competing organizations would be eliminated. While he did not deny there was room for multiple surveys, he claimed that "one solid organization" could meet all the demands for scientific and economic knowledge regarding the geography, geology, and natural resources of the West. And lest there be any doubt about which organization might play that role, Hayden wrote that it was "well known to all who are acquainted with the history of such surveys, and will be acknowledged by all unprejudiced persons, that the various organizations which have operated of late years have grown up directly or indirectly in connection with the work inaugurated and prosecuted by the survey under my charge, and have met with a measure of success somewhat according to their imitation of the methods and objects of this organization." In light of this and Powell's "determination to withdraw" from geological and geographical surveys and devote himself to ethnography, Hayden said the way was "happily open for the much needed reform, which will do away with the present anomalous state of things, and correct a long standing evil." He proposed that Schurz instruct Powell to restrict himself to ethnographic work and assign all of Powell's geological and geographical work to Hayden's survey. This "perfectly just and fair" arrangement would help "preserve both organizations from perils that now threaten their destruction."[44]

¶ Schurz declined to follow Hayden's suggestion. There was no real need to do so. By then, Powell had quite given up geological and geographical explorations, and the bulk of his survey's work in those directions concentrated on publishing what had already been done and making follow-up studies of doubtful points. Yet Hayden's proposal was both timely and nicely calculated; as Hayden's biographer puts it, "it offered Powell what he seemed to want most, appeased those in Congress who cried for consolidation, and paid homage to Schurz's desire for efficiency."[45] That Powell failed to embrace it, and probably discouraged Schurz from enacting it, indicates that he intended more than restricting himself to ethnology.

When his bid to capture Powell's geological and geographical work failed, Hayden went on with his scheming. The results quickly became evident. In a confidential letter to Marsh in mid-March 1878, the geologist John James Stevenson complained, "that infernal Hayden is once more on the rampage." Hayden had convinced Atkins to introduce resolutions of inquiry into the activities of the various western surveys. The action posed a new threat to the Wheeler Survey, to which Stevenson was attached, and Hayden had picked his congressional ally carefully. Now chair of the Committee on Appropriations, Atkins was in a position to see that his suggestion to look into the matter of "duplicate and triplicate work" was carried out, and on 8 March 1878 he submitted two resolutions to the House. Emphasizing the need for economy and efficiency, the resolutions called upon the War and Interior secretaries to report on "all public geological and geographical surveys conducted by or under the authority" of their departments. In response to the call for information, Hayden, Powell, and Humphreys submitted reports on the surveys under their direction. Though each disclaimed knowledge of any intentional duplication of effort with respect to other surveys, duplication was obvious.[46]

¶ As if reviving the issue of duplication would not be troublesome enough for the Wheeler and Powell Surveys, Hayden was also "using with great effect the letters which were given to him on Gardner's account in 1873." As Stevenson expressed it, the letters supporting Hayden during the 1874 battle with the Corps of Engineers had been given in spite of Hayden, not because of him. Stevenson wished they could all be taken back. Readily confessing a "deep personal interest" in the matter, he told Marsh that what was "wanted is to get some letters on the Engineers' side, with which to head off Hayden and his letters." Those who had previously written letters supporting Hayden need only explain that they done so "under a misapprehension."

¶ Thus far things were proceeding in what had become their customary fashion, with Hayden seeking yet again to push the army surveys out of geology and natural history, and those in the army engineer surveys responding as usual. Then Stevenson indicated a possible new front for the battle: "[Clarence] King said this morning that an excellent idea would be to have some senator move that the whole matter of these surveys be referred to the National Academy to report on the competence of the persons in charge of the several surveys." Though he considered it "an excellent suggestion," Stevenson recognized that the only way the NAS could resolve anything was if the leaders of the surveys could be bound to abide by its decision. He believed Hayden, for one, "would not consent to the reference as it ould [*sic*] mean sure death to him."[47]

¶ It was an intriguing idea, however, for those who would have liked nothing better than the "sure death" of Hayden's power. In the wake of the responses to Atkins's resolutions, it was an inviting tactic and a fairly simple matter to have Hewitt, who sat on the House Appropriations Committee and was a close friend of King, suggest such an idea. Thus, when the appropriating legislation for the Hayden and Powell Surveys was reported, it concluded with a charge in some ways similar to what Atkins had suggested the previous year: "And the National Academy of Sciences is hereby required, at their next meeting, to take into consideration the methods and expenses of conducting the above surveys [Hayden's and Powell's], and the surveys of the Land Office, and to report to Congress as soon thereafter as may be practicable a plan for surveying and mapping the Territories of the United States on such general system as will, in their judgment, secure the best results at the least possible cost; and also to recommend to Congress a suitable plan for the publication and distribution of the reports, maps, and documents, and other results of the said surveys." The charge was virtually unprecedented. While its charter designated the NAS as an advisory body for the government whenever called upon, in the decade and a half since the academy had been created the government had been slow to call upon it, and Congress rarely asked its advice. Soliciting its advice was so unusual that Garfield was unaware Congress had the legal authority to "require" the NAS to undertake investigations. When the charge became law that June, Hayden quickly recognized it as a dramatic threat to his survey.[48]

¶ Though Hewitt clearly sponsored the passage referring the surveys to the consideration of the NAS, the genesis of the idea is obscure. Hewitt later claimed motivation by a concern that, for lack of system, the surveys had become "defective in administration, contradictory and discordant in results, and devoid of that unity which can alone insure general excellence." But Hewitt was not consistently anxious for these virtues, and he was probably encouraged in this direction by King and Powell. Both had strong personal motivations for suggesting arbitration by the NAS, as both had a number of friends there on whom they could count for a sympathetic hearing. Hewitt was King's closest friend in the House and would also soon become a partner with King in several cattle-ranching ventures. King may have suggested to him, as he had to Stevenson, the advisability of referring the matter to the NAS. If King first broached the idea that March, the date coincides remarkably with the conclusion of his final report for the survey of the fortieth parallel. A new position would not have been out of order.[49]

¶ Powell was probably active in instigating the move as well. By this time, Powell and King were friends rather than opponents, and Powell counted Hewitt as one of his survey's "friends." As early as January 1877, Powell had called upon King's aid in securing his appropriation in terms that indicate an acquaintance of some standing: "I beg of you to come and help me pull through this year. You can do me great good in exactly the direction in which I am needing assistance." Moreover, Powell had been advocating reform in the western surveys since 1874. As the weakest of the three players in the field, Powell had the least to gain in the maintenance of the status quo and the most to gain from reform; Hayden's position was just the reverse, which helps explain his antipathy toward reform. Without disruptive reform, as the leader of the dominant survey Hayden could look forward to eventually encompassing or eliminating competitors like Powell. Fearing exactly that, Powell sought reform to remove the threat.[50]

¶ Hewitt's original proposal referred only to the Hayden and Powell Surveys, along with those of the General Land Office. When the passage came up for debate in the House on 13 June 1878 Hayden supporters Atkins and Thomas M. Patterson of Colorado were able to include consideration of the Wheeler Survey as well. Patterson also proposed amending the charge by asking for a recommendation on "which of the said scientific surveys is the most thorough, skillful, useful, and reliable." Even Atkins opposed this amendment, however, as "threatening to tear all the legislation on this subject to pieces," most likely, perhaps, by inviting an open brawl among the existing surveys for the nomination. Patterson agreed to withdraw this amendment if the War Department surveys were included in the review, to which Hewitt agreed.[51]

¶ Hewitt later stated that he had originally thought the geological and geographical surveys ought to be confided to the Corps of Engineers. Whether this was so or not, from the first the goal was suppression of the Interior Department surveys. This is all the more clear given that the main points of the charge were not strictly necessary. A "plan for surveying and mapping the Territories of the United States" had been promulgated by Secretary Delano in July 1874. Nor was there need for "a suitable plan for the publication and distribution of reports, maps, and documents, and other results of the said surveys" since that already occurred through the usual procedure of submission to the House and Senate committees for public printing. Yet, if the "said surveys" were to come to an end, a plan providing for the completion of the work they had on hand might be in order, and Hayden's survey had by far the most work in progress. The problem with the Interior Department's "plan for surveying and mapping the Territories of the United States" was that it presumed a major role for Hayden, having been drafted largely on his recommendations, and it was his role that many wanted to eliminate.[52]

¶ That eliminating Hayden was one of the original goals is even clearer from the fact that when the proposal to refer the survey question to the NAS first came up in Congress, both Hewitt and Garfield were amazingly well informed about the academy's plans. Both sought to amend the proposal by striking out the reference to the academy's "next regular meeting" and substituting "at their next meeting," on the understanding that it was to have an "immediate" meeting.[53] It is unlikely they would have known this unless they had been in communication with academy members. King and Powell are the most likely potential intermediaries.

¶ For the reformers, including the War Department surveys was not a bad idea. Nor was decreasing the army's role a bad idea from Hewitt's perspective, since he had made doing so one of his primary goals since entering the House in December 1875. But none of the would-be reformers had any desire to adopt Patterson's second amendment. If the choice were one of making comparisons of the existing surveys rather than a proposal for creating some new system of surveys, Hayden stood a much stronger chance of not only surviving but even vanquishing his opponents. Still, the issue was unclear enough to Atkins and Patterson that they were satisfied with ensuring that the emphasis of the NAS review would not be merely an attempt to suppress or reform the surveys in the Interior Department but would include the War Department as well. At the same time, their amendment enlarged the opportunity of civilian science, which was quite acceptable to the reformers. Even many of Hayden's opponents supported him on this principle. But it was a critical period. The phrasing of the issue clearly favored the interests of economy, while leaving a great deal of discretion concerning what aims a survey of the public domain should embrace. In the hands of the wrong committee, Hayden's organization could face a severe challenge.

¶ Unfortunately for Hayden, the death of Joseph Henry in May 1878 threw the selection of the committee's membership into the hands of a declared foe. Henry had been president of the NAS since 1867 and had done much to transform it from an insular, self-congratulatory circle to a scientific meritocracy. With his death, Marsh, as the academy's vice president, automatically became acting president. Marsh held a number of grievances against Hayden. One was his support of Cope. Another was a legacy of the 1874 battle with Wheeler, whom Marsh had supported. Hayden had sought to persuade him to reconsider, but Marsh perceived the effort as an attempt at blackmail and remained a supporter of the Corps of Engineer surveys. By 1878, he had even contracted to bring out his monograph on toothed birds as one of the volumes of the King Survey.[54] As acting president, Marsh wanted the NAS to take a more active role in national scientific affairs, and one of the first subjects to which the academy turned its attention was the federal surveys. With Marsh in charge, that attention did not view Hayden with any great favor, nor he it.

Hayden had long been skeptical about proposals to submit the western surveys to another committee. He was even less optimistic about any good coming from a study by the NAS, telling Scudder in late December 1877: "if you wish to kill a project outright with Congress get [the NAS] to propose it." Congress, Hayden pointed out, liked to make its own plans. But once Congress adopted this plan, Hayden had no choice but to defend his work and attempt to prevent his enemies from gaining control of the committee. He moved quickly to rally supporters. He had copies of the charge to the NAS printed up and sent them to his friends, urging them to attend the next meeting of the academy in New York. He was not without friends who could act for him in the NAS, yet he feared his friends were "liable to be *apathetic*, while a few enemies will be extraordinarily active." His own hopes depended upon the nature of the committee appointed, and he turned to Baird for help. As a member of the council of the NAS, Baird might be able to influence the membership of the committee. While he worried that Marsh might "consider this a good opportunity to pay off old scores," he was also suspicious of Newberry, telling Baird not to let him be appointed "on any consideration whatever." Hayden appealed to Baird's own interests as well. Baird had just been appointed to succeed Henry as secretary of the Smithsonian, and Hayden warned him that if "certain influences" got control of the western survey work, the Institution stood to lose an important source in natural history collections.[55]

¶ However, a surprise was in store for Hayden. He had assumed the committee would be appointed at the academy's November meeting, but Marsh did not wait until then. On 13 October, Hayden received a letter from Schurz transmitting a notice that the committee had been appointed and inviting him to submit a report for its consideration.[56] While Hayden explored the Yellowstone and implored his friends to attend the NAS meeting, his enemies appointed a committee that manifestly did not share an interest in preserving Hayden's organization. Setting himself as chair, Marsh named Dana, Newberry, William B. Rogers, William P. Trowbridge, Simon Newcomb, and Alexander Agassiz as members.

¶ In a statement clearly meant for public consumption, Marsh explained that in appointing the committee "it was obvious that I could not properly select as members any of those who had taken part in the controversy between the then existing government surveys." While none of those chosen was then directly connected with any of the western surveys, few met the condition of not having taken part in the controversy. Even fewer were well disposed toward Hayden. Dana was at best lukewarm, while Marsh, Newberry, and Agassiz were declared foes. Most had reason to favor quite different interests. The committee was drawn almost exclusively from the Northeast, that is, from the most urbanized and industrialized section of the country, and almost exclusively from the world of academics. Even then, only a small segment of the academic world was represented: Yale, Columbia School of Mines, and Harvard. Furthermore, five of the seven were geologists, while the only representative of biology had already expressed himself as opposed to its inclusion in geological surveys. In large part, the committee sought to advance the interests of one of its own, King, who belonged to their world by birth, academic training, and scientific and social achievement.[57]

¶ After a preliminary meeting in New York on 19 October, the committee presented its recommendations to the full membership of the NAS during a special business session at Columbia College on 6 November. "After a full discussion of three hours," the thirty-five members present, including Hayden, adopted the report by a vote of thirty-one to one. The report made three basic proposals: that the Coast Survey be transferred from the Treasury Department to the Interior, be renamed the Coast and Interior Survey, and be charged with the "entire mensuration of the public domain"; that a new organization be created under the Interior Department to be called the United States Geological Survey (USGS) and charged with "the study of the geological structure and economical resources of the public domain"; and that the General Land Office give up all surveying but retain responsibility for disposition and sale of the public lands. For surveying it would call on the Coast and Interior Survey, and for questions regarding classification and value of the lands, the USGS. This tripartite arrangement, said the report, would eliminate duplication and wasted effort and secure "perfect co-ordination and co-operation between the three branches."[58]

¶ Among the practical results of the NAS recommendations, three in particular deserve notice. First, all the present surveys in the West would suffer "discontinuance." Second, the army's role would be greatly reduced. Though it would be allowed to continue conducting surveys in cases of military necessity, the dominant role in western surveying would pass to the civilian sector. Finally, the recommendations left no place for zoology and botany. Natural history would be reduced to "necessarily connected paleontology," while the USGS devoted itself to "illustrating the resources and classification of the land, [and] reports upon general and economical geology."[59] In this, especially, the report repudiated much of Hayden's organization, the only survey that gave a major place to studies in zoology and botany.

¶ The committee had presented its recommendations to the academy membership as a unanimous report based on serious study and careful consideration of statements from the heads of the various surveys. This was a blatant fraud. Even before naming the committee, Marsh had already formulated the outlines of the plan that was eventually proposed and was sounding out opinions on it from committee members and, through Newcomb, from Schurz and Coast Survey superintendent Carlile Patterson. Originally, Marsh thought to suppress the conflict between the civilians and the military by separating their efforts and assigning them different aspects of the work, but Newcomb doubted this would work. Aside from practical difficulties, he worried about attempting to impose a decision without consultation. Familiar with the ways of Congress, he sought to proceed more diplomatically and advised Marsh that it was "essential" that the committee at least appear to have conferred with "the now existing authorities."[60]

¶ Newcomb feared Marsh "greatly overestimat[ed] the influence of the Academy as a body relative to that of the men who will be working against our plan in case they are dissatisfied with it." If Hayden, Wheeler, and Powell were all "satisfied with the report of the Academy it will be well," but there was "no reason to suppose that they will be unless we find out before hand exactly what they each will want." But if they were dissatisfied, "the strongest argument with which they could go before Congress would be that the Academy had decided on a plan in secret session and considered the whole subject without allowing them to be heard." Three days later, Marsh sent a notice to the secretaries of the War and Interior Departments informing them that a committee had been formed and inviting them to convey "any information in regard to the plans and wishes of your Department" with respect to the surveys. This provided the appearance of consultation, but none of the communications were received until after the committee had met. In any event, only one individual considered any significant changes advisable, and he already had good connections with the committee. H. G. Wright, acting chief of the Corps of Engineers, reiterated the army's argument of military necessity. J. A. Williamson, commissioner of the General Land Office, argued that any change in the methods of surveying the public lands for the purposes of establishing and transferring title would only "create confusion."[61]

¶ Nor did Hayden suggest much by way of modification. He began with a challenge. Writing that "however desirable might be some great comprehensive plan of surveys, which should include all the scientific organizations connected with the Government," Hayden claimed the question must inevitably arise: "is any such plan practicable at this time? Is the country ready for a Department or Bureau of Science?" If the answer was "No," then "we have simply to consider what plan may be most practicable and what one may meet the approval of a majority of Congress and the scientific men of the country?" Believing the answer was "No," Hayden went on to outline what *had* proved practicable. He stressed the completeness of his organization, citing testimony that "there was not such an organization in all Europe." He argued that if this were so, "material changes in the organization" were more apt to produce ill effects than good and only retard the progress of the western surveys. Still, Hayden recognized that some changes were likely to be proposed, among them combining the present distinct geological surveys under the Interior Department. He endorsed this proposal and called attention to his letter to Schurz, where he had made just such a proposal. And in a concession to the War Department, he wrote that if it should be decided to continue separate geological surveys in that department, the respective secretaries could determine the areas to be assigned to the different parties, as had been recommended in the 1874 report. He did not consider it advisable, however, "to divorce topography from geology" since "experience shows it to be impracticable as well as unwise."[62]

¶ What is most striking about Hayden's letter is what he hardly mentioned and was, in fact, one of the chief objections to his survey: the work he underwrote in zoology and botany. His only mention of these branches of natural history was an oblique reference that, once parties had been organized, naturalists might be added to them at "very little additional expense." Hayden had good reason not to call attention to this work, recognizing as he did that Congress's attention was focused on the economic benefits to be derived from surveys conducted "at the least possible cost" and that at least one member of the committee opposed work in zoology and botany in the surveys.[63] It was not that he did not consider such work a proper object of federal support. It was a matter of considering his audience.

¶ Powell's communication to the NAS committee differed markedly from the others. Rather than defend any existing organization, Powell castigated the entire system of surveys and called for thoroughgoing reform. Though he reserved the largest measure of criticism for the General Land Office, he began and ended with comments on the geological and geographical surveys, referring to statements he had made in response to Atkins's resolution of 8 March. There, Powell had argued that under the present arrangement two distinct cartographic systems were in use, which resulted in the construction of atlases on different scales that were inadequate for mutual use by the departments. If this situation was allowed to continue, the result would either be duplication of the entire area or two separate atlases of demarcated regions that would be of little or no use to the other department. "In view of all these facts," he had concluded, "it is manifest that the work should be unified and a common system adopted."[64]

¶ Writing that the labor should be divided on a "scientific basis," Powell advocated separating the geographical from the geological work. He further noted that "if ethnology, botany, and zoology are to be embraced in the general scientific survey" each of these "should have but a single organization, with a single head subordinated to the general plan." The present undifferentiated system, with its "multiplication of organizations for all of these purposes," was "unscientific, excessively expensive, and altogether vicious." It not only prevented "comprehensive, thorough, and honest research" but stimulated "unhealthy rivalry" and led to the production of "sensational and briefly popular" presentations rather than "solid and enduring results."[65]

¶ Claiming the government had a long tradition of funding scientific research "for the purpose of making many of the great industries of the people at large more remunerative and secure," Powell argued that any reorganization of the surveys should be allied with "the great industrial interests of the country, those relating to agriculture and mining." Such a survey would "always receive ample support because the results of its work will increase the national wealth and beneficially affect the largest proportion of the people." Any survey "divorced from these economic considerations, and devoted to research valuable chiefly for abstract science, must always be weak and have an uncertain tenure of existence." Powell buttressed his argument with a consideration of "the broad question of what should be the attitude of a government toward scientific surveys" and identified two principles. Government support "should be very limited and scrupulously confined to those objects of research which under ordinary circumstances could not or would not be undertaken by individuals." At the same time, the government had a right to expect results of "utilitarian value" for all classes in the population. On the basis of these principles Powell judged that zoology and botany were not proper subjects of government patronage. They already had "thousands," even "tens of thousands," of cultivators "who neither ask nor want the slightest assistance from the government," and their findings were rarely utilitarian. Apart from emergencies, there was no need to fund such research.[66]

¶ Powell concluded his reflections by stating that he did not intend to recommend any "specific plan of organization or specific method of survey." Nevertheless, the similarity between his recommendations and those of the NAS report goes beyond coincidence and is obviously the result of Powell's close consultation in the drafting of the committee's report. In fact, Powell had already proposed a plan for the future of western surveys in a document that would have revolutionary implications, his *Report on the Lands of the Arid Region of the United States*. Since at least 1874 Powell had been struck by the aridity of most of the lands west of the hundredth meridian and had begun to argue that that fact ought to be dominant in government land policy for the region. Four years later, he had come to some firmer conclusions, which he spelled out in *Lands of the Arid Region*. The basic thrust remained the same as in 1874. Land surveys in the region would only be remunerative if they emphasized economic geology. Irrigation was so fundamental to settlement and economic development in the arid regions that land legislation must set aside the traditional American sanctity of private property and insist that natural resources be used in a manner consistent with the public good. Following upon this, proper use of the arid lands required wholesale reform in the methods of parceling and selling public lands. Lands had to be disposed of according to the availability of water and their suitability for various agricultural uses. In short, the arid lands had to be dealt with scientifically, utilizing wise legislation, engineering of the greatest skill, and comprehensive planning.[67]

¶ Powell had not kept his ideas to himself. No sooner did the Sundry Civil Bill pass than he wrote Marsh forwarding several copies of his recently issued *Lands of the Arid Region* for the proposed committee's perusal. Along with them went a request to allow Powell to address the committee, once it had been formed, "setting forth what I deem to be the proper organization for the United States Geographical and Geological Surveys." It might seem bold to presume to send copies of a report and request that the members of the yet-to-be-named committee read "at least the first two chapters" by way of preparing themselves for "a clearer understanding of the plan which I shall propose." But it would not have been so bold for someone involved in the entire scheme from the beginning. The plan ultimately reported by Marsh's committee shows how involved Powell remained. Transferring General Land Office surveying to the Coast Survey answered his concern for an exact survey founded on secure determinations of position, while making possible the economy of skipping large areas of territory not susceptible for agricultural purposes. More directly relevant to Hayden, the proposed USGS was very similar to the geological survey Powell advocated: operations closely allied to, and circumscribed by, economic and utilitarian interests; scientific research sharply curtailed; and zoology and botany totally deleted. Little wonder the Coast Survey's Julius Hilgard reported to Marsh at the end of November that "Powell says the project is just what he wants."[68]

The NAS recommendations notwithstanding, it remained an open question whether, as Asa Gray commented to Hayden, Congress would "pay any attention" to the report or "treat it, as it, and the Departments do, Reports of Visiting Committees." Marsh and the others who had set the whole process afoot were determined to see to it that Congress *did* pay attention to their recommendations. Following the November meeting, Marsh went immediately to Washington. By the end of the week, he had secured endorsements from the Interior and Treasury secretaries, the army chief of staff, the superintendent of the Coast Survey, and the president himself. It was an auspicious beginning, and Agassiz congratulated him on his success. But he also warned: "Hayden is at work . . . making misrepresentations and not stating the whole."[69]

¶ Exactly what Hayden was doing is unclear. The whole affair had put him at a disadvantage, which he had to attempt to overcome as he sought to turn the situation to his benefit. While it soon appeared that he had mixed feelings, initially he expressed satisfaction with the NAS report. Writing Agassiz that it was "a remarkable piece of condensed thought," Hayden said it "must prove the foundation of organized science in Washington and on that account I voted for its adoption." Though he would have "preferred some modifications," Hayden could "not see how the Committee could have made any other report." But as Hilgard observed, Hayden faced a predicament: "altho' he knows that it is not *him*self that is thought of by the authors of the Report for Geological Director, [he] would certainly think it too soon to counteract it. *He* has to sink or swim by it, for the defeat of the Report is that of Hayden and Powell and is the triumph of the Engineers."[70] In the meantime, the plan's supporters labored to ease it through Congress.

¶ The first signs of dissatisfaction came from the Coast Survey and the Corps of Engineers. On 22 November, Patterson sent Marsh an "unofficial" letter backing away from the proposal to transfer the Coast Survey from the Treasury. Patterson feared a loss of independence in administering the Coast Survey if it should be transferred to the Interior Department and required to work in conjunction with the General Land Office. At the same time, he realized it would "not do to let any other regular organization be formed in the Interior Department for Interior Surveys," and so the Coast Survey would "observe a 'masterly inactivity.'"

¶ Patterson had taken a conservative position from the first, considering such a stance traditional in the Coast Survey. He admitted that the Coast Survey did not have an "intimate" connection with any government department and that as it finished its coastal work and moved into the country's interior it would probably naturally gravitate into the Interior Department until Congress eventually established a "Department of Public Works." But he feared antagonism from the Corps of Engineers, whom he characterized as a "very powerful body expending annually some eight millions of the Government money" who hoped eventually to receive responsibility for all surveys. Thus, he became alarmed in early January 1879 when he heard that the NAS was involved in "secret action[s]" and quickly fired off letters to Marsh and Newcomb asking for information of any action taken by any member of the Coast Survey that had "tended in the most remote degree to influence your opinion or that of any member of the Academy." Shielding Hilgard's role, Marsh admitted none, except the "unofficial" advice and "approval" Patterson himself had given when asked about "one or two points" by Newcomb.[71] The response, along with Marsh's assurance that nothing had been done in secret and that the Corps of Engineers had been kept fully informed and given every opportunity to make suggestions, sufficed to confirm Patterson in his "masterly inactivity."

¶ The engineers, on the other hand, decided to take the offensive. Fulfilling Newcomb's prophecy that they would protest strongly if they felt they had not received a fair hearing, General Humphreys, the Chief of Engineers, argued that by excluding all members of existing government surveys the committee had hardly anyone competent to pass judgment upon the western surveys. According to Humphreys, having the Coast Survey assume responsibility for all topographical surveying would increase the cost astronomically, compared to the economical work of the Corps of Engineers. However, supporters of the NAS plan easily dealt with the objection by pointing out that the cost of topographical and geographical surveys depended on the exactitude desired and the terrain to be studied. Powell argued that in contrast to the rugged and forested regions of the Atlantic and Pacific coasts, "more than nineteen-twentieths of the country to be surveyed is such that geographic work, including triangulation and topography, can be executed at very small expense," estimating an average cost of two dollars per square mile.[72]

¶ After the report was presented to the House on 2 December 1878, the Speaker referred it to the Committee on Appropriations the following day.[73] There, Hewitt took charge of it and, with King's assistance, drafted legislation incorporating the recommendations of the NAS report, probably working from drafts provided by Powell. Legislation reforming the surveys was inserted into the Legislative, Executive, and Judicial Expenses Bill, while an appropriation for the USGS was included in the Sundry Civil Bill. As chairman of the Appropriations Committee, Atkins reported the Legislative Expenses Bill on 10 February 1879. Among the few propositions in the bill over which there was "likely to be any serious contest," Atkins identified "the change proposed by the National Academy of Sciences in the mode of conducting our geological and geographical survey and land-parceling surveys." But as the first of three House proponents of the plan, Atkins called the proposal "the most important feature" in the bill and commended it to the House's "most careful attention."[74]

¶ The proposed change was indeed the object of "serious contest," yet the contest had little to do with the geological surveys per se. The problem lay with the proposed reforms to the land-parceling surveys. Apart from the notable exception of Peter Wigginton of California, almost every western representative and delegate opposed any changes in these surveys as being liable to impose excessive expenses upon settlers and disrupt entering and filing claims. Hewitt, the second member of the trio defending the plan, then rose to speak on 11 February. Relying heavily upon Powell's arguments, Hewitt identified reform in the land system as the only way to accommodate environmental realities in the remaining public lands. More significantly, he closely equated the geological surveys with a modern industrial economy, declaring that "the science of geology and the science of wealth are indissolubly linked together." Focusing on the nation's resources in coal and metals and their place in modern industry, Hewitt said the plan directed the attention of the geological surveys "to these immeasurable elements of national wealth . . . [and] to a rigid, profound study of these great fundamental problems of national progress." It had come "from the highest scientific authority in the land" and "commends itself to the judgment of the men who have been most energetic and successful in the development of our resources, the 'captains of industry' of our time." However, not all House members were convinced that "the highest scientific authority in the land" could be trusted on such an "intensely practical question" as the public land surveys. Minnesota's Mark Dunnell argued that overturning a "well understood" system and replacing it by an unknown and untested quantity with "new rules, [and] new methods," when settlers on the frontier "already [had] enough to contend with," required "practical argument and good sound reasoning rather than the scintillations of an excited imagination."[75] At this point, James Garfield, the third member of the trio supporting the proposed reforms, rose to speak.

¶ Garfield said nothing about the General Land Office surveys, the subject of such interest to most western representatives. Instead, he focused on the geological surveys, arguing that it was of the "utmost importance" that federal support of science be based on a "well-understood, well-reasoned, and well-defined system." From the beginning, his remarks resonated with themes Powell had made his own. Garfield called for limited federal involvement in science. Insisting the government should beware of becoming a competitor to private interests, he claimed scientific men generally preferred "to be let alone to work in free competition" and as a "general principle" the government "ought not to interfere in matters of science, but should leave its development to the free, voluntary action of . . . the people themselves." Garfield claimed that exceptions for this rule had clear mandates in the Constitution, as in the establishment of lighthouses or a "great popular interest" involving the whole community that unaided private enterprise could not accomplish, such as in protection from epidemic diseases or inquiries of such "great magnitude and cost" that private individuals could not successfully undertake them.

¶ Garfield identified the geological surveys as falling under the last category and thus as appropriate objects of federal support. Yet he argued Congress had been supporting them unwisely, that due to a lack of systematic forethought a "large part" of its support had been spent in "a way which has tended to discourage the private pursuit of science." By that he meant that much of the money had been used to support studies in natural history and the multiplication of scientific publications, areas Hayden supported and that Garfield claimed private interests were capable of supporting without government assistance. Garfield said it was "high time" for the government to restrict its scientific work "within the limits of the rules" he had laid down, consolidate the "scientific part of our work of survey under one responsible head," and limit appropriations for work "only in the direction of public necessity."[76]

¶ Garfield considered his speech a discussion of "the division of power in our American System into three classes, national, state and the reserved power of the people," and he believed he had "made more impression on the thoughtful men of the House" than he usually did. Powell was probably pleased with the speech as well since its principle of limited government involvement in science might have come directly from Powell's own arguments as adopted by the NAS report. Garfield need not have relied on the academy's report for his argument, however, since Powell had gone far in cultivating his friendship in the preceding couple years, so far that sometime after April 1878 he sent Garfield a copy of his *Lands of the Arid Region* with the request that he read at least "the first two chapters." Yet Garfield was a busy man, a man whose influence in the government was much solicited, and he struggled to keep up with his correspondence without the aid of a full-time secretary. Powell came to his assistance, even as he sought Garfield's aid. Beginning on 21 December 1878, Powell sent one of his own secretarial assistants around to Garfield's house a couple of days each week to help him keep up with his mail. The arrangement lasted until the end of the congressional session.[77]

¶ Though Hewitt's speech had met with "great applause," most western legislators remained opposed to any changes in the system of entering the public lands. Eventually, they forced deletion of all sections in the Legislative Bill dealing with reform of the land-parceling surveys. In comparison, the sections establishing the USGS and the attendant suppression of the Hayden, Powell, and Wheeler Surveys, attracted relatively little attention and were passed by the House on 25 February and sent to the Senate. The Sundry Civil Bill, with its appropriation for the USGS, had already passed the House with little debate the day before.[78]

¶ The plan narrowly escaped defeat in the Senate, and here Hayden's strategy begins to become apparent. The charge to the NAS had posed a serious challenge, and Hayden first responded by seeking to shape the committee and its report. When those efforts failed, he acted on two fronts. The next battle would have to be fought in Congress, and there he sought either to undermine support for the academy's proposal or to obtain its effects. After all, one result of enacting the academy plan would be the suppression of all the current surveys. As a competitor, Hayden did not lose sight of the goal but looked to the longer term. If it was impossible to prevent enactment of the proposal, it might be possible to capture it. He therefore assisted House opponents of the proposed changes to the General Land Office surveys in attacking the NAS report as the work of a "revolutionist," that is, Powell, and a "kangaroo report" that was opposed by a majority of the most prominent members of the academy. Simultaneously, Hayden laid plans to finesse the issue in the Senate.[79]

¶ When the Sundry Civil Bill came up for debate on the Senate floor, Aaron Sargent, one of Hayden's staunchest supporters, successfully proposed an amendment transforming the appropriation for the USGS into an appropriation for the Hayden Survey. Then, when the Legislative Bill was taken up on 1 March, the entire section establishing the USGS was deleted. Since the House and Senate bills contained a number of significant differences, however, they were referred to conference committees on 2 March, a day before Congress was to adjourn. In conference, it became apparent that the differences between the House and Senate versions of the Legislative Bill could not be resolved in time to be passed before the end of the session. At this point, Hewitt and Atkins, as House members of the conference committee, were able to insert the clauses of the House version of the Legislative Bill establishing the USGS into the Sundry Civil Bill. The next day, the last day of the legislative session, both the House and Senate accepted the conference report of the Sundry Civil Bill, and President Hayes signed it into law late that evening.[80]

¶ The legislation establishing the USGS was thus saved at the last hour, and many of Hayden's supporters voted for it in the end. They probably thought they were voting for Hayden since he had already secured the endorsement of nearly two-thirds of the members of the House and Senate for the new directorship. Newcomb later claimed that had King's supporters not acted quickly, Hayes might have nominated Hayden for the position the very next day, but that may be only hyperbole to emphasize their eventual victory.[81] What is clear is that Hayden had claimed the West as his territory and had developed and defended that territory for two and a half decades. Now challengers threatened to overrun it entirely, but they had not yet succeeded. If he had lost a battle, he had not yet lost the war. Mastery remained the goal, and the contest remained undecided. He could still redeem all and win complete victory over his opponents as the competition became a furious contest for the directorship of the USGS.

9 Generalist versus Technocrat

I have a stronger desire that what I have done may contribute to science than any personal reputation, though I wish both. —Hayden to Meek, 12 January 1856

Many persons who have seen me grow up from nothing imagine I should do for them the same servile things I did years ago, but I claim some respect now, or I let them alone. —Hayden to Leidy, 26 October 1872

In late December 1878 J. J. Stevenson warned Marsh: "If you expect to secure the appointment as Chief Geologist of the U.S. Surveys for any reputable geologist, . . . you will do well to make yourselves sure that the President will nominate the right man and that when nominated, that man will be confirmed by the Senate." Advising him to "have a paper signed by as many geologists as possible to back your candidate," Stevenson cautioned that he could not be "too prompt in this matter" since "Hayden has already made a long stride towards the position and unless something be done speedily he will be the man and nothing short of omnipotence can prevent it."[1]

¶ Stevenson's letter points to the question on which the whole competition for control of the federal surveys turned in the winter and spring of 1879: who was a "reputable geologist" competent to fulfill the function of director of a scientific department? Though the competition would speak of competence and focus on the question of the function of a director of science, ultimately the decision revolved on the issue of reputation. Understanding that competition, then, requires understanding the importance of reputation in the making and potential unmaking of a scientific career. Reputation underlies everything. Patronage is based on it, as are membership and status in the scientific community. If patronage was "the social system of pre-institutionalized science," reputation was at the heart of the system since patronage is more than the extension of material means. More fundamentally, it is a loan of the patron's reputation to the client. For this reason, the client's reputation is also important; it cannot be permitted to reflect discredit on the patron.[2]

¶ Reputation is also important within the scientific community, a community that deals in questions of truth and veracity and claims about the way things really are. The challenge facing the community as its members seek answers to these questions is how one can know when one has answers and statements that can be trusted as answers. This is difficult enough when doing one's own investigating; it is even more so when relying on another's work. Then the question becomes a personal one, and judgments of truth and falsity become assessments of credibility and trustworthiness, appraisals of character and reputation. Such questions were all the more important in the context of nineteenth-century science, as disciplines underwent the transition from individual patronage through nascent scientific institutions to the emergent professionalization of scientific careers in the 1870s. In asserting control over science and particular disciplines, members of the scientific community had to establish effective standards by which they could judge scientific practice and practitioners.[3]

¶ Even with the emergence of objective credentials as academic or professional degrees, such standards remained based on social recognition. Before their development, social recognition was the primary standard; an individual became a recognized scientist by virtue of being recognized as such by the scientific community. In extending such recognition to someone they knew, the members of the community passed judgment on the individual's character and practice. In extending recognition to someone they did not know personally, they relied on the testimony or judgment of character of known individuals. Even after having been received into the scientific community, an individual's relative status within that community could easily change over time, as judgments continued to be made about his or her practice and competency relative to changing standards of practice.[4] Hayden's career reflected all these elements, as his enemies brought him down using the same dynamics he had used to rise to prominence.

Hayden had long been concerned for his reputation. He had left his uncle's farm with little more than a desire to succeed, and his Oberlin classmates witnessed how this desire drove him. One noted that "his crude ambition struck me as being his strongest bent." Soon after graduating from Oberlin, he decided to pour his ambition into natural history. Thanks to Hall's patronage he was presented with and quickly grasped an opportunity to make a reputation as a western naturalist. Though as early as 1856 he wrote Meek of his "stronger desire that what I have done may contribute to science than any personal reputation," he immediately added, "I wish both." A decade later, as he closed the field season for his survey of Nebraska, he promised Meek that their names would "be ever identified" with the region's geology.[5]

¶ As a young collector cultivating patrons, Hayden seems to have known instinctively that his reputation and presentation were all-important, that they were all he could offer in exchange for preferment. He appeared eager, ambitious, enthusiastic, energetic, confident, friendly, and willing to be of service. He promoted himself while seeming flatteringly deferential to anyone who might be of service to him. It worked. People noticed and helped him. Nor was it all false. He was energetic and active. He brought back rich collections, developed geological skills, made astute observations, and learned how to elaborate theories to explain them. His stock rose, his reputation as a scientist spread, and he became the head of a popular government bureau. In 1873, his accomplishments earned his election to membership in the NAS, marking his inclusion among the scientific elite in the United States.

¶ Hayden experienced some difficulties negotiating the challenges of success, however, especially in maintaining good relations with those who had helped him. For instance, though he tried several times, he never succeeded in mending relations with Hall, who never forgave the wrong he felt Hayden had done him. Other difficulties were more of Hayden's own making. As he began to achieve success in leading his own survey in the late 1860s, he was not always generous in sharing credit and acknowledging his dependence on others. In 1869 Lesley informed him that the entomologist John L. LeConte, who had described many of Hayden's insect specimens for him, was "a little hurt" that Hayden had not seen fit to mention him or Newberry in a recent paper. It was a failure to keep his networks of support in good order, and Lesley advised him "to avoid all cause of dissatisfaction, because such men have the power to help spread your views and sustain them" and that apart from considerations of friendship and good will, "it is good policy to do much to maintain the kindest scientific relations with what the germans [*sic*] call your Fachgenossen—or fellow workers in your line." This was not the only time Hayden had such a failure pointed out to him. In part, he was overextended and sometimes neglected to perform ordinary services, such as send copies of reports or samples of specimens to those scientific societies that had been his earliest supporters. At different times, Leidy and Lesley both had occasion to remind him of such obligations regarding the Academy of Natural Sciences and the American Philosophical Society.[6]

¶ There was more to it than absentmindedness, however. In the early 1870s, as his fame and influence grew following his Yellowstone expeditions, Hayden began to change. In September 1872, Leidy warned him that "some of your friends and acquaintances begin to speak of you coldly. They say in general that you were once amiable and kind, but fear that prosperity is making you indifferent and arrogant."[7] The warning surprised Hayden, and he asked for Leidy's personal opinion: "do you see anything, or have you seen anything that pointed in that direction?" As for the opinions of others, Hayden had two explanations. On one hand, "many persons who have seen me grow up from nothing imagine I should do for them the same servile things I did years ago, but I claim some respect now, or I let them alone." Asserting there was "not a man on earth who has been a true friend to me all the way through" who could claim to have been deserted, Hayden insisted that in any case where he had seemed "indifferent or arrogant, there has been a *persistent* reason for it, not one neglect, not one rebuff alone, but a series of them." He also reminded Leidy of "how complicated my relations are getting to be with the world"; as a consequence he got a "'*sorehead*' every little while." It was impossible to comply with all the demands made upon him, and "reasonable requests on my part are not respected by some." His solution was to have "a fixed line of action and go through with it at all hazards."

¶ As a further explanation, Hayden referred to a "clique" in Philadelphia, "which meets one evening a week." He wrote Leidy that he had "left that clique for nearly two years" now, declaring that he had been "treated coldly as much for the warmth with which I defended your character and that of Prof. Baird, as for anything else." Yet he had "no doubt that my own character was discussed in much the same way." In the end, Hayden largely dismissed the issue and put his trust in the results of his work, convinced that they would constitute sufficient rebuttal of any criticism.[8] He was entrusting his personal reputation to his scientific reputation but failed to see the impact the former was making on the latter.

¶ His denials notwithstanding, Hayden did act impulsively and was sometimes quite oblivious to the effect his actions had on others. For instance, in 1872 he replaced Thomas Porter as survey botanist with John Coulter without warning or explanation. Porter felt his abrupt dismissal keenly. He had done all the botany for the previous two years "at the cost of a large amount of time and study, and without compensation" and wrote Hayden that he had counted on and made preparations for receiving the collections made in 1872 on the basis of an understanding from a letter received the previous spring.[9] More significantly, Hayden's demanding "some respect now" and his refusal to perform the "same servile things" he used to do signaled shifts in his personal and patronage relationships. They were getting much more complicated, and he did not navigate all the complications well. Indeed, he seems not even to have noticed some of them, yet they would ultimately have a serious impact on his career. If Hayden did not disturb the community in such a violently open manner as Cope and Marsh, he did violate good manners in a quieter but important way.

¶ In May 1872, Hayden wrote Hall, "I do not go to meetings any more." His explanation was simple—"I have a field now for the expenditure of all my surplus energy and more too"—but it was also dangerous. Meetings had become a problem, taking up too much of Hayden's time, but boycotting them was no solution. While an active scientist might find attending meetings difficult, deciding not to attend them at all was an unacceptable breach of etiquette for anyone who wished to be considered an active member of the scientific community. Not only would it contribute to the impression that he was becoming indifferent and arrogant, particularly as he was demanding respect, but it would also give critics a clear field to indict his behavior without effective hindrance. For someone who was already encountering complaints from occasional "soreheads" as well as being associated with a troublesome character like Cope, it was all the more important that he be seen to act the gentleman in scientific society. Refusing to join socially with that society because it drained his time and energies risked rupturing the network of relationships that supported the survey that now provided him with an outlet for all of his "surplus energy."[10] Since his patrons provided Hayden with access to power, the loss of patrons through changes in his personal relationships would mean a loss of that access. One of the more important of such changes occurred in his relationship with Baird and helps explain some of the difficulties Hayden experienced in the summer of 1878.

¶ Baird had initially put off Hayden's efforts to recruit him as a patron, but after seeing the results of Hayden's collecting with Meek in the Dakota Badlands in 1853, he eventually became a willing patron and cosponsor during Hayden's 1854–55 expedition to the Upper Missouri and remained one of Hayden's most important patrons and advisors for the next two decades. The relationship clearly benefited Hayden since Baird was able to provide a great deal of practical assistance. But like any patronage relationship, the benefits flowed both ways. Though he has long been recognized as one of the most important patrons of natural history in nineteenth-century America, it is easy to overlook the fact that Baird's cultivation of a wide network of client collectors was not the result of simple beneficence. While his patronage was remarkable in the number and extent of his clients, it was quite ordinary in that it was based on a fundamental element of self-interest. Baird was a patron to clients who served his interests, and his primary interest was his museum. He cultivated his client-collectors because he had to do so. There was a keen competition for the loyalty of good collectors in natural history. Baird did what he could and what he needed to do to retain his clients.[11] But since his primary interest remained in what they could contribute to his museum, they became in a sense outposts of that center of his empire.

¶ Baird presided over his empire with a single-minded focus. His refusal to involve himself in Hayden's disagreements with Warren in 1857 was typical of his focus. Baird refused to be sidetracked from his goals; he refused to get involved in quarrels he could either avoid or ignore. So long as others' disputes left his own domain undisturbed, he focused his efforts on that domain, tending it and building it up. Within his domain, however, he ruled, limited only by the constraints Henry imposed in permitting him to build up the museum. When he became secretary in his turn, Baird was able to give free rein to his penchant for complete authority and supervision. Always reluctant to share authority, he continued to show himself inventive in devising means to gain what he wanted and maintain his control over what he had, and he kept an even tighter rein on affairs at the Smithsonian than Henry had.[12]

¶ Baird was older than almost all of his clients, and the pattern that emerged between them was not one of partnership but of senior professor and junior student. According to the complaint of one former protégé who had worked with him closely for more than two decades, Baird did not tolerate peers well: "It is B's policy never to have one of his peers or betters about him—so that this establishment is simply a hatching house of henchmen who make an honest living by doing what they are told to do."[13] By the early 1870s, however, Hayden was beginning to reach the point of being one of Baird's peers. At the least, he was becoming a senior client, and almost a partner. He was demanding some respect. In the process, he stretched the bonds of their patronage relationship to the breaking point.

¶ As his survey assumed its mature shape from 1872 to 1874, it outgrew some of its earlier dependence on the Smithsonian's assistance. The incident of the undelivered boxes of minerals and fossils to Oberlin and Wooster Colleges in 1872 underlined something of this development, as did Hayden's recognition that he had to develop his own means of distributing publications and other materials rather than continue to rely on Baird and the Smithsonian to take care of such tasks for him. At the same time, the survey was providing many more things of use to Baird and the Smithsonian besides its collections in natural history, items such as photographs, bulletins and other reports, and patronage positions in which Baird could place new protégés. The high-water mark of this new partnership occurred during the Philadelphia Centennial Exhibition. Baird made extensive use of Hayden, calling upon him time and again for documents and other materials to present to foreign representatives in exchange for collections to be turned over to his national museum. At the same time, Hayden found Baird rather delinquent in ensuring reciprocation and had to ask repeatedly for explanations of what he could expect in return and when he might expect it.[14] Though their interests continued to overlap, they were growing apart. Hayden's interests focused more and more on his survey, while Baird's interests remained focused mostly on his own enterprises. To Baird, Hayden's survey was useful but not essential. The difference this made became apparent in the summer of 1878 when Baird failed to act as a patron to Hayden.

Hayden knew he faced the fight of his life from the time Congress referred the survey issue to the NAS. He knew he would have to impress people if his survey were to survive. But this presents a puzzle since he seems to have been ill prepared for the battle. Uncertain of what to do, he turned to his friends and patrons, asking them to think of some way to rescue him. Stranger still, at the time of greatest danger he seemingly abandoned the field of battle. Instead of staying in Washington for the summer to coordinate efforts on his own behalf, as Powell did, Hayden departed with his survey to revisit Yellowstone National Park, only returning just barely in time for the NAS meeting. He seems to have been unusually distracted and unsure of himself rather than a man at the height of his powers.[15]

¶ Part of the answer to the puzzle lies in his personal life. In the spring of 1878 Emma Hayden learned that her husband had syphilis. He had probably had the disease for several years by that time, and she probably learned of it as the result of a recent serious decline in his health. The revelation shattered her, and the blow to their marriage probably shook Hayden's confidence, as he found his private and public lives simultaneously threatened. In part, it seems Hayden responded by escaping to the West, the single remaining source of stability in his life. In particular, he returned to Yellowstone, which had played such a role in his public career. For Hayden, the trip was probably an effort to restore both physical and mental health. At the same time, his absence gave Emma time to work through her distress. Lacking records of their personal correspondence, we cannot know how he worried about how her struggle would turn out and whether their marriage would last. Yet he clearly had a great deal on his mind that summer as he pondered his future.[16]

¶ If the summer began with confusion, it ended with renewed determination, as he resumed the note Holmes had heard in late May: " 'Jim by the Jumpin Jingo' (or words to that effect) 'next winter we will have a *carriage*,' " referring to the carriage Powell used so effectively for lobbying. Though he began the summer ill and remained discouraged into the fall and wrote that he likely would not be able to attend the meeting of the NAS, several elements combined to revive him. One was a suspicion that Baird would fail him. He had been relying on Baird to influence the selection of the committee members, perhaps even by serving as one of its members, and to advise him about Marsh's intentions. When Baird simply responded that the meeting would not be held until 5 November, giving Hayden "ample opportunity for coming on and looking after matters" himself, he began to suspect Baird of preparing to "compromise" with his enemies.[17]

¶ Baird probably would not have expressed it that way, though it must have seemed so from Hayden's perspective. It was simply a clear case of the impact of their strained relations. Baird had no strong interest in helping Hayden fight this battle, and in the end he ducked it. Instead, on the day before the NAS meeting, Baird appealed to an excuse he frequently used to avoid unpleasant obligations and sent Hayden a short note informing him that due to "Mrs. Baird's indisposition, and urgent business" he would not be attending the meeting. Baird had nothing to gain in helping Hayden at this point. If he stood to lose some natural history specimens through a change in the geological surveys, this was more than offset by what he already had. His recent gains from the Centennial Exhibition remained without a permanent home, he still retained a large network of natural history collectors, and he already had a well-developed natural history collection in the Smithsonian, to which he was able to make large additions through his own Fisheries Commission surveys.[18] He could afford to sacrifice Hayden.

¶ A second factor that probably influenced Hayden was receipt of Schurz's letter transmitting the notice that the committee had been appointed and inviting him to submit a written statement. Hayden knew any statement had to be tailored to the committee membership, and it was exactly in this that he was frustrated. Schurz's letter was dated 3 October. Hayden probably received it on 14 October, the same day he received Baird's letter inviting him to look after matters himself. Yet as he wrote both Baird and Leidy that day, he did not know who the members were, so he did not know what to write. He asked both men for ideas. His letter to Baird seems self-pitying: "I do not know what to say or do. I do not wish to commit myself to anything and wish the whole matter were over." To Leidy, though, he revealed greater resolution, while still reflecting uncertainty as to tactics: "I am asked to make reply. I do not know what to say. Think up something for me. Gather outside opinions quietly. Will see you very soon."[19] He had transferred the role of patron from Baird to Leidy, but the change was fraught with significance. Unlike Baird, Leidy had no real influence in Washington.

¶ Hayden remained unaware of the committee's membership as late as 19 October, giving him at most ten days in which to adjust his report to its audience. Nor can learning their identities have been a source of comfort. Besides its chairman, it contained two declared foes, Newberry and Agassiz, who had sent Hayden some "frank . . . suggestions" the previous May about the "secondary" nature of zoological and botanical publications in a geological survey and the likelihood of their being a source of "great inconvenience and annoyance" if brought to the attention of Congress by Hayden's enemies. Agassiz's opposition to the survey's work in biology may have been more than a matter of principle. In the 1870s, he was devoting much of the wealth he was extracting from Michigan copper mines to giving shape to the dream of his father, Louis Agassiz, by building up the Museum of Comparative Zoology. Much more sensitive to balanced budgets than his father, he understandably looked with a jaundiced eye on governmental competitors in biology while expending tens of thousands of dollars annually on the museum. Among such competitors, Hayden and Baird ranked first. A limited government role in biology was obviously in Agassiz's interest since federal support of natural history would clearly have made it more expensive for him to complete his father's work.[20]

¶ Discovering he was on the committee, Hayden had attempted to blunt his objections by downplaying the survey's interest in biology. At the same time, proposing little by way of change was consistent with the feelings Hayden expressed over the summer. While he presumed from the first that referring the whole issue to the NAS would result in "some great plan" to "obliterate the present order of things," Hayden realized he needed to mobilize supporters to prevent such changes as would "destroy the individuality" of his organization. He argued privately as well as publicly that his survey was widely "acknowledged to be the most effective for this kind of work and ought to remain."[21] He would uphold and rely upon its reputation.

¶ Hayden attended the academy's November meeting, yet at first sight his behavior seems paradoxical. At each of its meetings, members were permitted to deliver papers on their recent work. Hayden took advantage of this privilege to present three papers: one on the topography of Two Ocean Pass in Wyoming, another on evidence of true glaciers in the Wind River Range, and an outline of his plan for a general geological map of the territories. They have been seen as evidence of his continuing poor judgment; "none of his topics conveyed the resounding impression he needed—of a dynamic scientist, an imaginative administrator, or even of a capable man at the height of his powers who was looking for wider responsibilities." It might appear that under the circumstances only the third would have made any impact on his hearers.[22] However, this is to forget that the papers *were* representative of Hayden's recent work, and if he was to impress people it would have to be with his work. The first two presented findings of his most recent expedition, while the third presented plans for the future, no doubt an elaboration of his recent success in the *Atlas of Colorado.* Furthermore, all of the topics possessed the advantage of being noncontroversial.

¶ It is also important to remember Hayden's position at the time. All summer he had sought to learn the dispositions of academy members toward his survey. But while he questioned his Washington office about Powell's actions and urged Baird and Leidy to find out what they could through "quiet, careful inquiries," Hayden also told Baird that he desired "the fight shall be as easy as possible consistent with the preservation of the organization." In short, he did not wish to create any more disturbance than necessary. This explains his strategy both during and after the meeting. He knew he faced a serious challenge. He also knew that bucking the political currents too strenuously risked losing everything. So he adopted a policy Newcomb later aptly described as "leaving the cultivation of the tree to others, while . . . making his pole to knock down the fruit."[23]

¶ Hayden had long sought to defeat his competitors in the western surveys by arguing on the basis of their duplication of his work, which he believed the strongest line to take with Congress. At the same time, he thought he was making progress convincing congressmen that dividing the country into sections for different surveys was impractical and unscientific, and the only reasonable plan was a single survey under one head. Though he clearly would have preferred a different plan than that presented by Marsh's committee, his immediate strategy at the academy meeting was quiet listening. He took no part in the general discussion of the plan, yet evidently voted for it.[24] Once the plan had been adopted and presented to Congress, he quietly provided friends there with ammunition against elements of the plan with which he disagreed. All the while, he sought either to co-opt the proposal into his own survey or win the nomination for the new position. In either case, his claim to his ultimate goal, the continuance of *his* survey, whether in its present form or in the newly proposed USGS, rested on his image as a reputable senior statesman of science. It was this image that opponents attacked.

Stevenson's warning to Marsh in late December was accurate. Hayden had indeed been busy soliciting letters testifying to his fitness to head any new geological survey that might be established. Collecting testimonial letters had become second nature to Hayden, and he had built up a sizable file of them from diverse sources. Now he oiled up his solicitation machinery once more with a new gift to offer, his *Atlas of Colorado*. As summer began in 1878, Hayden issued strict orders that the scarce copies of the most recent printing of the *Atlas* not go out without his permission, but that winter he sent them out in a flurry of activity. They went to editors of journals and newspapers, to colleges and scientific societies, to scientists and industrial interests. All could add their mite or more to support his cause. The aim could not be clearer than in a note from Baird. Advising Hayden that the geologist T. Sterry Hunt sought a copy of Hayden's atlas, he wrote: "He has Clarence King's and is desirous of getting yours. Had you not better send it to him?"[25]

¶ After so many years of soliciting testimonials, Hayden knew what he wanted his supporters to say in their letters, and he was not at all shy about giving directions. To his friend Archibald Geikie, he wrote that he wanted letters arguing for his appointment as director of the USGS on the basis of his "long service as a pioneer and the builder up of the important survey under my charge, its long services, and the struggles it has passed through." Two weeks later, Hayden wrote again, asking Geikie "to address a letter to the President of the United States as a foreign scientific worker, requesting my appointment to the Directorship of the new survey." Once again, he suggested the tone: "You could state the general satisfaction my appointment would give the scientific men of Europe, the merit of my work." American correspondents received similar instructions. Asking the ethnologist Lewis Morgan, a longtime acquaintance from Rochester and now a member of the NAS, for a letter of support, Hayden told him: "Speak of my long service in this work in the West, long before any others now living were in the field, the influence of my work on the Educational interests as well as scientific at home and abroad, and state that it would greatly [*sic*] to the interests of the Government to continue my work in the new Office, etc."[26]

¶ At the end of December Hayden gathered together a number of the better letters he had received over the course of the previous half-decade and published extracts from forty-one of them in early 1879. The compilation, *Extracts from Letters and Notices of Eminent Scientific Men and Journals in Europe and America, commendatory of the United States Geological and Geographical Survey of the Territories*, formed an impressive testimonial to his accomplishments, with endorsements from some of America's and Europe's best-known scientists. Their content emphasized exactly the points that Hayden wanted. They lauded the quality of his survey's scientific work, explaining that it was viewed as an "exemplar" of government geological surveys by scientists throughout Europe. The letters also praised the efficiency of his organization, noting that it was "most economical" and "most prolific" in results, and they celebrated Hayden's ability at managing the labor of a large scientific staff. Finally, virtually to a man, the letters' authors all stressed how

Hayden's reports reflected credit on American science and the American government as its patron. Titles could impress, so Hayden identified the authors in terms that underlined the significance of their opinions. Dates were not always helpful, however, and to his opponents' chagrin Hayden omitted them for most of the letters. Though most referred to the *Atlas of Colorado*, and so dated from circa 1878, some were from much earlier in the decade, and a number of those now firmly in King's camp found themselves quoted as enthusiastic supporters of Hayden's survey.[27]

¶ Stevenson was mistaken, however, in thinking Marsh remiss in his efforts to ensure the ultimate success of his plan. On the contrary, he and other King supporters had made their preference known among Washington power brokers weeks earlier. King had been seeking a new position since the previous spring and had revealed his desire for another government position as early as February 1878, a month before he suggested to Stevenson the advisability of referring the whole survey issue to the NAS and three months before Atkins reported legislation to do exactly that. Some of his friends proposed him as successor to Henry as secretary of the Smithsonian. Others doubted the advisability of this so long as he remained active as a mining consultant. He quickly identified his own preference when Marsh's committee set to work, journeying to Cambridge during September 1878 to visit J. D. Whitney, his old boss from the California survey, and ask "in all frankness" if Whitney was likely to be a candidate for director should Congress create a new geological survey. When Whitney "decidedly said no" King asked if he could count on Whitney's support. As King later remembered it, Whitney gave "every appearance of great cordiality" in assuring him that he was the "*only person to be thought of*" (emphasis in original). King also used the summer to inform some of his European acquaintances of his quest for a new position; at least one of them passed the word on to Hayden by the end of October.[28]

¶ In early December 1878, King made a visit to Washington during which he "look[ed] over the ground very fully" and came away convinced that "in all probability" he would receive the appointment as head of the USGS. Though he knew Hayden was "moving Heaven and Earth to get the President's support" in case the new position should be approved by Congress, King believed he had "the inside track." He had some reason for confidence. A member of one of New York City's oldest social clubs, King moved in elite circles, and his supporters enjoyed a number of important social ties to Schurz and Hayes. As a result, he decided to modify his campaign strategy, telling geologist Samuel Franklin Emmons, "I no longer think it necessary to have any letters written against the present incumbent," that is, Hayden; he would rely on "letters in my behalf."[29]

¶ Like Hayden, King knew just the sort of letters he wanted. Writing Marsh to ask him to arrange for a letter from the faculty at Yale, he gave detailed instructions. He told Marsh to be sure to stress his experience, especially the twelve years spent in charge of the survey of the fortieth parallel, and to insist upon three points: that he had "a practical and intimate knowledge of economic geology," that he had "enough executive faculty to manage the business," and that his "relations to the scientific men of the land are such that I can gain the cooperation of good men." (In his letter to the president, Marsh enumerated just those points, in virtually the same order King listed them, as did the majority of other writers who supported King.) Finally, King also sought a "letter of general recommendation" signed by all the members of the NAS committee on surveys, which would have constituted an emphatic statement that he was the man for whom the proposed USGS was designed.[30]

¶ The evident confidence King manifested at the end of December in this letter gives rise to an interesting question when it is juxtaposed against one of the rebuffs he received in his quest for testimonial letters. Although he eventually built up a strong file of letters supporting his nomination, as he called upon his various social, business, and academic connections, he also experienced some unexpected disappointments. J. D. Whitney administered one of the sharpest after having second thoughts about his own candidacy and about supporting King, once the prospect of a new federal survey seemed more likely. Not only did Whitney refuse to sign a letter recommending King, but he also prevented the faculty of Harvard from sending a collective letter. This caused consternation among King's supporters and led to speculation as to Whitney's own aims regarding the directorship. Whitney even went so far as to suggest that Hayden was more likely to be of service to Harvard as head of the USGS than King was.[31] This refusal of support from one of the nation's leading geologists raises a question: did King really have such a lead on his "inside track" by mid-December that Hayden had no chance of receiving the appointment?

¶ Marsh probably explained that King was the candidate the NAS had in mind when he went to Washington in November 1878 to promote its proposal to Hayes and members of the administration. It is clear that a primary reason for King's visit to Washington in early December 1878 was to advance his own candidacy and make the acquaintance of influential officials he did not already know. However, it is probably too much to conclude that by mid-December Hayes had already made up his mind to appoint King on the condition that his sponsors could muster strong enough endorsements to offset Hayden's popular support. It also seems unlikely that Hayden was soon made aware that he would not receive the appointment. The strongest evidence cited for this position consists of a visit Hayes made to Hayden's survey offices on 20 December 1878, during which Hayes offered him an appointment as juror at an international geological conference in Paris, and a letter to Hayes from Postmaster General David Key of 4 January 1879 responding to Hayes's "anxiety that Mr. Hayden should be provided for." Did Hayes and Hayden discuss the proposed USGS, and did Hayden recognize the offer of an honorary appointment as a consolation prize and realize the president had no intention of appointing him director of the USGS?[32]

¶ Whether or not Hayes had essentially decided to appoint King if the appointment could be shown politically supportable seems impossible to know on the basis of available evidence. Not only is it unknown what transpired between the two men during Hayes's visit to Hayden's office, but it is not clear that Key's letter refers to F. V. Hayden, and there were numerous Haydens in Washington. It is clear, however, that Hayden and King and their mutual supporters all continued to act as if the question *was* still undecided and subject to influence, as if their opponents *could be* and *had to be* defeated. For instance, only a few weeks *after* Hayes's visit Hayden published the *Extracts.* King and his supporters adopted much the same attitude. Powell, Newcomb, William B. Rogers, Wolcott Gibbs, and Grove Karl Gilbert all joined King in prompting waves of letters from university faculties and working scientists as well as politicians, businessmen, and literary figures, all recommending

King's appointment. And if King had foresworn negative campaigning, many of his supporters happily took on the burden; their letters supporting King added points against Hayden. Nor did they feel confident they could let up their campaign until two days before Hayes announced King's appointment.[33]

¶ In the meantime, King pushed for the creation of the USGS in Congress. While he manifested an aversion to it, King was no stranger to political maneuvering. As his admirer and friend Henry Adams wrote, King "knew the congressman." He also knew that "to get a man red hot you must go at him white hot," so he willingly returned to Washington in January and took a direct role in lobbying congressmen for passage of the NAS committee's plan. His actions were partly in response to Newcomb's urgent calls for his presence and partly to ensure the creation of a position he dearly wanted. Passage of the proposal was much more important for King than for Hayden. Hayden had a survey; King no longer did. But if King was to act as the spokesman of disinterested science and not appear merely self-seeking in promoting reform of the federal surveys, he may have thought it necessary to mute his own campaign for appointment as director of the proposed USGS. If that was not enough, he had another reason for maintaining a low profile into mid-January; until he resigned his position on 18 January 1879, King remained technically attached to the Army Corps of Engineers, which opposed the proposal for which he was so ardently laboring. Therefore, as he sought testimonials at the turn of the year he told J. D. Whitney, "My lips are now sealed as to why I desired letters at this time."[34]

By mid-February, it appeared the USGS would go through. Some of King's supporters, however, were less confident about his becoming its director, as Hayden's early efforts seemed about to pay off. At this point, Newcomb writes, the actions of a handful of men, some three or four of those "most interested to secure Mr. King's appointment," were critical. They privately intimated to Schurz that "the scientific men interested might have something to say on the subject." Indeed, they did, and together they blocked Hayden's appointment. As their major spokesman, Powell spoke of competency and purpose in science, but behind his words lay a vision of science in the federal government quite different in important respects from the vision Hayden and his allies shared. His words were also highly personal in nature and helped make the fight for the directorship "a remarkably bitter struggle."[35]

¶ Given Powell's key role in the whole affair, a mystery seems to remain in Hayden's confusion over the identity of his most important rival. In spite of learning that King was a candidate as early as October, Hayden seems not to have recognized him as a serious opponent until mid-January. Instead, he first focused on Powell as his most important challenger. This would have been an entirely natural mistake, however. By 1878, Hayden knew Powell as a familiar and dangerous foe. He had been very aware that Powell's decision to stay in Washington most of the previous summer was calculated to do him harm, and he was no doubt aware that Powell had joined with Marsh and the proponents of the NAS plan. Add to this the fact that King purposely kept his own campaign low key until mid-January, even stating that he did not seek the position, and it becomes quite reasonable that Hayden focused attention on the one survey leader in Washington obviously supporting creation of the new bureau. This is particularly understandable since Powell gave no public indication of his own intentions until 20 February 1879, ten days after the Legislative Expenses Bill had been reported to the House. On that day, he asked Atkins for an appropriation of twenty thousand dollars in the Sundry Civil Bill to enable him to continue his ethnological work under the supervision of the Smithsonian. When Atkins reported the bill four days later, it contained the clause Powell sought. This may very well have caught Hayden by surprise. Since at least early December 1878 he had been trying to make peace with Powell, to no avail.[36] Not in the least interested in making peace with Hayden, Powell was about to escalate hostilities.

¶ By 20 February Powell was convinced Congress would approve the legislation creating the USGS. Yet he was deeply concerned about the "most vigorous efforts" being made by Hayden to receive the appointment as director, and he urged upon Marsh "the most vigorous efforts in Mr. King's behalf."[37] How vigorous Powell could be soon became clear as he took direct aim at Hayden's character as a public servant and as a scientist. Powell feared Newcomb's analysis of Hayden's policy was about to become a prophecy; now that others had successfully cultivated the tree, Hayden seemed about to snatch away its fruit.

¶ On 10 March 1879, Powell wrote T. Sterry Hunt, "my winter has been filled with work." His letter to Hunt was only one element of his main work: ensuring the enactment of as much of the NAS plan as possible and the appointment of King to head the USGS. On 4 March, the first part of this work was finished, and now Powell was concentrating on the second. Explaining that he was doing "all in my power to present [King's] merits to the President," Powell entreated Hunt, "if you know of anything else you can do to secure Mr. King's appointment I hope you will not fail to act."[38]

¶ Besides stirring up others to seek new letters of recommendation from the nation's colleges and scientists, Powell and his staff added their names to King's supporters, writing Hayes within days of his signing the Sundry Civil Bill. With the passage of the bill came the time to present credentials and seek private appointments, and both camps did their best to bring supporters to Washington to press their respective cases. Throughout February and into the first half of March they fortified the testimonial letters with personal interviews with Hayes and Schurz. In early March, Hayden obtained an interview with William K. Rogers, the president's longtime friend, advisor, and private secretary, preparatory to an interview with Hayes. He also made arrangements for Leidy, Cope, and the Princeton geographer Arnold Guyot to come to Washington to support his candidacy. Marsh, Powell, and Newcomb all had at least one interview with Hayes. So did Brewer, who argued that King was the rightful heir to Charles Hoffmann's system of topographical mapping in mountain regions, and Newberry, whom Hayes had appointed to head the Ohio state geological survey in 1869 and seems to have particularly trusted.[39]

¶ On the day Hayes signed the bill creating the USGS, Powell sent a letter to Atkins, ostensibly in response to a petition circulated in the House the previous day supporting Hayden's appointment to head the new bureau. Powell had not given up his larger plan of reforming the government's stance toward the western lands, and creation of the USGS was but one element of that plan. Seeking to unite Atkins to this purpose, he reminded Atkins of "the responsible duty" Atkins had assumed in "inaugurating this highly commendable reform" and expressed certainty that "the appointment of a suitable person [to head the USGS] must be a subject of profound solicitude" to him.

¶ Hayden, said Powell, was entirely unsuitable. Pointing out that many of the objects of reform proposed by the Appropriations Committee had been "seriously attacked and crippled" by opposition in the House, Powell charged that Hayden had been prominent among the opponents of reform. He had helped raise "false issues," while "his friends and supporters in the House and Senate endeavored to insert amendments favorable to him personally; . . . from the beginning to the end his sole concern has been to advance himself personally and to defeat the true objects and intents of the measure." In short, Powell called into question Hayden's performance as a public servant. Accusing him of opposing reform for his own personal benefit, Powell declared that "if Dr. Hayden is appointed all hope of further reform in the system of land surveys is at an end or indefinitely postponed." In light of this, Powell urged Atkins to inform both Schurz and Hayes of any information he might have about the opponents' activities and to encourage the other members of the Appropriations Committee to do likewise, "in order to defeat if possible all efforts which may be made to secure Dr. Hayden's appointment."[40]

¶ Getting Atkins's support would be helpful, but he was a Democrat and chair of the House Appropriations Committee, and Hayes was engaged in a fierce battle with that very committee and party over unacceptable conditions in both the army and the legislative, executive, and judicial appropriations bills. For real congressional influence with the president, Powell turned to Garfield. Fellow Ohioans, Hayes and Garfield had long been friendly, sharing several common political aims, including civil service reform. Additionally, Hayes owed his election to Garfield, who had served as one of the Republican congressional members on the special commission that decided the disputed election. In a masterful letter and memorandum that showed he knew exactly what notes to hit to gain his purpose, Powell wrote Garfield three days after writing to Atkins. Fulfilling a promise to provide more information on a topic on which they had already spoken, he made a scathing attack on Hayden's character as a public servant and his scientific and executive ability as head of his survey.[41]

In 1874, the contest had been between a military and a civilian vision of who should have jurisdiction over science. Hayden had cast himself as defender of the rights of civilian scientists, and to that standard he had rallied the vast majority of civilian scientists, including a number who did not always care for everything he did or represented. William D. Whitney, one of his ardent supporters at the time, had summed up the issue as a question of whether responsibility for the promotion of science ought to be left "to the leisure of army officers" or placed in the hands of "men fitted for it by natural gift and particular education—men whose lives are devoted to it, whose reputation depends upon it, and who bring to it a zeal and enthusiasm certainly not inferior to the best which the votaries of any profession display."[42] In 1879, the battleground had shifted and the conflict was tighter. Now two rival civilian visions competed for the same limited resources. Now Hayden represented an older, generalist vision, while Powell spoke for a newer, narrower, technocratic one. The contrast between the two reveals how much the world of government science had changed.

¶ For over two and a half decades Hayden had poured his considerable energies into the creation and elaboration of his dream of a great natural history survey of the trans-Mississippi region, contributing to the "scientific and material interests" of the entire West, from "the Arctic Circle to the Isthmus of Darien." Having chosen to devote the rest of his working days to this effort, he had devoted them as well to ensuring that those who joined him in the enterprise might do so with "confidence in the permanency of the work" as a way of making careers for themselves. His vision included scientific concerns, and he sincerely desired that his name be "ever identified with the Geology of this country." Yet his vision went far beyond geology and geography to embrace all of natural history and a wide variety of other interests. His practice testifies that there was nothing artificial in his appeal to the multifaceted "interest[s] and sympath[ies] of all classes of intelligent people of our country from Maine to Florida," to whom he addressed his survey's publications.[43] In part, it derived from his philosophy of doing what was practicable in the context of an unreadiness for a "Bureau of Science." But it also sprang from a genuine interest in doing as much as possible.

¶ Hayden sympathized with the interests and admired the efforts of specialist science but saw little reason to limit his survey to geology when, "at very little additional expense," it could prosecute and advance efforts on a wider scale. He dismissed Powell's argument, and by implication Garfield's echoing of it, that government should not sup-

port efforts in zoology and botany. They only mirrored the sentiments of Agassiz and Marsh, who were hardly representative: "They are rich and can get along without Govt. aid, but all are not so situated." Instead, he agreed with John L. LeConte that "many places explored by Government surveys will not be visited by the unremunerated students of Natural History, upon whom Zoology and Botany mostly depend for their advancement. Consequently no material can be obtained for study, unless . . . Government employees collect the specimens."[44]

¶ Hayden's generalist vision was now under serious attack. In his harsh criticisms of Hayden, Powell raised the standard of a new vision, ironically one that had become possible in great measure because of Hayden's success. Though the essential elements of Powell's vision have to be extracted from his rhetoric, they are quite apparent in the "abstract" on the Hayden Survey that he sent Garfield. When this is laid alongside his *Report on the Surveys* presented to the NAS committee, Powell's alternative vision of government science is clear.

¶ Powell advocated a vision in which the head of a scientific bureau possessed more than ordinary competence and expertise in all fields under his jurisdiction. Hayden, said Powell, was not such a man, and he denounced Hayden as a fraud and a charlatan, equally incompetent to instigate good scientific work or judge its merits and suitability for his survey. Powell attributed all the good qualities the work of the Hayden Survey possessed to Hayden's more capable assistants, who were able to do scientific and useful work in spite of Hayden rather than because of him. Hayden himself, Powell charged, "frittered away splendid appropriations upon work which was intended purely for noise and show," designed to be "scattered broadcast over the United States and Europe with his name blazoned on them and to attract the attention of every accessible class of scientific people as well as the wonder-loving populace."

¶ While admitting that Hayden had displayed "intense zeal and untiring energy in his expeditions," Powell claimed he possessed neither "the capacity nor qualifications" necessary "to do something for science." Even "the basis of all geological work," a good map, was beyond Hayden's ability, wrote Powell, asserting that the *Atlas of Colorado*, the "masterpiece" of Hayden's survey, owed little to Hayden. "The whole plan or scheme of the work," he said, "was copied after Clarence King's." It was King, not Hayden, who was "the pioneer and founder of a whole system of survey work which was novel and original, exactly suited to the region and which though it may be susceptible of improvement will on the whole be the only practicable system for the far west."[45]

¶ Powell was a very capable man, as capable at ignoring, twisting, and distorting facts as he was at marshaling them for argumentative purposes. His characterization of Hayden exhibits all these traits. In claiming that there was "not a third rate scientist in America" who did not know Hayden for a "charlatan," he ignored the numerous first-rate scientists in America and Europe who had supported Hayden. These included Hall, Dana, Hilgard, Newberry, and Meek, who had all joined in nominating and electing him to the NAS in 1873, when election depended upon the performance of original scientific investigations. When Powell gave King all the credit for pioneering a "whole system of survey work which was novel and original, exactly suited to the region," he neglected to mention that King had borrowed the system from Hoffmann, the true developer of the triangulating method for surveying mountainous regions. Nor did Powell mention that besides Gardner and Wilson, Hoffmann had also instructed Hayden Survey geographer Henry Gannett in his methods. Finally, in charging that Hayden's meddling in the scientific work of the survey had disgusted and embittered both Marvine and Gardner, he neatly selected two men no longer with the Hayden Survey. Marvine had been a staunch supporter of Hayden but was now dead and could not rebut the charge.[46] Gardner had other reasons to be bitter with Hayden, reasons that had nothing to do with scientific mapping. Nor did Powell mention that Wilson, geographer under J. D. Whitney and then King before joining Hayden with Gardner, *stayed* with Hayden after Gardner left, moving up to take Gardner's position. If Hayden had caused so much dissension in his scientific corps, it seems unlikely he would have commanded as much loyalty among them as he usually did.

¶ Yet Powell's contrasting of Hayden with King was significant. In his letter to Marsh's committee, Powell had closely linked the future of government science with "the great industrial interests of the country" as the means of ensuring its "ample support." This made it essential that the director of the survey inspire confidence in those circles. This agreed with Powell's vision of the future of development in the West, as presented in his *Report on the Lands of the Arid Region*. There he presented a very different vision from the one typically found in Hayden's reports. Where Hayden frequently made suggestions on how individuals could help themselves in settling the West, Powell insisted that the ordinary individual was incapable of coping with conditions in the arid lands, that henceforth wise legislation, engineering of the greatest skill, and comprehensive planning were necessary.[47] His vision required a technocrat, not a populist, a specialist rather than a generalist, a scientific laborer instead of a promoter and entrepreneur. It needed a Clarence King, not a Ferdinand Hayden.

¶ Hayden and the vision he represented were not without their defenders, however. Unfortunately, most of the evidence of the ways in which his supporters presented him to Hayes is missing; several years after losing the competition for the appointment, Hayden requested that all the letters and papers in Hayes's possession relating to his pursuit of the directorship of the USGS "be done up in a close package" and sent to him.[48] This was evidently done, and the letters subsequently became lost with most of the rest of the private papers still in Hayden's possession when he died. While both sides admitted that "Hayden letters" greatly outnumbered "King letters," only a handful of the former have survived, making them all the more important for understanding how Hayden's supporters presented his claims for the position.

¶ They did so vigorously. Where Powell attacked Hayden as a fraud and a charlatan, Cope attacked the leaders in the movement to nominate King as a "clique," and King as someone who had improperly compromised his integrity as a government employee.[49] Unfortunately, these arguments did not address the nexus of the decision, which was based on science closely allied with prospective economic benefit. Still, Hayden's defenders clearly reveal that the issue was not merely a question of competence as a scientist but the function of a director of a scientific bureau. And since Hayden had proved himself a good director, the question of his reputation was all the more critical: could he inspire confidence? His claim to head the USGS certainly did not rest on his efforts to nurture it. But neither he nor his supporters ever argued that he had created or sponsored it. Rather, they argued that it was largely due to his efforts and accomplishments that the USGS was even possible. His claim rested on his accomplishments as a senior scientist and public servant. These, said his supporters, did inspire confidence.

¶ J. Peter Lesley's letter to Hayes makes this quite clear. Though Lesley admitted it would be "absurd" to call Hayden a "great geologist," if the geological surveys were to be "subjected to one chief" he felt "strongly impelled" to request that "Hayden's claims to such a position be not entirely overlooked." Lesley did not appeal to Hayden's ability as a geologist. Instead, he appealed to Hayden's many years of service; his "inexhaustible energy, fairness in the treatment of subordinates, and really broad views"; his "extraordinary executive abilities and a certain evident sterling honesty and singleness of purpose *in the direction of science*" (emphasis in original). These qualities had sufficed to keep "many who dislike him personally his staunch friends and supporters as [being] a *pioneer geologist* of the very highest rank."

¶ Lesley considered Hayden's career as a "pioneer geologist" one of his greatest attributes. That career, Lesley claimed, accounted in large part for "much of the popularity and consequent progress of my science on this side of the Atlantic." Hayden was "*the man*," Lesley declared emphatically, "who by his unaided and undisciplined pluck and force of will commenced twenty years ago the survey of the territories, and has been ever since unswervingly and most successfully enlarging and organizing and glorifying that immense survey, until other and better geologists have been inspired and helped to come in and appropriate parts of it to themselves." Lesley argued that "*To set aside such a hero, now*, because more exact workers have taken the field, and find their interest in exposing his mistakes (the best of us have made quite as many and as flagrant ones) and the personal peculiarities of the man (we all have some such) I think would not resound to the benefit or to the honor of geology."[50]

¶ Princeton geographer Arnold Guyot stressed the same attributes in his letter to Hayes, emphasizing the "high estimation" in which foreign scientists held the Hayden Survey and their unanimous praise for the "rapidity & perfection" of its reports. Such results, he said, indicated a rare combination of qualities in the survey's leader: "Scientific knowledge of what is wanted, discrimination in selecting his aids [*sic*], judgement in training them, administrative ability, energy and above all that enthusiasm for the work, which shrinks from no obstacles or personal sacrifices, to reach the best results attainable." Any change of leadership, Guyot warned, "would be a misfortune for science & a detriment to the best interest of the Government."[51]

¶ Leidy and Cope echoed these sentiments in letters to Schurz. Drawing on more than twenty-five years of acquaintance with Hayden, Leidy commended the "untiring, economical and able manner in which he has conducted geological surveys in the western territories" as well as "the character of his many published reports, and . . . the almost universally favorable criticisms of his work by the highest authorities of all countries." On the basis of these qualities, Leidy asserted that "no one is better qualified" for the position of director of the USGS. Cope was more explicit and enumerated three points supporting Hayden's candidacy: that he knew more of the geology of the West than any other man, "being the founder of the system in the largest part, as at present in use among all of our geologists"; that in conducting his survey he did not seek to represent any "clique or locality" but drew his subordinates from "all parts of the country," rather than simply a few of the "great schools"; and that in spite of twenty-five years of experience and "much temptation," Hayden was "free from all taint of corruption." None of these, asserted Cope, could be said of King, who, even if he was personally unobjectionable, was "unfortunate in the companions he is now in," men who "represent the pretentious type among American scientists, whose aspirations are far beyond their merits."[52]

¶ The appeals to Schurz in support of Hayden fell on deaf ears but not because King was obviously the better man or because Schurz held Hayden's close friendship with the disgraced Delano against him.[53] Schurz had good reason to believe Powell's contention that giving Hayden the position as it had been created might have meant an end to the larger aim of reform in the General Land Office. Hayden's actions in supporting congressional opponents to reforms in the public land surveys probably provided reason enough for Schurz to suspect he would not be the appropriate choice to have an ex officio seat on a committee to study the public land laws with an eye to their revision. By mid-March, while Hayden may have enjoyed the support of the preponderance of scientists across the country, he enjoyed the support of very few people who counted in Washington. They had mostly opted for King.

¶ Hayes probably had little personal interest in either candidate. He had more important concerns during the final weeks of the Forty-fifth Congress and into the summer of the special session that followed. He had hoped to follow Congress's adjournment with a two-month trip to California, but that proved impossible when Congress adjourned without approving appropriations for the army or the legislative, executive, and judicial offices. Then, during the weeks of the special session, Republicans and Democrats deadlocked in a budget battle as Hayes vetoed bill after bill because of clauses limiting federal authority to regulate elections, while Garfield stood as an important bulwark for the administration, keeping House Republicans in line. Nowhere in his diaries for these months did Hayes make any mention of King, Hayden, or the USGS.[54]

¶ One thing, however, did bear some relationship to their contest while simultaneously revealing how insightful Powell's line of attack was. Hayes cared greatly about preserving executive privilege. In the spring and summer of 1879 he not only fought to preserve the right of the federal government to guarantee free elections but continued his long-standing fight for civil service reform and the right of the executive branch to appoint officials free of the dictation of members of Congress. He believed that people should not look to congressmen to get them jobs and that congressmen should not expect to get people positions with patronage. In an interview with President Hayes the night before sending his abstract on the Hayden Survey to Garfield, Powell drew particular attention to Hayden's practices in securing congressional support for his appropriations. The following day, he urged Garfield to draw upon his own knowledge of Hayden's methods and make the same points with Hayes, claiming the president "questioned me on this matter especially." There can be little doubt of the impression Powell sought to make: that Hayden obtained congressional favor in return for patronage positions, publications, and photographs. Though his morality was clearly selective here, in light of his own practices, Powell's urging of this approach upon Hayes, and particularly the mention of appropriations, shows effective timing.[55] He knew how to get Hayes's attention that March when the House was making appropriations contingent upon acceptance of provisions that the president strongly opposed, that is, a quid pro quo.

¶ The efficacy of Powell's line of attack and its impact upon Hayes's decision finds further corroboration in a letter Hayes received the week before Powell's interview. To the chagrin of King and his supporters, thanks to J. D. Whitney's protest no "Harvard letter" supported King. But probably thanks to someone who planted the idea in Hayes's mind, Hayes himself requested advice from Harvard's president, Charles W. Eliot. In his response, Eliot pulled no punches. Neither did he make much distinction between what he had observed and what he had from hearsay. What he wrote damned Hayden's cause.

¶ Eliot offered opinions on four men: J. D. Whitney, King, Hayden, and Nathaniel S. Shaler. All but Hayden were known to Eliot personally, and Whitney and Shaler were both on the faculty at Harvard. Though he asserted that Whitney was "the fittest man in the country for the position," it seems as if Eliot sought a respectable way to move Whitney out of Harvard because he characterized him as "a man of absolute integrity, independent to a fault, quick-tempered and sensitive,—a somewhat troublesome subordinate, but a very considerate, just, and generous superior." Whitney was not a candidate, however, and Eliot moved on to King. While he considered King's scientific attainments inferior to Whitney's, Eliot called him a man of "experience and success in public surveys" and claimed that his appointment would also "be regarded by American scientific men as well-earned, as creditable to the government, and as full of promise for the future of the Survey." Eliot also considered Shaler "an active, energetic man, up-right, honorable, and of excellent ability" but not ready to take on so responsible a position.

¶ Though he claimed no personal knowledge of Hayden, Eliot had no hesitation in condemning him. He began by asserting that Hayden was "with Congressmen, the leading candidate for the position," as if that itself were an offense. In Eliot's opinion, one contrary to a number of scientists on his own faculty, including Whitney, Hayden "[did] not command the confidence of men of science." His only basis for this was hearsay, the gossip of "scientific men" revolving around Hayden's alleged "ignorance, his scientific incapacity, and his low habits when in camp." For Hayes, the last would have been particularly serious.

Unfortunately for Hayden, Lesley's letter of support helped give the charge substance, mentioning as it did "his often disagreeable and violent and dictatorial manners, which have won against him many powerful and bitter enemies," hardly elements to give promise of his ability to win widespread cooperation. Reinforced by Schurz's recommendation, which all parties realized would be telling, Hayes gave the nod to King.[56]

¶ King's nomination, announced on 20 March, distressed Hayden and his supporters. But all was not yet lost. The Senate still had to confirm the nomination, and Hayden's patrons there made one last effort to defeat King. Only slight traces of what occurred survive, but it seems to have been an uphill battle. When the Senate Committee on Public Lands met on 1 April 1879, it voted unanimously to support King's nomination. The strongest objection to his confirmation was the charge that while in the employ of the government he had "made examinations of mining property for private persons, and given opinions as an expert." His supporters countered that he had merely been exercising a "right," which had never been legally denied, "to practice his profession as a mining engineer" and give opinions in cases submitted to him. Two days later, the Senate confirmed King's appointment as the first director of the USGS. Once again, the principal objection focused on his having served as a mining expert for private concerns while employed by the government. And once again, his defenders met the accusation, not by denying the charge, but by urging that "he had not in any manner neglected his public duties or taken advantage of his public position to further his personal schemes." At the same time, they urged his "eminent fitness for the position." However, to supporters of reform the objections may have seemed so many *endorsements* of King, evidence that he manifestly possessed the confidence of the "captains of industry" and "the great industrial interests of the country." During the debate, "the probable result became so apparent . . . that no division was called for."[57]

¶ In fact, by this time no division was needed. Surprisingly, King's opponent had become his supporter. Why? During the early months of 1879 Hayden desperately sought to gain the appointment as head of the USGS. He believed he deserved it, that he had earned it as the rightful recognition of his accomplishments. But he also feared that if he did not win the position his "career in Western work" would be "cut short off." It was probably this fear, as much as anything else, that gave urgency to his efforts.[58] Yet it is also possible that Hayes offered some sort of concession that led Hayden, in the end, to support his chief rival.

¶ Hayden had an interview with Hayes sometime around 15 March. By the nineteenth, King's supporters finally felt confident that he would "undoubtedly be appointed" head of the USGS, as he was the following day. Did Hayes forewarn Hayden? Did they come to some sort of agreement or understanding? Probably. It seems the most reasonable way to understand Hayden's comment to the geologist Alexander Winchell on 21 March: "King was duly confirmed without much difficulty. I aided as much as I could." Why aid his adversary unless an understanding had been reached? And what would more likely have appealed to Hayden than provisions for him to continue his work and prevent his being "cut short off"? Exactly such an arrangement was reached, and Hayden continued in his letter to Winchell that he was waiting for details about his own appointment. He had too much political support for Hayes simply to cast him aside. Even in defeat he landed on his feet, receiving an appointment as one of six USGS geologists and an appropriation to close out his survey's work.[59]

¶ Still, the result bitterly disappointed Hayden and his supporters. After reading of King's confirmation, Washington Townsend, now retired from Congress, wrote Hayden that he had hoped the appointment would be given to Hayden, in view of his "long service in State and National geological surveys and the excellent work that has emanated from your office, and which has been so highly appreciated and commended both at home and abroad, and the high rank which you hold amongst the geologists of the world." All of these "seemed to . . . entitle you to the position." Townsend held out the hope that "the time will come when the services you have rendered the government and the cause of geological science will be properly appreciated, and that you will be placed in a position to which I think you are justly entitled." But Hayden had few expectations of the kind. Instead, it was time to clean out his office and begin closing down his operations. The day after King's confirmation was announced, he wrote Leidy asking, "Will you have room for 50 or 75 volumes of books? Can you store them in your house? When you get through with them they could go to the Academy perhaps."[60]

¶ Accepting a subordinate position was undeniably a consolation prize and not easy for Hayden. This was particularly so because he had been firmly convinced he should and would have the appointment. In December, he had written Geikie: "I have been assured that no one but myself would get the Chief directorship of the new bureau, if it is formed." He repeated the claim five weeks later, asserting "*I can say confidentially*, that there is no doubt of my appointment," and again at the end of May. Yet only in the last letter did he state that Hayes had promised to appoint him, and even then he did not claim he had the promise from the president himself but only through friends. By now, however, Hayden was bitterly discouraged and not at all happy with his prospects for the future.[61] He was also very tired.

10

The Sun Sets on Hayden's West

As the smoke cleared after the battle, the vanquished began to count their casualties. The editors of the *American Naturalist* considered their interests particularly hard hit. Though he had earlier attempted to persuade coeditor Cope that it was "no use now to criticize the action of the Nt. Aca. in [the] Naturalist,"[1] Alpheus Packard had good reason to regret implementation of the plan. Instead of consolidating the Hayden, Wheeler, and Powell Surveys, Congress had created a new geological survey, appropriating only "a little more than each of the other surveys [had] formerly received." As he read the effect, "the work is apparently to be greatly curtailed, and science and the best interests of the western people will, in a corresponding degree suffer."

¶ An entomologist, Packard's own interests would be among the first to feel the impact, all because of the actions of "two or three naturalists who have been conspicuous in shaping legislation in this whole matter." The result was the cutting off of zoological and botanical work as part of the geological surveys. "This," he lamented, "is to be deprecated by biologists throughout the country, who are probably unaware how much has been done to influence those in authority at Washington, and to prejudice them against giving national aid to these sciences." Packard attributed the outcome to "narrow, local private jealousies, rather than from any generous, catholic, scientific spirit." He was one of the first to know from experience what Cope meant when he commented on the last-minute passage of the bill establishing the USGS: "a large number of scientific men will now have the opportunity to repent at leisure their apathy in having allowed the substitution of one organization in place of three or four, which will, in all probability, not receive from Congress even the third of the aid which the surveys have been accustomed to obtain."[2]

¶ Packard contrasted this "new feature in the history of science" in the United States with the more liberal practice that had prevailed since the Lewis and Clark Expedition. Such patronage had "added immensely to the prestige of American biological science" at "little extra expense" to the surveys. Packard had hoped that "the largest, best known survey" in the United States and Europe would have won its director the privilege of extending and completing the work "in the manner already begun," for it had "won the warmest sympathy and interest from the leading geologists and palaeontologists of Europe" for being conducted "in a liberal, catholic way, and so as to promote and diffuse among the people who are paying for the work done, a knowledge of the natural resources of the Far West." But this had not happened. Instead, a "grave injustice" had been done; another man had been given charge of the new survey, and the scope of the work was to be curtailed. Packard was sure that if Henry, "the lamented promoter of American science in its broadest spirit," had still presided over the NAS "the result would have been far different."[3]

¶ Whatever might have happened had Henry still lived, Packard was only partly correct in identifying a "new feature in the history of science" in the United States. The geological and exploratory surveys had always been closely tied to economic interests, and there can be little doubt such interests were generally uppermost in legislators' minds when making such appropriations. Several years later, when Marsh appealed to Hewitt in the interest of basic science to take some action to preserve the USGS from attacks being made in the interest of economy, Hewitt responded that all he had ever sought was to secure a survey that would yield "a good geological and topographical map of the United States." Having "never contemplated the establishment of a scientific publication department for original research," Hewitt would only promise to do what he could "to prevent injury to that portion of the work which is really valuable and productive."[4] For Hewitt, that meant work with obvious economic utility. Powell and Marsh had done their work too well.

¶ At the same time, the nomination and confirmation of King as director of the USGS was a choice of a narrower vision of the federal patronage of science. In labeling Hayden a "pioneer geologist" Lesley pointed to how it had become possible to make that choice. Hayden had done a great deal to advance interest in geology in the federal government. Though not the only geologist in federal employ, nor even the most talented as a scientist, he was a talented entrepreneur and possessed an extraordinary skill at self-promotion united with an ability to seize opportunities. By multiplying the beneficiaries of his enterprise, he had multiplied its possibilities and its supporters, successfully beaten off repeated challenges, and firmly established the principle of civilians directing science for the public good. Without his work of nearly twenty-six years laying the foundations, not only of a large portion of western geology but also of the practice of geology within a thoroughly civilian context in the federal government, there would have been little for "more exact workers," inspired by his success and the fields he opened, "to come in and appropriate parts of" for themselves.

¶ Hayden left college with a burning desire to make a name for himself and quickly identified natural history and explorations in the American West as territories ripe with opportunities in which he might do so. Having equipped himself with the rudiments of expeditionary geology and natural history, Hayden perceived a vast field rich for a scientific harvest. What he lacked in financial resources he made up for in enthusiasm and energy as he labored untiringly to develop and nourish a variety of constituencies to support his goals and his organization. Recognizing, and for the most part sharing, the wide spectrum of interests in the American West, Hayden recruited capitalists and developers, settlers and educators, congressmen and scientists as well as a broad spectrum of the general public by uniting their interests to his and offering a product that appealed to the "interest and sympathy of all classes of intelligent people of [the] country from Maine to Florida" and beyond the nation's shores.[5]

¶ Hayden's persistent effort and unceasing promotion of the utility of his survey, as well as his talent for identifying attractive opportunities and quickly skimming off the cream of interesting results, earned him increased appropriations from Congress. Those appropriations in turn enabled him to expand his networks of interests and enhance his organization's technical expertise through the recruitment and retention of skilled personnel. Adept at orchestrating and exploiting public opinion to support his endeavors as well as some of the cruder aspects of the politics of patronage, Hayden maneuvered between the shoals of the demands of officeholders and office seekers and the contrasting demands of his scientific clientele. But the greatest measure of his success was in mobilizing a coalition of civilian scientific interests that not only succeeded in neutralizing the powerful bureaucratic opposition of the War Department but managed to wrest control from the military and establish it in a civilian department of the government.

¶ In his first and only annual report as director of the USGS, King wrote that with the founding of the new survey geology had taken the remaining step "necessary to give the highest efficiency and most harmonious balance to the national geological work." The science had escaped being "dragged in the dust of rapid exploration" with the founding of the different surveys in 1867 and instead had taken "a commanding position in the professional work of the country." Now it had finally witnessed the foundation of a "permanent bureau charged with the investigation and elucidation of the geological structure and mineral resources and productions of the United States."[6] King and Hayden both contributed to this transformation, but by opening new patterns of patronage Hayden did the most to break new ground. It would have been quite a different matter to create the USGS as a civilian bureau without a pattern of surveys wholly separate from military sponsorship. If King's had been the only survey created in 1867 there very likely would not have been an institutional foundation on which to erect the USGS as a civilian bureau. While much of the task of consolidating the surveys fell to King, there might have been little for the bureaucrat to organize had the enthusiast not gone before him.

¶ In some ways, the wrong man was chosen to head the USGS. King found his new position uncomfortable. It did not furnish sufficient income for his needs nor did it afford him sufficient opportunity to conduct scientific work of his own. Rather, he found himself tied down with the tasks of organizing a scientific bureau. More significantly, King was never at ease with the political necessities of his position and disdained waiting on political society as part of the rough and tumble of Washington politics. This was a sphere in which Hayden had reveled and in which he had accomplished his most important work in building his survey. It was also a world King's successor relished with a quiet intensity. Powell's tenure as head of the USGS from 1880 to 1894 confirms the role of the entrepreneur. During the first half of this period Powell won a vast increase in funding and responsibility for the USGS largely through his entrepreneurial talents. Even the difficulties he experienced during his later years point to the importance of entrepreneurship; in large measure they were the result of his departure from the cardinal rule that science was best supported by the public when its promoters highlighted economic benefits rather than the increase of knowledge.[7]

¶ Hayden's career, then, is best understood as that of a public entrepreneur of science. By the successful application of entrepreneurial techniques he developed his survey into one of the most admired nationally supported geological surveys of its time in the world and carved out a niche for civilian science in the federal government. At the same time, his career illustrates a number of features in the changing environment for science in the United States and the federal government. When Hayden began his survey of Nebraska in 1867 he was charged with a multiplicity of tasks beyond the investigation of geological resources, tasks that embraced a wide range of interests in the western territories. In 1879, however, the duties of the USGS narrowly focused upon economic geology: "the classification of the public lands and examination of the Geological Structure, mineral resources and products of the national domain."[8]

¶ These changes reflect how the West, the country's attitude toward it, and the practice of science had all changed significantly in the intervening years. The late 1870s saw the beginning of a leveling off from the rate of rapid advance in mineral production during the preceding decades. At the same time, the West had become rapidly populated and was no longer such a wide-open frontier. Though local "boosters" and western representatives continued to stress the abundance of land and opportunities in the region, the best opportunities for individuals had already been taken. Though few were willing to listen, Powell spoke the truth in his assertions that almost all of the land that could be exploited using agricultural techniques appropriate for eastern conditions had already been claimed. The period of rapid development had largely passed, yielding to a more deliberate pace, and Powell's

Lands of the Arid Region and *Report on the Methods of Surveying* manifest a recognition of the need to take a new approach toward the public lands.

¶ The decade and a half after the Civil War had also seen significant changes in scientific practice. An example of this changed environment can be seen in two letters: one from 1865, the other from 1874. In the first, composed over the course of several days, Lesquereux wrote Lesley that much as it might be desirable to retire from the chase of rapid publication of scientific papers in order to give time for ideas to mature, such a thing was hardly possible in "an epoch of Railroads, where every body who can not get a place in the cars is running along in a mad carreer [*sic*] and where those who want to reach a desired end have to take the same course or to be left far behind." If Lesley took the time to "sit down quietly and *brood over your soul's eggs*" (emphasis in original), he "would probably find when they are hatched and the chickens grown up that they are already sold in the market and that the discovery of the species does not now belong to you." Telling Lesley it was necessary to "live as our generation lives," Lesquereux insisted that as scientists they had to "put forward and publish as fast as we get them those scraps of science which we owe to study, observation and experience." Though ideas might indeed be perfected if one later had time, he urged Lesley not to hesitate from fear of incompleteness or errors in what he might write: "We can never be perfect. We must learn from others and let others learn from us. Our own errors and mistakes are encouraging to many who are glad to see and to know better than we do. Science profits even from our blunders."[9]

¶ Writing only a few years later to General Humphreys, King expressed a rather different opinion, indicative of a dawning age. Explaining his reasoning for not issuing annual reports of progress comparable to those of the Hayden Survey, King told Humphreys that "the day has passed in geological science when it is either decent or tolerable to rush into print with undigested field operations ignoring the methods and appliances in use among advanced investigators." King explained it was his intention to give his work "a finish which will place it on an equal footing with the best European publications, and those few which have redeemed the wavering reputation of our American investigators."[10] Another view of scientific practice was operative here.

Rather than enthusiastic pioneering, King advocated careful, deliberate study.

¶ King considered his role in the establishment of the USGS in an analogous way. He later wrote that his "most important contribution" to science and the "only important fact" of his twenty-year career in Washington was the role he played in the "crushing of the old system of personal surveys" and putting an end to what geologist James D. Hague called "the feudal period of Federal Scientific Expeditions."[11] Yet just as the feudal period in European history cannot be dismissed as "the Dark Ages," but was instead a formative period that preserved much of the culture of an earlier day while laying the foundations for the Renaissance and period of nation-states that succeeded it, so too it is unjust to dismiss Hayden and his survey as if they belonged to the Dark Ages of federal science.

¶ Hayden's peers had a more subtle appreciation of the role he played in developing a permanent place for science in the federal establishment. The elements they identified as forming his most important contributions were not his scientific writings, though these were not denigrated and were not nearly as worthless as Powell claimed in the heat of battle, but his entrepreneurial accomplishments. In a memoir he read before the NAS nearly seven years after Hayden's death, former Hayden Survey geologist Charles A. White wrote: "When a man has devoted his life to some special branch of science it is comparatively easy for some one to write an exhaustive and accurate estimate of the value of his labors, upon the basis of his published works; but the writings of Dr. Hayden alone do not afford the means of properly estimating the value of his services to science. He wrote no exhaustive treatises, but he made it possible for many others to prepare and publish such, and the scientific reputation of a considerable number of men was largely accomplished by means of the opportunities he created. Nearly fifty persons whose names have become known to science were from time to time more or less directly connected with the surveys under his direction, no less than thirteen of whom are, or were when living, members of this Academy." White had no doubt that "the labors of Dr. Hayden, directly or indirectly, accomplished more for the general advancement of geological science in America than those of any one else. Indeed, I think it may be truthfully said that the present

United States Geological Survey is a consequence of his labors, and that it would not now be in existence if Dr. Hayden's work had re-

mained unaccomplished."[12]

¶ Lesley also appreciated Hayden's role in this context, writing that he would be remembered as someone who "opened a new world in the far West to intelligent curiosity and detailed exploration." Lesley pointed especially to the "indescribable power [Hayden] exercised over a great number of minds. . . . Whatever Hayden asked for from the people, the politicians, and the Governors of the new States and Territories was allowed to be useful and desirable, and the means placed at his disposal." Hayden was the scientific manifestation of "the curiosity, the intelligence, the energy, the practical business talent of the western people. . . . He exactly met the wants of the Great West."[13] The comments of both men point clearly to Hayden's entrepreneurial practice. The practice of the War Department could never have had such an effect. It operated under a different philosophy, and its publications were mainly for departmental use and neither printed in large numbers nor given widespread distribution.

¶ Even J. D. Whitney comprehended Hayden in these terms. Whitney was not uncritical of Hayden's work, but he recognized merit as well, especially in view of the obstacles Hayden had to overcome. After his own experience with the geological survey of California, Whitney could sympathize with the pressures Hayden experienced as a public scientist. When Hayden applied to him for support during the 1874 conflict with Wheeler, Whitney was more than happy to come forward on Hayden's behalf. As he told his brother William D. Whitney, the only "fault" he had to find with Hayden was that he operated "too much in a B.S. light." But Whitney could excuse this, having learned it was "the only way to be popular in this country and get his work continued. Men who tell a plain, unvarnished tale are not to be listented [*sic*] [to] in this country."[14]

¶ Even if some of the most eminent figures in American science could appreciate the value of, or at least the reasons for, Hayden's entrepreneurial practice, the narrowing of vision in the relationship of government to science was real and not merely an artifact of hindsight or a function of Powell's arguments. A comparison of the charge of the USGS with the instructions given King for the survey of the fortieth parallel or, even better, those given Hayden for the survey of Nebraska quickly reveals the difference.

¶ It can also be seen in the trade press, as Raymond's writings in the *Engineering and Mining Journal* during the 1870s attest. A staunch advocate of government patronage of science, during the early part of the decade Raymond had no trouble supporting Hayden and the Hayden Survey. Though occasionally critical of Hayden's scientific competence in certain areas, Raymond had not seen any reason to hold that against him at the time, particularly in light of his "energetic and indefatigable" efforts in leading the survey. But when the bill creating the USGS was passed, Raymond threw his support behind King. For Raymond, the issue was scientific expertise and practice. As he put it, "if the new Director is wise, he will understand that his primary object must be to ascertain and make known the resources of the public lands. . . . Let him imitate the sagacity of Clarence King, who published first of all his volume on the Mining Industry, and last of all his theoretical deductions in continental geology." Since King was a candidate for the position, who better could imitate him? It comes as no surprise that Raymond applauded King's nomination, revealing that he had had King in mind all the time, as "the very best man who could have been selected."[15]

¶ The only question remaining is why scientists sought to have the patronage relationship with the federal government narrowed in the first place. In fact, they did not. This is unequivocally clear in the case of the natural historians, who were now to be cut off. It was also true of the supporters of King and the new order. They did not seek a *narrowing* of patronage but *control* of it for their own vision of how science ought to be practiced. It was a disciplinary fight over control of access to careers. The question of what sort of science the federal government ought to support was simply part of a larger quest to control scientific careers, which was not at all limited to federal science. As leading figures in the American scientific community promoted professionalization within science in the latter third of the nineteenth century, they sought both the right to judge competency within the profession and the ability to influence or control funding. Their goals included raising the standards of practice and heightening appreciation for academic training in the developing scientific departments of the nation's leading colleges and universities.[16] It was no accident that of the three candidates Eliot thought even marginally qualified to head the USGS two of them taught at his school, Harvard, and the other was trained at Yale. This brings the whole issue around, once more, to entrepreneurial concerns.

¶ Hayden's chief creation was establishing a means of practicing a career. By the end of the 1870s, there was very little debate about the appropriateness of geology and geography in the service of the federal government, nor even that these were most appropriately civilian disciplines. With necessity presumed, the question of why the federal government should fund science was posed in a different context. Legislators' answers had always revolved on the presumption of economic benefit. In this sense, while Hayden had modified the environment for the practice of science in the federal establishment, some of its most fundamental features remained unchanged. Economic issues remained paramount, and Powell seized upon them to displace Hayden from his "warm place."

¶ Powell would ultimately change his tune when challenged on his own practice of funding basic science to the apparent neglect of practical economic utility. Then he would pick up Hayden's theme, arguing that much of what the government did would never be done by private individuals. Far from echoing the arguments of Agassiz and Marsh, Powell would echo Hayden, stating that valuable as the contributions of private scientific philanthropy were, "a hundred millionaires could not do the work in scientific research now done by the General Government."[17] But all this was in the future.

¶ Hayden, meanwhile, never lost his interest in the West. Appointed as one of six USGS geologists and assigned the completion of his survey's reports, he labored at the task for the next four years, though he never completed his long-contemplated synthesis of his geological explorations. When his health began to fail, Hayden sought a chance to go west again in 1883. In what proved a vain hope that fieldwork would be restorative, he spent parts of the next three summers working with Peale in Montana. However, his health gradually deteriorated, and by late 1886 he was largely confined to bed. On 31 December 1886, Hayden resigned his position, concluding nearly thirty years of service as government naturalist, geologist, and explorer. He died nearly a year later, on 22 December 1887, and was buried in his wife's family plot in Woodland Cemetery in West Philadelphia.[18]

¶ While fondly remembered by friends and scientific associates, who composed several touching memorials, in subsequent years Hayden was either largely forgotten by the USGS, apart from those who had been members of the Hayden Survey, or remembered only in ridicule. Having suffered the misfortune of dying before either of his enemies, Hayden became one of history's "losers." Though familiar with rewriting history and his story to his own advantage, Hayden did not live long enough to rewrite his final chapters, and subsequent historians of the USGS and biographers of King and Powell have been too concerned with magnifying the accomplishments of their heroes to give Hayden and his career the consideration they deserve. The nadir, no doubt, was the burlesque satire the USGS's "Pick and Hammer Club" produced in 1965 and 1971, which caricatured Hayden as an explorer in pursuit of fame who passed himself off as "a gentleman and a scholar" by trading on fraudulent scientific credentials and the public's taste for "scenic wonders." Yet in spite of such historical prejudice and oversight, on occasion even those largely concerned with celebrating the achievements of the USGS's first two directors have recognized Hayden's contributions, even if they have consigned them to a footnote observing that his "most important administrative contribution" was "successfully institutionalizing the earth sciences within the Interior Department." That was indeed one of Hayden's major accomplishments, and his struggles toward this end are replete with lessons in the history of American science, particularly on the relationship of science and the federal government.[19]

¶ Students of entrepreneurship have long recognized that successful innovation requires not only the recognition of an opportunity but also that innovation must be matched to felt social needs and the existence of a social power willing to act as patron and devote resources to the enterprise. Hayden's career clearly illustrates that successfully situating innovation and entrepreneurialism in the context of the federal government required the construction of a conjunction between diverse interests to secure a recognition of felt social needs and the commitment of resources through federal patronage of science. At the same time, it also helps explain why Hayden experienced only temporary success. Having won a firm place for science, he became eminently dispensable when the commitment of resources followed newfelt needs.

¶ When Dupree wrote his classic study on the history of the relationship of science and the federal government he expressed the hope that his work would provide the foundation for the erection of a national science policy to be carried out by the newly founded National Science Foundation. Even though his book traced the history of that relationship as having evolved largely ad hoc, Dupree viewed that development as moving toward, and indeed demanding, increased order as the importance of science in both American society and American government increased.[20] In many ways, Hayden's career supports Dupree's conclusions. But it also supports a major theme in Walter McDougall's study of the drive for space exploration: the seeming inherent irrationality of some elements of federal scientific policy.

¶ NASA's adoption of manned space missions rather than less expensive and less dangerous unmanned ones seems to have been determined more on the grounds of political appeal than scientific utility or need. But the apparent paradox is easily explained in the realization that scientific rationality is not the only operative rationality and is sometimes less important than other forms of rationality in political questions. Hayden knew that well. He knew the importance of appealing to a wide variety of potential supporters. Though Powell libelously charged that Hayden's mind was "utterly untrained to severe scientific logic and analysis—is incoherent and purposeless," there was more than a little purpose to Hayden's logic and operations, as Powell well knew. That logic had enabled Hayden to develop a five-thousand dollar grant into one of the most admired geological and geographical surveys of its time and to challenge successfully a long-standing military tradition of surveys. Powell's appreciation of the logic and purpose represented in Hayden's practice is quite evident in Powell's own practice as director of the USGS. Dupree sees Powell's directorship as corresponding ever more closely to what he terms the "ideal government bureau," the traits of which he sees emerging in the latter quarter of the nineteenth century. But short of possessing the security of an "organic act" establishing his organization, a goal toward which he consistently labored,

Hayden's practice was in many respects identical to Powell's as described by Dupree.[21]

¶ More significantly, Hayden's practice illustrates something of the context in which the characteristics of the "ideal bureau" were identified and forged. As the relationship between civilian scientists and their public patrons tentatively took on a new form, a number of issues were up for grabs. So, too, was the control of scientific and bureaucratic careers. There was no quiet place to work out these issues in terms of a rational science policy for a rapidly developing nation. They were dealt with instead in the context of continuing and frequently bitter battles for appropriations. Some stratagems worked, others failed. But at all times the contenders had to keep one eye on their opponents and the other on the opportunity for scientific or political advantage. Sometimes the last two were identical, frequently not. Hayden's greatest legacy was in the success with which he played the game. He bridged the distances between scientific and political interests and established a secure ground for practicing geology and geography within a thoroughly civilian context in the federal government, winning a vast new territory in which succeeding generations of scientists could make secure careers.

Notes

ABBREVIATIONS USED IN THE NOTES

Am. J. Sci.	*American Journal of Science*
BDA	*The Biographical Dictionary of America*
BUSGGST	*Bulletin of the United States Geological and Geographical Survey of the Territories*
Cong. Rec.	*Congressional Record*
DAB	*Dictionary of American Biography*
DSB	*Dictionary of Scientific Biography*
Eng. Min. J.	*Engineering and Mining Journal*
FVH	Ferdinand V. Hayden
Proc. ANSP	*Proceedings of the Academy of Natural Sciences of Philadelphia*
Proc. APS	*Proceedings of the American Philosophical Society*
RG	Record Group, National Archives and Records Administration, Washington DC
RU	Record Unit, Smithsonian Institution Archives, Washington DC
Trans. APS	*Transactions of the American Philosophical Society*

INTRODUCTION

1. *U.S. Statutes at Large* 14 (1867): 457; Henry Adams, *The Education of Henry Adams* (n.p., 1918; reprint, Boston: Houghton Mifflin, 1961), 312; Mary C. Rabbitt, *Minerals, Land and Geology for the Common Defense and General Welfare*, vol. 1, *Before 1879* (Washington DC: GPO, 1979), 159.
2. *U.S. Statutes at Large* 14 (1867): 470; Rabbitt, *Minerals*, 159; Baird to Wilson, 9 Mar. 1867, National Archives, RG 49, General Land Office Records, Division "D," "Mails and Files," Series 17, Register of Letters Received, vol. 137; Baird to FVH, 9 Mar. 1867, National Archives, RG 57, Records of the Geological Survey, "Records of the Geological and Geographical Survey of the Territories ('Hayden Survey'), 1867–79" (henceforth, RG 57H).

3. Mike Foster, *Strange Genius: The Life of Ferdinand Vandeveer Hayden* (Niwot CO: Roberts Rinehart, 1994), esp. chap. 25.

4. William Cronon, George Miles, and Jay Gitlin, "Becoming West: Toward a New Meaning for Western History," in *Under an Open Sky: Rethinking America's Western Past*, ed. William Cronon, George Miles, and Jay Gitlin (New York: W. W. Norton, 1992), 8–9, 14–15; Donald Worster, *Rivers of Empire: Water, Aridity, and the Growth of the American West* (New York: Pantheon, 1985); Worster, *An Unsettled Country: Changing Landscapes of the American West* (Albuquerque: Univ. of New Mexico Press, 1994).
5. Wallace Stegner, "Thoughts in a Dry Land," in *Where the Bluebird Sings to the Lemonade Springs: Living and Writing in the West* (New York: Random House, 1992), 52.
6. Cronon, Miles, and Gitlin, "Becoming West," 6–7.
7. Rodman W. Paul, *The Far West and the Great Plains in Transition, 1859–1900* (New York: Harper & Row, 1988), 1; Patricia Nelson Limerick, *The Legacy of Conquest* (New York: W. W. Norton, 1987), 28.
8. Ann Shelby Blum, *Picturing Nature: American Nineteenth-Century Zoological Illustration* (Princeton: Princeton Univ. Press, 1993); Barbara Novak, *Nature and Culture: American Landscape and Painting, 1825–1875* (New York: Oxford Univ. Press, 1980); John F. Sears, *Sacred Places: American Tourist Attractions in the Nineteenth Century* (New York: Oxford Univ. Press, 1989); William H. Truettner, ed., *The West as America: Reinterpreting Images of the Frontier, 1820–1920* (Washington DC: Smithsonian Institution Press, 1991); Carol Clark, *Thomas Moran: Watercolors of the American West* (Fort Worth TX: Amon Carter Museum of Western Art, 1980); Joni Louise Kinsey, *Thomas Moran and the Surveying of the American West* (Washington DC: Smithsonian Institution Press, 1992); Peter B. Hales, *William Henry Jackson and the Transformation of the American Landscape* (Philadelphia: Temple Univ. Press, 1988).
9. Robert H. Wiebe, *The Search for Order, 1877–1920* (New York: Hill & Wang, 1967); Alan Trachtenberg, *The Incorporation of America* (New York: Hill & Wang, 1982), 2–3; Burton J. Bledstein, *The Culture of Professionalism* (New York: W. W. Norton, 1976).
10. Leonard G. Wilson, "The Emergence of Geology as a Science in the United States," *Journal of World History* 10 (1967): 416–17; Nathan Reingold, "American Indifference to Basic Research: A Reappraisal," in *Nineteenth-Century American Science: A Reappraisal*, ed. George H. Daniels (Evanston IL: Northwestern Univ. Press, 1972), 38–62.
11. Roger Cooter and Stephen Pumfrey, "Separate Spheres and Public Places:

Reflections on the History of Science Popularization and Science in Popular Culture," *History of Science,* 32 (1994): 237, 242; Bruno Latour, *Science in Action* (Cambridge MA: Harvard Univ. Press, 1987), 108ff.

12. See, A. J. G. Cummings and Larry Stewart, "The Case of the Eighteenth-Century Projector: Entrepreneurs, Engineers, and Legitimacy at the Hanoverian Court in Britain," in *Patronage and Institutions: Science, Technology, and Medicine at the European Court, 1500–1750,* ed. Bruce T. Moran (Rochester NY: Boydell Press, 1991), 235–38, and the essays in this work generally.
13. For example, Mario Biagioli, *Galileo, Courtier: The Practice of Science in the Culture of Absolutism* (Chicago: Univ. of Chicago Press, 1993) and Paula Findlen, *Possessing Nature: Museums, Collecting, and Scientific Culture in Early Modern Italy* (Berkeley: Univ. of California Press, 1994).
14. Thurman Wilkins (with the help of Caroline Lawson Hinkley) *Clarence King: A Biography,* rev. ed. (Albuquerque: Univ. of New Mexico Press, 1988); William Culp Darrah, *Powell of the Colorado* (Princeton: Princeton Univ. Press, 1951); Paul Meadows, *John Wesley Powell: Frontiersman of Science* (Lincoln: Univ. of Nebraska Press, 1952); Wallace Stegner, *Beyond the Hundredth Meridian: John Wesley Powell and the Second Opening of the West* (Boston: Houghton Mifflin, 1954; New York: Penguin, 1992), and John Upton Terrell, *The Man Who Rediscovered America: A Biography of John Wesley Powell* (New York: Weybright & Talley, 1969).
15. Among those studies that have explored the entrepreneurial activities of bureaucrats and scientists, see, e.g., Robert E. Kohler, *Partners in Science: Foundation Managers and Natural Scientists, 1900–1945* (Chicago: Univ. of Chicago Press, 1991); and the essays in Ronald Rainger, Keith R. Benson, and Jane Maienschein, eds., *The American Development of Biology* (New Brunswick NJ: Rutgers Univ. Press, 1991); in Wiebe E. Bijker, Thomas P. Hughes, and Trevor J. Pinch, eds., *The Social Construction of Technological Systems: New Directions in the Sociology and History of Technology* (Cambridge MA: MIT Press, 1987); and in Jameson W. Doig and Erwin C. Hargrove, eds., *Leadership and Innovation: A Biographical Perspective on Entrepreneurs in Government* (Baltimore: Johns Hopkins Univ. Press, 1987), whose preface suggested the general characteristics mentioned in the following paragraphs.
16. J. D. Cox to A. A. Wright, 24 Feb. 1888; Manly Root to Wright, 31 Mar. 1888; A. Harper to Wright, 21 Mar. 1888, Smithsonian Archives, RU 7085, Marcus Benjamin Papers; William Henry Jackson, *Time Exposure: The Autobiography of William Henry Jackson* (New York: G. P. Putnam's Sons, 1940), 236; Mike Foster, "The Permian Controversy of 1858: An Affair of the Heart," *Proc.* APS 133 (1989): 371.

17. Doig and Hargrove, *Leadership and Innovation*, 8; Latour, *Science in Action*, 155.

18. Latour, *Science in Action*, 13–15, 146ff.
19. Henrika Kuklick and Robert E. Kohler, eds., *Science in the Field*, *Osiris*, 11 (special issue, 1996).
20. J. Peter Lesley, "Obituary Notice of Ferdinand Vandiveer Hayden, M.D., Ph.D., LL.D.," *American Philosophical Society Miscellaneous Pamphlets*, 26 (1888): 61; William Henry Jackson, quoting Hayden, in *The Diaries of William Henry Jackson, Frontier Photographer* (Glendale CA: Arthur H. Clark, 1959), 240.

1. GEOLOGICAL SURVEYS

1. George Otis Smith, "A Century of Government Geological Surveys," in *A Century of Science in America, with special reference to the American Journal of Science, 1818–1918*, ed. Edward Salisbury Dana et al. (New Haven: Yale Univ. Press, 1918), 193.
2. A. Hunter Dupree, *Science in the Federal Government: A History of Politics and Activities* (Cambridge MA: Harvard Univ. Press, Belknap Press, 1957; Baltimore: Johns Hopkins Univ. Press, 1986); Stephen P. Turner, "The Survey in Nineteenth-Century American Geology: The Evolution of a Form of Patronage," *Minerva* 25 (1987): 282–330; Wilson, "Emergence of Geology," 416–37.
3. Biagioli, *Galileo*, 11, 16, 54ff.
4. Biagioli, *Galileo* 353, 19; Bruno Latour, "Give Me a Laboratory and I Will Raise the World," in *Science Observed: Perspectives on the Social Study of Science*, ed. Karin D. Knorr-Cetina and Michael Mulkay (London: Sage, 1983), 141–70.
5. Dorinda Outram, "New Spaces in Natural History," in *Cultures of Natural History*, ed. N. Jardine, J. A. Secord, and E. C. Spary (Cambridge: Cambridge Univ. Press, 1996), 249–65; Nathan Reingold, "Definitions and Speculations: The Professionalization of Science in America in the Nineteenth Century," in *Science, American Style*, ed. Nathan Reingold (New Brunswick NJ: Rutgers Univ. Press, 1991), 25–53.
6. Reingold, "Definitions and Speculations," 31–35; Reingold, "Reflections on Two Hundred Years of Science in the United States," in *Science, American Style*, 13–23. On the role of local institutions, see J. Kirkpatrick Flack, *Desideratum in Washington: The Intellectual Community in the Capital City, 1870–1900* (Cambridge MA: Schenkman, 1975), and Stanley M. Gural-

nick, *Science and the Ante-Bellum American College* (Philadelphia: American Philosophical Society, 1975).

7. Guralnick, *Science*, 149–50; Guralnick, "Sources of Misconception of the Role of Science in the Nineteenth-Century American College," *Isis* 65 (1974): 352–66; Guralnick, "The American Scientist in Higher Education, 1820–1910," in *The Sciences in the American Context*, ed. Nathan Reingold (Washington DC: Smithsonian Institution Press, 1979; Charlotte M. Porter, *The Eagle's Nest: Natural History and American Ideas, 1812–1842* (Tuscaloosa: Univ. of Alabama Press, 1986); Rosenberg, *No Other Gods*.
8. On the popularity of natural history, see David Elliston Allen, *The Naturalist in Britain: A Social History* (London: Ebenezer Baylis & Son, 1976); Lynn Barber, *The Heyday of Natural History, 1820–1870* (Garden City NY: Doubleday, 1980); Lynn L. Merrill, *The Romance of Victorian Natural History* (New York: Oxford Univ. Press, 1989); and William Martin Smallwood, in collaboration with Mabel Sarah Coon Smallwood, *Natural History and the American Mind* (New York: Columbia Univ. Press, 1941). On geology, see Roy Porter, *The Making of Geology: Earth Science in Britain, 1660–1815* (London: Cambridge Univ. Press, 1977) and Dennis R. Dean, "The Influences of Geology on American Literature and Thought," in *Two Hundred Years of Geology in America*, ed. Cecil J. Schneer (Hanover NH: Univ. Press of New England, 1979), 289–303. On ornithology, see Paul Lawrence Farber, *The Emergence of Ornithology as a Scientific Discipline: 1760–1850* (Dordrecht: D. Reidel, 1982). On the breakup of natural history, see David Elliston Allen, "The Lost Limb: Geology and Natural History," in *Images of the Earth: Essays in the History of the Environmental Sciences*, ed. L. J. Jordanova and Roy S. Porter (Chalfont St. Giles: British Society for the History of Science, 1979), 200–206.
9. Barber, *Heyday of Natural History*, 57–59.
10. Susan Faye Cannon, "Humboldtian Science," in *Science in Culture: The Early Victorian Period* (New York: Science History Publications, 1978), 75–78; Allen, *Naturalist in Britain*, 122–23; Sally Gregory Kohlstedt, "Curiosities and Cabinets: Natural History Museums and Education on the Antebellum Campus," *Isis* 79 (1988): 407; and Kohlstedt, "Parlors, Primers, and Public Schooling: Education for Science in Nineteenth-Century America," *Isis* 81 (1990): 428–34.
11. Patsy A. Gerstner, "A Dynamic Theory of Mountain Building: Henry Darwin Rogers, 1842," *Isis* 66 (1975): 26–37; Martin J. S. Rudwick, *The Great Devonian Controversy: The Shaping of Scientific Knowledge among Gentlemanly Specialists* (Chicago: Univ. of Chicago Press, 1985), 379–81, 396–97.

12. George H. Daniels, *Science in American Society: A Social History* (New York: Alfred A. Knopf, 1971), 126–35, 141.
13. Robert H. Silliman, "The Hamlet Affair: Charles Lyell and the North Americans," *Isis* 86 (1995): 541–61; Robert H. Dott Jr., "Lyell in America—His Lectures, Field Work, and Mutual Influences, 1841–1853," *Earth Science History* 15 (1996): 128.
14. George P. Merrill, ed. and comp., *Contributions to a History of American State Geological and Natural History Surveys*, Smithsonian Institution, United States National Museum, *Bulletin 109* (Washington DC: GPO, 1920), 363ff, 459ff, 150, 139; Merrill, *The First One Hundred Years of American Geology* (New Haven: Yale Univ. Press, 1924), chaps. 3–6; and Michele L. Aldrich, "American State Geological Surveys, 1820–1845," in *Two Hundred Years*, 133–44; quoted in William M. Jordan, "Geology and the Industrial-Transportation Revolution in Early to Mid Nineteenth-Century Pennsylvania," in *Two Hundred Years*, 92–93; Dean, "Influences of Geology," 293–97.
15. On the general characteristics of state surveys, see Merrill, *First One Hundred Years*, and Aldrich, "American State Geological Surveys"; James Hall to B. W. Kumler, n.d., quoted in Merrill, *First One Hundred Years*, 297.
16. Wilson, "Emergence of Geology," 416–17; Hyman Kuritz, "The Popularization of Science in Nineteenth-Century America," *History of Education Quarterly* 21 (1981): 260–61; William H. Goetzmann, *New Lands, New Men: America and the Second Great Age of Discovery* (New York: Viking Penguin, 1986), 186–89.
17. C. K. Yearley Jr., *Enterprise and Anthracite: Economics and Democracy in Schuylkill Country, 1820–1875* (Baltimore: Johns Hopkins Univ. Press, 1961), 98, quoted in Jordan, "Geology and the Industrial-Transportation Revolution," 97; Aldrich, "American State Geological Surveys," 134.
18. Donald M. Scott, "The Popular Lecture and the Creation of a Public in Mid-Nineteenth-Century America," *Journal of American History* 66 (1980): 791–809; Edward Lurie, *Louis Agassiz: A Life in Science* (Baltimore: Johns Hopkins Univ. Press, 1988), esp. chaps. 4–6.
19. Sally Gregory Kohlstedt, "The Nineteenth-Century Amateur Tradition: The Case of the Boston Society of Natural History," in *Science and Its Public: The Changing Relationship*, ed. Gerald Holton and William A. Blanpied (Dordrecht: D. Reidel, 1976), 173–90; and Kohlstedt, "The Geologists' Model for National Science," *Proc. APS*, 118 (1974): 179–80; Merrill, *Contributions*, 327, 363.
20. George H. Daniels, *American Science in the Age of Jackson* (New York: Columbia Univ. Press, 1968).

21. Herman LeRoy Fairchild, *The Geological Society of America, 1888–1930: A Chapter in Earth Science History* (New York: Geological Society of America, 1932), 31–36; Patsy A. Gerstner, "Henry Darwin Rogers and William Barton Rogers on the Nomenclature of the American Paleozoic Rocks," in *Two Hundred Years,* 178; Kohlstedt, "Geologists' Model," 179–95; Kohlstedt, *The Formation of the American Scientific Community: The American Association for the Advancement of Science, 1848–60* (Urbana: Univ. of Illinois Press, 1976), chap. 3.
22. Kohlstedt, *Formation,* 70–76.
23. Nathan Reingold, ed., *Science in Nineteenth-Century America: A Documentary History* (Chicago: Univ. of Chicago Press, 1964), 169; Mark Beach, "Was There a Scientific Lazzaroni?" in *Nineteenth-Century American Science,* 128–29, 117 n. 4. Contemporaries agreed the Lazzaroni consisted of Bache, Joseph Henry, John Fries Frazer, Wolcott Gibbs, Benjamin Apthorp Gould, James Dwight Dana, Louis Agassiz, Benjamin Peirce, and Cornelius Conway Felton; Beach, "Was There a Scientific Lazzaroni," 118–19.
24. Henry to Bache, 9 Aug. 1838, in *Science in Nineteenth-Century America,* 83, 85; Beach, "Was There a Scientific Lazzaroni," 121ff.
25. Kohlstedt, *Formation,* 78–79, 84, chaps. 6–7, passim; Beach, "Was There a Scientific Lazzaroni," 128–29, 132; Dupree, *Science,* 29–33, 43, 53.
26. Hugh Richard Slotten, *Patronage, Practice, and the Culture of American Science: Alexander Dallas Bache and the U.S. Coast Survey* (Cambridge: Cambridge Univ. Press, 1994), chaps. 5–7.
27. Slotten, *Patronage,* 5, 107, 129–30, 135; Dupree, *Science,* 80, 136–48; Miller, *Dollars for Research,* 41–47; and Beach, "Was There a Scientific Lazzaroni," 128–31.
28. Mary P. Winsor, *Reading the Shape of Nature: Comparative Zoology at the Agassiz Museum* (Chicago: Univ. of Chicago Press, 1991), 3, 67–71, 89–90.
29. Winsor, *Reading the Shape,* 68; Lurie, *Louis Agassiz,* chaps. 4–6.
30. Porter, *Eagle's Nest,* 129.
31. Rudwick, *Great Devonian,* 438–45; Steven Shapin, *A Social History of Truth: Civility and Science in Seventeenth-Century England* (Chicago: Univ. of Chicago Press, 1994), 27, 126, 241–42; Porter, *Making of Geology,* 215.
32. Biagioli, *Galileo,* 64ff.
33. Paul Lucier, "Commercial Interests and Scientific Disinterestedness: Consulting Geologists in Antebellum America," *Isis* 86 (1995): 253–54, 264–65.
34. Hamilton Cravens, "American Science Comes of Age: An Institutional Perspective, 1850–1930," *American Studies* 17 (1976): 56.

35. John C. Fitzpatrick, ed., *Journals of the Continental Congress, 1774–1789*, vol. 28, *1785* (Washington DC: GPO, 1933), 378.

36. The best introduction to the surveys and explorations of the American West through the first three-quarters of the nineteenth century remains William H. Goetzmann, *Exploration and Empire: The Explorer and the Scientist in the Winning of the American West* (New York: W. W. Norton, 1966); Frank N. Schubert, *Vanguard of Expansion: Army Engineers in the Trans-Mississippi West, 1819–1879* (Washington DC: GPO, 1980) provides a brief introduction to the western surveys and their multiple goals and effects.

37. Dupree, *Science*, 93, 99; Findlen, *Possessing Nature*, 292.

38. William A. Deiss, "The Making of a Naturalist: Spencer F. Baird, the Early Years," in *From Linnaeus to Darwin: Commentaries on the History of Biology and Geology*, ed. Alwyne Wheeler and James H. Price (London: Society for the History of Natural History, 1985), 142. The material in these paragraphs on Baird comes from this essay and William Healey Dall, *Spencer Fullerton Baird: A Biography* (Philadelphia: J. B. Lippincott, 1915); Deiss, "Spencer F. Baird and His Collectors," *Journal of the Society for the Bibliography of Natural History*, 9 (1980): 635–45; and E. F. Rivinus and E. M. Youssef, *Spencer Baird of the Smithsonian* (Washington DC: Smithsonian Institution, 1992).

39. Dall, *S. F. Baird*, 14, 41, 72–80, 156–66; Rivinus and Youssef, *Spencer Baird*, 41–44; Dupree, *Science*, 56–61; Goetzmann, *Exploration and Empire*, 235–40; Blum, *Picturing Nature*, 122–57.

40. Deiss, "Baird and His Collectors," 635–45; Rivinus and Youssef, *Spencer Baird*, 57–58 and chap. 8.

41. Deiss, "Baird and His Collectors," 635–45; Rivinus and Youssef, *Spencer Baird*, chap. 8.

42. Rivinus and Youssef, *Spencer Baird*, 83.

43. Goetzmann, *Exploration and Empire*, 281.

44. Dupree, *Science*, 94–95, 99–100; Goetzmann, *Exploration and Empire*, 303, 99; Vincent Ponko Jr., "The Military Explorers of the American West, 1838–1860," in *North American Exploration*, ed. John Logan Allen, vol. 3, *A Continent Comprehended* (Lincoln: Univ. of Nebraska Press, 1997), 396, 402; William Goetzmann, *Army Exploration in the American West, 1803–1863* (New Haven: Yale Univ. Press, 1959), chap. 7.

45. See Dupree, *Science*, chap. 7.

46. Dupree, *Science*, 134–35.

47. Morton Keller, *Affairs of State: Public Life in Late Nineteenth Century America* (Cambridge MA: Harvard Univ. Press, Belknap Press, 1977), 85; Dupree,

Science, 91; Dupree, "Science Policy in the United States: The Legacy of John Quincy Adams," *Minerva* 28 (1990): 261.

48. U.S. Bureau of the Census, *The Statistical History of the United States: From Colonial Times to the Present* (New York: Basic Books, 1976), 22.
49. *Statistical History*, 606, 600, 590; William Thomas Hogan, S.J., *Economic History of the Iron and Steel Industry in the United States* (Lexington MA: D. C. Heath, 1971), 1:25; W. H. Dennis, *A Hundred Years of Metallurgy* (Chicago: Aldine, 1963), 97; Douglas Alan Fisher, *The Epic of Steel* (New York: Harper & Row, 1963), 128–29; Hales, *William Henry Jackson*, 68.
50. Rabbitt, *Minerals*, 180; John Hoyt Williams, *A Great and Shining Road: The Epic Story of the Transcontinental Railroad* (New York: Random House, 1988), 43–48.
51. David Dary, *Entrepreneurs of the Old West* (Lincoln: Univ. of Nebraska Press, 1986), 230–31; Hales, *William Henry Jackson*, 48.
52. Dary, *Entrepreneurs*, 227, 254, 255–56; Henry Nash Smith, *Virgin Land: The American West as Symbol and Myth* (Cambridge MA: Harvard Univ. Press, 1978), 174–75; Paul, *Far West*, 94.
53. James A. Ward, *Railroads and the Character of America, 1820–1887* (Knoxville: Univ. of Tennessee Press, 1986), 94.
54. Editors, "Introductory," *American Naturalist* 1 (1867): 1–4.
55. Richard A. Bartlett, *Great Surveys of the American West* (Norman: Univ. of Oklahoma Press, 1962), xiv.
56. Clarence King, *Report of the Geological Exploration of the Fortieth Parallel* (Washington DC: GPO, 1878), 1:xi; Goetzmann, *Exploration and Empire*, 437.
57. Darrah, *Powell*, 78–82.
58. A. A. Humphreys to William W. Belknap, 23 Apr. 1874, in U. S. Grant, *Message from the President of the United States, in Answer to a Resolution of the House of April 15, 1874. Transmitting a Report from the Secretary of War, Relative to Geographical and Geological Surveys West of the Mississippi*, 43rd Cong., 1st sess., 1874, H. Exec. Doc. 240 (henceforth, Grant, *Geographical and Geological Surveys*), 3.
59. George M. Wheeler, *Preliminary Report Concerning Explorations and Surveys Principally in Nevada and Arizona* (Washington DC: GPO, 1872), 11–12, 60–61.
60. Goetzmann, *Exploration and Empire*, 469.

2. MAKING OF A FRONTIER NATURALIST

1. See Foster, *Strange Genius*, esp. chaps. 1–3, 24. I gladly rely on Foster's biography of Hayden for much of what follows regarding the details of

Hayden's life. For Hayden's family background, see Foster, *Strange Genius*, chap. 2.

2. A. Harper to A. A. Wright, 21 Mar. 1888, and W. B. Williams to Wright, 15 Mar. 1888, copies in RU 7085.
3. Foster, *Strange Genius*, chap. 4.
4. Foster, *Strange Genius*, chap. 4; Guralnick, *Science*, ix–x, 159; and Guralnick, "American Scientist," 106.
5. Foster, *Strange Genius*, 28–32.
6. Foster, *Strange Genius*, 31, 33.
7. Foster, *Strange Genius*, 33–34.
8. FVH to James Hall, 29 Jan. 1853, James Hall Correspondence, New York State Archives, Accession No. KW12835; Foster, *Strange Genius*, 35–36; Jerome R. Ravetz, *Scientific Knowledge and Its Social Problems* (Oxford: Clarendon Press, 1971), chap. 3.
9. FVH to Hall, 29 Jan. 1853, Hall Correspondence.
10. Allen, *Naturalist in Britain*, 17–18; Jane R. Camerini, "Wallace in the Field," in *Science in the Field*, 47–48.
11. John M. Clarke, *James Hall of Albany: Geologist and Palaeontologist, 1811–1898* (n.p., 1923; reprint, New York: Arno Press, 1978), 244; "Academy of Natural Sciences," *Philadelphia Public Ledger*, 10 March 1890, 5.
12. Foster, *Strange Genius*, 35. On the popularity of natural history in the nineteenth century, see Allen, *Naturalist in Britain*; Daniels, *American Science in the Age of Jackson*; John C. Greene, *American Science in the Age of Jefferson* (Ames: Iowa State Univ. Press, 1984); and Bruce Greenfield, *Narrating Discovery: The Romantic Explorer in American Literature, 1790–1855* (New York: Columbia Univ. Press, 1992).
13. Hall to FVH, 16 Jan. 1853, Ferdinand V. Hayden Papers, 1846–1865, MS 3154, Western Reserve Historical Society, Cleveland, Ohio (henceforth, Hayden Papers, Cleveland); Hall to Joseph Leidy, 10 Apr. 1853, Ewell Sale Stewart Library, The Academy of Natural Sciences of Philadelphia, Manuscripts/Archives, Collection 1-B, Leidy Papers, Xeroxes from College of Physicians (henceforth, Leidy Coll. 1-B); Joseph T. Gregory, "North American Vertebrate Paleontology, 1776–1976," in *Two Hundred Years*, 308.
14. Foster, *Strange Genius*, 39; Deiss, "Making of a Naturalist," 141; Baird to FVH, 22 Feb. 1853; Hall to FVH, 27 Feb. 1853, Hayden Papers, Cleveland; FVH to Hall, 29 Jan. 1853, Hall Correspondence; Dall, *S. F. Baird*, 182.
15. Hall to FVH, 27 Feb. 1853, Hayden Papers, Cleveland; Newberry to Hall, 23 Mar. 1853, Hall Correspondence; FVH to Hall, 3 Mar. 1853, George P. Merrill Papers, Library of Congress; Foster, *Strange Genius*, 40–41; Cliff-

ord M. Nelson, "Meek at Albany, 1852–58," *Earth Sciences History* 6 (1987): 40–46.

16. FVH to Hall, 3 Mar. 1853, Merrill Papers; FVH to Baird, 16 Feb. 1853, Smithsonian Archives, RU 7002, Spencer F. Baird Papers; Mike Foster, "Ferdinand Vandeveer Hayden as Naturalist," *American Zoologist* 26 (1986): 343–44.

17. FVH to Hall, 3 Mar. 1853, Merrill Papers; FVH to Hall, 28 Apr. 1853, J. V. Howell Collection, American Heritage Center, University of Wyoming, Laramie, Acc. 1684 (henceforth, Howell Collection); FVH to Meek, 29 Apr. 1853, Smithsonian Institution, RU 7062, Fielding B. Meek Papers, 1843–1877.
18. Hall to FVH, 16 Jan. 1853, Hayden Papers, Cleveland; FVH to Hall, 10 May 1853, in *Science in Nineteenth-Century America*, 169–71; FVH to Hall, 6 May 1853; FVH to Hall, 16 May 1853; Meek to Hall, 28 May 1853 and 19 June 1853, all in Hall Correspondence; Meek to Leidy, 12 Nov. 1856, Leidy Coll. 1-B; Meek, "Notebook 1853," RU 7062 (henceforth, Meek, "Notebook 1853"), 80–83, 134, 156–57; Foster, *Strange Genius*, 50–52; John E. Sunder, *The Fur Trade on the Upper Missouri, 1840–1865* (Norman: Univ. of Oklahoma Press, 1965), 23–25, 64–68, 127–29, 151–55; Kuklick and Kohler, "Introduction," in *Science in the Field*, 3, 7; Camerini, "Wallace in the Field," 44–65; Brian W. Dippie, *Catlin and His Contemporaries: The Politics of Patronage* (Lincoln: Univ. of Nebraska Press, 1990), 25–27, 58–61.
19. Stuart McCook, "'It May Be Truth, But It Is Not Evidence': Paul du Chaillu and the Legitimation of Evidence in the Field Sciences," in *Science in the Field*, 182; Rudwick, *Great Devonian*, 48.
20. James A. Secord, *Controversy in Victorian Geology: The Cambrian-Silurian Dispute* (Princeton: Princeton Univ. Press, 1986), 4; Rudwick, *Great Devonian*, 46.
21. Secord, *Controversy*, 25–26; James D. Dana, *New Text-Book of Geology, Designed for Schools and Academies*, 2d ed. (New York: Ivison, Blakeman, Taylor, 1874), 40–41.
22. Dana, *New Text-Book*, 356; Rudwick, *Great Devonian*, 39–40; Anne Larsen, "Equipment for the Field," in *Cultures of Natural History*, 358–77.
23. Meek, "Notebook, 1853," 113–16.
24. Hayden, *Geological Report of the Exploration of the Yellowstone and Missouri Rivers, 1859–'60* (Washington DC: GPO, 1869), vii–viii; Meek, "Notebook 1853," 24–30, 152–57; Gilbert F. Stucker, "Hayden in the Badlands," *American West* 4 (1967): 41.
25. FVH to Hall, 19 Mar. 1853; Meek to Hall, 28 May 1853, Hall Correspon-

dence; Spencer F. Baird, *Directions for Collecting, Preserving, and Transporting Specimens of Natural History* (Washington DC: Smithsonian Institution, 1854), 24–25; Baird, *Hints for Preserving Objects of Natural History* (Carlisle PA, Gitt & Hinckley, 1846), 10.

26. Dana, *New Text-Book*, 357; James Hall and F. B. Meek, "Descriptions of New Species of Fossils, from the Cretaceous Formations of Nebraska," *Memoirs of the American Academy of Arts and Sciences*, 5 (1854): 379–411.
27. Joseph Leidy to Hall, 20 Apr. 1853, Hall Correspondence; Hayden, "A brief sketch of the geological and physical features of the region of the upper Missouri," in Lieut. G. K. Warren, *Explorations in the Dacota Country, in the Year 1855*, 34th Cong., 1st sess., 1856, S. Exec. Doc. 76 (henceforth, Hayden, "A brief sketch . . . of the upper Missouri"), 75.
28. Baird, *Directions for Collecting* (1859); Meek, "Notebook 1853," 113–16; Allen, *Naturalist in Britain*, 130–36; Foster, *Strange Genius*, illustration opposite p. 180; FVH to Baird, 13 May 1867, RU 7002.
29. Foster, *Strange Genius*, 52–53.
30. Hall and Meek, "Descriptions of New Species of Fossils" (1854), 379.
31. Hall to Leidy, 8 Jan. 1854, Leidy Coll. 1-B.
32. FVH to Hall, 6 May 1853; Meek to Hall, 28 May 1853; Meek to Hall, 19 June 1853, Hall Correspondence; Foster, *Strange Genius*, 46.
33. Hall to Leidy, 14 Dec. 1853, Leidy Coll. 1-B; FVH to Leidy, 11 Jan. 1854, Ewell Sale Stewart Library, The Academy of Natural Sciences of Philadelphia, Manuscripts/Archives, Collection 1, Leidy Papers (henceforth, Leidy Coll. 1); Baird to FVH, 14 Jan. 1854, Smithsonian Archives, RU 53, Assistant Secretary, 1850–1877.
34. FVH to Leidy, 11 Jan. 1854, Leidy Coll. 1.
35. FVH to Meek, 4 Mar. 1854, RU 7062; Baird to FVH, 3 Feb. 1854 and 15 Mar. 1854, RU 53; FVH to Baird, 8 Feb. 1854, 23 Feb. 1854, 5 Mar. 1854, 20 Mar. 1854, and 10 Apr. 1854, RU 7002.
36. FVH to Baird, 14 Apr. 1854, 10 Apr. 1854, 20 Mar. 1854, and 5 Mar. 1854, RU 7002.
37. Baird to FVH, 22 Apr. 1854, RU 53; FVH to Baird, 26 Apr. 1854, RU 7002.
38. FVH to Baird, 26 Apr. 1854 and 5 May 1854, RU 7002; typescript of a contract between Alfred J. Vaughan and F. V. Hayden; typescript of a memo of S. F. Baird, 11 May 1854, The F. V. Hayden Collection, American Heritage Center, University of Wyoming, Laramie.
39. Hayden, *Geological Report . . . 1859–'60*, viii; Baird to FVH, 9 May 1854 and 20 May 1854, RU 53; FVH to Baird, 13 May 1854 and 4 June 1854, RU 7002; Foster, *Strange Genius*, 59, 66.

40. FVH to Baird, 11 Nov. 1854, RU 7002; Frederick Martin Brown, "Hayden's 1854–55 Missouri River Expedition," *Denver Westerners Roundup* 27, no. 3 (May–June 1971): 3–66.

41. FVH to Baird, 2 July 1854, RU 7002; Baird to FVH, 12 June 1855, RU 53; FVH to Meek, 4 Mar. 1854, 1 July 1854, 11 Nov. 1854, and 25 Jan. 1856, RU 7062.
42. Foster, *Strange Genius*, 66; Sunder, *Fur Trade*, 176–77.
43. FVH to Baird, 9 Feb. 1855, 6 Apr. 1855, 10 May 1855, and 10 July 1855, RU 7002; Foster, *Strange Genius*, 63.
44. FVH to Baird, 11 Nov. 1854, 17 Nov. 1854, 26 Nov. 1854, 6 Dec. 1854, and 9 Feb. 1855, RU 7002; Baird to FVH, 2 Dec. 1854, RU 53; Goetzmann, *Exploration and Empire*, 309; Foster, *Strange Genius*, 64; Robert W. Johannsen, "Stephen A. Douglas and the Territories in the Senate," in *The Frontier, the Union and Stephen A. Douglas* (Urbana: Univ. of Illinois Press, 1989), 105.
45. FVH to Baird, 9 Feb. 1855, RU 7002; FVH to Leidy, 9 Feb. 1855, Leidy Coll. 1; Leidy to FVH, 8 July 1855, Library of the College of Physicians at Philadelphia, Historical Collections, Joseph C. Leidy Jr. Papers, "Memoir of Joseph Leidy Senior" (call number Z10/214 box 2), copy of letter attached to p. 325. Baird's response, as recorded in his outgoing correspondence, is quite illegible, but Hayden quickly moved on to other proposals.
46. Clifford M. Nelson and Fritiof M. Fryxell, "The Ante-bellum Collaboration of Meek and Hayden," in *Two Hundred Years*, 190; FVH to Meek, 1 July 1854, 12 Jan. 1856, and 25 Jan. 1856, RU 7062; FVH to Baird, 2 July 1854, 3 July 1854, 11 Nov. 1854, 6 Apr. 1855, 10 May 1855, 10 July 1855, and 26 Dec. 1855, RU 7002; FVH to George Engelmann, 4 Mar. 1856, George Engelmann Papers, Missouri Botanical Garden Archives, St. Louis, Missouri; Foster, *Strange Genius*, 68–70.
47. Foster, *Strange Genius*, 69; FVH to Baird, 4 Mar. 1856, RU 7002; FVH to Leidy, 13 Oct. 1870, Leidy Coll. 1.
48. FVH to Hall, 30 Jan. 1856; Hall to FVH, draft, 22 Apr. 1856, Hall Correspondence; FVH to Baird, 4 Mar. 1856, RU 7002; Foster, *Strange Genius*, 68–69; Nelson, "Meek at Albany," 44–46.
49. Warren, "Portion of journal kept by Lt. Warren in 1856," Gouverneur Kemble Warren Papers, 1848–1882, New York State Library, Manuscripts and Special Collections (henceforth, Warren, "1856 Journal"), 22 Apr.; FVH to Baird, 20 Mar. 1856 and 22 Mar. 1856, RU 7002; Foster, *Strange Genius*, 67–71.
50. Warren, "1856 Journal," 22 Apr.; Hayden, "A brief sketch . . . of the upper Missouri," 66–79.

51. Meek and Hayden, "Descriptions of New Species of Gasteropoda from the Cretaceous Formations of Nebraska Territory," *Proc.* ANSP 8 (1856): 63–69; "Descriptions of New Species of Gasteropoda and Cephalopoda from the Cretaceous Formations of Nebraska Territory," *Proc.* ANSP 8 (1856): 70–72; "Descriptions of Twenty-eight New Species of Acephala and One Gasteropod, from the Cretaceous Formations of Nebraska Territory," *Proc.* ANSP 8 (1856): 81–87; "Descriptions of New Species of Acephala and Gasteropoda, from the Tertiary Formations of Nebraska Territory," *Proc.* ANSP 8 (1856): 111–26; Rudwick, *Great Devonian*, 141–43.
52. FVH to Baird, 21 Apr. 1856, 18 June 1856, and 11 July 1856, RU 7002; Warren, "1856 Journal," 22 Apr.; Warren to FVH, 4 Nov. 1856, in Merrill, *First One Hundred Years*, 712–13; Foster, *Strange Genius*, 73, 75; Frank N. Schubert, "Troublesome Partnership: Gouverneur K. Warren and Ferdinand V. Hayden on the Northern Plains in 1856 and 1857," *Earth Sciences History* 3 (1984): 144–45.
53. FVH to Baird, 11 Feb. 1857, 4 Mar. 1857, 14 Mar. 1857, and 28 Mar. 1857, RU 7002; Foster, *Strange Genius*, 77; Merrill, *First One Hundred Years*, 503; FVH to Leidy, 6 Dec. 1856, Leidy Coll. 1; Warren, "Lieut. Warren's official journal commanding explorations in Nebraska, 1857," 19 July; in Gouverneur Kemble Warren Papers, 1848–1882, New York State Library, Manuscripts and Special Collections, see, e.g., Hayden, "Notes Explanatory of a Map and Section Illustrating the Geological Structure of the Country Bordering on the Missouri River," *Proc.* ANSP 9 (1857): 109–16; clipping from *National Intelligencer*: Warren to the "Editors of the *National Intelligencer*," 15 Mar. 1858, RU 7062; Meek and Hayden, "Descriptions of New Species of Gasteropoda," 65–66; "Descriptions of New Species of Gasteropoda and Cephalopoda," 70.
54. Foster, *Strange Genius*, 75, 57; FVH to Leidy, 23 Jan. 1856, 27 Nov. 1856, 6 Dec. 1856, and 17 Jan. 1857, Leidy Coll. 1.
55. Constance McLaughlin Green, *Washington*, vol. 1, *Village and Capital, 1800–1878* (Princeton: Princeton Univ. Press, 1962), 200, 209, 223–24; Richard A. Bartlett, "Scientific Exploration of the American West, 1865–1900," in *North American Exploration*, 3:461–62.
56. Foster, *Strange Genius*, 75–76, 98; Dupree, *Science*, 98; Foster, "Hayden as Naturalist," 345; Herman J. Viola, *Exploring the West* (Washington DC: Smithsonian Institution, 1987), 147; *DSB*, s.v. "Meek, Fielding Bradford," by Ellis L. Yochelson; "Regulations of the Potomac Side Naturalists Club," 10–11, Smithsonian Archives, RU 7210, "Potomac Side Naturalists' Club, *Circa* 1858–1866."

57. FVH to Baird, 5 July 1857, 21 Aug. 1857, 29 Aug. 1857, 1 Nov. 1857, 5 Nov. 1857, 23 Nov. 1857, 2 Dec. 1857, and 13 Dec. 1857, RU 7002; Baird to FVH, 28 Nov. 1857, RU 53; Schubert, "Troublesome Partnership," 146; Foster, *Strange Genius*, 77–81.
58. Rivinus and Youssef, *Spencer Baird*, 71–74, 84–85, 162.
59. Meek and Hayden, "Remarks on the Lower Cretaceous Beds of Kansas and Nebraska," *Proc. ANSP* 10 (1858): 257; Meek and Hayden, "Geological Explorations in Kansas Territory," *Proc. ANSP* 11 (1859): 8.
60. Foster, *Strange Genius*, 48.
61. Rudwick, *Great Devonian*, 46–48.
62. Foster, *Strange Genius*, 82, 107–9; Nelson and Fryxell, "Ante-bellum Collaboration," 187, 191–92; Meek and Hayden, "Descriptions of New Species of Acephala and Gasteropoda"; Meek and Hayden, "Descriptions of New Lower Silurian, (Primordial), Jurassic, Cretaceous, and Tertiary Fossils, Collected in Nebraska," *Proc. ANSP*, 13 (1861): 415–47.
63. Meek and Hayden, "Remarks on the Lower Cretaceous Beds of Kansas and Nebraska," 256–58; Meek and Hayden, "Geological Explorations in Kansas Territory," 21–22; Meek and Hayden, "Descriptions of New Species of Acephala and Gasteropoda," 111; FVH to Baird, 13 May 1854, 20 Mar. 1856, 22 Mar. 1856, 17 May 1857, and 29 Aug. 1857, RU 7002; FVH to Hall, 11 Oct. 1856, Hall Correspondence; Hall to Joseph Henry, 12 Aug. 1858 and 15 Oct. 1858, Hall to Henry, copy, 15 Oct.[?] 1858, James Hall Papers, New York State Library, Manuscripts and Special Collections (henceforth, Hall Papers); Foster, *Strange Genius*, 94–99; Nelson, "Meek at Albany," 44–46.
64. FVH to Baird, 22 May 1859 and 13 June 1859, RU 7002.
65. FVH to Baird, 13 June 1859 and 28 June 1859, RU 7002.
66. FVH to Baird, 24 Aug. 1859 and 13 Oct. 1859, RU 7002; W. F. Raynolds, "Journal, Yellowstone & Mo. Ex. Expdn., W. F. Raynolds, Capt. of Engrs, Commanding," 11, 26, and 27 Sept. 1859, William Raynolds Papers, The Yale Collection of Western Americana, Beinecke Rare Book and Manuscript Library, Yale University.
67. Raynolds, "Journal," 23, 27 Nov. 1859 and 6 Feb. 1860.
68. Baird to Leidy, 14 Feb. 1856, Leidy Coll. 1-B; Academy of Natural Sciences of Philadelphia to American Philosophical Society, 19 Mar. 1888, American Philosophical Society Archives; FVH to Leidy, 19 Dec. 1860, Leidy Coll. 1; Peale, "Biographical Sketch of F. V. Hayden," 32; Hayden, "Contributions to the Ethnography and Philology of the Indian Tribes of the Mis-

souri Valley," *Trans. APS*, n.s., 12 (1863): 231–461; McCook, "'It May Be Truth,'" 184.

69. *DAB*, 1963–64 ed., s.v. "Stevens, Isaac Ingalls," by Joseph Schafer; FVH to Hall, 16 May 1853, Hall Correspondence; Sunder, *Fur Trade*, 153; Isaac I. Stevens to Baird, 22 Oct. 1855; Stevens to Capt. Van Vliet, 22 Oct. 1855, Smithsonian Archives, RU 26, Secretary of the Smithsonian; "Journal of Dr. Elias J. Marsh: Account of a Steamboat Trip on the Missouri River, May-August, 1859," *South Dakota Historical Review* 1 (1936): 81.
70. Foster, *Strange Genius*, 140–41.
71. FVH to Leidy, 7 Mar. 1862, 3 Apr. 1862, and 3 May 1862, Leidy Coll. 1; *DSB*, s.v. "Cope, Edward Drinker," by Joseph M. Maline. On Hayden's first contact with Cope, I thank Mike Foster, who directed my attention to Meek to Newberry, 7 Nov. 1862, and Meek to Hayden, 18 June 1862 and 25 June 1862, in RU 7062.
72. Hayden, "Physics and Hydraulics of the Mississippi River," *Am. J. Sci.*, 2d ser., 33 (1862): 181–89; "Colorado River of the West," *Am. J. Sci.*, 2d ser., 33 (1862): 387–403; "United States Government Surveys," *Am. J. Sci.*, 2d ser., 34 (1862): 98–101; Foster, *Strange Genius*, 142.
73. FVH to Leidy, 12 May 1863 and 10 Apr. 1863, Leidy Coll. 1; Foster, *Strange Genius*, 144.
74. Foster, *Strange Genius*, chap. 12; FVH to Leidy, 12 May 1863, Leidy Coll. 1; Foster, "Hayden as Naturalist," 345; "Regulations of the Potomac Side Naturalists Club," 10, RU 7210.
75. Foster, "Hayden as Naturalist," 345; Baatz, "'Squinting at Silliman,'" 224; FVH to Leidy, 7 May 1865, 18 Aug. 1865, 30 Sept. 1865, 1 Oct. 1865, and 22 Nov. 1865, Leidy Coll. 1; FVH to Cadwalader Biddle, 26 July 1872, University of Pennsylvania Archives, *Minutes of the Board of Trustees of the University of Pennsylvania*, 11:167; Foster, *Strange Genius*, 151–52.
76. Charles A. White, "Memoir of Ferdinand Vandeveer Hayden, 1829–1887," *National Academy of Sciences, Biographical Memoirs* (Washington DC: National Academy of Sciences, 1893), 3:401–2; Edward Potts Cheyney, "External History of the University of Pennsylvania," in *Universities and Their Sons: University of Pennsylvania*, ed. Joshua L. Chamberlain (Boston: R. Herndon, 1901), 118–19; Foster, *Strange Genius*, 152–53; FVH to Leidy, 7 May 1865, Leidy Coll. 1.
77. *Catalogue of the Trustees, Officers, and Students of the University of Pennsylvania, 1865–1866* (Philadelphia: Collins, 1866), 23; University of Pennsylvania Archives, UPC 6, Auxiliary School of Medicine Records, 1865–1889, "Faculty Minutes," 15 Mar. 1870.

78. Hayden, "United States Government Surveys," 98, 99, 101; Hayden, *Geological Report . . . 1859–'60*, chap. 13; Merrill, *First One Hundred Years*, 506; Leidy to FVH, 20 Aug. 1866; James D. Dana to FVH, 20 Oct. 1866, RG 57H.
79. Baird to FVH, 13 Jan. 1867, RG 57H.
80. Jane Camerini, "Remains of the Day: Early Victorians in the Field," in *Victorian Science in Context*, ed. Bernard Lightman (Chicago: Univ. of Chicago Press, 1997), 355–56, 372; FVH to Baird, 15 Jan. 1867, RU 7002.

3. SURVEY OF NEBRASKA

1. Baird to FVH, 9 Mar. 1867, RG 57H. Baird referred to Hayden's *On the Geology and Natural History of the Upper Missouri. Being the substance of a report made to Lieut. G. K. Warren, T.E.U.S.A.* (Philadelphia: C. Sherman & Son, 1862).
2. Foster, *Strange Genius*, 154; FVH to Baird, 8 Mar. 1867 and 10 Mar. 1867, RU 7002.
3. FVH to Henry, 9 Mar. 1867, RU 26. At first, there was some confusion about whom to write to—the governor of Nebraska or the commissioner of the General Land Office—and some ended up writing a letter to both Governor Saunders and Commissioner Wilson. Humphreys to Alvin Saunders, 11 Mar. 1867; Warren to FVH, 13 Mar. 1867; Raynolds to Saunders, 13 Mar. 1867; Dana to FVH, 11 Mar. 1867, RG 57H.
4. FVH to Wilson, 16 Mar. 1867 and 18 Mar. 1867, RG 49; Wilson to FVH, 10 Apr. 1867, RG 57H.
5. FVH to Wilson, 16 Apr. 1867 and 3 May 1867, RG 49.
6. Wilson to FVH, 4 May 1867 and 29 Apr. 1867, RG 57H.
7. Wilson to FVH, 29 Apr. 1867 and 10 May 1867, RG 57H.
8. FVH to Meek, 7 May 1867, RU 7062; Wilson to FVH, 29 Apr. 1867, RG 57H; FVH to Meek, 7 May 1867 and 9 May 1867, RU 7062.
9. FVH to Meek, 7 May 1867, 9 May 1867, and 15 May 1867, RU 7062.
10. FVH to Baird, 12 Apr. 1867 and 13 May 1867, RU 7002.
11. Baird to FVH, 14 May 1867, RU 53; FVH to Baird, 17 May 1867, RU 7002.
12. FVH to Wilson, 20 May 1867 and 17 June 1867, RG 49; Wilson to FVH, 25 June 1867, RG 57H.
13. Wilson to FVH, 29 Apr. 1867, RG 57H; FVH to Leidy, 5 June 1867, Leidy Coll. 1; FVH to Baird, 5 June 1867 and 6 June 1867, RU 7002.
14. Wilson to FVH, 15 July 1867, RG 57H; Voucher #1, with FVH to Wilson, 24 Sept. 1867, RG 49.
15. FVH to Baird, 13 June 1867, RU 7002; FVH to Meek, 7 May 1867, 9 May 1867, and 15 May 1867, RU 7062; Smithsonian Archives, RU 7098, "Bio-

graphical Information File," Theodore N. Gill folder; FVH to Wilson, 17 June 1867; receipt from General Land Office to FVH, 1 July 1867; FVH to Wilson, 24 July 1867 and 24 Sept. 1867, RG 49.

16. FVH to Wilson, 17 June 1867, RG 49; FVH to Baird, 13 June 1867, RU 7002; Hayden, "First Annual Report of the United States Geological Survey of the Territories, Embracing Nebraska," in *First, Second, and Third Annual Reports of the United States Geological Survey of the Territories for the Years 1867, 1868, and 1869, under the Department of the Interior* (Washington DC: GPO, 1873) (henceforth, "First Annual Report"), 14; Meek to FVH, 2 Sept. 1867 and 15 Oct. 1867, RG 57H.
17. FVH to Wilson, 1 July 1867, in Hayden, "First Annual Report," 7.
18. FVH to Wilson, 30 July 1867, 8 Aug. 1867, and 22 Aug. 1867, RG 49.
19. FVH to Wilson, 24 Sept. 1867, RG 49.
20. FVH to Wilson, 9 Oct. 1867, RG 49.
21. FVH to Wilson, 9 Oct. 1867, 2 Nov. 1867, 7 Nov. 1867, and 6 Dec. 1867, RG 49.
22. Wilson to FVH, 29 Apr. 1867, RG 57H; FVH to Wilson, 8 May 1867 and 1 July 1867, RG 49; Hayden, "First Annual Report," 16, 17, 22, 25–27, 29, 40ff, 49, 56.
23. FVH to Wilson, 16 Mar. 1867, 5 July 1867, 30 July 1867, 22 Aug. 1867, and 2 Nov. 1867, RG 49; FVH to Leidy, 25 June 1867 and 23 July 1867, Leidy Coll. 1.
24. FVH to Meek, 9 Oct. 1867 and 2 Nov. 1867, RU 7062.
25. Foster, *Strange Genius*, 161.
26. Wilson to FVH, 29 Apr. 1867, RG 57H.
27. FVH to Meek, 7 May 1867, 9 May 1867, and 15 May 1867, RU 7062; Hayden, *On the Geology and Natural History of the Upper Missouri*, 11; Meek and Hayden, "Geology of Nebraska—Important Discoveries," *Mining and Statistic Magazine* 10 (1858): 293.
28. FVH to Wilson, 1 July 1867, RG 49; Wilson to FVH, 15 July 1867, RG 57H; Hayden, "First Annual Report," 7, 23.
29. Hayden, "A brief sketch . . . of the region of the upper Missouri," 69; Hayden, "First Annual Report," 9.
30. FVH to Wilson, 24 July 1867 and 30 July 1867, RG 49; Hayden, "First Annual Report," 11–12, 64.
31. Hayden, "First Annual Report," 12, 14, 10.
32. Hayden, "First Annual Report," 14–15; Smith, *Virgin Land*, 179.
33. Hayden, "First Annual Report," 40, 8, 24, 46.
34. Hayden, "First Annual Report," 8, 64, 13.

35. Hayden, "First Annual Report," 15, 16, 27.
36. Smith, *Virgin Land,* 178–79; Hayden, "First Annual Report," 63.
37. Hayden, "First Annual Report," 58–59.
38. Hayden, "First Annual Report," 21, 32.
39. FVH to Wilson, 17 June 1867, RG 48; FVH to Baird, 17 June 1867, RU 7002.
40. FVH to Baird, 8 Oct. 1867, RU 7002.
41. Wilson to FVH, 18 Dec. 1867, RG 57H.
42. *DAB,* 1959 ed., s.v. "Englemann, George," by George P. Merrill; s.v. "Horn, George Henry," by Leland Ossian Howard; *DSB,* s.v. "Scudder, Samuel Hubbard," by Melville H. Hatch.
43. Merrill, *First One Hundred Years,* 432; *DAB,* 1959 ed., s.v. "LeConte, John Lawrence," by Leland Ossian Howard, and s.v. "Lesquereux, Leo," by Joseph Ewan; Chester A. Arnold, "Paleobotany," in *A Short History of Botany in the United States,* ed. Joseph A. Ewan (New York: Hafner, 1969), 103–8; J. Peter Lesley, "Memoir of Leo Lesquereux, 1806–1889," *National Academy of Sciences, Biographical Memoirs* (Washington DC: National Academy of Sciences, 1895), 3:187–212; Lesquereux to FVH, 7 Dec. 1867, RG 57H.
44. Torrey to FVH, 30 Dec. 1867, RG 57H.
45. FVH to Meek, 9 Oct. 1867, RU 7062.
46. Joseph S. Wilson, *Report of the Commissioner of the General Land Office on the Extension of the Geological Survey to Different Localities of the Public Domain,* 40th Cong., 2nd sess., 1868, H. Misc. Doc. 136.
47. *U.S. Statutes at Large,* 15 (1868): 119; Wilson to FVH, 14 Apr. 1868, RG 57H; FVH to Meek, 1 Aug. 1868, RU 7062.

4. HARNESSING INTERESTS

1. Richard E. Neustadt, foreword to *Leadership and Innovation,* vii; on the characteristics of entrepreneurs in public service, see Doig and Hargrove, "'Leadership' and Political Analysis," in *Leadership and Innovation,* 8.
2. Doig and Hargrove, "'Leadership,'" 9–10.
3. Doig and Hargrove, "'Leadership,'" 11.
4. Cravens, "American Science," 56; "Geological Explorations in the Territories," *New York Times,* 6 July 1868.
5. FVH to Wilson, 9 July 1868, RG 49; Wilson to FVH, 28 July 1868, RG 57H; *U.S. Statutes at Large,* 15 (1869): 306.
6. Foster, *Strange Genius,* 175.
7. Rabbitt, *Minerals,* 187; *U.S. Statutes at Large,* 16 (1870): 306; Hayden, *Preliminary Report of the United States Geological Survey of Wyoming and Portions of Contiguous Territories, (Being a Second Annual Report of Progress,) conducted*

under the Authority of the Secretary of the Interior (Washington DC: GPO, 1871), 6–7.

8. Foster, *Strange Genius*, 179–80.
9. Rabbitt, *Minerals*, 171; Hayden, "Third Annual Report of the United States Geological Survey of the Territories," in *First, Second, and Third Annual Reports*, 106–7; Hayden, *Preliminary Report of . . . Wyoming*, 6.
10. Bartlett, *Great Surveys*, 22.
11. For a brief sketch of early explorations of Yellowstone in 1863–70, especially by local Montanans, see *Yellowstone and the Great West: Journals, Letters, and Images from the 1871 Hayden Expedition*, ed. Marlene Deahl Merrill (Lincoln: Univ. of Nebraska Press, 1999), 11–13. For a more complete treatment, see Aubrey L. Haines, *The Yellowstone Story: A History of Our First National Park*, vol. 1 (Yellowstone National Park: Yellowstone Library and Museum Association, in cooperation with Colorado Associated Univ. Press, 1977), esp. 60ff, 84–137; Paul Andrew Hutton, *Phil Sheridan and His Army* (Lincoln: Univ. of Nebraska Press, 1985), 163–64; Langford, "The Wonders of the Yellowstone," *Scribner's Monthly* 2 (1871): 128.
12. Haines, *Yellowstone Story*, 137–38; Foster, *Strange Genius*, 201–6, 238–39; Roderick Nash, *Wilderness and the American Mind* (New Haven: Yale Univ. Press, 1982), 110–11; FVH to J. Peter Lesley, 13 Feb. 1871, American Philosophical Society Library, Philadelphia, Pennsylvania, J. Peter Lesley Papers, Correspondence; *U.S. Statutes at Large*, 16 (1871): 503.
13. Hutton, *Phil Sheridan*, 164; Goetzmann, *Exploration and Empire*, 406ff.
14. Hayden, *Preliminary Report of the United States Geological Survey of Montana and Portions of Adjacent Territory Being a Fifth Annual Report of Progress* (Washington DC: GPO, 1872), 3–9.
15. "The Yellowstone Expedition," *New York Times*, 18 September 1871; Katherine E. Early, *"For the Benefit and Enjoyment of the People": Cultural Attitudes and the Establishment of Yellowstone National Park* (Washington DC: Georgetown Univ. Press, 1984), 19; Alvred Bayard Nettleton to FVH, 27 Oct. 1871, RG 57H. For more on the role of the Northern Pacific's promotion of the national park, see Haines, *Yellowstone Story*, chaps. 5–6; and Kinsey, *Thomas Moran*, 58–63.
16. Foster, *Strange Genius*, 222–23; Hayden, "The Hot Springs and Geysers of the Yellowstone and Firehole Rivers," *Am. J. Sci.*, 3d ser., 3 (1872): 105–15, 161–76; Rabbitt, *Minerals*, 198, 200; *U.S. Statutes at Large*, 17 (1872): 162; Hayden, *Preliminary Report of . . . Montana*, 162.
17. Hayden, *Sixth Annual Report of the United States Geological Survey of the Territories, Embracing Portions of Montana, Idaho, Wyoming, and Utah; Being a Report*

of Progress of the Explorations for the Year 1872 (Washington DC: GPO, 1873), 1, 7–8.

18. Hayden, *Sixth Annual Report*, 6.
19. Goetzmann, *Exploration and Empire*, 433; DAB, 1959 ed., s.v. "Gardiner, James Terry," by Ray Palmer Baker. For unknown reasons, Gardner both formerly and latterly spelled his name as "Gardiner"; I adopt the spelling he used with the Hayden Survey.
20. Hayden, *Annual Report of the United States Geological and Geographical Survey of the Territories, Embracing Colorado, Being a Report of Progress of the Exploration for the Year 1873* (Washington DC: GPO, 1874), 1.
21. See Foster, *Strange Genius*, 241.
22. Goetzmann, *Exploration and Empire*, 517; see annual reports for these years; Hayden, *Annual Report . . . 1873*, 2.
23. Hayden, *Annual Report . . . 1873*, 2; *Sixth Annual Report*, 10; *Preliminary Report of . . . Wyoming*, 6–7.
24. Hayden, *Sixth Annual Report*, 10.
25. Hayden, *Preliminary Report of . . . Wyoming*, 7.
26. Hayden, *Preliminary Report of . . . Wyoming*, 7; Dodge to FVH, 20 Sept. [1871?]; R. S. Elliott, circular of the Kansas Pacific Railway Company, 18 Aug. 1870, RG 57H.
27. R. S. Elliott, "On the industrial resources of Western Kansas and Eastern Colorado," in Hayden, *Preliminary Report of . . . Wyoming*, 442–58; Elliott to FVH, 4 Jan. 1870, 19 Jan. 1872, and 26 Jan. 1872, RG 57H.
28. Hinchman to FVH, 22 Jan. 1871, RG 57H; FVH to Columbus Delano, 27 Jan. 1873, National Archives, RG 48, Records of the Department of the Interior, Records of the Patents and Miscellaneous Division, General Records, Entry 128, "Letters Received Relating to the Geological Survey and Its Predecessors, 1868–80" (henceforth, RG 48).
29. David Sievert Lavender, *The American Heritage History of The Great West* (New York: American Heritage Publishing, 1965), 350; Anne Farrar Hyde, *An American Vision: Far Western Landscape and National Culture, 1820–1920* (New York: New York Univ. Press, 1990), 147–61.
30. Lamborn to FVH, 19 Aug. 1873; Palmer to FVH, 30 May 1878, RG 57H.
31. Bloomfield to D. W. C. Peters, 9 Feb. 1870; Samuel Rumell to FVH, 23 Jan. 1871; George E. Marsh to FVH, 4 Dec. 1871; George Hadden to FVH, 4 Jan. 1877, RG 57H. On the interest of the mining press, see Anonymous [John A. Church?], "Congress and Science," *Eng. Min. J.* 13 (1872): 361–62; and [Rossiter W. Raymond], "Preliminary Report of the United States

Geological Survey of Montana and Portions of Adjacent Territories, being a Fifth Annual Report of Progress," *Eng. Min. J.* 13 (1872): 376.

32. Hayden, *Preliminary Report of . . . Wyoming*, 7.
33. "James Stevenson, Late Executive Officer United States Geological Survey—A Noted Explorer and Collector," *Washington National Tribune*, 2 August 1888; "Obituary: Col. James Stevenson," *New York Times*, 26 July 1888; FVH to Baird, 21 Nov. 1869, RU 7002; Keller, *Affairs of State*, 255, 266; *Biographical Directory of the American Congress, 1774–1927*, s.v. "Logan, John Alexander," 69th Cong., 2nd sess., 1928, H. Doc. 783, 1235 (Washington DC: GPO, 1928); and James Pickett Jones, *John A. Logan: Stalwart Republican from Illinois* (Tallahassee: Univ. Presses of Florida, 1982), chaps. 5, 7–8, passim.
34. *BDA*, 1906 ed., s.v. "Dawes, Henry Laurens," and *DAB*, 1936 ed., s.v. "Dawes, Henry Laurens," by Claude M. Fuess; Allan Peskin, *Garfield: A Biography* (Kent OH: Kent State Univ. Press, 1978), esp. 148, 434; FVH to Baird, 14 Sept. 1872, RU 52; *DAB*, 1936 ed., s.v. "Sargent, Aaron Augustus," by P. O. Ray; Townsend to FVH, 6 Oct. 1875, 20 Oct. 1875, 26 June 1876, and 17 June 1878; Townsend to Zachariah Chandler, 20 Oct. 1875, RG 57H.
35. Watson Gilder to FVH, 24 Jan. 1872; Moran to FVH, 24 May 1872, RG 57H; FVH to Lesley, 30 Jan. 1874 (seems to be misdated, and probably from early Jan. 1879), Lesley Papers; Sargent to FVH, 3 Mar. 1872 and 8 Mar. 1872, RG 57H.
36. "A Public Necessity," *Yankton Press*, 12 Dec. 1871; Armstrong to FVH, 20 Dec. 1871, RG 57H.
37. Thomas to FVH, 12 July 1873, RG 57H; Hayden, *First, Second, and Third Annual Reports*, 3; Samuel L. Boardman, "Government Explorations and Surveys," *Maine Farmer: Agriculture, Mechanic Arts, Literature, News, &c.*, 23 May 1874.
38. Algernon S. Paddock to FVH, 12 July 1876; J. B. Packer to FVH, 29 Jan. 1871; James C. Campbell to Martin Maginnis, 23 Jan. 1876; D. H. Gilmour to Maginnis, 24 Feb. 1876, RG 57H.
39. W. E. Wilson to FVH, 6 Mar. 1874, RG 57H.
40. Wm. W. Jefferies to FVH, 6 June 1873; Monroe to FVH, 18 Mar. 1873, RG 57H.
41. On the Hayden-Monroe friendship, see FVH to Monroe, 14 Oct. 1872; Monroe to FVH, 26 Oct. 1872, photocopy, Hayden Collection; on the mineral specimens, see FVH to Monroe, 2 Jan. 1872 and 18 July 1873, Hayden Collection.

42. Circular No. 2, Office U.S. Geological Survey of the Territories, 1872; Marcou to FVH, 13 Nov. 1874; Alexander Agassiz to FVH, 11 Jan. 1873; Frederic Ward Putnam to FVH, 17 Jan. 1873; J. I. Williams to FVH, 24 Jan. 1873; P. R. Uhler, certificate of receipt, 24 Feb. 1871, RG 57H.
43. FVH to Leidy, 30 Jan. 1874, 1 Mar. 1874, 14 Feb. 1875, and 5 June 1875, Leidy Coll. 1.
44. H. D. Smalley to FVH, 13 Jan. 1874; Willard Fiske to FVH, 20 Jan. 1874, RG 57H.
45. Leidy to FVH, 18 Mar. 1873; Lesley to FVH, 1 Feb. [year unknown], RG 57H.
46. Hyatt to FVH, 17 Nov. 1866; Packard to FVH, 4 Oct. 1867, RG 57H.
47. George Ghurber to FVH, 28 Dec. 1869; "The Prairie Farmer" to Cyrus Thomas, 25 Oct. 1873; William Bross to FVH, 25 Feb. 1870; John A. Church to FVH, 3 Feb. 1877; Jesse G. Randall to FVH, 27 Feb. 1871; Boardman to FVH, 14 May 1874 and 19 May 1874, RG 57H.
48. W. W. Harding to FVH, 29 Mar. 1875; Louis Nell to FVH, 31 May 1878 and 6 June 1878; O. W. Gray to FVH, 16 Feb. 1874; E. C. Bridgman to FVH, 22 Nov. 1875; Clements to FVH, 27 Mar. 1877; Adams to FVH, 3 Jan. 1875, RG 57H.
49. Kelley to FVH, 13 Mar. 1876, RG 57H.
50. Gooding to FVH, 15 Apr. 1878; Anker to FVH, 21 Nov. 1877, RG 57H.
51. Goetzmann, *Exploration and Empire*, 517, and *New Lands, New Men*, 409; Turner, "Survey in Nineteenth-Century," 290, 291.

5. POSITIONS, PATRONAGE, AND PROFESSIONALS

1. Keller, *Affairs of State*, 238, 239, 256.
2. FVH to Wilson, 20 May 1867, RG 49.
3. Sid H. Nealy to FVH, 29 Apr. 1875; D. P. Holloway to FVH, 27 Apr. 1877, RG 57H; FVH to James Hall, 30 Mar. 1877, Hall Correspondence.
4. Rush [Taggart] to Dear Sister Clem, 14 Oct. 1872, William Rush Taggart Collection, American Heritage Center, University of Wyoming, Laramie; FVH to Monroe, typescript, 20 May 1872 and 14 Oct. 1872, Hayden Collection.
5. Hayden, *Preliminary Report of . . . Montana*, 3; FVH to George Allen, 13 Apr. 1871, *Yellowstone and the Great West*, 29; William Henry Holmes, "Random Records of a Lifetime, 1846–1931," unpublished manuscript, 10 June 1929, 3:43, National Museum of American Art/National Portrait Gallery Library, Smithsonian Institution, Washington DC; Hayden, "Geological Survey of the U.S. Territories: Prof. Hayden's Expedition," *Tribune*, 5 June 1871; Hayden, *Sixth Annual Report*, 1, 5.

6. W. H. West to FVH, 17 May 1872, RG 57H; Hayden, *Sixth Annual Report*, 5.

7. Holman to FVH, 8 Mar. 1873; Holman Jr. to FVH, 3 May 1875; Alcorn to FVH, 6 Mar. 1876; Bullitt to FVH, 16 Jan. 1875; Baker to FVH, 16 June 1878, RG 57H.
8. Holmes, "Biography of Cyrus Thomas, Ph.D." in "Random Records," 14: 61–66; Baird to FVH, 11 Feb. 1870, RU 7002.
9. Savage to FVH, 26 Nov. 1871 and 22 Jan. 1872, with notes from Samuel C. Pomeroy to Savage; John J. Ingalls to FVH, 16 Apr. 1873, RG 57H. Peskin, *Garfield*, 22ff, 45ff; James A. Garfield, *The Diary of James A. Garfield*, ed. Harry James Brown and Frederick D. Williams, vol. 2, *1872–1874* (East Lansing: Michigan State Univ. Press, 1967), 14 n. 42, 109 n. 277; Garfield to FVH, 4 Apr. 1872, RG 57H.
10. Hayden, *Sixth Annual Report*, 5; Wakefield to "Martie" Wakefield, 26 May 1872, 10 June 1872, 1 Aug. [1872], 27 July 1872, 14 July 1872, and 16 Aug. 1872, Edmund Burritt Wakefield Collection, Hiram College Archives, Hiram College, Hiram, Ohio.
11. Atkinson to Garfield, 23 Mar. 1873, RG 57H.
12. Atkinson to FVH, 13 June 1874, RG 57H; Hayden, *Ninth Annual Report of the United States Geological and Geographical Survey of the Territories, Embracing Colorado and Parts of Adjacent Territories* (Washington DC: GPO, 1877), 10; Gardner to FVH, 18 Sept. 1875, in "The Old Man of the Mountains," *Rocky Mountain News* (Denver), 21 Sept. 1875.
13. Hurlbut to Stevenson, 6 Feb. 1878, RG 57H.
14. Bonnie Skell Hardwick, "Science and Art: The Travel Writings of the Great Surveys of the American West after the Civil War" (Ph.D. diss., Univ. of Pennsylvania, 1977), 3, 154–55, 220; Ernest Ingersoll, *Knocking Round the Rockies* (New York: Harper & Brothers, 1883; reprint, Norman: Univ. of Oklahoma Press, 1994), 3.
15. Thurman Wilkins, *Thomas Moran: Artist of the Mountains* (Norman: Univ. of Oklahoma Press, 1966), 58–59; Clark, *Thomas Moran*, 12; William H. Truettner, *National Parks and the American Landscape* (Washington DC: Smithsonian Institution, 1972), 86; Thomas Moran, *Home-Thoughts, From Afar: Letters of Thomas Moran to Mary Nimmo Moran* (East Hampton, NY: East Hampton Free Library, 1967), 130; Nettleton to FVH, 16 June 1871, RG 57H.
16. Herbert Oliver Brayer, *William Blackmore: A Case Study in the Economic Development of the West*, vol. 1, *The Spanish Mexican Land Grants of New Mexico and Colorado, 1863–1878* (Denver: Bradford-Robinson, 1949), 73; Blackmore to FVH, 2 Dec. 1869 and 18 Feb. 1871, RG 57H.

17. Blackmore to FVH, 3 June 1872, RG 57H; Sidford Hamp, "With Hayden on the Yellowstone: The Letters of Sidford Hamp," *Brand Book*, ed. Dabney Otis Collins (Denver: Westerners, 1949), 243; Herbert Oliver Brayer, ed., "Exploring the Yellowstone with Hayden, 1872: Diary of Sidford Hamp," *Annals of Wyoming* 14 (1942): 268, 271–72; Brayer, *William Blackmore*, 1:23.
18. Hayden, *Eleventh Annual Report of the United States Geological Survey of the Territories, Embracing Idaho and Wyoming* (Washington DC: GPO, 1879), xx; House Committee on the Public Lands, *Geographical and Geological Surveys West of the Mississippi*, 43d Cong., 1st sess., 1874, H. Rept. 612, 33; Gray to FVH, 27 Mar. 1877, RG 57H; Dupree, *Science*, 198; F. V. Hayden, ed., *Extracts from Letters and Notices of Eminent Scientific Men and Journals in Europe and America, Commendatory of the United States Geological and Geographical Survey of the Territories* (Washington DC: GPO, 1879), 5, 12.
19. Jackson, *Time Exposure*, 237.
20. Jackson, *Time Exposure*, 223; Ingersoll to FVH, 3 June 1874, 16 Dec. 1874, 10 Mar. 1875, and 7 Mar. 1876; Barber to FVH, 1 May 1875; Kellogg to FVH, 28 Apr. 1872; Platt to FVH, 10 Sept. 1872 and 9 June 1874, RG 57H.
21. Ewan, *Rocky Mountain Naturalists*, 67–72; Porter to FVH, 23 Nov. 1871, 21 Feb. 1872, 17 Feb. 1872, and 25 Mar. 1872, RG 57H.
22. Hayden, *Sixth Annual Report*, 5–8; Baird to FVH, 17 May 1873, RG 57H.
23. Dupree, *Science*, 94; Lesley to FVH, 9 Feb. 1871, RG 57H; FVH to Philip Reese Uhler, 24 Dec. 1872, by permission of the Ernst Mayr Library, Museum of Comparative Zoology Archives, Harvard University.
24. Hayden, "Third Annual Report," 107; Hayden, *Preliminary Report of . . . Wyoming*, 3; Joseph Henry, 13 Feb. 1872, Smithsonian Archives, RU 7001, Joseph Henry Collection; FVH to Baird, 14 Sept. 1872 and 8 Oct. 1872, RU 52.
25. Hayden, "Third Annual Report," 199; R. A. F. Penrose, "Memoir of Persifor Frazer," *Bulletin of the Geological Society of America* 21 (1910): 6–7; Persifor Frazer, "The Life and Letters of Edward Drinker Cope," *American Geologist* 26 (1900): 124–25.
26. Hayden, *Preliminary Report of . . . Wyoming*, 6.
27. Nancy K. Anderson, "'The Kiss of Enterprise': The Western Landscape as Symbol and Resource," in *West as America*, 237; Hales, *William Henry Jackson*, 67, 71; Jackson, *Time Exposure*, 187; FVH to Leidy, 6 Aug. 1870, Leidy Coll. 1.
28. The complete Yellowstone expedition that year totaled eighty-three men: Hayden's corps of thirty-two, Barlow and Heap's force of eleven, and a

shared army escort of forty. *Yellowstone and the Great West,* ed. Merrill, 18; FVH to Wilson, 2 Nov. 1867, RG 49; FVH to Baird, 8 June 1871, in RU 52; Charles Janeway Stillé to FVH, 14 Mar. 1871; Jeanes to FVH, 14 Mar. 1871, RG 57H; *BDA,* 1906 ed., s.v. "Adams, Robert"; *DAB,* 1928 ed., s.v. "Adams, Robert," by Charles H. Lincoln; anonymous, Smithsonian Archives, RU 7230, Department of Geology Biographical File.

29. Hayden, *Sixth Annual Report,* 1; Hoffmann to FVH, 1 Feb. 1872; Rudolph Hering to Hilgard, 15 Apr. 1872; Lee E. Brown to FVH, 18 Feb. 1876 and 27 Apr. 1878; Guyot to FVH, 19 Apr. 1877; Adams to FVH, 3 May 1878, RG 57H.
30. *DAB,* 1936 ed., s.v. "Egleston, Thomas," by Edna Yost; Egleston to FVH, 28 Feb. 1871, RG 57H; Hayden, *Preliminary Report of . . . Montana,* 3.
31. Dana to FVH, 3 Apr. 1872, 29 Apr. 1872, and 18 Sept. 1872, RG 57H.
32. Hayden, *Sixth Annual Report,* 7–8. On the findings, see Lesquereux, "Lignitic Formation and Fossil Flora," 350, and Meek, "Paleontological Report," 435–62, both in Hayden, *Sixth Annual Report*; Lesquereux, "The Lignitic Formation and Its Fossil Flora," 367–78, and Cope, "Report on the Vertebrate Paleontology of Colorado," 434, both in Hayden, *Annual Report . . . 1873*; and Cope, "Review of the Vertebrata of the Cretaceous Period Found West of the Mississippi River," *BUSGGST* 2 (1874): 16.
33. Hayden, *Sixth Annual Report,* 5; D. P. Heap to FVH, 7 Nov. 1871; J. E. Hilgard to FVH, 30 Oct. 1871, RG 57H.
34. Hayden, *Sixth Annual Report,* 5.
35. Wakefield to "Martie" Wakefield, 24 May 1872, Wakefield Collection; James T. Gardner to FVH, 23 Feb. 1873; Bechler to FVH, 13 July 1878; Lorenzo Brentano to FVH, 12 July 1878, RG 57H; E. B. Wakefield, "Up the Yellowstone," unpublished lecture, 13–14, Wakefield Collection.
36. Hering to Hilgard, 15 Apr. 1872, RG 57H.
37. Charles F. Hoffman to FVH, 3 Apr. 1872, RG 57H; *DAB,* 1936 ed., s.v. "Gannett, Henry," by Robert M. Brown; Gannett to FVH, 19 Feb. 1872, RG 57H.
38. Goetzmann, *Exploration and Empire,* 513; Hayden, *Sixth Annual Report,* 10.
39. Hayden, *Sixth Annual Report,* 10; Mike Foster, "A. D. Wilson," in Franklin Rhoda, *Summits to Reach: Report on the Topography of the San Juan Country* (Boulder CO: Pruett Publishing, 1984), 120–21; Gardner to FVH, 2 Mar. 1873, RG 57H.
40. Gardner to FVH, 4 Feb. 1873; Chittenden to FVH, 10 Jan. 1873, RG 57H.
41. On the dates and details of Marvine's career, see John W. Powell, "Biographical Notice of Archibald Robertson Marvine," *Bulletin of the Philosophi-*

cal Society of Washington 2 (1876): appendix 10, p. 53; Gardner to FVH, 23 Feb. 1873 and 8 Mar. 1873, RG 57H.

42. Gardner to FVH, 2 Mar. 1873, RG 57H.
43. Stevenson to FVH, 6 Jan. 1875, Merrill Papers.
44. Gannett to FVH, 19 Feb. 1872 and 3 Jan. 1873, RG 57H.
45. Hayden, *Sixth Annual Report*, 10; Samuel Chittenden to Amanda Chittenden, 28 Feb. 1873, Chittenden Family Papers, Special Collections Department, Duke University Library, Durham, North Carolina; FVH to Samuel H. Scudder, 8 Nov. 1877, Scudder Papers, Boston Society of Natural History Records, Lyman Library, Museum of Science, Boston.
46. C. F. Maynard to Baird, 2 Feb. 1873; Lesquereux to FVH, 2 May 1872, RG 57H.
47. Lesquereux to FVH, 12 Dec. 1870 and 26 Nov. 1872, RG 57H.
48. FVH to Meek, 9 Feb. 1872, 19 May 1872, 14 Sept. 1872, 30 May 1873, 8 Sept. 1873, 19 June 1875, and 7 Apr. 1876, RU 7062.
49. Allen to FVH, 31 Dec. 1872, 7 Jan. 1873, 13 Jan. 1875, 16 Dec. 1876, and 13 Mar. 1875, RG 57H.
50. Allen to FVH, 28 Sept. 1875, 10 Oct. 1875, and 23 Dec. 1877, RG 57H; Frank Luther Mott, *History of American Magazines, 1865–1885* (Cambridge MA: Harvard Univ. Press, 1938), 14.
51. Simon Newcomb, *The Reminiscences of an Astronomer* (Boston: Houghton, Mifflin, 1903), 168.
52. G. B. Chittenden to [Amanda Chittenden], 24 May 1874, from MSS #B-33 Chittenden Family Papers, 1785–1981, in the Whitney Library of the New Haven Colony Historical Society, New Haven, Connecticut; Gill to FVH, 1 Feb. 1875; Coues to FVH, 19 May 1875, RG 57H; *U.S. Statutes at Large*, 19 (1876): 120; FVH to Meek, 9 Dec. 1875, RU 7062

6. EXECUTIVE OF SCIENCE

1. FVH to Baird, 9 Sept. 1873, RU 7002.
2. Contract of N. P. Davis with U. S. Geological Survey of the Territories, 12 Oct. 1874, RG 57H; FVH to Columbus Delano, 21 Nov. 1873, RG 48.
3. Ingersoll, *Knocking Round the Rockies*, 17; Albert C. Peale, "The United States Hayden Exploring Expedition," *Illustrated Christian Weekly* 6, no. 35 (1876): 412.
4. Dary, *Entrepreneurs*, 40; Peale, "United States Hayden Exploring Expedition," 412; G. B. Chittenden to Amanda Chittenden, 1 June 1873, Chittenden Papers, Duke.
5. Ingersoll, *Knocking Round the Rockies*, 19–20, 23; Peale, "United States Hay-

den Exploring Expedition," 412; Jackson, *Diaries*, 212; Hales, *William Henry Jackson*, 132; Eugene Ostroff, *Western Views and Eastern Visions* (Washington DC: Smithsonian Institution Traveling Exhibition Service, 1981), 21–22.

6. Ostroff, *Western Views*, 17–18.
7. Hales, *William Henry Jackson*, 72; Albert C. Peale, "Personal notes, 1975," National Archives, RG 57, Geologist's Field Notebooks on Microfiche, Microfiche No. 1972, June 1–6; G. B. Chittenden to Amanda Chittenden, 1 June 1873, Chittenden Papers, Duke.
8. "The Yellowstone Expedition," *New York Times*, 18 Sept. 1871; Hayden, *Preliminary Report of . . . Montana*, 17; Hales, *William Henry Jackson*, 101; *Yellowstone and the Great West*, 128, 260 n. 15.
9. Hales, *William Henry Jackson*, 113; Goetzmann, *Exploration and Empire*, xi.
10. Jackson, *Diaries*, 222–23, 225–26.
11. *New York Times*, 18 Jan. 1875; Chittenden to Amanda Chittenden, 30 Sept. 1874, Chittenden Papers, New Haven.
12. Cope, "A General Sketch of the Ancient Life," in Hayden, *Preliminary Report of . . . Montana*, 322.
13. Hayden, *Annual Report . . . 1873*, 62; Rhoda to "Sully" (Mr. Sullivan, Hayden's secretary), 13 June 1875, RG 57H; Peale, "Personal Notes, 1875," 13 Aug.
14. Ostroff, *Western Views*, 15, 19.
15. Jackson, *Diaries*, 242.
16. Annie P. Cope to FVH, 22 Sept. 1872 and 25 Sept. 1872, RG 57H; Gannett to FVH, 1 Aug. 1874, RG 57H; Holmes, "Random Records," vol. 4, pt. 1: 76–77; vol. 2: 47.
17. FVH to Wilson, 9 Sept. 1868, RG 49; affidavit of Jn.[?] Bubb, 1st Lt., Fourth Infantry, 30 Oct. 1870; affidavit of Stephen D. Hovey, 28 Oct. 1876, RG 57H.
18. Bechler to FVH, 8 July 1875, RG 57H.
19. Samuel H. Scudder to FVH, 9 Jan. 1869; West to Commandant, 12 Sept. 1872; FVH to Delano, 27 Jan. 1873, RG 57H; FVH to Leidy, 29 Sept. 1872, 2 Oct. 1872, and 2 Aug. 1866, Leidy Coll. 1.
20. FVH to Commanding Officer, Fort Custer, Montana, 30 Aug. 1878; affidavit of A. D. Wilson, 26 Apr. 1879, RG 57H; Albert C. Peale, "Diary," National Archives, RG 57, Geologist's Field Notebooks on Microfiche, Microfiche No. 1978, 28, 29, 31 Aug. [1878].
21. Peale, "Personal Notes, 1875," 23 June; 3, 31 July; 7, 11, 14, and 20 Aug.
22. Peale, "Personal Notes, 1875," 21 Aug.; David Grey, "The Hayden Survey:

Gardner and Gannett Unite Their Parties, and Are Attacked by Renegade Indians," *Chicago Inter-Ocean*, 8 Sept. 1875.

23. FVH to Zachariah Chandler, 2 June 1876, RG 48; Elliott Coues, "Au Revoir(?)" *Rod and Gun* 8 (1876): 299.

24. FVH to Leidy, 15 June 1873, Leidy Coll. 1.
25. Lesquereux to FVH, 5 Mar. 1872, 12 Sept. 1872, and 19 Sept. 1872, RG 57H.
26. Lesquereux to Lesley, 18 May 1873 and 23 Sept. 1873, Lesley Papers.
27. Gardner to FVH, 23 Feb. 1873 and 2 Mar. 1873, RG 57H.
28. Gardner to FVH, 2 Mar. 1873; Holmes to FVH, 13 June 1875, RG 57H.
29. Hayden, *Sketch of the Origin and Progress of the United States Geological and Geographical Survey of the Territories* (Washington DC: GPO, 1877), 5.
30. Chittenden to FVH, 27 July 1875; Holmes to FVH, 13 June 1875, RG 57H; Chittenden to [Amanda Chittenden], [1876], Chittenden Papers, New Haven; Chittenden to [Amanda Chittenden], 15 Aug. [1876], Chittenden Papers, Duke; Mike Foster, "Editor's Preface," in Rhoda, *Summits to Reach*, 3.
31. [Wakefield] to [Martie Wakefield], 7 July 1872, Wakefield Collection; Archibald R. Marvine, "U. S. Geological Survey of the Territories, Middle Park Division, Journal, A. R. Marvine, 1873," Department of the Interior, United States Geological Survey, Geologic Records, Denver, USGS Field Records Library, Accession No. 1963, 65–66, 67, 71, 75–79; Hayden, *Ninth Annual Report*, 10; *Tenth Annual Report of the United States Geological and Geographical Survey of the Territories* (Washington DC: GPO, 1878), xxi.
32. FVH to Leidy, 23 Jan. 1856, Leidy Coll. 1; Baird to FVH, 13 Jan. 1867; Marsh to FVH, 12 Mar. 1867, 27 Jan. 1868, 10 Mar. 1869, and 27 Mar. 1869; Cope to FVH, 28 Jan. 1868, RG 57H.
33. FVH to Leidy, 1 Sept. 1870 and 7 Sept. 1870; Marsh to FVH, 8 Sept. 1870, Leidy Coll. 1.
34. FVH to Leidy, 13 Oct. 1870, 12 Nov. 1870, and 13 Nov. 1870, Leidy Coll. 1; Leidy to FVH, 1 Nov. 1870, RG 57H.
35. FVH to Baird, 3 Apr. 1871, RU 52; Cope to FVH, 19 Feb. 1872, RG 57H; Ronald Rainger, "The Bone Wars: Cope, Marsh and American Vertebrate Paleontology, 1865–1900," in *The Ultimate Dinosaur*, ed. Byron Preiss and Robert Silverberg (New York: Bantam Books, 1992), 292.
36. Leidy to FVH, 18 Sept. 1872, RG 57H; FVH to Leidy, 2 Oct. 1872 and 29 Sept. 1872, Leidy Coll. 1.
37. Cope to Lesley, 17 Aug. 1872; Marsh to Lesley, 24 Aug. 1872 and 28 Aug. 1872, Lesley Papers; Rainger, "Bone Wars," 9–10.
38. Cope to FVH, 14 Feb. 1873 and 18 Feb. 1873, RG 57H; FVH to Leidy, 26 Apr.

1873, Leidy Coll. 1; Gardner to FVH, 4 Feb. 1873, RG 57H; FVH to Leidy, 8 Apr. 1873, Leidy Coll. 1-B.

39. Marsh to FVH, 3 Dec. 1873, RG 57H.
40. FVH to Marsh, 8 Dec. 1873, Hayden Collection.
41. Cope to FVH, 8 Feb. 1874, RG 57H; Hayden, *Annual Report . . . 1873*, 13.
42. FVH to Marsh, 8 Dec. 1873, Hayden Collection; FVH to LeConte, 25 Mar. 1877, John Lawrence LeConte Papers: 1812–1897, American Philosophical Society, Philadelphia.
43. FVH to Baird, 3 July 1873, 16 July 1873, and 12 Sept. 1873, RU 7002.
44. FVH to Baird, 12 Sept. 1873, RU 7002.
45. G. B. Chittenden to Amanda Chittenden, 7 June 1873, Chittenden Papers, Duke; Chittenden to Amanda Chittenden, 1 Mar. 1874, Chittenden Papers, New Haven.
46. Bechler to FVH, 25 Aug. 1875; Holmes to FVH, 3 Oct. 1875, RG 57H; Gardner to [Anne Terry Gardner], 17 Sept. 1875 and 28 Oct. 1875, James Terry Gardiner Collection, New York State Library, Albany, New York; Gardner, *Report upon the Southern Coal and Iron Field of Colorado Territory, by James T. Gardner, Geographer of U.S. Geological and Geographical Survey of the Territories, 1875* (Colorado Springs CO: Out West Printing & Publishing, 1875); Endlich to FVH, 31 Aug. 1875, RG 57H.
47. "The Hayden Survey: The Recent Attack on Gardner's Division—Were the Scientific Gentlemen More Frightened Than Hurt?" *New York Herald*, 28 Sept. 1875; "The Hayden Survey: The Work Accomplished by Wilson's Division—The Alleged Reflection of Professor Hayden on the Gardner Party Denied," *New York Herald*, 29 Sept. 1875; Henry Gannett to FVH, 5 Oct. 1875 and 15 Oct. 1875, RG 57H.
48. [Gardner] to [Anne Terry Gardner], 28 Oct. 1875, Gardiner Collection; Josiah D. Whitney, "Geographical and Geological Surveys," *North American Review* 121 (1875): 37–85, 270–314.
49. [Gardner] to [Anne Terry Gardner], 28 Oct. 1875, Gardiner Collection.
50. Holmes, "Random Records," 2:29; Bechler to FVH, 8 July 1875, RG 57H.
51. Brayer, *William Blackmore*, 1:73, 271; Blackmore to FVH, 2 Dec. 1869; "H." to N. P. Banks, 8 Feb. 1873, RG 57H.
52. On Swallow, see Foster, "Permian Controversy"; FVH to Meek, 3 June 1869, RU 7062; on Wheeler and the Army Corps of Engineers, see Foster, *Strange Genius*, 254–55, and chap. 8 of this work.
53. "The Hayden Survey: A Visit to the Offices of the Surveying Corps," *New York Times* 27 Apr. 1875.
54. Lesquereux to FVH, 12 Dec. 1870 and 29 Dec. 1873, RG 57H.

55. See Jackson, *Time Exposure*, 221.
56. Endlich to FVH, 3 Feb. 1877, RG 57H.
57. Henry W. Elliott to FVH, 23 Aug. 1875; Endlich to FVH, 30 Oct. 1875, RG 57H; Endlich to FVH, 9 May 1878, Merrill Papers; Foster, "Fred Endlich," in *Summits to Reach*, 131–32, 135–38.

58. Foster, "Fred Endlich," 134; Holmes to Peale, 11 May 1875, Howell Collection.
59. Benjamin Perley Poore, *Perley's Reminiscences of Sixty Years in the National Metropolis* (Philadelphia: Hubbard Brothers, 1886), 2:261–63; G. B. Chittenden to [Amanda Chittenden], 2 Nov. 1873, 1 Mar. 1874, and 24 May 1874, Chittenden Papers, New Haven.

7. PUBLISHING AND PUBLICIZING

1. Geikie, "Ferdinand Vandeveer Hayden," *Nature* 37 (1888): 326; Larry T. Spencer, "Filling in the Gaps: A Survey of Nineteenth Century Institutions Associated with the Exploration and Natural History of the American West," *American Zoologist* 26 (1986): 379.
2. *Catalogue of the Publications of the U.S. Geological and Geographical Survey of the Territories*, ed. F. V. Hayden, 3d ed., rev. to 31 Dec. 1878 (Washington DC: GPO, 1879), 4.
3. On the myriad chores involved in scientific publishing through the Government Printing Office in the mid-nineteenth century, see Blum, *Picturing Nature*, chap. 5.
4. Lesquereux to FVH, 9 Jan. 1870, RG 57H; Hayden, *Sixth Annual Report*, 13.
5. FVH to G. B. Chittenden, 29 Sept. 1875, Chittenden Papers, New Haven; FVH to Leidy, 1 Sept. 1870, 5 Nov. 1870, and 20 Sept. 1872, Leidy Coll. 1.
6. Bartlett, *Great Surveys*, 20, 118; Cope to FVH, 4 Jan. 1870 and 2 Feb. 1871, RG 57H.
7. Hayden, "Second Annual Report of the United States Geological Survey of the Territories," in *First, Second, and Third Annual Reports*, 77; Lesley to FVH, 24 Feb. 1869, RG 57H.
8. Sandra Ireland Oliver, "Ferdinand V. Hayden: Scientist or Charlatan? The Wyoming Years" (master's thesis, Univ. of Wyoming, May 1978), 53; Bartlett, *Great Surveys*, 58–59; Goetzmann, *Exploration and Empire*, 501.
9. Charles L. Batten Jr., *Pleasurable Instruction: Form and Convention in Eighteenth-Century Travel Literature* (Berkeley: Univ. of California Press, 1978), 1, 3, 5–6, 8, 46; Cannon, *Science in Culture*, 75, 87.
10. Hicks, "The Development of the Natural History Essay," 162, 7; Regis, *Describing Early America*, xi; Paul Brooks, *Speaking for Nature: How Literary Na-*

turalists from Henry Thoreau to Rachel Carson Have Shaped America (Boston: Houghton Mifflin, 1980); Hildebidle, *Thoreau,* 5, 26–31, 54.

11. Batten, *Pleasurable Instruction,* 14, 82; Hildebidle, *Thoreau,* 40–41, 30–31.
12. Peggy Champlin, *Raphael Pumpelly: Gentleman Geologist of the Gilded Age* (Tuscaloosa: Univ. of Alabama Press, 1994), 73–74.
13. Brooks, *Speaking for Nature,* 45–48; [Henry Adams?], "King's Mountaineering in the Sierra Nevada," *North American Review* 114 (1872): 446.
14. Mike Foster, "Hayden in Wonderland: Exploring Yellowstone," *Timeline: A Publication of the Ohio Historical Society* 6 (1989): 36–47; Champlin, *Raphael Pumpelly,* 131–32; Foster, *Strange Genius,* 212ff; Hayden, *Sixth Annual Report,* 5; John Tallmadge, "From Chronicle to Quest: The Shaping of Darwin's 'Voyage of the Beagle,'" *Victorian Studies* 23 (1980): 341.
15. Hayden, *Annual Report . . . 1873,* 13.
16. Lesley to FVH, 24 Feb. 1869; Packard to FVH, 20 Mar. 1873 and 17 Feb. 1870; Dana to FVH, 13 Jan. 1870 and 22 Dec. 1869, RG 57H.
17. William Bross to FVH, 25 Feb. 1870, RG 57H.
18. "Congress and Science," *Eng. Min. J.* 13 (1872): 361–62; *DAB,* 1935 ed., s.v., "Raymond, Rossiter Worthington"; *BDA,* 1906 ed., s.v. "Raymond, Rossiter Worthington"; *National Cyclopaedia of American Biography,* s.v., "Raymond, Rossiter Worthington," 45; [Raymond], "Preliminary Report of the United States Geological Survey of Montana," 376.
19. [Raymond], "Annual Report of the United States Geological and Geographical Survey . . . for the year 1873," 74.
20. FVH to Baird, 8 June 1871, RU 52; FVH to Leidy, 8 June 1871, Leidy Coll. 1-B.
21. Wilson to FVH, 29 Apr. 1867, RG 57H; FVH to Wilson, 9 July 1868, RG 49; FVH to Jacob D. Cox, 16 Oct. 1869, RG 48; *U.S. Statutes at Large,* 17 (1872): 131; FVH to Columbus Delano, in Joseph Leidy, *Contributions to the Extinct Vertebrate Fauna of the Western Territories* (Washington DC: GPO, 1873), 1.
22. FVH to Meek, 9 Feb. 1872, RU 7062; Cope to FVH, 28 Nov. 1871; Lesquereux to FVH, 23 Dec. 1871 and 5 Mar. 1872, RG 57H; Cyrus Thomas, *Synopsis of the Acrididae of North America* (Washington DC: GPO, 1873).
23. FVH to Leidy, 20 Sept. 1872, Leidy Coll. 1; FVH to Meek, 9 Apr. 1871, RU 7062; Hayden, "Letter to the Secretary," in Leidy, *Contributions to the Extinct Vertebrate Fauna,* i.
24. Hayden, "Letter to the Secretary," in Alpheus Spring Packard, *A Monograph on the Geometrid Moths or Phalaenidae of the United States* (Washington DC: GPO, 1876), iii.

25. Hayden, *Sixth Annual Report*, 5; Hayden, "Letter to the Secretary," in Packard, *Monograph on the Geometrid Moths*, iii.
26. Lesquereux to Lesley, 7 Sept. 1872, Lesley Papers.
27. FVH to Leidy, 3 May 1862 and 30 Sept. 1870, Leidy Coll. 1; Leidy to FVH, 1 Nov. 1870; Cope to FVH, 28 Nov. 1871, 19 Feb. 1872, and 13 Nov. 1872, RG 57H.
28. FVH to Leidy, 23 Apr. 1873 and 26 Apr. 1873, Leidy Coll. 1.
29. Cope to FVH, 26 Nov. 1873, RG 57H.
30. Cope to FVH, 1 Dec. 1873, RG 57H.
31. Hayden, "Prefatory Note," *BUSGGST* 2 (1874): 1; *Catalogue of the Publications*, 24; FVH to Scudder, 10 Dec. 1875, 21 Mar. 1877, 7 June 1877, and 7 July 1878, Scudder Papers, Boston.
32. Goetzmann, *Exploration and Empire*, 527–28.
33. Goetzmann, *Exploration and Empire*, 527–28; Powell to James A. Garfield, 7 Mar. 1879, National Archives, RG 57, "Geographical and Geological Survey of the Rocky Mountain Region" (henceforth, RG 57P).
34. Hayden, "Prefatory Note," *BUSGGST* 4 (1878): iii–iv; Powell to Garfield, 7 Mar. 1879, RG 57P.
35. Hayden, *Annual Report . . . 1873*, 9; *Catalogue of the Publications*, 33–35.
36. Hardwick, "Science and Art," 3.
37. Paul, *Far West*, 94–95; Hayden, "Coal and Iron in Colorado," *Rocky Mountain News* (Denver), 27 Nov. 1867.
38. Paul, *Far West*, 7ff; Reid to FVH, 26 May 1869, RG 57H.
39. Reid to FVH, 31 Oct. 1871; Barnard to FVH, 4 Mar. 1874, 20 Oct. 1875, and 16 Mar. 1876, RG 57H; "Peale, A. C. (M.D.), 1871–72 Diaries," 7 Aug. 1871 and 14 Sept. 1871, Yellowstone National Park Manuscript Collection, Yellowstone National Park.
40. Thomas to FVH, 29 Aug. 1873 and 9 Aug. 1873, RG 57H.
41. Mott, *History of American Magazines*, 5; R. W. Gilder to FVH, 11 Sept. 1871; Abbott to FVH, 19 Apr. 1875, RG 57H; Albert C. Peale, "The United States Hayden Exploring Expedition," *Illustrated Christian Weekly* 6 (1876): 277–78, 388, 412–23, 460–61.
42. Hardwick, "Science and Art," 197; E. Motz, "Prof. Hayden's Expedition," *New York Times*, 7 Sept. 1873.
43. Scott, "Popular Lecture," 791.
44. Foster, "Hayden in Wonderland," 38, 246; Chairman of Committee on Lectures, Young Men's Christian Association, [name illegible] to FVH, 3 Oct. 1871; Francis A. Stout to FVH, 21 Nov. 1872; D. C. Haskell to FVH, 29 Apr. 1877, RG 57H.

45. Darrah, *Powell*, 182; "Western Scenery: Interesting Facts Concerning Our National Parks," *New York Times*, 16 Apr. 1874.

46. Scott, "Popular Lecture," 802–3; Hayden, "Our Great West, and the Scenery of Our Natural Parks," *Journal of the American Geographical Society of New York* 6 (1874): 196–211.
47. Washington Townsend to FVH, 19 Dec. 1873; John Gibbs to FVH, 23 Jan. 1873; O. M. Wilson to FVH, 18 Dec. 1872 and 18 Feb. 1874; Ingersoll to FVH, 12 Apr. 1875, RG 57H.
48. Blum, *Picturing Nature*, esp. xxix, 48, 62–63, chaps. 4 and 8.
49. Martin J. S. Rudwick, "The Emergence of a Visual Language for Geological Science, 1760–1840," *History of Science* 14 (1976): 149–50, 156; Blum, *Picturing Nature*, 167.
50. Meek to FVH, 9 Mar. 1869, RG 57H; Meek to Baird, 9 Mar. 1869, RU 7002.
51. FVH to Scudder, 10 Dec. 1875, Scudder Papers, Boston.
52. Hayden, "Prefatory Note," in Elliott Coues, *Fur-Bearing Animals: A Monograph of North American Mustelidae* (Washington DC: GPO, 1877), iv.
53. FVH to Leidy, 25 July 1866, Leidy Coll. 1; Leidy to FVH, 20 Aug. 1866, RG 57H.
54. Ostroff, *Western Views*, 12, 13.
55. Ostroff, *Western Views*, 13; FVH to Wilson, 2 Nov. 1867, RG 49; Jackson, *Time Exposure*, 187.
56. Ostroff, *Western Views*, 13; anonymous, "Sun-Pictures of Rocky Mountain Scenery," *Am. J. Sci.*, 2d ser., 50 (1870): 125.
57. Ostroff, *Western Views*, 21, 22; William Culp Darrah, *Stereo Views: A History of Stereographs in America and Their Collection* (Gettysburg PA: Times and News Publishing, 1964), 9; William C. Darrah, *The World of Stereographs* (Gettysburg PA: W. C. Darrah, 1977), 6, 45; "Interpretive Chronology—Stereos, American History and Popular Culture, 1850–1914," in *Points of View: The Stereograph in America—A Cultural History*, ed. Edward W. Earle (Rochester NY: Visual Studies Workshop Press, 1979), 38–58; Hales, *William Henry Jackson*, 48, 122.
58. William H. Jackson to FVH, 1 Aug. 1870, RG 57H; Darrah, *Stereo Views*, 36, 81; Darrah, *World of Stereographs*, 24, 45; Hales, *William Henry Jackson*, 88, 124.
59. O. M. Wilson to FVH, 18 Dec. 1872, RG 57H; "The Hayden Survey: A Visit to the Offices of the Surveying Corps," *New York Times*, 27 Apr. 1875.
60. Teese to FVH, 5 May 1877, RG 57H.
61. Dana to FVH, 30 Nov. 1872 and 8 Aug. 1871; Agassiz to FVH, 25 Feb. 1873; Francis A. Stout to FVH, 13 Nov. 1872 and 5 Feb. 1873; Ingersoll to FVH, 16

Dec. 1874; Cyrus Thomas to FVH, 22 July 1873; Benjamin R. Cowen to FVH, 3 Nov. 1873, RG 57H; Joseph Henry to FVH, 2 Feb. 1867; Baird to FVH, 27 Nov. 1877 and 2 Feb. 1878, Smithsonian Archives, RU 33, Office of the Secretary, 1865–1891, Outgoing Correspondence; J. E. Toustellotte to FVH, 1 Mar. 1873, RG 57H.

62. Stevenson to FVH, 25 Dec. 1874 and 6 Jan. 1875, Merrill Papers.
63. Gilder to FVH, 24 Jan. 1872; L. Abbott to FVH, 19 Apr. 1875; I. Appleton to B. R. Cowen, 14 May 1872, RG 57H.
64. Robert H. Lamborn to FVH, 16 Nov. 1871; Robert E. Strahorn to FVH, 11 Nov. 1878, RG 57H.
65. Moran to FVH, 11 Mar. 1872, RG 57H; "Fine Arts: Mr. Thomas Moran's 'Great Canon of the Yellowstone,'" *New-York Daily Tribune*, 4 May 1872.
66. Kinsey, *Thomas Moran*, 43, 86–88; Clarence Cook, "Art at the Capitol," *Scribner's Monthly* 5 (1873): 499; Truettner, *National Parks*, 86; Moran, *Home-Thoughts*, 133, 137; [Hayden?], "List of Members and Collaborators of the Survey for 1873," *BUSGGST* 1 (1873): 4; Moran to FVH, 28 June 1873 and 31 Mar. 1873, RG 57H.
67. Hyde, *American Vision*, 7–9, chap. 5; Hayden, *The Yellowstone National Park, and the Mountain Regions of Portions of Idaho, Nevada, Colorado and Utah* (Boston: L. Prang, 1876); Kinsey, *Thomas Moran*, 88–91; Clark, *Thomas Moran*, 43–45.
68. Sears, *Sacred Places*, 3–4, chaps. 6–7; Novak, *Nature and Culture*, 18; Joshua C. Taylor, foreword to Truettner, *National Parks*, 7.
69. Zechariah Chandler to FVH, 29 Nov. 1875, RG 57H.
70. U. S. Grant, *Additional Appropriation for the Executive Departments of the United States at the Centennial Exhibition*, 44th Cong., 1st sess., 1876, H. Exec. Doc. 148, 23–24.
71. J. S. Ingram, *The Centennial Exposition, Described and Illustrated . . .* , (Philadelphia: Hubbard Brothers, 1876), 148–49; Grant, *Additional Appropriation*, 24.
72. Runkle to FVH, 19 June 1876, RG 57H.
73. Baird to FVH, 19 June 1876 and 3 July 1876, RG 57H.
74. E. A. Barber to Wm. H. Jackson, 18 Oct. 1876; Baird to FVH, 5 July 1876, 31 July 1876, 28 Oct. 1876, 11 Nov. 1876, 16 Nov. 1876, and 21 Nov. 1876, RG 57H.
75. Baird to FVH, 3 July 1876; Guyot to FVH, 20 Feb. 1877; Packard to FVH, 29 Apr. 1878; Putnam to FVH, 16 Dec. 1878; Alexander Agassiz to FVH, 5 July 1878; F. M. Pierson to FVH, 17 Aug. 1878, RG 57H.
76. Elliott to FVH, 2 Dec. 1876, RG 57H.

8. COMPETING IN A CHANGING ENVIRONMENT

1. FVH to Meek, 2 Nov. 1867, RU 7062.

2. *U.S. Statutes at Large*, 20 (1878): 230.
3. Motz, "Prof. Hayden's Expedition"; Everts to FVH, 14 Feb. 1872, RG 57H; [John A. Church?], "Dr. Hayden's Discoveries," *Eng. Min. J.*, 14 (1872): 313.
4. FVH to Meek, 4 Mar. 1854, RU 7062; Secord, *Controversy*, 30, 121; Rudwick, *Great Devonian*, 141–43, 150.
5. FVH to Baird, 14 Sept. 1872, RU 52.
6. House, *Geographical*, 30, 34; FVH to Delano, 27 Jan. 1873, RG 48.
7. FVH to Delano, 25 Apr. 1874, in Grant, *Geographical and Geological Surveys*, 10; FVH to Leidy, 31 Dec. 1872, Leidy Coll. 1; Clare[nce King] to Gardner, 15 Feb. 1873, Gardiner Collection; FVH to Delano, 27 Jan. 1873, RG 48.
8. Benjamin Peirce, *Report of the Superintendent of the United States Coast Survey, Showing the Progress of the Survey During the Year 1872* (Washington DC: GPO, 1875), 1–2, 39–40; Gustavus A. Weber, *The Coast and Geodetic Survey: Its History, Activities and Organization* (Baltimore: Johns Hopkins Univ. Press, 1974, reprint of 1923 edition), 8; Gardner to FVH, 1 Feb. 1873, RG 57H.
9. Gardner to FVH, 6 Feb. 1873, RG 57H; Peirce, *Report . . . the Year 1872*, 1–2; Peirce, *Report of the Superintendent of the United States Coast Survey, Showing the Progress of the Survey During the Year 1873* (Washington DC: GPO, 1875), 44.
10. Gardner to FVH, 6 Feb. 1873 and 8 Mar. 1873, RG 57H; FVH to Gardner, 10 Mar. 1873, Gardiner Collection.
11. House, *Geographical*, 32–33, 71.
12. House, *Geographical*, 32, 39, 71–72.
13. Thomas to FVH, 9 Aug. 1873, in RG 57H; FVH to Baird, 16 July 1873; Baird to FVH, 28 July 1873, RU 7002.
14. Thomas to FVH, 6 June 1873, 12 July 1873, 22 July 1873, 24 July 1873, and 26 Aug. 1873, RG 57H.
15. FVH to Monroe, 18 July 1873, Hayden Collection; FVH to Baird, 9 Sept. 1873, RU 7002.
16. House, *Geographical*, 1.
17. Belknap to President [Grant], 27 Apr. 1874; Humphreys to Belknap, 23 Apr. 1874; Delano to Grant, 28 Apr. 1874; FVH to Delano, 25 Apr. 1874, all in Grant, *Geographical and Geological Surveys*. For the quotations from Grant, see pp. 1–2.
18. House, *Geographical*, 11, 28; Endlich to FVH, 30 Oct. 1875 and 9 May 1877, RG 57H.
19. House, *Geographical*, 19–37, passim.

20. House, *Geographical*, 51–52, 54, 62–69, 71, 73–77.
21. House, *Geographical*, 16–17.
22. House, *Geographical*, 59–60.
23. Belknap to [Delano], 18 June 1874, RG 57H; House, *Geographical*, 32; FVH to Delano, 22 June 1874, RG 48.
24. Delano to FVH, 1 July 1874, RG 57H.
25. House, *Geographical*, 54–55.
26. [James T. Gardner] to [Anne Terry Gardner], 3 June 1874 and [23 June 1874], Gardiner Collection; Darrah, *Powell*, 180, 184; Stegner, *Beyond the Hundredth Meridian*, pt. 3.
27. Garfield, *Diary*, 2:265; 2:36 n. 132; Darrah, *Powell*, 248; Meadows, *John Wesley Powell*, 70; Terrell, *Man Who Rediscovered*, 182.
28. Ansel Walling, Samuel Randall, and William Holman, *Cong. Rec.*, 44th Cong., 1st sess., 1876, 4, pt. 5:4100.
29. *U.S. Statutes at Large*, 19 (1876): 120.
30. FVH to Meek, 21 July 1876, 10 July 1876, and 17 July 1876, RU 7062.
31. *Cong. Rec.*, 44th Cong., 1st sess., 1876, 4, pt. 5:4097.
32. *Cong. Rec.*, 44th Cong., 1st sess., 1876, 4, pt. 5:4102.
33. *Cong. Rec.*, 44th Cong., 2d sess., 1877, 5, pt. 3:1793.
34. *Cong. Rec.*, 44th Cong., 2d sess., 1877, 5, pt. 3:1878.
35. For Wheeler, see Julius Seelye and Gustave Schleicher, *Cong. Rec.*, 44th Cong., 2d sess., 1877, 5, pt. 3:1878–79; for Hayden, see Washington Townsend, Nathaniel Banks, James Belford, and James Monroe, *Cong. Rec.*, 44th Cong., 2d sess., 1877, 5, pt. 3:1950–52; *U.S. Statutes at Large*, 19 (1877): 350.
36. Ari Hoogenboom, *The Presidency of Rutherford B. Hayes* (Lawrence: Univ. Press of Kansas, 1988), 118; Hans Trefousse, *Carl Schurz: A Biography* (Knoxville: Univ. of Tennessee Press, 1982), 235, 240; Powell to Schurz, 22 May 1877, in Powell, *Geological and Geographical Surveys*, 45th Cong., 2d sess., 1878, H. Exec. Doc. 80, 8.
37. Powell, *Geological and Geographical Surveys*, 8–11.
38. Newberry to Garfield, 20 Jan. 1877, copy of letter with Powell to Newberry, 25 Jan. 1877, RG 57P.
39. Goetzmann, *Exploration and Empire*, 419–24.
40. Foster, *Strange Genius*, 285–86; Goetzmann, *Exploration and Empire*, 424, 492.
41. FVH to Schurz, draft, 25 June 1877, RG 57H.
42. Schurz to FVH, 2 Aug. 1877; A. Bell to FVH, 9 Nov. 1877, RG 57H; Holmes to Peale, 5 June 1877, Howell Collection.

43. FVH to Schurz, 15 Nov. 1877, RG 48; Foster, *Strange Genius*, 288; FVH to Delano, 25 Apr. 1874, in Grant, *Geographical and Geological Surveys*, 11.

44. FVH to Schurz, 15 Nov. 1877, RG 48.

45. Foster, *Strange Genius*, 288.

46. Stevenson to Marsh, 15 Mar. 1878, Othniel Charles Marsh Papers, Manuscripts and Archives, Yale University Library; *Cong. Rec.*, 45th Cong., 2d sess., 1878, 7, pt. 2:1593; Powell, *Geological and Geographical Surveys*; Hayden, *Geological and Geographical Surveys*, 45th Cong., 2d sess., 1878, H. Exec. Doc. 81; and A. A. Humphreys, *Surveys by the War Department*, 45th Cong., 2d sess., 1878, H. Exec. Doc. 88.

47. Stevenson to Marsh, 15 Mar. 1878, Marsh Papers.

48. *Cong. Rec.*, 45th Cong., 2d sess., 1878, 7, pt. 5:4560, 4899; FVH to Scudder, 21 July 1878, Scudder Papers.

49. *Cong. Rec.*, 45th Cong., 3d sess., 1879, 8, pt. 3:1203; David McCullough, *The Great Bridge* (New York: Simon & Schuster, 1972), 373–77, 388–96, 415–16; Wilkins, *Clarence King*, 256–57; Henry Nash Smith, "Clarence King, John Wesley Powell, and the Establishment of the United States Geological Survey," *Mississippi Valley Historical Review* 34 (June 1947): 43 n. 18; Darrah, *Powell*, 243.

50. Foster, *Strange Genius*, 289, 292–93; Powell to King, 23 Jan. 1877, RG 57P; Smith, "Clarence King," 41–42.

51. *Cong. Rec.*, House, 45th Cong., 2d sess., 1878, 7, pt. 5:4560.

52. *Cong. Rec.*, 45th Cong., 3d sess., 1879, 8, pt. 3:1204; "Instructions for the government of the Geological and Geographical surveys of the Territories of the United States, (authorized by Acts of Congress to be made under the direction of the Secretary of the Interior), in the preparation of suitable maps for the construction of an Atlas of said Territories," Department of the Interior, Washington DC, 1 July 1874, accompanying Delano to FVH, 1 July 1874, RG 57H; FVH to Delano, 22 June 1874, RG 48; Foster, *Strange Genius*, 294–95.

53. *Cong. Rec.*, 45th Cong., 2d sess., 1878, 7, pt. 5:4560.

54. Dupree, *Science*, 147; FVH to Marsh, 20 Apr. 1874; Marsh to FVH, draft, Apr. 1874, Marsh Papers; Smith, "Clarence King," 42–43.

55. FVH to Scudder, 29 Dec. 1877, Scudder Papers; FVH to Leidy, 21 July 1878, Leidy Coll. 1; FVH to Scudder, 21 July 1878, Scudder Papers; FVH to Baird, 22 July 1878, 27 Aug. 1878, and 20 Sept. 1878, RU 7002; Rivinus and Youssef, *Spencer Baird*, 127.

56. Schurz to FVH, 3 Oct. 1878; Marsh to Schurz, copy, 28 Sept. 1878, RG 57H;

FVH to Schurz, 20 Oct. 1878, in *Surveys of the Territories*, 45th Cong., 3d sess., 1878, H. Misc. Doc. 5 (henceforth, House, *Surveys of the Territories*), 11.

57. O. C. Marsh, *Report of National Academy of Sciences*, 45th Cong., 1st sess., 1879, H. Misc. Doc. 5, 7; Rabbitt, *Minerals*, 264; Schuchert and LeVene, *O. C. Marsh*, 256.
58. Marsh, *Report of NAS*, 6–8; *Proceedings, National Academy of Sciences* 1, pt. 2 (1878): 146; House, *Surveys of the Territories*, 2–4.
59. House, *Surveys of the Territories*, 3–4.
60. Marsh, *Report of NAS*, 7–8; Marsh to Newcomb, telegram 17 Oct. [1878], Simon Newcomb Papers, Library of Congress; Marsh to Wm. B. Rogers, 12 Oct. 1878, Marsh Papers; Newcomb to Marsh, 18 Oct. 1878; 5 Oct. 1878, Newcomb Papers; Newcomb to Marsh, 25 Sept. 1878, Marsh Papers.
61. Newcomb to Marsh, 25 Sept. 1878, Marsh Papers; Marsh to Schurz, 28 Sept. 1878, RG 57H; House, *Surveys of the Territories*, 7, 10.
62. House, *Surveys of the Territories*, 11–12.
63. House, *Surveys of the Territories*, 12; Alexander Agassiz to FVH, 9 May 1878, RG 57H.
64. John Wesley Powell, *Report on the Methods of Surveying the Public Domain* (Washington DC: GPO, 1878), 4.
65. Powell, *Report on the Methods of Surveying*, 5.
66. Powell, *Report on the Methods of Surveying*, 12–14.
67. Powell, *Report on the Methods of Surveying*, 16; Powell to Marsh, June 1878, Marsh Papers; House, *Geographical*, 53; Foster, *Strange Genius*, 289; John Wesley Powell, *Report on the Lands of the Arid Region of the United States, With a More Detailed Account of the Lands of Utah*, ed. Wallace Stegner (Cambridge MA: Harvard Univ. Press, Belknap Press, 1962; originally printed as 45th Cong., 2d sess., 1878, H. Exec. Doc. 73), 7–8, and passim.
68. Powell to Marsh, June 1878, Marsh Papers; Powell, *Report on the Methods of Surveying*, 5–7, 12; Hilgard to Marsh, 28 Nov. 1878, Marsh Papers.
69. Gray to FVH, 27 Nov. 1878, RG 57H; Rabbitt, *Minerals*, 275; Schuchert and LeVene, *O. C. Marsh*, 254; Agassiz to Marsh, 17 Nov. 1878, Marsh Papers.
70. FVH to Agassiz, 15 Nov. 1878, Agassiz Papers, by permission of the Ernst Mayr Library, Museum of Comparative Zoology Library, Archives, Harvard University, Cambridge, Massachusetts; Hilgard to Marsh, 28 Nov. 1878, Marsh Papers.
71. Patterson to Marsh, 22 Nov. 1878; Hilgard to Marsh, 28 Nov. 1878; Newcomb to Marsh, 5 Oct. 1878; Patterson to Marsh, 11 Jan. 1879; Patterson to Newcomb, 11 Jan. 1879; Marsh to Patterson, 13 Jan. 1879, Marsh Papers.

72. John Wesley Powell, *Cost of Geographical Surveys*, 45th Cong., 3d sess., 1879, H. Exec. Doc. 72, 3; Powell to Garfield, copy, 18 Feb. 1879, RG 57P.
73. The legislative history of the academy's survey plan has been reported a number of times; see Smith, "Clarence King," 37–58; Goetzmann, *Exploration and Empire*, chap. 16; Rabbitt, *Minerals*, chap. 14; Thomas G. Manning, *Government in Science: The U.S. Geological Survey, 1867–1894* (Lexington: Univ. of Kentucky Press, 1967), chap. 2; and esp. Foster, *Strange Genius*, chap. 23.
74. *Cong. Rec.*, 45th Cong., 3d sess., 1879, 8, pt. 1:28; pt. 2:1169–70, 1204, 1211; Wilkins, *Clarence King*, 261–62; Darrah, *Powell*, 246–49; Allan Nevins, *Abram S. Hewitt, With Some Account of Peter Cooper* (New York: Harper and Brothers, 1935; New York: Octagon Books, 1967), 408–9; Powell to Schurz, 23 Dec. 1878, RG 57P.
75. *Cong. Rec.*, 45th Cong., 3d sess., 1879, 8, pt. 2:1197, 1200–1208, 1562.
76. *Cong. Rec.*, 45th Cong., 3d sess., 1879, 8, pt. 2:1209–10.
77. Garfield, *Diary*, 4:181; Powell, *Report on the Methods of Surveying*, 4, 5, 12–15; Powell to Garfield, n.d., James A. Garfield Papers, Library of Congress; Garfield, *Diary*, 4:158–72, 198–203ff; Joseph Stanley-Brown, "Memorandum concerning Joseph Stanley-Brown's Relations with General Garfield, New York, June 24, 1924," Papers of Joseph Stanley-Brown, Library of Congress.
78. *Cong. Rec.*, 45th Cong., 3d sess., 1879, 8, pt. 2:1207–8, 1559–67, pt. 3:1864–71, 1906–9.
79. Thomas Patterson, Dudley Haskell, and John Baker, *Cong. Rec.*, 45th Cong., 3d sess., 1879, 8, pt. 2:1207, 1560, 1563.
80. *Cong. Rec.*, 45th Cong., 3d sess., 1879, 8, pt. 3:2084–85, 2182, 2283, 2301–3, 2409; Foster, *Strange Genius*, 311–12.
81. Newcomb, *Reminiscences*, 258.

9. GENERALIST VERSUS TECHNOCRAT

1. Stevenson to Marsh, 20 Dec. 1878, Marsh Papers.
2. Biagioli, *Galileo*, 4, 16, 19, 54ff, 87–89, 353.
3. Steven Shapin, "The House of Experiment in Seventeenth-Century England," *Isis* 79 (1988): 404; Shapin, *Social History*, 126; see Rainger, Benson, and Maienschein, *American Development*.
4. Rudwick, *Great Devonian*, 420; Shapin, *Social History*, 241–42.
5. A. Harper to A. A. Wright, 21 Mar. 1888, RU 7085; FVH to Meek, 12 Jan. 1856 and 2 Nov. 1867, RU 7062.
6. FVH to Hall, 3 Dec. 1867, 19 Sept. 1868, 18 Dec. 1868, and 20 June 1869,

Hall Correspondence; Lesley to FVH, 9 Mar. 1869 and 1 Feb. [year unknown]; Leidy to FVH, 18 Mar. 1873, RG 57H.

7. Leidy to FVH, 2 Sept. 1872, Leidy Coll. 1.
8. FVH to Leidy, 26 Oct. 1872, Leidy Coll. 1.
9. Porter to FVH, 3 Dec. 1872 and 21 Feb. 1872, RG 57H.
10. FVH to Hall, 17 May 1872, Hall Correspondence; Camerini, "Wallace in the Field," 44–45, 48, 63–64, 65; Findlen, *Possessing Nature,* 131, 365; Baatz, "'Squinting at Sillliman,'" 238.
11. Rivinus and Youssef, *Spencer Baird,* chap. 8, passim, esp. 95; Deiss, "Baird and His Collectors," 635, 638–40, 642; Dall, *S. F. Baird,* 289–93.
12. Rivinus and Youssef, *Spencer Baird,* 71–74, 162, and chaps. 12, 13, and 17.
13. Rivinus and Youssef, *Spencer Baird,* 163, 168.
14. FVH to Baird, 6 Dec. 1876, RU 52.
15. Foster, *Strange Genius,* 299–303.
16. Foster, *Strange Genius,* 301; FVH to Martin B. Anderson, 12 July 1878, Martin B. Anderson Papers, University of Rochester Library.
17. Holmes to Peale, 31 May 1878, Howell Collection; FVH to Baird, 22 July 1878, 27 Aug. 1878, and 20 Sept. 1878, RU 7002; Baird to FVH, 18 Sept. 1878, RG 57H; FVH to Leidy, 2 Sept. 1878 and 4 Oct. 1878, Leidy Coll. 1.
18. Baird to FVH, 4 Nov. 1878, RU 33; Rivinus and Youssef, *Spencer Baird,* 47–49.
19. Schurz to FVH, 3 Oct. 1878, RG 57H; FVH to Baird, 14 Oct. 1878, RU 7002; FVH to Leidy, 14 Oct. [1878], Leidy Coll. 1.
20. FVH to Baird, telegram, 19 Oct. 1878, RU 7002; FVH to Schurz, 29 Oct. 1878, RG 48; FVH to Baird, 22 July 1878 and 27 Aug. 1878, RU 7002; Agassiz to FVH, 9 May 1878, RG 57H; G. R. Agassiz, ed., *Letters and Recollections of Alexander Agassiz with a Sketch of His Life and Work* (Boston: Houghton Mifflin, 1913), 219–31; Winsor, *Reading the Shape,* 174–75.
21. FVH to Samuel Scudder, 7 July 1878 and 21 July 1878, Scudder Papers.
22. Foster, *Strange Genius,* 301.
23. G. B. Chittenden to FVH, 26 June 1878; F. M. Pearson to FVH, 17 Aug. 1878, RG 57H; FVH to Baird, 22 July 1878 and 27 Aug. 1878, RU 7002; FVH to Leidy, 4 Oct. 1878, Leidy Coll. 1; Newcomb to Marsh, 6 Jan. 1879, National Academy of Sciences–National Research Council Central Policy Files, National Academy of Sciences, Committee on Plan for Surveying and Mapping U.S. Territories, 1873–1878, Washington DC.
24. FVH to Samuel Scudder, 29 Dec. 1877, 30 Dec. 1877, and 8 Jan. 1878, Scudder Papers; *Proceedings, National Academy of Sciences,* vol. 1, pt. 2 (1878): 140.

25. F. M. Pierson to FVH, 17 Aug. 1878; Baird to FVH, 24 Jan. 1879, RG 57H.

26. FVH to Geikie, 24 Jan. 1879 and 4 Feb. 1879, Geikie Papers, quoted by permission of Edinburgh University Library, Special Collections, University of Edinburgh; Carl Resek, *Lewis Henry Morgan: American Scholar* (Chicago: Univ. of Chicago Press, 1960), 61, 133; FVH to Morgan, 3 Feb. 1879, Lewis H. Morgan Papers, Department of Rare Books and Special Collections, Rush Rhees Library, University of Rochester.

27. Hayden, *Extracts from Letters and Notices*, 6, 7, 21, and passim.

28. Agassiz to Newcomb, 22 Apr. 1878, Newcomb Papers; Wilkins, *Clarence King*, 259; King to J. D. Whitney, 16 Jan. 1879, William D. Whitney Papers, Manuscripts and Archives, Yale University Library; King to William Brewer, 15 Jan. 1879, Huntington Library, San Marino, California, HM 27832 (quoted by permission of the Huntington Library, San Marino, California); Ferdinand Zirkel to King, 14 Nov. 1878, Rutherford B. Hayes Papers, Rutherford B. Hayes Presidential Center, Spiegel Grove, Fremont, Ohio; Foster, *Strange Genius*, 317; FVH to Geikie, 24 Jan. 1879, Geikie Papers.

29. King to Emmons, 30 Dec. 1878, Clarence King Papers, American Philosophical Society, Philadelphia; Edward K. Spann, *The New Metropolis: New York City, 1840–1857* (New York: Columbia Univ. Press, 1981), 213–14; Foster, *Strange Genius*, 317.

30. King to Marsh, 2 Jan. [1879], Marsh Papers; Marsh to Hayes, 14 Jan. 1879, Hayes Papers.

31. King to George J. Brush, 16 Jan. 1879, Brush Family Papers, Manuscripts and Archives, Yale University Library.

32. Foster, *Strange Genius*, 319–21; Key to Hayes, 4 Jan. 1879, Hayes Papers.

33. King to Marsh, 2 Jan. [1879], Marsh Papers; Gilbert to Newberry, 10 Jan. 1879, RG 57P; Rogers to Gibbs, 26 Feb. 1879; Gibbs to Marsh, 28 Feb. 1879, Marsh Papers; Foster, *Strange Genius*, 317–18; Charles W. Eliot to Hayes, 28 Feb. 1879; J. J. Stevenson to Hayes, 6 Mar. 1879, Hayes Papers; Powell to Garfield, 7 Mar. 1879, Garfield Papers.

34. Adams, *Education*, 416, 311; Wilkins, *Clarence King*, 101, 261–69; Patricia O'Toole, *The Five of Hearts: An Intimate Portrait of Henry Adams and His Friends, 1880–1918* (New York: Ballantine Books, 1990), 65–66, 70–73; Newcomb to Marsh, 7 Dec. 1878; King to Newcomb, 26 Dec. 1878, Newcomb Papers; King to Whitney, 16 Jan. 1879, William D. Whitney Papers; Wilkins, *Clarence King*, 263.

35. King to Marsh, 2 Jan. [1879], Marsh Papers; Trefousse, *Carl Schurz*, 248; Newcomb, *Reminiscences*, 258–60; Newcomb to Marsh, 14 Mar. 1879,

Marsh Papers; James D. Hague, "Biographical Sketch of Clarence King," [1887?], 12, RU 7085.

36. FVH to Geikie, 24 Jan. 1879, Geikie Papers; Packard to FVH, 14 Jan. 1879, RG 57H; FVH to Geikie, 31 May 1879, Geikie Papers; Packard to FVH, 1 Jan. 1879, RG 57H; Asa Gray to FVH, 22 Jan. 1879, RG 57H; King to William H. Dall, 19 Feb. 1879, Smithsonian Archives, RU 7073, William H. Dall Papers, 1865–1927; Powell to Atkins, 20 Feb. 1879, RG 57P; *Cong. Rec.*, 45th Cong., 3d sess., 1879, 8, pt. 3: 1864–68; Darrah, *Powell*, 248; FVH to Lewis H. Morgan, 6 Feb. 1879 and 28 Feb. 1879, Morgan Papers.

37. Powell to Marsh, 20 Feb. 1879, RG 57P.
38. Powell to Hunt, 10 Mar. 1879, RG 57P.
39. Powell to Marsh, 20 Feb. 1879; William B. Rogers to Wolcott Gibbs, 26 Feb. 1879, Marsh Papers; Grove K. Gilbert to Hayes, 5 Mar. 1879; Clarence E. Dutton to Hayes, 5 Mar. 1879; Powell to Hayes, 7 Mar. 1879, Hayes Papers; FVH to J. D. Whitney, 13 Mar. 1879, Whitney Papers; Ari Hoogenboom, *Rutherford B. Hayes: Warrior and President* (Lawrence: Univ. Press of Kansas, 1995), 302; FVH to Leidy, 14 Mar. 1879, Leidy Coll. 1; Cope to Leidy, 16 Mar. 1879, Leidy Coll. 1-B; Newcomb to Marsh, 14 Mar. 1879, Marsh Papers; Hoogenboom, *Rutherford B. Hayes*, 218.
40. Powell to Atkins, 4 Mar. 1879, RG 57P.
41. Hoogenboom, *Rutherford B. Hayes*, 277, 359, 361; Garfield, *Diary*, 3:379, 425; Powell to Garfield, 7 Mar. 1879, Garfield Papers.
42. FVH to J. D. Whitney, 16 May 1874, Whitney Papers; [William D. Whitney], "Who Shall Direct the National Surveys," *Nation*, 18 (1874): 328.
43. Hayden, *Preliminary Report of . . . Wyoming*, 6–7; *Sixth Annual Report*, 10; FVH to Meek, 2 Nov. 1867, RU 7062; Hayden, *Sixth Annual Report*, 6.
44. FVH to LeConte, 27 Feb. 1879, LeConte Papers; LeConte to FVH, 14 Feb. 1879, RG 57H.
45. Powell to Garfield, 7 Mar. 1879, Garfield Papers.
46. "Minutes of the Stated Session of the National Academy of Sciences held in Washington, April 15th, 16th, 17th, 18th, 1873," 400, National Academy of Sciences, N. A. S. Minutes, 1863–1882, Washington DC; Edwin Tenney Brewster, *Life and Letters of Josiah Dwight Whitney* (Boston: Houghton Mifflin, 1909), 236–37, 309–10; Marvine to J. D. Whitney, 7 May 1874, Whitney Papers.
47. Powell, *Report on the Methods of Surveying*, 12; Powell, *Lands of the Arid Region*, 7–8, and passim.
48. FVH to W. K. Rogers, 20 Sept. 1882, Hayes Papers.

49. Cope to Schurz, 15 Mar. 1879, Hayden Collection.

50. Lesley to Hayes, 10 Feb. 1879, Lesley Papers.

51. Guyot to Hayes, 18 Feb. 1879, Hayden Collection.

52. Leidy to Schurz, 13 Mar. 1879; Cope to Schurz, 15 Mar. 1879, Hayden Collection.

53. Wilkins, *Clarence King*, 266–70; Terrell, *Man Who Rediscovered*, 211; Darrah, *Powell*, 251.

54. Rutherford B. Hayes, "Fourth Annual Message," in *The State of the Union Message of the Presidents, 1790–1966*, ed. Fred L. Israel (New York: Chelsea House, 1967), 2:1419; Hayes to William D. Howells, 30 Dec. 1878, William D. Howells Papers, Houghton Library, Harvard University, Cambridge, Massachusetts; Hoogenboom, *Rutherford B. Hayes*, chap. 22.

55. Hayes, *Diary and Letters*, 430, 497; Powell to Garfield, 7 Mar. 1879, Garfield Papers; Powell to Eugene Hale, 24 Jan. 1877, RG 57P.

56. Eliot to Hayes, 28 Feb. 1879, Hayes Papers; Lesley to Hayes, 10 Feb. 1879, Lesley Papers.

57. Smith, "Clarence King," 55; E. G. Robinson to FVH, 21 Mar. 1879, RG 57H; "Clarence King to be Confirmed: The Senate Committee Unanimously in his Favor," *New York Tribune*, 2 Apr. 1879; "Clarence King Confirmed," *New York Tribune*, 4 Apr. 1879.

58. FVH to Lewis H. Morgan, 3 Feb. 1879, Morgan Papers; FVH to Leidy, 14 Mar. 1879, Leidy Coll. 1.

59. James C. Pilling to Howell, 19 Mar. 1879, RG 57P; Foster, *Strange Genius*, 320–21; FVH to Winchell, 5 Apr. 1879, Alexander Winchell Papers, Bentley Historical Library, University of Michigan, Ann Arbor; FVH to Leidy, 5 Apr. 1879, Leidy Coll. 1; *U.S. Statutes at Large*, 20 (1879): 395.

60. Townsend to FVH, 4 Apr. 1879, RG 57H; FVH to Leidy, 5 Apr. 1879, Leidy Coll. 1.

61. FVH to Geikie, 13 Dec. 1878, 24 Jan. 1879, and 31 May 1879, Geikie Papers.

10. SUN SETS ON HAYDEN'S WEST

1. Packard to FVH, 1 Jan. 1879, RG 57H.
2. A. S. Packard Jr., "Scientific News," *American Naturalist* 13 (May 1879): 344; [E. D. Cope], "Scientific News," *American Naturalist* 13 (Apr. 1879): 275.
3. Packard, "Scientific News," 344–45.
4. Hewitt to Marsh, 3 May 1886, Marsh Papers.

5. Hayden, *Sixth Annual Report*, 5.
6. Clarence King, *First Annual Report of the United States Geological Survey* (Washington DC: GPO, 1880), 4–5.
7. Goetzmann, *Exploration and Empire*, 594; Wilkins, *Clarence King*, 254–55, 262–63, 265–66, 286–88; Dupree, *Science*, chaps. 10–11; Manning, *Government*, chaps. 4–9; Clifford M. Nelson, "Paleontology in the United States Federal Service, 1804–1904," *Earth Sciences History* 1 (1982): 48–57.
8. *U.S. Statutes at Large*, 20 (1879): 394–95.
9. Lesquereux to Lesley, 21, 28, and 30 Jan. 1865, Lesley Papers.
10. King to Humphreys, 25 Feb. 1874, in Goetzmann, *Exploration and Empire*, 458.
11. King to Marcus Benjamin, 21 Aug. 1887, RU 7085; Hague, "Biographical Sketch of Clarence King," 12.
12. White, "Memoir of Ferdinand Vandeveer Hayden," 407–8.
13. Lesley, "Obituary Notice of Ferdinand Vandiveer Hayden," 60–61.
14. J. D. Whitney to FVH, 20 Feb. 1870, RG 57H; W. D. Whitney to J. D. Whitney, 12 May 1874; Archibald Marvine to J. D. Whitney, 7 May 1874; J. D. Whitney to W. D. Whitney, 13 May 1874, Whitney Family Papers. "B. S. light" is undoubtedly a reference to Benjamin Silliman Jr., meaning he considered Hayden to be closely allied with speculators' interests; see Gerald Taylor White, *Scientists in Conflict: The Beginnings of the Oil Industry in California* (San Marino CA: Huntington Library, 1968).
15. [Raymond], "Preliminary Report of the United States Geological Survey of Montana," 376; [Raymond], "The Consolidated Surveys," 159; Raymond, "The New Director of the United States Geological Survey," *Eng. Min. J.* 27 (15 Mar. 1879): 179.
16. Winsor, *Reading the Shape*, 196; Toby A. Appel, "Organizing Biology: The American Society of Naturalists and Its 'Affiliated Societies,' 1883–1923," in *American Development*, 88–89; Blum, *Picturing Nature*, 119–20. Besides Appel's essay, all the essays in *American Development* present individuals who acted as entrepreneurs in shaping science, esp. Rainger, "Vertebrate Paleontology as Biology: Henry Fairfield Osborn and the American Museum of Natural History," 223–28.
17. Powell to W. B. Allison, 26 Feb. 1886, in Manning, *Government*, 136–37.
18. King, *First Annual Report of the USGS*, 14; Peale, "Biographical Sketch of F. V. Hayden," 21–22; Clifford M. Nelson, Mary C. Rabbitt, and Fritiof M. Fryxell, "Ferdinand Vandeveer Hayden: The U.S. Geological Survey Years, 1879–1886," *Proc. APS* 125 (1981): 238–43.

19. Nelson, Rabbitt, and Fryxell, "Ferdinand Vandeveer Hayden," 242 n. 27, 243 n. 33.

20. Dupree, *Science*, vii–ix; xviii.

21. Walter A. McDougall, . . . *The Heavens and the Earth: A Political History of the Space Age* (New York: Basic Books, 1985), chap. 15; Powell to Garfield, 7 Mar. 1879, RG 57P; Dupree, *Science*, 158–60, 211.

Select Bibliography

The following is a very brief bibliography of some of the books and articles I found most useful in studying Hayden and his survey.

Allen, John Logan, ed. *North American Exploration.* Vol. 3, *A Continent Comprehended.* Lincoln: Univ. of Nebraska Press, 1997.

Baatz, Simon. "'Squinting at Silliman': Scientific Periodicals in the Early American Republic, 1810–1833." *Isis* 82 (1991): 223–44.

Barber, Lynn. *The Heyday of Natural History, 1820–1870.* Garden City NY: Doubleday, 1980.

Bartlett, Richard A. *Great Surveys of the American West.* Norman: Univ. of Oklahoma Press, 1962.

Biagioli, Mario. *Galileo, Courtier: The Practice of Science in the Culture of Absolutism.* Chicago: Univ. of Chicago Press, 1993.

Blum, Ann Shelby. *Picturing Nature: American Nineteenth-Century Zoological Illustration.* Princeton: Princeton Univ. Press, 1993.

Brayer, Herbert Oliver, ed. "Exploring the Yellowstone with Hayden, 1872: Diary of Sidford Hamp." *Annals of Wyoming* 14, no. 4 (1942): 252–98.

Brown, Frederick Martin. "Hayden's 1854–55 Missouri River Expedition." *Denver Westerners Roundup* 27 (1971): 3–66.

Cravens, Hamilton. "American Science Comes of Age: An Institutional Perspective, 1850–1930." *American Studies* 17 (1976): 49–70.

Dall, William Healey. *Spencer Fullerton Baird: A Biography, Including Selections From His Correspondence with Audubon, Agassiz, Dana, and Others.* Philadelphia: J. B. Lippincott, 1915.

Daniels, George H. *American Science in the Age of Jackson.* New York: Columbia Univ. Press, 1968.

———, ed., *Nineteenth-Century American Science: A Reappraisal.* Evanston IL: Northwestern Univ. Press, 1972.

Darrah, William Culp. *Powell of the Colorado.* Princeton: Princeton Univ. Press, 1951.

Deiss, William A. "The Making of a Naturalist: Spencer F. Baird, the Early Years." In *From Linnaeus to Darwin: Commentaries on the History of Biology and Geology*, edited by Alwyne Wheeler and James H. Price. London: Society for the History of Natural History, 1985.

———. "Spencer F. Baird and His Collectors." *Journal of the Society for the Bibliography of Natural History* 9 (1980): 635–45.

Destler, Chester McArthur, ed. "Diary of a Journey into the Valleys of the Red River of the North and the Upper Missouri." *Mississippi Valley Historical Review* 33 (1946–47): 425–42.

Dupree, A. Hunter. *Science in the Federal Government: A History of Politics and Activities*. Cambridge MA: Harvard Univ. Press, Belknap Press, 1957; Baltimore: Johns Hopkins Univ. Press, 1986.

Foster, Mike. "Ferdinand Vandeveer Hayden as Naturalist." *American Zoologist* 26 (1986): 343–49.

———. "Hayden in Wonderland: Exploring Yellowstone." *Timeline: A Publication of the Ohio Historical Society* 6 (August–September 1989): 36–47.

———. "The Permian Controversy of 1858: An Affair of the Heart." *Proceedings of the American Philosophical Society* 133 (1989): 370–90.

———. *Strange Genius: The Life of Ferdinand Vandeveer Hayden*. Niwot CO: Roberts Rinehart, 1994.

Goetzmann, William H. *Army Exploration in the American West, 1803–1863*. New Haven: Yale Univ. Press, 1959; Lincoln: Univ. of Nebraska Press, Bison, 1979.

———. *Exploration and Empire: The Explorer and the Scientist in the Winning of the American West*. New York: W. W. Norton, 1966.

———. *New Lands, New Men: America and the Second Great Age of Discovery*. New York: Viking Penguin, 1986.

[Hamp, Sidford]. "With Hayden on the Yellowstone: The Letters of Sidford Hamp." In *Brand Book* [yearbook], 1948 ed., edited by Dabney Otis Collins. Denver: Westerners, 1949.

Howell, J. V. "Geology Plus Adventure: The Story of the Hayden Survey." *Journal of the Washington Academy of Sciences* 49 (1959): 220–24.

Jackson, William Henry. *The Diaries of William Henry Jackson, Frontier Photographer: to California and Return, 1866–67; and with the Hayden Surveys to the Central Rockies, 1873, and to the Utes and Cliff Dwellings, 1874*. Edited by LeRoy R. Hafen and Ann W. Hafen. Glendale CA: Arthur H. Clark, 1959.

———. *Time Exposure: The Autobiography of William Henry Jackson*. New York: G. P. Putnam's Sons, 1940.

Kinsey, Joni Louise. *Thomas Moran and the Surveying of the American West.* Washington DC: Smithsonian Institution Press, 1992.

Kuritz, Hyman. "The Popularization of Science in Nineteenth-Century America." *History of Education Quarterly* 21 (1981): 259–74.

Manning, Thomas G. *Government in Science: The U.S. Geological Survey, 1867–1894.* Lexington: Univ. of Kentucky Press, 1967.

McLaird, James D., and Lesta V. Turchen. "Exploring the Black Hills, 1855–1875: Reports of the Government Expeditions, Part III: 'The Scientist in Western Exploration: Ferdinand Vandiveer Hayden.'" *South Dakota History* 4 (1974): 161–97.

Merrill, George P., ed. and comp. *Contributions to a History of American State Geological and Natural History Surveys.* Washington DC: GPO, 1920.

———. *The First One Hundred Years of American Geology.* New Haven: Yale Univ. Press, 1924.

Merrill, Marlene Deahl, ed. *Yellowstone and the Great West: Journals, Letters, and Images from the 1871 Hayden Expedition.* Lincoln: Univ. of Nebraska Press, 1999.

Miller, Howard S. *Dollars for Research: Science and Its Patrons in Nineteenth Century America.* Seattle: Univ. of Washington Press, 1970.

Nelson, Clifford M. "Meek at Albany, 1852–58." *Earth Sciences History* 6 (1987): 40–46.

———. "Paleontology in the United States Federal Service, 1804–1904." *Earth Sciences History* 1 (1982): 48–57.

Nelson, Clifford M., and Mary C. Rabbitt. "The Role of Clarence King in the Advancement of Geology in the Public Service, 1867–1881." In *Frontiers of Geological Exploration of Western North America,* edited by Alan E. Leviton, Peter U. Rodda, Ellis L. Yochelson, and Michele L. Aldrich. San Francisco: Pacific Division, American Association for the Advancement of Science, 1982.

Nelson, Clifford M., Mary C. Rabbitt, and Fritiof M. Fryxell. "Ferdinand Vandeveer Hayden: The U.S. Geological Survey Years, 1879–1886." *Proceedings of the American Philosophical Society* 125 (1981): 238–43.

Nelson, Clifford M., and Ellis L. Yochelson. "Organizing Federal Paleontology in the United States, 1858–1907." *Journal of the Society for the Bibliography of Natural History* 9 (1980): 607–18.

Pike, Donald G. "Four Surveyors Challenge the Rocky Mountain West: Fighting Bureaucracy and Indians in a Wild Land." *American West* 9, no. 3 (1972): 4–13.

Rabbitt, Mary C. *Minerals, Land and Geology for the Common Defense and General Welfare.* Vol. 1, *Before 1879.* Washington DC: GPO, 1979.

Rivinus, E. F., and E. M. Youssef. *Spencer Baird of the Smithsonian.* Washington DC: Smithsonian Institution Press, 1992.

Schneer, Cecil J., ed. *Two Hundred Years of Geology in America.* Hanover NH: Univ. Press of New England, 1979.

Schubert, Frank N. "Troublesome Partnership: Gouverneur K. Warren and Ferdinand V. Hayden on the Northern Plains in 1856 and 1857." *Earth Sciences History* 3 (1984): 143–48.

Slotten, Hugh Richard. *Patronage, Practice, and the Culture of American Science: Alexander Dallas Bache and the U.S. Coast Survey.* Cambridge: Cambridge Univ. Press, 1994.

Smith, Henry Nash. "Clarence King, John Wesley Powell, and the Establishment of the United States Geological Survey." *Mississippi Valley Historical Review* 34 (1947): 37–58.

Stegner, Wallace. *Beyond the Hundredth Meridian: John Wesley Powell and the Second Opening of the West.* Boston: Houghton Mifflin, 1954; New York: Penguin, 1992.

Terrell, John Upton. *The Man Who Rediscovered America: A Biography of John Wesley Powell.* New York: Weybright & Talley, 1969.

Thurston, William. "Establishment of the U.S. Geological Survey." *Journal of the Washington Academy of Sciences* 61 (1971): 7–12.

Turner, Stephen P. "The Survey in Nineteenth-Century American Geology: The Evolution of a Form of Patronage." *Minerva* 25 (1987): 282–330.

Wilkins, Thurman, with the help of Caroline Lawson Hinkley. *Clarence King: A Biography.* Rev. and enl. ed. Albuquerque: Univ. of New Mexico Press, 1988.

Wilson, Leonard G. "The Emergence of Geology as a Science in the United States." *Journal of World History* 10 (1967): 416–37.

Index